CATASTROPHE

CATASTROPHE

How Obama, Congress, and
the Special Interests Are Transforming . . .
a Slump into a Crash,
Freedom into Socialism,
and a Disaster into a
CATASTROPHE . . .
and How to Fight Back

DICK MORRIS
and EILEEN McGANN

HARPER

An Imprint of HarperCollins*Publishers*
www.harpercollins.com

HarperCollins books may be purchased for educational, business, or sales promotional use. For information, please write: Special Markets Department, HarperCollins Publishers, 10 East 53rd Street, New York, NY 10022.

FIRST EDITION

Library of Congress Cataloging-in-Publication Data has been applied for.

ISBN: 978-0-06-177104-0

09   10   11   12   13   DIX/RRD   10   9   8   7   6   5   4   3   2   1

To Eugene J. Morris.,
98.5 years old and an inspiration to us both

CONTENTS

INTRODUCTION
Take Back Our Country

> We are today in the middle of the greatest catastrophe—the greatest catastrophe due almost entirely to economic causes—of the modern world.
>
> —JOHN MAYNARD KEYNES, 1931

It's time to take back our country.

Now.

It's that simple. It's that urgent.

It's time to take it back from President Barack Obama, before he fully implements his radical political agenda—one that threatens our liberty, endangers our livelihood, and jeopardizes our very safety and security.

Obama has canceled the war on terror and declared a war on prosperity.

It's a catastrophe.

Make no mistake about it: We now have a socialist in the White House. Barack Obama firmly believes in government control of our major industries, a hallmark of European socialism. Watch him. First it was the banks, then the auto industry. What's next? He'll keep going until the federal government owns or dominates every major American business and sets the salaries for all employees.

Using the global economic crisis as an excuse to revolutionize our economy and institutionalize pervasive and perverse changes masquerading as "reforms," Obama wants to change our way of living, working, and even thinking.

He's committed to orchestrating an extraordinary redistribution of wealth, significantly raising taxes on those who make more than $200,000 a year while providing tax credits and other advantages to those who don't. He intends to create a dual tax system: on one side there will be those who pay an enormous amount of taxes, and on the other there will be those who pay nothing at all but are regularly and directly subsidized by the increased taxes of those who do. Think France.

Obama plans to expand the role, size, and cost of government vastly and to regulate each and every aspect of corporate and commercial conduct. It's only a matter of time before political correctness, too, will be legislated, and the policing of acceptable personal conduct will become yet another role of the government. Everything is on the table. Remember that both his chief of staff, Rahm Emanuel, and his secretary of state, Hillary Clinton, have warned that we shouldn't "waste" a good crisis like the one we're in.

"Waste" a crisis? What do they mean? Well, apparently the Obama administration sees the current atmosphere of economic turmoil and uncertainty as a great opportunity to make sweeping changes that wouldn't otherwise be acceptable to the American public. Changes the American left has been dreaming about for years. So now, under the guise of solving the crisis, Obama can pass and fund just about anything. Just take a look at his nearly trillion-dollar stimulus bill—and all of the outrageous earmarks that were wedged into it by Congress as the price of passage.

And it's not just the economy: Obama has virtually ended the war on terror. His administration doesn't even utter the words. In recent testimony before Congress, Department of Homeland Security secretary Janet Napolitano actually referred to "man-caused" disasters, pointedly avoiding the word "terrorism." [1] Obama's appointments to the Justice Department have been people who are determined to root out, investigate, and expose not the terrorists themselves but those who protect us from them. Guantánamo has become a resource center for terrorists; a new one is freed every week. And Obama is reversing our long-term commitment to Israel—and instead giving almost a billion dollars to Hamas.

Let's face it: his policies are a catastrophe, and we need to stop him.

It's also time to take our country back from the Democratic Congress, which has undergone an embarrassing transformation from a do-nothing body into a rubber-stamp annex of the Obama White House: 535 elected officials who didn't even bother to read the details before they authorized almost a trillion dollars in stimulus spending that their constituents will have to pay for. A Democratic Congress that, in the middle of the gravest financial disaster since the Great Depression, bargained for billions in additional outrageous earmark spending programs to please their contributors and lobbyist friends, without a look back at the needs of their constituents. Just to whet your appetite (or, should we say, spoil it), here are a few of the worst expenditures of taxpayer money contained in that stimulus bill:

$200,000   to fund a tattoo removal clinic in California[2]
$190,000   for the Buffalo Bill Historical Center in Wyoming[3]
$2,192,000   for the Center for Grape Genetics in Geneva, NY[4]
$1,791,000   to fund Swine Odor & Manure Management Research in Iowa[5]

The malfeasance of the Congress is in itself a catastrophe. We need to clean house (and Senate) and replace the self-serving automatons with elected officials who genuinely understand that their job—their only purpose—is to serve the people who elect them, not the people who pay for their campaigns. People who understand that they, too, will be thrown out if we see more of the same. It's about time we had representatives in Washington who root for the people back home, instead of conspiring against them with their generous lobbyist pals.

On a recent episode of Glenn Beck's Fox News show, an organizer of a tea party protest in St. Louis indicated that members of Congress had been invited to the event in order to give them a chance to meet with their "board of directors"—the voters who elected them and who should be able to advise them about the needs of the district. She had it right. That's how it should be, and it's a good way to think about Congress: we hire them, we pay them, and they should be accountable to us. Unfortunately, most of them don't think that way at all. The only boards of directors that our representatives routinely meet with are the corporate ones, who decide who their political action committees will contribute to.

We desperately need to take back Congress and make it accountable to us, the voters—not the banks, credit card companies, defense contractors, and other special interests that have been running the show for way too long.

Can we do it? Well, to quote our president: Yes, we can!

There's a lot more we can do to make Congress more accountable and more constituent-friendly. One important step would be to work hard to keep the political dynasties from taking up space in Congress. It's not just that it's usually their family name recognition that gets them elected; it's that the dynastic politicians come with a special kind of baggage: generations of hangers-on, people who have been given favors and jobs over the years who watch out for them and make it difficult for insurgents to take them on successfully at the polls. You know the names we're talking about: Kennedy, Dodd, Clinton, Dole, to name a few.

While we're at it, we should look at the growing number of spouses of members of the House and Senate who are invited to sit on corporate boards—and paid very well for doing so. Is this a backdoor way of paying the members?

But that's not all. It's also time to take back our country from the Wall Street masters of the universe, whose insatiable greed led them to create a dangerously unstable environment for American businesses and investors—until their house of cards crashed, taking the wealth of millions of shareholders, investors, and average Americans with them . . . and they turned to the government for a bailout.

The AIGs, the Citibanks, the Lehmans, and the rest of the unfortunately familiar Wall Street roster of shame created an unprecedented catastrophe—with the help of many in Congress, who contributed to that catastrophe by recklessly deregulating banks and financial institutions and ignoring the growing signs of economic catastrophe because they did not want to offend their patrons.

Those same institutions that are now broke poured millions into the campaign coffers of those in Congress who should have been watching out for the investors who needed protection instead of watching out for their donors. Is it any coincidence that the chairman of the Senate Banking Committee, Connecticut senator Christopher Dodd, was the number one recipient of AIG money and that company executives aggressively urged top-level employees to contribute to him as soon as it was clear he would be the next chairman of the committee? Within three days, the group had raised $160,000. Now questions have been raised about whether Dodd returned the favor when he agreed to insert language into an amendment to the stimulus bill to permit the retention of bonuses that had already been awarded. It's a legitimate question: at first Dodd vehemently denied that he had had anything to do with the language that was so favorable to AIG, but he later admitted that he had reluctantly agreed to the change after the Treasury Department asked him to do so.

That's the way things work in Washington, and that's why we have to take it back.

It's our country. It's our Congress. It's our government. We can't simply cede them to the people who want to destroy our values or follow instructions from their corporate patrons.

We've seen what happens when greedy companies like Countrywide Financial lure customers into unconscionable mortgages that they know they can't afford. Many believe that Countrywide's unscrupulous practices— the writing of hundreds of thousands of subprime mortgages that were doomed to end in default and the baiting of customers with initially low interest rates that eventually ballooned into unaffordable notes—was the detonator that triggered the financial meltdown that we are now witnessing. Now those unfortunate people are lining up in foreclosure court and losing their homes by the thousands. Meanwhile, the Countrywide executives, who walked out with hundreds of millions of dollars in bonuses, have found a new business. Many of the former top executives at Countrywide (except for CEO Angelo Mozilo) have started a new company. Guess what it does? Buys up notes from failed financial institutions and then sells them again.

Having profited in the glory days of the subprime mortgages, these scoundrels are now buying many of them out—and exploiting the failure of the mortgage market for their own profit.

We need to take our country away from these predators, who have caused so much emotional and financial pain. They should be banned from having anything to do with mortgages. Forever.

When we take our country back, that should be high on our agenda.

Now is the time, as we reclaim our country, our Congress, and our right to determine our system of government, for us to join together to prevent an Obama-inspired class war. Because that's where we're headed.

It is the cruelest of ironies that, at this time and place in our history—when America desperately needs a president committed to reigniting economic growth—instead we've elected one who is more interested in dividing us by class and redistributing our wealth than he is in creating more of it.

Because now is not the time to govern by ideology. Not in the middle of an unprecedented economic meltdown.

And now is not the time to accept or reject solutions based only on whether they fit an extremist political agenda. Not while we are drowning in the worst economic disaster since the Great Depression, with record unemployment rates, staggering numbers of home foreclosures, decimated 401(k)s, and rising numbers of tent cities and shantytowns for the homeless.

And now is especially no time to accept or reject solutions based on whether they fit or don't fit a particular philosophical agenda. The trendy economic populism we hear from the White House will do nothing but turn neighbors, families, and friends against one another. Americans don't want that. We can't afford that. It may sound tough for President Obama to say he'll take every legal step possible to get back the AIG bonuses (the ones his administration initially okayed), but do we really want to encourage populist vigilantes to hire buses to bring ACORN community organizers and the press on a tour of the homes of the AIG employees? That's what happened in Connecticut after Obama made his remarks. What does this do to the children of these people when they see protests outside their homes, their previously safe havens?

It's not going to help us to condone this vigilantism. We can face our problems only by coming together as a nation and facing, with confidence, the storms that surround us. But our president would have 95 percent of us turn on the other 5 percent in an economic civil war, making class conflict the engine of our economic and tax policy.

Obama may speak eloquently about working together, but he doesn't really seem to understand the fundamental necessity of support and respect for *all* sectors of our economy. Not just those who are at the core of the

Democratic Party, not just those who are union members, not just those who are the poorest among us, but all of us.

Thus far, Obama's behavior in office suggests that he has a flawed—and sometimes arrogant—approach to government. He needs the cooperation of business, yet he spurns it because of his class bias. He is desperate for more investors in our nation's stocks and bonds, yet he hounds these potential investors, overregulates them, and taxes them because they have too much money. Does he really think that this will work?

Anxious to stimulate consumer spending, Obama would raise taxes on the most prodigious consumers—the wealthy—by almost 50 percent. Eager to return to the days of prosperity and opportunity, he leads us, instead, into his notion of entitlement.

We want to make capitalism work. He wants to replace it with socialism.

But Barack Obama is only our president, not our dictator. Even armed with top-heavy majorities in both houses of Congress, he cannot get around the fact that we still live in a democracy. We are still a free people. The more we understand what he's doing to us—and why he's doing it—the more we can defend ourselves and reverse his disastrous course in 2010, when the congressional elections will offer us the next opportunity.

But we need to start today—by remembering that it's our country and taking it back.

Right now, in the darkness of the recession, that might seem difficult, even impossible. At the moment, reemerging into the light of prosperity is our primary concern. We all have immediate worries: our jobs, our families, our homes, our future.

But the very policies designed to extricate us from this hellish economy are those that will keep us in the darkness. Obama's spending—his massive, massive spending—will not hasten the end of the recession. What it will do is ensure a period of rampant inflation and, likely, yet another recession after that, before the inflation can be cured.

Yet, as desperate as our agony is today, it is not our major threat.

Only when we come out of the darkness, blinking in the light of a more normal economy, will the true nature of our catastrophe become apparent.

Unless we act today, we'll be returning to a very different world.

Will the bank on the corner be run by the government? Will it be like the Bureau of Motor Vehicles? Will we be able to get loans for cars and houses without passing a political loyalty test or a government-sponsored means test to establish our need?

And will our doctors be free to treat us as they wish, or will they have to check with Washington to find out what medications are approved and which procedures they can offer?

Will we be free to listen to talk radio as it explores alternatives to socialism, or will it have been forced off the air?

At our workplace, will we be coerced into joining unions that represent the Democratic Party but not us?

And will our country be dominated politically by a coalition of those who pay no taxes, while the rest of us are powerless to protest when the government takes two-thirds of our income?

These are the real stakes.

As John F. Kennedy said in his inaugural address, "In the long history of the world, only a few generations have been granted the role of defending freedom in its hour of maximum danger. I do not shrink from this responsibility—I welcome it."

Nor can any of us afford to shrink from the present task, which demands our attention, our energy, our commitment, and our resolve, We, too, must welcome this challenge. And we must prove worthy of meeting it.

We need to attack Barack Obama's socialist agenda in ways big and small. Between now and the elections of 2010, we must fight and win the special elections that will be called to fill vacancies in Congress. We need to demonstrate the revitalized power of opposition to socialism in the off-year elections in New Jersey and Virginia. And we must mobilize opinion, particularly in the districts of the marginal Democratic senators and congressmen—the frauds who run like moderates and then vote like socialists. We need to lay the basis for their defeat in 2010 and make them think twice before they vote to curtail our freedoms and give away our health care.

We must strike terror into the hearts of the Democrats in Congress who rubber-stamp Obama's programs, so that we can slow his momentum. Those who perpetuate his radicalism must fear for their seats as we stir public anger at their actions in their districts.

Don't worry if you don't live in a district with an election coming soon or with a phony Democratic moderate. In a very real sense, these days we're all in one district—our money, work, conversation, and anger carry across state and district lines. We will be heard!

And, when 2010 comes, we'll be ready to take our country back. We will know the stakes. And we won't be conned by a moderate-sounding president whose idea of change is the end of freedom and the dawn of socialism.

That's not change we can believe in.

This book is a call to action. At the end of each chapter, we suggest specific actions that can help us regain our country.

Join us in this most necessary and urgent work.

In his provocative book *Liberty and Tyranny*, Mark Levin speaks of the "soft tyranny" of government regulation. No longer will we be blind to that threat.

Not if we work together.

To quote Obama: NOT THIS TIME.

I

HOW OBAMA IS CAUSING A CATASTROPHE

Obama's tax increase will trigger a stock market crash and devastate the already slumping real estate industry. A selling psychology often feeds on itself and can induce a market-wide panic. So the nearer Obama gets to power the faster the markets are likely to dip. So look for a sharp downturn as election day approaches and especially in the period between a Democratic victory and inauguration day. Obama will doubtless blame the drop on the outgoing Bush administration, but it would be his own tax plans that send the markets into a tizzy.

—From *Fleeced*
by Dick Morris and Eileen McGann
written February 2008
published June 2008

OBAMA'S WAR ON PROSPERITY

Last year, in *Fleeced*, we predicted the disaster in which we now find ourselves. But who could have predicted the steps Barack Obama would take to turn this disaster into a catastrophe?

President Obama pledges to bring us back to prosperity, to end the recession. But his policies are likely to do the opposite—possibly casting us into a full-scale, long-lasting depression. At the very least, his huge spending will bring inflation and even more economic pain. And, in so many ways, Obama's program undermines the very business confidence that will be essential to restoring normal economic activity.

We are hostage to an ideologue who wants to use this crisis—not solve it—to promote his dogmatic agenda.

How did we let things get this far?

HIDING IN PLAIN SIGHT: HOW OBAMA GOT INTO POWER

From the moment he first realized he could win the presidency, Barack Obama has known exactly what he would do in the Oval Office. He just wasn't sure how to pull it off.

He told us his agenda with unusual specificity and elaboration. He hid nothing. He pulled no punches. Not for him the tack taken by Charles de Gaulle as the anxious French pressed him for his agenda before assuming power in 1957. "When I achieve power," de Gaulle replied haughtily, "I will know what to do with it." Obama not only knew what he wanted to do; he told everyone who would listen. If he hid his program, he did it in plain sight.

But most of America wasn't listening. Enthralled by his charisma and the trappings of his candidacy, they tuned out his program and mindlessly applauded his sound bites. Willfully suspending skepticism, they eagerly believed his superficial promises to change the way Washington worked, to exclude the lobbyists and special interests, and to end partisan bickering. Only after he was elected, when we started to see him appoint lobbyist after lobbyist and ride roughshod over the Republican opposition, did we come to realize that these vague commitments were just the window dressing on his program. The parsley around the meat.

But his program was never obscured. In a mind-numbing series of debates with his fellow Democrats, he spelled it out for us all to hear.

But we weren't paying attention to the boring programmatic details. How much more exciting it was to focus on the fact that we were witnessing the end of the color bar that first blighted America centuries ago, when the early slaves stepped onto these shores in chains. How much more thrilling to watch Barack Obama overcome the inevitable nominee, Hillary Clinton, by outsmarting her, defeating her, and making a mash of her strategy. What a relief to watch Mrs. Clinton's ill-conceived focus on experience, in what was clearly a moment that called for change, backfire on her.

But what change did Obama represent? The truth was hard for us to accept: that the man who was marching inexorably to the White House was a genuine radical from Harvard and Chicago. We heard the rantings of Reverend Jeremiah Wright and the stories Sean Hannity told about William Ayers, but we wouldn't believe the clues. The conclusion was too horrible. Were we really about to elect a man who would change not just Washington but our values, our nation, and our own lives?

But the program lay out there in the sun day after day. It never varied. Obama never temporized. He trimmed his tax proposals from time to time and waffled on details of his national security stance, but the basic thrust of his administration was as clear on the day he announced his candidacy in Springfield, Illinois, as it was when he spelled it out in his first address to Congress as president.

Most presidential candidates don't bother. Bill Clinton, George H. W. Bush, Richard Nixon, Jimmy Carter, and John F. Kennedy all took office with only a vague idea of what they would do with the power. George W. Bush told us what he had in mind, but the agenda was so limited that it never much mattered. In our recent past, only Lyndon Johnson and Ronald Reagan took office with as clear an idea of what they wanted to achieve. And, like both of these presidents, Obama did not trouble to hide his proposals as he campaigned for the job. Like Johnson and Reagan, Obama let it all hang out.

Didn't he plainly and frankly tell us that he would:

- Socialize health care

- Raise taxes sharply on those making over $200,000

- Raise capital gains taxes on high-income people

- Block the repeal of the estate tax

- Raise the Social Security payroll tax so everyone (or practically everyone) will have to pay it on his or her whole income

- Rebuild our infrastructure regardless of cost

- Pour money into alternative energy sources but go slow on nuclear power

- Pull out of Iraq

- End tough interrogations of terror suspects

- Dramatically increase federal spending

- Weaken the standards in the No Child Left Behind Act

- Push legislation allowing unions to organize without secret ballots

- Call for immigration legislation granting amnesty to most illegal immigrants already here

- Extend health care benefits to all legal immigrants, even those recently legitimized by his own amnesty plan

- Sharply increase aid to states and cities

- Change the ownership and rules of talk radio

- Shift our stance from support of Israel to greater sympathy for the Palestinian position

- Increase regulation of business

- Do more to regulate executive pay

- Weaken welfare reform

- Cut taxes for 95 percent of Americans while raising them sky high on the rest.

- Tax hedge fund and real estate partnership earnings as ordinary income

- Cap and trade legislation to charge utilities and industries for their carbon output

- Revise NAFTA and restrict free trade

This agenda was not new. It was a greatest-hits collection that revived proposals made by the Democratic-union Left for the past thirty years. But since Lyndon Johnson, and especially in the wake of Ronald Reagan, no Democratic president had dared to embrace it. Even with a Democratic Congress, Bill Clinton pursued only a small part of the liberal program.

Politics, after all, is the art of the possible—and, in political terms, the labor/left agenda was clearly impossible.

Obama camouflaged his domestic agenda behind the single overshadowing position of opposition to the war in Iraq. His emphasis on this theme—as opposed to the changes he contemplated at home—distracted us from the essential radicalism of his agenda. Obama may not have been another Bill Ayers or Jeremiah Wright, but he was clearly another Walter Mondale, Jimmy Carter, and Michael Dukakis. He just couldn't let anyone know.

The swelling casualty count in Iraq disenchanted Americans and distracted them from the importance of preserving our national security. Isolationism and obliviousness to the obvious costs of a premature pullout became the order of the day. As public opinion moved to the left, driven by the incompetence of George W. Bush's war strategy, Obama seemed to offer a reasonable alternative. His antiwar position—once easily dismissed as turning tail—now looked like a rational position.

The war was an issue that would ratify Obama's liberalism as centrist, and it gave him the opportunity to hide his radical domestic agenda behind his antiwar rhetoric. As Hillary's more security-minded position stalled in the mud, Obama's idealistic stance rode a national wave of war fatigue.

But then a funny thing happened: We started to win in Iraq. Guided by the new strategy of General David Petraeus and the surge in troop strength, the issue began to go away. By the late summer of 2008, Obama was left high and dry by the shifting tide—and his radical agenda threatened to attract newfound, and unwelcome, attention.

OBAMA'S CAMPAIGN: SAVED BY THE CRISIS

When the stock market began its long, dismal crash to the bottom on September 29, 2008, it saved the Obama campaign. The Democratic nominee had never really recovered from the loss of the Iraq issue, and for a moment Sarah Palin's exciting debut seemed to put Obama on the ropes. But when the market fell apart on Bush's watch, Obama was saved.

From there, the Democrat coasted. He encountered a momentary speed bump when a plumber named Joe did what the rest of the country had failed to do: read Obama's program. Accused of raising taxes, the Democrat admitted that he was, in fact, trying to redistribute income. But in the trauma of the crisis nobody listened, and Obama scored his massive victory.

There is, however, one consolation: in a democracy, no victory lasts forever. The American people are watching Obama closely. His promises of recovery have been so bold that waiting to see if he manages to keep them has become a new national pastime. But the programs he has launched are likely to dig us deeper into the hole than we were when he took office. That's why it's crucial for us to understand what he's doing to our country—so that we can reject his socialist agenda in the congressional elections of 2010.

"NEVER LET A SERIOUS CRISIS GO TO WASTE" —RAHM EMANUEL

Having won the presidency, carried a top-heavy majority in the House, and filled the Senate with sixty Democrats, Obama knew he could count on easy sailing in Congress. He would have no problem getting most of the new spending programs he wanted passed during his term (or two) in office. He would likely succeed where Clinton had failed and pass health care reform.

But Obama had more—a lot more—in mind. He had no interest in a typical Democratic presidency, with the focus on incremental change that characterized the Carter and Clinton years. He wanted to be a president in the mold of Lyndon Johnson or even Franklin D. Roosevelt. He wanted to pass everything, and he wanted to do so right away.

Just as the economic crisis showed him the way to win the election, now it pointed the way to pass his program. He merely had to rebrand his radical/socialist agenda as an economic recovery package.

Taking a page from Rahm Emanuel, his chief of staff, Obama decided he wouldn't "let a serious crisis go to waste." Far from being wasted, this crisis would be put to a cynical use—to catalyze the most dramatic change in American politics and economics since the 1930s. When Obama got finished "solving" the crisis, nothing would ever be the same again.

Suddenly everything was possible! No need to wait year after year to pass the programs on the environment, energy, welfare, education, health care, higher education, veterans, infrastructure, and urban problems that

Democrats had been pushing for years. Do it all at once! Jam through eight years of new spending proposals in one year! For that matter, do it in one week!

By cramming every Democratic spending fantasy into one bill—into that Trojan horse called "the stimulus package"—Obama could have it all, up front. No waiting.

It was just like the game urban social work agencies have played for years. The antipoverty storefront of the 1960s became the community development program of the 1970s. In the 1980s it morphed into an empowerment zone. Under Clinton it became a job training center, under Bush a tutoring program for No Child Left Behind. Same storefront. Same staff. Same clientele. Just a different shingle hanging outside.

So now Obama could put his entire agenda on the table at once, declare a national crisis, and jam it through. No time for debate. No time even to print the bill so members could read what they were voting for. *Emergency!*

Despite the empirical evidence that spending and one-shot tax cuts don't work, Obama couldn't resist. He finally had a chance to take advantage of Keynesian economic theory, to get Congress to pass all of his pet spending bills—his fantasies about renovating schools, computerizing health records, rebuilding roads and bridges, spreading broadband access, widening health care coverage of children and the unemployed, increasing scientific research, building alternative energy sources, and so on in the name of stimulating the economy, and so on. Suddenly everything was a stimulus measure.

Obama must have known that his stimulus package would do little to end the recession. He must have realized that the simple Keynesian approach wouldn't work. But he didn't care. He wanted the spending. He wanted the social programs. He wanted government to grow, and this was his excuse for doing it.

The wonderful thing about a spending/stimulus package is that it doesn't really matter what you spend the money on. A check is a check is a check. It doesn't matter if you're hiring a teacher or a cop or a scientist or an artist or a dishwasher. The goal is to spend money, and it doesn't much make a difference what the money is buying. So Obama invited the House and Senate Democrats to name their pet projects; whatever they were, he'd put them in the package.

It was like inviting an alcoholic in for a drink. And Congress was a thirsty drunk.

The proposals came fast and furious. The total cost was $787 billion. The stimulus bill itself ran 1,071 pages. Not that any member of Congress had time to read it, because the text didn't reach them until a few hours before they had to pass it.

And here it is in all its gory glory!

OBAMA'S STIMULUS PACKAGE

Program	Funding
Accountability	*$323,500,000*
Department of Agriculture, Office of Inspector General	$22,500,000
Department of Commerce, Office of Inspector General	$10,000,000
National Oceanic and Atmospheric Administration, Office of Inspector General	$6,000,000
Department of Justice, Office of Inspector General	$2,000,000
NASA, Office of Inspector General	$2,000,000
Defense Department. Office of Inspector General	$15,000,000
Department of Energy, Office of Inspector General	$15,000,000
Department of the Treasury, Inspector General for Tax Administration	$7,000,000
General Services Administration, Office of Inspector General	$7,000,000
Recovery Act Accountability and Transparency Board	$84,000,000
Small Business Administration, Office of Inspector General	$10,000,000
Department of Homeland Security, Office of Inspector General	$5,000,000
Bureau of Indian Affairs, Office of Inspector General	$15,000,000
Environmental Protection Agency, Office of Inspector General	$20,000,000
Department of Labor, Office of Inspector General	$6,000,000
Department of Health and Human Services, Office of Inspector General related to the Office of the National Coordinator for Health Information Technology	$17,000,000
Department of Education, Office of Inspector General	$14,000,000
Corporation for National and Community Service, Office of Inspector General	$1,000,000
Social Security Administration, Office of Inspector General	$2,000,000
Government Accountability Office salaries and expenses	$25,000,000

Program	Funding
Department of Veterans Affairs, Office of Inspector General	$1,000,000
State Department, Office of Inspector General	$2,000,000
Department of Transportation, Office of Inspector General	$20,000,000
Department of Housing and Urban Development, Office of Inspector General	$15,000,000
Aid to People Affected by Economic Downturn	*$36,910,807,000*
Rural Housing Service, Rural Housing Insurance Fund Program direct loans and unsubsidized guaranteed loans	$11,672,000,000
Rural Housing Service, Housing & Community Facilities Program	$130,000,000
Special Supplemental Nutrition Program for women, infants, and children (WIC)	$500,000,000
School lunch programs for schools where at least 50 percent of students qualify for free or reduced price meals	$100,000,000
Food bank commodity assistance program	$150,000,000
Temporary increase in benefits under the Supplemental Nutrition Assistance Program (food stamps)	$19,900,000,000
Food distribution program on Indian reservations	$5,000,000
Federal Crop Insurance Act: Agricultural Disaster Assistance Program	
Farm operating loans	$173,367,000
Direct farm operating loans	$20,440,000
IRS health insurance tax credit administration	$80,000,000
Emergency food and shelter	$100,000,000
Bureau of Indian Affairs job training and housing improvement programs	$40,000,000
Indian Home Loan Guarantee Program	$10,000,000
Community service employment for older Americans	$120,000,000
Extra funding for state unemployment insurance	$150,000,000
State reemployment services for the jobless	$250,000,000
Child care assistance for low-income families	$1,651,227,000
Child care assistance for low-income families through state programs	$255,186,000
Child care assistance for low-income families to improve infant and toddler care	$93,587,000
Community Service Block Grant Program	$1,000,000,000
Social Security Act funding	50,000,000
Social Security Administration processing of disability and retirement workloads	$460,000,000

Program	Funding
Aid to State and Local Governments	*$58,355,000,000*
State administrative expenses to carry out increase in food stamp program	$295,000,000
Economic development assistance programs	$150,000,000
Violence against women prevention and prosecution programs	$225,000,000
Office of Justice Programs state and local law enforcement assistance (Edward Byrne Memorial Justice Assistance Grants)	$2,000,000,000
State and local law enforcement assistance grants to improve criminal justice systems, assist crime victims, and mentor youth	$225,000,000
Southern border and high-intensity drug trafficking areas	$30,000,000
ATF Project Gunrunner	$10,000,000
State and local law enforcement assistance to Indian tribes	$225,000,000
Crime victim assistance	$100,000,000
Rural drug crime program	$125,000,000
Internet crimes against children initiatives	$50,000,000
Community Oriented Policing Services (COPS) grants	$1,000,000,000
Justice Department salaries and expenses for administration of police grant programs	$10,000,000
Community Development Financial Institutions Fund for financial assistance, training and outreach to Native American, Hawaiian, and Alaskan native communities	$100,000,000
Local and state fire station upgrades and construction	$210,000,000
Disaster assistance direct loans (may exceed $5,000,000 and may be equal to not more than 50 percent of local government annual budget if the government lost 25 percent or more in tax revenues)	
State Fiscal Stabilization Fund to avoid cutbacks and layoffs (82 percent must be used for education; 18 percent may be used for public safety and other government services; the latter part may be used for repairs and modernization of K–12 schools and college and university buildings)	$53,600,000,000
Business	*$870,000,000*
Rural Business Cooperative Service, rural business program account	$150,000,000
Small Business Administration salaries and expenses, microloan program, and improvements to technology systems	$69,000,000
Surety bond guarantees revolving fund	$15,000,000
Small business loans	$636,000,000

Program	Funding
Education	
State grants for adult job training	$500,000,000
State grants for youth job training and summer employment opportunities	$1,200,000,000
Dislocated worker job training	$1,250,000,000
YouthBuild program for high school dropouts who reenroll in other schools	$50,000,000
Job training in emerging industries	$250,000,000
Job training in the renewable energy field	$500,000,000
Head Start programs	$1,000,000,000
Early Head Start program expansion	$1,100,000,000
Education for the disadvantaged, elementary and secondary education	10,000,000,000
Education for the disadvantaged, school improvement grants	$3,000,000,000
Education impact aid	$100,000,000
School improvement programs	$650,000,000
Innovation and improvement of elementary and secondary schools	$200,000,000
Special education funding under the Individuals with Disabilities Education Act	$12,200,000,000
Pell grants for higher education	$15,840,000,000
Institute of Education data systems	$245,000,000
Institute of Education state data coordinators	$5,000,000
Dislocated worker assistance national reserve	$200,000,000
School improvement grants awarded based on the number of homeless students identified in a state	$70,000,000
Student aid administrative costs	$60,000,000
Energy	*$41,400,000,000*
Energy efficiency and conservation block grants	$3,200,000,000
Weatherization Assistance Program (increases maximum income level and maximum assistance)	$5,000,000,000
State energy program	$3,100,000,000
Advanced batteries manufacturing, including lithium-ion batteries, hybrid electrical systems, component manufacturers, and software designers	$2,000,000,000
Modernize electricity grid	$4,400,000,000
Electricity grid worker training	$100,000,000
Fossil energy research and development	$3,400,000,000

Program	Funding
Uranium Enrichment Decontamination and Decommissioning Fund	$390,000,000
Department of Energy science programs	$1,600,000,000
Advanced Research Projects Agency	$400,000,000
Innovative technology loan guarantee program	$6,000,000,000
Western Area Power Administration construction and maintenance	$10,000,000
Bonneville Power Administration borrowing authority	$3,250,000,000
Western Area Power Administration borrowing authority	$3,250,000,000
Leading edge biofuel projects	$500,000,000
Federal building conversion to "high-performance green buildings"	$4,500,000,000
Energy-efficient federal vehicle fleet procurement	$300,000,000
Health Care	*$18,830,000,000*
Indian Health Service information technology and telehealth services	$85,000,000
Indian health facilities	$415,000,000
Grants for public health centers	$500,000,000
Construction, renovation, equipment, and information technology for health centers	$1,500,000,000
National Health Service Corps	$75,000,000
Addressing health professions workforce shortage	$425,000,000
National Institutes of Health grants and contracts to renovate nonfederal research facilities	$1,000,000,000
National Institute of Health grants and contracts for shared resources and equipment for grantees	$300,000,000
National Institutes of Health fund to support scientific research	$7,400,000,000
National Institutes of Health Common Fund	$800,000,000
National Institutes of Health renovations of high-priority buildings at the Bethesda, MD, campus, and other locations	$500,000,000
Comparative effectiveness research	$300,000,000
Comparative effectiveness research by the National Institutes of Health	400,000,000
Comparative effectiveness research by the Department of Health and Human Services	$400,000,000
Office of the National Coordinator for Health Information Technology	$1,680,000,000
National Coordinator for Health Information Technology's regional or subnational efforts	$300,000,000
Department of Commerce health care information enterprise integration activities related to the Office of the National Coordinator for Health Information Technology	$20,000,000

Program	Funding
Department of Health and Human Services computer and information technology security	$50,000,000
Department of Health and Human Services Prevention and Wellness Fund	$1,000,000,000
Department of Health and Human Services Prevention and Wellness Fund immunization program	$300,000,000
Department of Health and Human Services Prevention and Wellness Fund evidence-based clinical and community-based prevention strategies	$650,000,000
Department of Health and Human Services Prevention and Wellness Fund reduction in incidence of health care–associated infections	$50,000,000
Rehabilitation services and disability research	540,000,000
State grants for rehabilitation services and disability research	$18,200,000
Rehabilitation services in independent living centers	$87,500,000
Rehabilitation services for older blind individuals	$34,300,000
Other	*$2,147,000,000*
Census Bureau programs	$1,000,000,000
Digital-to-analog television converter box program	$650,000,000
President shall establish arbitration panel under FEMA public assistance program to expedite recovery efforts from Hurricanes Katrina and Rita	
Requirement that Department of Homeland Security uniforms be manufactured and sewn together by U.S. fabric and apparel companies	
National Endowment for the Arts grants	$50,000,000
Department of Labor salaries and expenses	$80,000,000
Additional awards to existing AmeriCorps grantees	$83,000,000
AmeriCorps program salaries and expenses	$5,200,000
AmeriCorps program administrative costs of expansion	$800,000
National security trust appropriation	$40,000,000
Social Security Administration health information technology research	$40,000,000
Filipino World War II veterans compensation	$198,000,000
Science and Technology	*$13,142,000,000*
Farm Service Agency salaries and expenses to maintain and modernize the information technology system	$50,000,000
Distance learning, telemedicine, and broadband program	$2,500,000,000

Program	Funding
National Telecommunications and Information Administration: Broadband Technology Opportunities Program	$4,690,000,000
National Institute of Standards and Technology scientific and technical research and services	$220,000,000
National Institute of Standards and Technology construction of research facilities	$360,000,000
National Oceanic and Atmospheric Administration operations, research, and facilities	$230,000,000
National Oceanic and Atmospheric Administration procurement, acquisition and construction	$600,000,000
National Aeronautics and Space Administration science	$400,000,000
National Aeronautics and Space Administration aeronautics	$150,000,000
National Aeronautics and Space Administration exploration	$400,000,000
National Aeronautics and Space Administration cross agency support	$50,000,000
National Science Foundation research and related activities	$2,500,000,000
National Science Foundation education and human resources	$100,000,000
National Science Foundation major research equipment and facilities construction	$400,000,000
National Science Foundation, Office of Inspector General	$2,000,000
Department of Veterans Affairs hiring and training of claims processors	$150,000,000
Department of Veterans Affairs information technology systems	$50,000,000
State Department technology security upgrades	$252,000,000
U.S. Agency for International Development (USAID) technology	$38,000,000
Transportation and Infrastructure	*$98,325,000,000*
Agriculture buildings and facilities and rental payments	$24,000,000
Agricultural Research Service buildings and facilities	$176,000,000
Natural Resources Conservation Service watershed and flood prevention programs	$290,000,000
Natural Resources Conservation Service, Watershed Rehabilitation Program	$50,000,000
Rural Utilities Service Water and Waste Disposal Program	$1,380,000,000
Defense Department facilities operation and maintenance, Army	$1,474,525,000
Defense Department facilities operation and maintenance, Navy	$657,051,000
Defense Department facilities operation and maintenance, Marine Corps	$113,865,000
Defense Department facilities operation and maintenance, Air Force	$1,095,959,000

Program	Funding
Defense Department facilities operation and maintenance, Army Reserve	$98,269,000
Defense Department facilities operation and maintenance, Navy	$55,083,000
Defense Department facilities operation and maintenance, Marine Corps Reserve	$39,909,000
Defense Department facilities operation and maintenance, Air Force Reserve	$13,187,000
Defense Department facilities operation and maintenance, Army National Guard	$266,304,000
Defense Department facilities operation and maintenance, Air National Guard	$25,848,000
Army research development, test, and evaluation	$75,000,000
Navy research development, test, and evaluation	$75,000,000
Air Force research development, test, and evaluation	$75,000,000
Defensewide research development, test, and evaluation	$75,000,000
Defense Department medical facilities repair and modernization including energy efficiency	$400,000,000
Army Corps of Engineers investigations	$25,000,000
Army Corps of Engineers construction	$2,000,000,000
Army Corps of Engineers, Mississippi River and tributaries	$375,000,000
Army Corps of Engineers operations and maintenance	$2,075,000,000
Army Corps of Engineers regulatory program	$25,000,000
Army Corps of Engineers formerly utilized sites remedial action program	$100,000,000
Bureau of Reclamation water and related resources, including inspection of canals in urbanized areas	$900,000,000
Central Utah Project water programs	$50,000,000
California Bay Delta restoration	$50,000,000
Nondefense environmental cleanup	$483,000,000
Defense environmental cleanup	$5,127,000,000
Federal buildings and courthouses	$750,000,000
Border stations and land ports of entry	$300,000,000
Department of Homeland Security headquarters consolidation	$200,000,000
Customs and Border Protection nonintrusive inspection systems	$100,000,000
Customs and Border Protection tactical communications equipment and radios	$60,000,000
Border security fencing, infrastructure, and technology	$100,000,000

Program	Funding
Land border ports of entry construction	$420,000,000
Immigration and Customs Enforcement tactical communications equipment and radios	$20,000,000
Transportation Security Administration checked baggage and checkpoint explosives detection machines	$1,000,000,000
Coast Guard shore facilities and aids to navigation facilities	$98,000,000
Coast Guard alteration of bridges	$142,000,000
FEMA public transportation and railroad security	$150,000,000
FEMA port security grants	$150,000,000
Bureau of Land Management maintenance and restoration of facilities, trails, lands, abandoned mines, and wells	$125,000,000
Bureau of Land Management construction of roads, bridges, trails and facilities, including energy-efficient retrofits	$180,000,000
Wildland fire management and hazardous fuels reduction	$15,000,000
U.S. Fish and Wildlife Service maintenance and construction of wildlife refuges and fish hatcheries and for habitat restoration	$165,000,000
U.S. Fish and Wildlife Service roads, bridges, and facilities, including energy efficient retrofits	$115,000,000
National Park Service facilities and trails	$146,000,000
Historically black colleges and universities preservation	$15,000,000
National Park Service road construction, cleanup of abandoned mines on parkland, and other infrastructure	$589,000,000
U.S. Geological Survey facilities and equipment, including stream gauges, seismic and volcano monitoring systems, and national map activities	$140,000,000
Bureau of Indian Affairs construction of roads, schools, and detention centers	$450,000,000
Superfund site cleanup	$600,000,000
Leaking underground storage tank cleanup	$200,000,000
Clean water state revolving fund grants	$4,000,000,000
Safe drinking water capitalization grants	$2,000,000,000
Brownfields projects	$100,000,000
Diesel emission reduction grants and loans	$300,000,000
Forest Service road, bridge, and trail maintenance; watershed restoration; facilities improvement; remediation of abandoned mines; and support costs	$650,000,000
Wildfire mitigation	$500,000,000

Program	Funding
Smithsonian Institution repairs	$25,000,000
Construction, renovation, and acquisition of Job Corps Centers	$250,000,000
Social Security Administration's National Computer Center replacement	$500,000,000
Military construction, Army: child development centers and warrior transition complexes	$180,000,000
Military construction, Navy and Marine Corps: child development centers and warrior transition complexes	$280,000,000
Military construction, Air Force: child development centers and warrior transition complexes	$180,000,000
Military hospital construction and energy conservation investments	$1,450,000,000
Military construction, Army National Guard	$50,000,000
Military construction, Air National Guard	$50,000,000
Family housing construction, Army	$34,507,000
Family housing operation and maintenance, Army	$3,932,000
Family housing construction, Air Force	$80,100,000
Family housing operation and maintenance, Air Force	$16,461,000
Temporary expansion of military homeowner assistance program to respond to mortgage foreclosure and credit crisis, including acquisition of property at or near military bases that have been ordered closed.	$555,000,000
Veterans Affairs hospital maintenance	$1,000,000,000
National Cemetery Administration for monument and memorial repairs	$50,000,000
State extended care facilities, such as nursing homes	$150,000,000
State Department diplomatic and consular programs for domestic passport and training facilities	$90,000,000
International Boundary and Water Commission: Rio Grande levee repairs	$220,000,000
Additional capital investments in surface transportation, including highways, bridges, and road repairs	$1,298,500,000
Administrative costs for additional capital investments in surface transportation	$200,000,000
Capital investments in surface transportation grants to be awarded by other administration	$1,500,000
Federal Aviation Administration infrastructure	$200,000,000
Grants-in-aid for airports	$1,100,000,0 00
Highway infrastructure investment	$26,725,000,000
Highway infrastructure investment in Puerto Rico	$105,000,000

Program	Funding
Highway infrastructure funds distributed by states	$60,000,000
Highway infrastructure funds for the Indian Reservation Roads Program	$550,000,000
Highway infrastructure funds for surface transportation technology training	$20,000,000
Highway infrastructure to fund oversight and management of projects	$40,000,000
High-speed rail capital assistance	$8,000,000,000
National Railroad Passenger Corporation capital grants	$850,000,000
National Railroad Passenger Corporation capital grants for security	$450,000,000
Federal Transit Administration capital assistance	$6,800,000,000
Public transportation discretionary grants	$100,000,000
Fixed guideway infrastructure investment	$750,000,000
Capital investment grants	$750,000,000
Shipyard grants	$100,000,000
Public housing capital improvements	$3,000,000,000
Public housing renovations and energy conservation investments	$1,000,000,000
Native American housing block grants	$510,000,000
Community development funding	$1,000,000,000
Emergency assistance for the redevelopment of abandoned and foreclosed homes	$2,000,000,000
Additional capital investments in low-income housing tax credit projects	$2,250,000,000
Homelessness prevention and rehousing	$1,500,000,000
Assistance to owners of properties receiving Section 8 assistance	$2,000,000,000
Grants and loans for green investment in section 8 properties	$250,000,000
Lead hazard reduction	$100,000,000

Source: Michael Grabell and Christopher Weaver, "The Stimulus Plan: A Detailed List of Spending," ProPublica.org, February 13, 2009, www.propublica.org/special/the-stimulus-plan-a-detailed-list-of -spending.

It's all a big spender could ever wish for—an orgy of outlays.

But even that much spending wasn't enough for Obama and his hungry Democrats. As soon as Congress passed the stimulus bill, it went to work on a supplemental appropriations bill and added another $410 billion to the spending frenzy.

Obama had promised that he would eliminate earmarks. In his campaign against John McCain, he excused his own earmarks as a political necessity, making plain his desire to reform the system if he were elected. But enthusiasm for the avalanche of spending overcame his commitments and Obama signed the bill—even though it contained 9,287 earmarks, whose cost totaled $12.8 billion.[6]

These earmarks made a mockery of the reform Obama claimed as his mantra. But even as he violated his promises by signing the earmark-laden bill, he issued recommendations to Congress to avoid earmarks in the future, clinging to his image as an apostle of fiscal responsibility.

Take a look at some of these earmarks and gauge for yourself how fiscally responsible our president really is:

OBAMA: TONE DEAF TO EARMARKS

Earmarks in President Obama's 2009 budget

$1,049,000	for control of Mormon crickets in Utah[7]
$200,000	to fund tattoo removal clinic in California[8]
$190,000	for the Buffalo Bill Historical Center in Wyoming[9]
$2,673,000	for the Wood Education and Research Center[10]
$300,000	to promote women's sports in Boston[11]
$206,000	to promote "wool research"[12]
$2,192,000	for the Center for Grape Genetics, Geneva, NY[13]
$1,791,000	to Swine Odor & Manure Management Research, Iowa[14]
$45,000	for weed removal in Berkshire, MA[15]
$469,000	for a fruit fly facility in Hawaii[16]
$800,000	for oyster rehabilitation in Alabama[17]
$4,545,000	for wood utilization research in Michigan[18]
$75,000	to create a "totally teen zone" for teens in Albany, Georgia[19]
$300,000	for research on migrating loons[20]

$900,000	for Chicago planetarium pushed by Rahm Emanuel[21]
$190,000	to buy trolleys in Puerto Rico[22]
$380,000	for lighthouse renovation in Maine[23]
$7,800,000	for sea turtle research in Hawaii[24]
$2,600,000	to monitor the population of Hawaiian Monk Seals[25]
$1,500,000	for research on pelagic fisheries in Hawaii[26]
$650,000	for beaver research and management in Mississippi and North Carolina[27]
$1,700,000	for a honey bee factory in the Rio Grande Valley[28]

Combined, the stimulus package and the Supplemental Appropriations Bill have left us with a deficit of at least $1.8 trillion for this year—a figure equal to 12 percent of the nation's gross domestic product (GDP).[29] Other, possibly more accurate estimates put it at $2 trillion, or 14 percent of GDP.[30]

Never since World War II has our deficit been even remotely that high. When the deficit crested at 4.7 percent of GDP in 1992, Bill Clinton had to focus all his energies on bringing it down. Now its size exceeds comprehension. In the worst of its economic recession, Japan tried supporting all manner of public works—to no avail—and swelled its deficit to 10 percent of GDP. But 12 percent and rising is a new peacetime record.

So anxious were Obama and Congress to pass their grand long-term spending plans while the light was green that they didn't even take care to spend it in 2009 to combat the recession we're facing today. According to the Congressional Budget Office (CBO), only 23 percent of the money from the stimulus package will be spent in the fiscal year that ends on October 1, 2009.[31]

For example, of the $28 billion to be spent on road construction projects, only $9.6 billion will be spent by 2020.[32] And of the $16.8 billion for renewable energy, only $2.5 billion will be spent in 2009.[33] Precisely what good spending so many years from now will do for today's economy is a mystery.

TAKING HIS TIME: WHEN OBAMA'S STIMULUS WILL BE SPENT

Fiscal Year	Amount Spent
2009	$185 billion
2010	$399 billion
2011	$134 billion
2012	$36 billion
2013	$28 billion
2014	$22 billion
2015*	$5 billion

*After 2015 the tax cuts are projected to increase government revenue by a few billion dollars each year until 2019.
Source: Congressional Budget Office.

But in Washington no one asks such questions. It's much easier just to vote yes.

IS OBAMA'S PROGRAM SOCIALISM?

In our era of breathless, hyperventilated politics, we often attach easy labels to our politicians without worrying too much about whether they're truly justified. In the 1950s, anyone who leaned the slightest bit to the left was pilloried as a Communist; any liberal legislation, including civil rights and Medicare, was condemned as "creeping socialism."

So it's wise to ask: Is it unjust to call Barack Obama a "socialist"?

No. He's earned it.

Historically, the adjective "socialist" has referred to people who believe that the government should own the means of production. As we'll see later, Obama may indeed be deliberately angling to take over the financial sector, giving him an unparalleled opportunity to spread his influence throughout the economy. But he has yet to give any evidence of wanting to take all of private industry and put it under public ownership.

In modern geopolitics, however, the term "socialist" refers broadly to the Social Democratic ideology followed by the left-leaning political parties of Western Europe, who want to expand the role of government in their countries. They want to establish a broader cradle-to-grave social welfare system and to widen the influence of public institutions.

The best shorthand to determine where a nation is on the capitalist/socialist scale is to measure how much of its economy is in the public sector—in other words, what percentage of its GDP comes from government spending. By this measure, the United States has ranked well to the right of almost every other major industrialized country in the world, with the sometime exception of Japan.

The following list compares prominent nations in the proportion of their GDPs that go to government:

TOTAL GOVERNMENT SPENDING AS A PERCENTAGE OF GDP

Sweden	57.0%
France	54.0%
Italy	48.6%
Netherlands	47.1%
Germany	47.5%
United Kingdom	43.7%
Canada	40.1%
Japan	37.5%
United States	36.4%

Source: Forbes.

These data, of course, predate the Obama administration. To measure the impact his program on our standing in the socialist landscape, let's do some simple math:

HOW OBAMA IS MAKING THE UNITED STATES A SOCIALIST DEMOCRACY

Pre-Obama

Total U.S. GDP	$14,000 billion
Total government spending	$5,096 billion (36.4%)

Additional government spending under Obama

Stimulus package	$ 787 billion
Supplemental appropriations	410 billion
Estimated health care spending	625 billion
Total new Obama spending	$1,822 billion
New percentage of GDP from government	49.4%

Now compare this table with the preceding one. Whereas U.S. government spending once accounted for 36.4 percent of our economy, it is now rising to 49 percent—sending us soaring past Britain and Germany and nestling in right under France—the very model of a modern socialist democracy!

So when it comes to Barack Obama's spending programs, "socialist" is no political slur. It's a simple description.

THE STIMULUS PACKAGE THAT DOESN'T STIMULATE

With so much of the spending in his program deferred until years from now, Obama's stimulus package won't really do much to stimulate the economy. Rather, it will create a whole new set of problems for our country down the road. In two or three years, it is likely to create massive inflation, which will necessitate a new, government-induced recession to get prices back in check.

Obama's stimulus bill was a spending program, not an economic recovery program. And that's a crucial difference.

To understand this, it's helpful to review a bit of economic history.

The theory that spending equals stimulus was first popularized by the British economist John Maynard Keynes. Writing in the 1930s, he theorized that government should run deficits in times of depression to pump money into the economy and surpluses during times of inflation and prosperity to pull money out and avoid upward pressure on prices.

Before Keynes, economists had advised balancing the budget, particularly during tough economic times. The classical economists felt that running a deficit would undermine confidence in the economy and cause businesses to sit on their hands and not invest. A balanced budget, they reasoned, would induce businessmen to feel greater confidence in the economy and to put up their money for new jobs.

The classical theory was daft. Like the doctors of old who bled their patients with leeches to drain off evil spirits, the classical economists weakened the markets by raising taxes and cutting spending. Like the poor patients being bled years ago, however, the economy needed more blood, not less. It needed more spending and lower taxes, not the opposite.

The flaws of classical economic theory became glaringly apparent under President Herbert Hoover. After the stock market crash at the end of 1929, the economy seemed to be pulling out of depression as 1931 dawned. But then the economists started to bleed the patient. In order to attract more gold into the country (at that point the United States was still on the gold standard) and generate confidence in the U.S. currency, the Federal Reserve Board raised interest rates two points. To cut the deficit, Hoover raised income taxes on the top bracket from 25 percent to 63 percent and on the bottom bracket from 1 percent to 1.5 percent. To make matters even worse, Congress responded to the depression by passing the Smoot-Hawley Tariff Act in 1930, imposing sky-high tariffs to kill off foreign competition and protect American jobs. The result, of course, was to provoke retaliation from other countries and dry up foreign trade, depriving the economy of the stimulus that exports would have provided.

These "cures" made the disease worse, and the depression resumed with a vengeance. The stock market crashed. Unemployment soared to 23 percent. And by the time FDR took over in March 1933, banks were failing across the country.

Onto this stage burst the new theories of what became known as Keynesian economics. Keynes reasoned that if government increased spending on public works and other projects, more jobs would be created. The increase in the number of jobs and the extra paychecks flowing into consumers' pockets would get the economy going again. The process was called "priming the pump." The point was not to replace the private sector but to shock it back into working as it should. Like a shock from a defibrillator, the money would induce the economy to pump normally.

But it turned out that there was one problem with Keynsian economics: it didn't work. During the 1930s—its heyday—large, persistent deficits did not end the depression. They helped a bit, lessening unemployment and easing the pain, but they failed to bring back prosperity.

The lesson of the 1930s is that when government provides jobs through deficit spending, the people who get regular paychecks are personally insulated from the worst of the depression; but the rest of the world gets little help from the change, if any. The government jobs created during the 1930s did little to stimulate the rest of the economy. The cycle Keynes predicted—in which government spending would increase purchasing power, generate more consumer spending, expand production, and lead to more private employment—never really happened.

Not until World War II broke out in 1939 did the American economy recover from the Great Depression and begin its rapid march back to full employment—a trend catalyzed by increased defense contracts and expansion of the military. The unemployed of the 1930s became the soldiers of the 1940s.

And when the war finally came to America in December 1941, the federal government's purchases and contracts pushed the economy to full employment in a hurry.

So why wouldn't Obama's stimulus package have the same effect as the World War II spending?

Two reasons: First, because government spending during World War II was incomparably higher than anything we could contemplate today. Even though Obama is running a budget deficit that may rise to 13 percent of GDP, that doesn't compare with the 30 percent deficit we ran in 1942.

Second, because in the 1940s contractors and businessmen knew that the war would go on for a while and that the new government orders wouldn't dry up. So they didn't hesitate to spend money to expand their production capacity and hire new workers. Today, everyone knows that Obama's stimulus package is a one-shot affair. Even if he passes a second package, everyone knows it won't last as long as America's four-year involvement in World War II.

But why didn't Keynes's theories work in the 1930s? If taxpayers got refunds and workers got paychecks, why didn't they spend the money? Why didn't they flock to the stores to buy new products and services? And why didn't that surge in demand lead to big increases in employment as businessmen raced to take advantage of the swelling market?

Because people have brains. They're not animals who respond automatically to stimulation; they know what's going on. In the 1930s, they realized that the new jobs the government gave out could end at any moment. They knew the tax refund checks they got were one-shot gifts that wouldn't come around again. Their anxiety over the future paralyzed their ability to respond to the economic stimulus of the moment the way the economists had hoped.

Likewise, business executives of the time knew that any sudden bump-up in sales was due not to an end of the recession but to the artificial, one-shot stimulus provided by the government. Once it was spent, it'd be back to the same old depression. And so, rather than taking the revenue generated by momentary sales upticks and investing it in new factories or hiring additional workers, they put the money into safe Treasury bills and waited for better times.

What about tax cuts? Were they a better way of implementing Keynes's theories? Did refund checks in the mail create the demand Keynes craved?

The experience with one-shot tax reduction or stimulus checks has been even more dismal that that with spending increases.

Earlier in 2008, faced with a faltering economy, George W. Bush and the Republican Congress approved a stimulus check program for American taxpayers. More than $100 billion went out, an average of $950 per family.[34] What happened? Nothing. The economy remained flat. Later, academics concluded that only 10 to 20 percent of the money had actually been spent on new goods and services.[35] The rest was just used to pay down bills or reduce debt—neither of which created any jobs.

In the past two decades, Japan has faced a very similar challenge. Saddled with a protracted recession with no growth and stubborn unemployment, the Japanese government has been borrowing like crazy, spending money on public works projects year after year—with no real effect.

It was a sobering comedown for the once-thriving nation. In the 1980s, the Japanese economy soared. In the four years 1987 through 1991, the country's GDP rose by 31 percent. Yet in the fourteen years that followed— from 1991 until 2005—it rose by only 10 percent!

The Japanese economy made slight gains in 2006 and 2007, but when

GROSS DOMESTIC PRODUCT IN JAPAN

Year	GDP, Current Prices (in Billions of Yen)	GDP, 1990 Prices (in Billions of Yen)
1987	349,760	368,906
1988	373,973	391,808
1989	399,998	410,282
1990	430,040	430,040
1991	458,299	446,371
1992	471,064	450,981
1993	475,381	452,339
1994	479,260	455,254
1995	483,220	461,951
1996	499,861	480,073
1997	507,271	484,379
1998	514,595	494,847
1999	495,227	468,421
2000	501,068	481,692
2001	496,777	482,560
2002	489,618	483,715
2003	490,544	490,788
2004	496,058	504,129
2005	502,457	513,630

Source: IMF Financial Statistics Yearbook.

the global economy caved in, the Japanese crash was worse. In the last quarter of 2008, according to CNN, the Japanese economy shrank at an annual rate of 12.7 percent.[36]

It wasn't that the Japanese government wasn't trying to stimulate the economy all those years. It was following the same, futile Keynesian path that Obama is pursing—with no effect.

Here is the dismal history of Japanese efforts to spend their way into prosperity:

WHEN JAPAN TRIED OBAMA'S PROGRAM[37]

1992 As the stock market sinks 60 percent, Japan launches a Keynesian economic stimulus program, passing an $85 billion stimulus package (approximately double it to get the U.S. equivalent). Net result: investment keeps falling and unemployment rises. By the end of the year, Japan's debt-to-GDP ratio is 68.6 percent.

1993 Japan spends $117 billion on public works and small businesses and announces widespread tax cuts, along with a program of deregulation and decentralization. Result: the economy gets worse; GNP shrinks by 0.5 percent.

  Later in 1993, the government spends $59 billion on low-interest home financing, "social infrastructure," and business. The economy doesn't respond. By the end of the year, Japan's debt-to-GDP ratio reaches 74.7 percent.

Is any of this beginning to sound familiar?

1994 The government passes a new $150 billion stimulus package, including a one-year income tax, public investment, aid to small businesses, and employment support. The economy remains stagnant; the country's prime minister, Morihiro Hosokawa, resigns amid a corruption scandal. By the end of the year, the country's debt-to-GDP ratio rises to 80.2 percent.

1995 The new government spends $137 billion on another stimulus program. No improvement.

1996 Facing a huge and growing deficit, the Japanese government raises the consumption (sales) tax from 3 percent to 5 percent. The economy goes from bad to worse.

1998 Japan passes another stimulus package, this time worth $128 billion. It doesn't work. Later that year, it passes yet another stimulus, the largest ever: $195 billion. By the end of the year, the country's debt-to-GDP ratio reaches an astonishing 114.3 percent.

1999 The government passes a new stimulus package of $70 billion. The debt-to-GDP ratio reaches 128.3 percent.

Source: Wall Street Journal.

All told, Japan spent about $1 trillion (double it to find the U.S. equivalent) in trying to jump-start its economy. By April 2009, the debt-to-GDP ratio was an incredible 217 percent. What did it get for its trouble? An average growth of .6 percent a year!

All that trouble for nothing.

So how can anyone still believe that the Keynsian approach—which didn't work in the United States in the 1930s, in Japan in the 1990s, or again in the United States in 2008—stands any chance of working in 2009?

Yet Keynesian economics remains the conventional wisdom—not of economists anymore, but of the mainstream media. As the economist Mark Skousen writes in his book *The Big Three in Economics,* "If a country falls into a military conflict, a deep slump, or other crisis, the Keynesian model immediately comes to the forefront: maintain spending at all costs, even if it means significant deficit financing. The misleading Keynesian notion that consumer spending, rather than saving, capital formation, and technology drives the economy, is still very much in vogue in the halls of government and in financial circles." [38]

The *Wall Street Journal* points to a key flaw behind the model: "Keynesian 'pump-priming' in a recession has often been tried, and as an economic stimulus it is overrated. The money that the government spends has to come from somewhere, which means from the private economy in higher taxes or borrowing. The public works are usually less productive than the foregone private investment." [39]

But don't take our word for it. A wide range of economic experts is already on the record as disagreeing with Obama and predicting failure for his stimulus package.

TOP ECONOMISTS SAY NO TO OBAMA'S STIMULUS PROGRAM

GARY BECKER, WINNER OF THE NOBEL PRIZE IN ECONOMICS:
"I tend to believe that [estimates of stimulus from government spending] are excessive. They will be put together hastily, and are likely to contain a lot of political pork and other inefficiencies. For another thing . . . it is impossible to target effective spending programs that primarily utilize unemployed workers, or underemployed capital. Spending on infrastructure, and especially on health, energy, and education, will mainly attract employed persons from other activities to the activities stimulated by the government spending. The net job creation from these and related spending is likely to be rather small. In addition, if the private activities crowded out are more valuable than the activities hastily stimulated by this plan, the value of the increase in employment and GDP could be very small, even negative." [40]

ERNIE GROSS, PROFESSOR OF ECONOMICS, CREIGHTON UNIVERSITY:
"We're creating a real problem for 2010 and beyond in terms of inflation, tax rates, and certainly in terms of debt." [41]

GEORGE REISMAN, AUTHOR OF *CAPITALISM: A TREATISE ON ECONOMICS*:
"That [increasing government spending to stimulate growth] is a view held by a large school of economists, perhaps the majority school, for the last 60 years or so. That's the Keynesian school, but there are other economists, like

the Austrian school, which holds a very different position. . . . In their view, an essential requirement to a sound economy is balanced budgets with small government."[42]

ROBERT BARRO, PROFESSOR OF ECONOMICS, HARVARD UNIVERSITY:

"This is probably the worst bill that has been put forward since the 1930s. I don't know what to say. I mean it's wasting a tremendous amount of money. It has some simplistic theory that I don't think will work, so I don't think the expenditure stuff is going to have the intended effect. I don't think it will expand the economy. And the tax cutting isn't really geared toward incentives. It's not really geared to lowering tax rates; it's more along the lines of throwing money at people."[43]

ARNOLD KLING, MERCATUS CENTER FINANCIAL MARKETS WORKING GROUP:

"[T]he risks of a large stimulus, compared with a small stimulus, are:

1. It is harder to spend larger amounts quickly and cost-effectively.

2. There is a greater risk that we will run into a "sudden stop," in which foreign investors are no longer willing to fund our deficits.

3. There is a risk that fiscal stimulus, large or small, is actually ineffective, so that a large stimulus only means a large failure.

4. There is a risk that much of the spending will kick in after a recovery is underway.

5. The government's capacity to deal with an emergency, such as a major natural disaster or a foreign attack, will be limited, because its credit worthiness will be damaged.

6. There is a risk that government will absorb a permanently higher share of GDP. Policymakers will be reluctant to cut public spending for fear of causing a downturn. Moreover, it will be difficult politically to cut public spending."[44]

THOMAS SARGENT, PROFESSOR OF ECONOMICS, NEW YORK UNIVERSITY:

"The calculations that I have seen supporting the stimulus package are back-of-the-envelope ones that ignore what we have learned in the last sixty years of macroeconomic research."[45]

(*continued on next page*)

GREG MANKIW, PROFESSOR OF ECONOMICS, HARVARD UNIVERSITY:

"My advice to Team Obama: Do not be intellectually bound by the textbook Keynesian model. Be prepared to recognize that the world is vastly more complicated than the one we describe in Econ 101. In particular, empirical studies that do not impose the restrictions of Keynesian theory suggest that you might get more bang for the buck with tax cuts than spending hikes." [46]

EUGENE FAMA, PROFESSOR OF FINANCE, UNIVERSITY OF CHICAGO BOOTH SCHOOL OF BUSINESS:

"Unfortunately, bailouts and stimulus plans are not a cure. The problem is simple: bailouts and stimulus plans are funded by issuing more government debt. (The money must come from somewhere!) The added debt absorbs savings that would otherwise go to private investment. In the end, despite the existence of idle resources, bailouts and stimulus plans do not add to current resources in use. They just move resources from one use to another." [47]

JOHN TAYLOR, PROFESSOR OF ECONOMICS, STANFORD UNIVERSITYV

"The theory that a short-run government spending stimulus will jump-start the economy is based on old-fashioned, largely static Keynesian theories. These approaches do not adequately account for the complex dynamics of a modern international economy, or for expectations of the future that are now built into decisions in virtually every market." [48]

As this book goes to press in April 2009, the nation's jobless rate continues its upward climb. The economy swallowed the 2009 part of the stimulus package, burped, and went nowhere.

But the more the economy stagnates despite Obama's medicine, the more he will sap his own credibility. The more unemployment data pile up and jobless claims grow week by week, the more the president's ratings will plummet.

And the more likely it is that we can turn things around in the election of 2010!

MISERY INDEX:
THE UPWARD, UNRELENTING
MARCH OF UNEMPLOYMENT

Month	Jobless Rate
August 2008	6.1%
September 2008	6.1%
October 2008	6.5%
November 2008	6.7%
December 2008	7.2%
January 2009	7.6%
February 2009	8.1%
March 2009	8.5%
April 2009	8.9%

FIGHTING THE RECESSION:
WHAT OBAMA SHOULD HAVE DONE

So what *should* Obama have done?

The classic conservative answer, revealed as on tablets from Mount Sinai by the economic giant Milton Friedman in the 1980s, held that money supply and monetary policy were the key. Friedman warned against looking to Keynesian economics to stimulate demand; the more government borrows, he reasoned, the less is available to the private sector, which actually has to create the jobs. And any short-term effect of massive deficit spending will be obviated by fears about the inflation it will cause.

Instead, Friedman said, use monetary policy—interest rates—to increase the supply of money and credit. Work on the supply side, not the demand side, of the economy. Give businesses the low interest rates to borrow the capital they need to expand, and get government out of the way.

But the problem is that interest rates today, as in Elton John's song, are already "too low for zero." Faced with the onset of the recession, the Federal Reserve Board has cut them as close to zero as you can get. Yet the recession has only deepened. And the deeper it gets, the more prices drop. After all, when no one wants to buy, prices go down. But with prices dropping by 3 or 4 percent a year, even a 0 percent interest rate is really 3 or 4 percent! (If money is worth 4 percent more each year—because prices have fallen by that much—why borrow money at 0 percent interest? Even at that price, it means you can't take advantage of the rising value of the currency.)

Cutting interest rates has done little to solve the recession. Credit has continued to dry up. And with confidence in the economy at historic lows, no one wants to borrow anyway.

So if Keynesian demand stimulation won't work and Friedman's monetary policy was ineffective, what *will* work? In the years since Keynes, economists have developed what's known as the Theory of Rational Expectations. Simply priming the pump—and hoping for the water to flow—clearly doesn't work on its own, they reasoned. Beyond that, you have to convince people that the future is bright—that they *can* afford to buy that new car or flat-screen TV after all.

Without that confidence, those who get the stimulus money will just thank their lucky stars and use the money to pay down their credit cards or student loans or mortgages or car loans or home equity lines of credit. After all, who knows if a windfall like that will ever come again? And none of these uses for the money will do the slightest to stimulate the economy.

The need was not for a one-shot stimulation of the economy but for some long-term basis for rationally buying into the idea that the economy was recovering.

That's the key: it all comes down to confidence. If you're afraid you're going to lose your job, you save your money and don't spend anything you don't have to. That makes the economy drop even more—and only increases the chance that you might actually lose your job!

If Obama had offered the prospect of a real change in the economic environment, rational people would have responded. A short-term rise in sales due to a stimulus or a tax cut wouldn't be enough to encourage discerning businessmen to invest in new plants or equipment. But how about a cut in the capital gains tax? Or a cut in the income tax? If you knew that in the future you would have to pay only 10 percent—not the current 15 percent—in capital gains taxes on your investment earnings, wouldn't that encourage you to invest? If you knew you'd have to pay only 30 percent of your income in taxes—not the current 35 percent—wouldn't that encourage you to spend more?

One-shot tax refunds are as useless as one-shot spending increases. But permanent tax cuts, which can encourage long-term growth, send a real message to rational people that better times are coming.

Anxious to use the crisis as a pretext to expand government, Obama criticized the idea of permanent tax cuts, particularly for the wealthy, saying that it was just this sort of policy that got us into the current mess. He was determined, he insisted, to break with the "failed approaches" of the past.

But it wasn't George W. Bush's tax cut that caused the recession. His tax cuts pulled us out of the recession of 2001–2002, which hit us right after Osama bin Laden flew a plane into the global economy and knocked it down. Largely because of these tax cuts, the economy grew for five years.

The Bush tax cuts didn't cause the budget deficits of the first decade of this century either. Even though Bush cut taxes for the rich (the top 10 percent of earners), their share of total tax payments rose from 64.89 percent in 2001 to 70.79 percent in 2006.[49] In total, the richest 1 percent of the nation actually paid more money overall because of Bush's policies—an amount rising from $301 billion a year in 2001 to $408 billion in 2006.[50] In fact, it's precisely because the drop in tax rates stimulated the economy that the lower rates brought in more revenue than the higher ones had.

But Obama wouldn't let all those inconvenient facts get in the way. He wasn't about to give up his big chance to use the crisis as an excuse to grow the government. And he certainly wasn't about to use it to shrink it!

OBAMA TRASH-TALKS THE ECONOMY

Even with top-heavy majorities in both houses of Congress, Obama couldn't be absolutely certain that he'd manage to get his big spending legislation passed. In the House, of course, he could do whatever he wanted: His majority there would pass anything, and the House Republicans—the best-dressed hostages in the world—could only sit back and watch the legislation sail through.

But the Senate was a different story. There, too, he had an ample majority, but there were still forty-one Republicans that stood in his way. To bring his proposals to a vote, he needed sixty senators—and that means he couldn't do it with Democrats alone.

So Obama needed to heat up the sense of crisis. He had to make his stimulus program a do-or-die proposition. "Pass this plan or you'll plunge us into the abyss" became the administration's daily message. In one speech, Obama used the word "crisis" more than twenty times. Intent on raising the level of anxiety for political purposes, he was seemingly oblivious to the effect his words were having on the economy. What little consumer spending that survived the crash of the last quarter of 2008 dried up; business pulled in its horns.

The president said the sky was falling, so everybody looked up.

Here's a sample of the language Obama has used to describe the economic crisis to the American people—language that has only increased our collective sense of fear and deepened the recession.

HOW OBAMA DEEPENED THE RECESSION . . . WITH HIS SPEECHES

"We are in the worst financial crisis since the Great Depression, and a lot of you, I think, are worried about your jobs, your pensions, your retirement accounts." [51]

—October 7, 2008

"But I think what unifies this group is a recognition that we are experiencing an unprecedented, perhaps, economic crisis that has to be dealt with, and dealt with rapidly." [52]

—January 23, 2009

"I want to say a few words about the deepening economic crisis that we've inherited." [53]

—Kicking off an event on jobs, energy reform, and climate change, January 26, 2009

"We've inherited a terrible mess." [54]

—Arguing for his stimulus plan, February 4, 2009

"We've inherited an economic crisis as deep and dire as any since the Great Depression." [55]

—February 10, 2009

"By any measure, my administration has inherited a fiscal disaster." [56]

—At an event calling for government contracting reform, March 4, 2009

"There are a lot of individual families who are experiencing incredible pain and hardship right now." [57]

—March 13, 2009

This was good politics but rotten economics. The more Obama described the economic situation as the "worst financial crisis since the Great Depression," the more he fanned the very flames his stimulus package was supposedly meant to extinguish. He was yelling "FIRE!" in a crowded theater, stampeding an already damaged economy into a panic-driven recession.

Didn't he know what he was doing? Of course he did. It's the fundamental mission of the president to keep Americans looking forward, energized, optimistic. But Obama needed to pass his radical big spending package. Curing the recession was not his end; it was his *means* to the end. The end was bigger government.

But Obama's insistence on the negative, and the harm it has done to the economy, is really a classic case of shooting oneself in the foot. His every pessimistic comment delays the time when the economy will rebound—and makes his eventual political defeat more likely.

INFLATION: THE REAL COST OF OBAMA'S POLICIES

The Obama spending package (aka the stimulus plan) won't just increase the national debt and burden every subsequent generation with massive interest payments. In the next few years it is also likely to cause runaway inflation.

Indeed, inflation, not the recession, may be the true economic catastrophe of our times.

Most economists agree that Obama's spending programs will cause huge inflation—particularly because they are to be funded by borrowing (or printing) money.

The economist Barry Elias, for example, believes that inflation may come in the next two to three years. Here's why.

According to the Federal Reserve Board, from October 2008 through February 2009 the supply of money in circulation (plus that held in reserve by financial institutions) grew by 271 percent.[58] That's right—it almost tripled. Yet car sales didn't triple. Home sales didn't triple. Consumer spending didn't triple. In fact, mostly they dropped.

So what happened to all that extra money? Where is it?

It's parked on the sidelines of the economy, in the equivalent of economic parking garages, waiting to come out. Right now, the economic weather is still too bad to go out driving. With layoffs on the rise and sales on the decline, no one dares to spend what money they have. People are paying down their debts or putting their money into Treasury bills.

But when the sun comes out, so will the money—and all at once.

Anthony Karydakis, a contributor to CNN, explains the danger in a graphic way:

The Fed prints, say, $7 trillion worth of $100 bills (representing roughly 50 percent of the size of the economy's current GDP) and all of those bills are neatly stacked up in a large room, the windows and doors of which are all locked—no bills are taken out of the room. As a result, all of that enormous amount of newly printed money stays inactive, not generating any additional economic activity (although that would have presumably been the Fed's original intent for doing so). No increase in spending and demand for goods and services are generated, hence no inflation. This is very close to the reality confronting the Fed today.[59]

Right now, an awful lot of Americans are following the Posturepedic Savings Plan (PSP)—that is, stuffing cash under their mattresses. But when the economy improves, all that money is going to come out at once, as consumers head out to buy new goods and services. All those purchases they'd deferred—a new car to replace their cranky old one, new furniture for their threadbare living room, a new house for their growing family—all of these pent-up consumer desires will come out at once.

And too much money will be chasing too few goods, leading to huge inflation.

The financial community clearly expects inflation. That is why long-term interest rates are now so much higher than short-term rates. Investors are pretty confident that inflation won't be a problem as long as the recession rages. There's more likely to be deflation. But once it ends, they can see inflation coming a mile away.

So even though interest rates on very-short-term Treasury bills are only one quarter of one percent, the Treasury has to pay 2.94 percent to get people to lend it money for ten years.[60] And the average mortgage interest rate for a 15-year loan (at fixed rates) is 4.61 percent.[61] Why? Because we expect to be hit with inflation.

Because banks aren't lending no matter how large their reserves are, the stimulus money remains parked on the sidelines. But when the banks decide the climate is right to start lending, huge inflation will be the likely result.

As Karydakis notes, "The Fed is acutely aware of the need to start mopping up that excess liquidity, very quickly after the economy starts showing signs of making a gradual comeback."[62]

But inflationary psychology can be a hard habit to kick. Once consumers see inflation, they start demanding higher salaries, even asking their bosses to put cost-of-living wage adjustments into their compensation package. Employers, desperate to meet the new demand for their company's services, don't have time to argue. They can't fire their workers, because once unemployment starts dropping there's too much risk that they'll have to scramble to find replacements and end up falling behind their competitors in market share. So they give in—and the inflationary wage/price spiral takes over.

Karydakis mentions the need to "start mopping up that excess liquidity" as soon as the economy improves. What would probably happen in such a circumstance is that the Fed would try to buy up the extra money in circulation. To do that, however, the Federal Reserve would need to sell debt—Treasury bills—in the open market. The T-bills would soak up part of the money in circulation, keeping it from being spent and causing more inflation.

Right now, to stimulate the economy, the Fed is paying those who buy T-bills a measly one-quarter of one percent interest. Buy $100,000 in Treasury bills, and after a year you'll see only $250 as a return on your investment. Yet despite these low rates people are flocking to buy T-bills. Why? Because the U.S. government is the strongest in the world—and therefore the safest place to park your money while the recession runs its course.

As soon as the recession eases, however, all demand will disappear for T-bills that pay such little interest. Instead people will want to *spend* their money, or to invest it in more profitable ventures. The Fed will have to raise T-bill rates to competitive levels to induce people to take their money out of circulation and buy T-bills with it instead. And there's the rub: the higher interest rates climb, the more of a drag on the economy they become.

So to borrow the money to pay for Obama's "stimulus package," we will have to raise interest rates which will undo any good his stimulus spending may have done.

And the only way to cure an inflationary spiral, once it takes effect, is to induce a recession!

As a nation, our last experience with persistent inflation came during the 1970s, when the big deficits we ran to pay for the Vietnam War and the residue of the Great Society (all without a tax increase) led to double-digit inflation. No matter how often President Gerald Ford spoke of the need to "WIN" (Whip Inflation Now), his pathetic efforts came to naught.

The result was a period of what became known as "stagflation": inflation continued, but economic growth lagged. Unemployment and prices rose at the same time. The only remedy, it turned out, was a new recession—this time caused by the government.

The man behind it was Paul Volcker, who was appointed chairman of the Federal Reserve by President Jimmy Carter (to Carter's credit). It was after Volcker raised interest rates to close to 20 percent that inflation finally stopped. But of course Volcker had to nearly kill the economy to do it. The recession of 1980–1982 was one for the history books: unemployment rose rapidly, and bankruptcies soared. It took three years to tame the inflation beast, during which the nation endured a recession almost as bad as our current one.

This is the pleasant prospect Obama has in store for us. And it's totally unnecessary!

The cause of this coming calamity is Obama's excess spending binge and the skyrocketing deficits his plan will cause. This "cure" is certain to cause both inflation and a future recession—while doing little or nothing to stimulate an early end to the recession we're in right now. It's all an excuse to allow Obama to pursue his big-government dreams. And what a catastrophe it's going to cause!

THE WILD CARD: DOUBTS ABOUT CURRENCY

So far, we've been talking about conventional economics: things Obama should have foreseen but didn't. But there is an added, and even scarier, dimension: in the unfolding economic disaster, people may lose faith in the world's currencies.

During the Great Depression, the currencies of the world were tied to the price of gold. Standing behind every national Treasury department was a commitment to buy the local currency back, at a fixed price, in exchange for gold. Nobody needed to worry about the currency losing its value as long as they could take away as much gold as their currency could buy (and they could carry) whenever they wanted.

But as the depression deepened, Great Britain went off the gold standard. With British currency the strongest in the world, London decided it wanted flexibility to inflate the currency to fight the deflation of the depression, even if it didn't have enough gold to cover the extra money.

Its action led investors around the world to fear that their currency might also go off the gold standard. It was his desire to reassure the markets on this point that led Herbert Hoover to the disastrous tax increases and interest rate hikes of 1931 that deepened the depression.

When he took office, Franklin D. Roosevelt followed Britain's lead and abandoned the gold standard. Whereas dollar bills used to bear the legend "Silver Certificate," marking them as redeemable in silver or gold, now they simply read "Federal Reserve Note." But the credibility of the United States and the United Kingdom were such that nobody minded.

After the United States abandoned the gold standard, the rest of the world followed suit. But in the current recession, the United States is borrowing money at a pace surpassed only by the World War II deficits—and once again the rest of the world is following in our footsteps. China, Russia, the United Kingdom, Japan, and the European Union are all borrowing money like mad to stimulate their own economies.

SPENDING THEIR WAY TO INFLATION

(Percentage of GDP Spent on Stimulus)

	2009	2010
China	3.2%	2.7%
United States	2.0	1.9
Germany	1.5	2.0
Japan	1.4	0.4

Source: "How No 3 China Is Gaining on US and Japan," LookingForWords.com, http://lookingforwords.com/2009/04/01/current-affairs/how-no-3-china-is-gaining-on-us-and-japan/.

Some estimates suggest that global borrowing to pay for government and corporate spending will total $10 trillion this year. But the rest of the world doesn't have $10 trillion to invest. In fact, it doesn't have much to lend us at all.

China, the leading lender to the United States, is finding that its exports are down by more than one-third as the recession stops Americans from buying Chinese products. Without foreign currency coming in at a rapid pace, China has slowed its purchases of Treasury bills. And China needs to spend its extra cash on stimulating its own economy. Economists estimate that the total amount Chinese businesses will borrow this year will come to more than $2 trillion on its own.

So what happens when everyone wants to borrow and no one has money to lend? The word "borrowing" then becomes a euphemism for printing money. Uncle Sam won't be able to borrow the $1.75 trillion he may need this year, so he'll print new money to cover the difference. (And, no, the money isn't literally printed. It's virtual money, created when the Fed lets banks lend money that doesn't exist.) And every other country in the world will do the same. After all, they're even less creditworthy than we are.

China, which holds more than $700 billion of our debt, is clearly worried about the chances of an inflationary spiral in the United States. If prices should get out of hand, the value of its investments in Treasury bills would be decimated. The interest rates on the T-bills it is holding wouldn't go up, but the worth of the bills would drop steeply. For this reason, China is insisting on short maturities on its Treasury debt so it can raise interest rates each time they roll over as a hedge against inflation.

When Chinese officials wondered publicly about the credibility of the American debt China is holding, the media attacked them. Obama and Secretary of State Clinton rushed to reassure the Asian powerhouse that its investments were secure. But China's doubts make sense, and they're worth listening to.

In the meantime, the Fed just keeps on increasing the money supply. On March 18, 2009, it announced a new trillion-dollar program of purchasing T-bills and issuing credit to banks in an effort to put more money into circulation.

As with its efforts to date, the Fed can give banks money, but it cannot make them lend. More likely, the banks will continue to park their money on the sidelines and bring it all out when conditions improve. The Fed will then be faced with the daunting, and likely impossible, task of mopping up all the surplus currency it is creating.

But by just printing money—not even really borrowing it—we face the frightening prospect of a global loss of confidence in currency. This unprecedented situation could bring back barter and other off-currency transactions and could spell total disaster for the markets. Nobody really knows what the effect of such a loss of confidence would be. We may be about to find out!

AROUND THE CORNER: TAX INCREASES

But we do know what's around the corner: big tax increases. It isn't just that Obama's stimulus package won't work. His tax policies are ensuring that it won't! Everything Obama is giving with his stimulus spending, he's taking away with the tax increases he's proposing.

With his right hand, Obama is offering business increased tax incentives and reductions. But with the left he is proposing to raise income, estate, and payroll taxes on those same businessmen in two years. He promotes real estate sales by offering first-time home buyers a tax credit. But then he proposes cutting the tax deduction for mortgage interest in two years!

Knowing the magnitude of the coming tax hikes, households making more than $200,000 a year aren't spending money in response to Obama's stimulus enticements. They're hunkering down, trying to conserve their assets so they'll be able to afford the tax increases they know he has in store for them.

And what increases they will be!

First, he'll increase the top brackets to 35 percent and 39.6 percent respectively—a 9 percent hike for the first group and a 13 percent rise for the second.

Then he'll impose the FICA Social Security payroll tax on all income over $250,000 per year. (He has yet, as of this writing, to submit a proposal to Congress, but he promised to raise these taxes in his campaign, and when it comes to tax hikes he usually keeps his word.) For these taxpayers, it will mean paying an extra 6.5 percent tax if they're employed (and an equal amount by their employer) or, more likely, a 13 percent tax increase if they're self-employed.

And he'll cut the amount that taxpayers making more than $200,000 a year can deduct on their taxes (for home mortgages, charitable donations, state and local taxes, and so on) by 30 percent.

Add in state and local levies that are going up all over the country, and that means a high-income taxpayer will have to pay more than 60 percent of his or her income in taxes.

Politically, Obama is making sure to gouge only the top wage earners in the nation. But economically the impact of these hikes will be huge. It's that top 1 percent who pay 41 percent of all income taxes in the United States; the top 5 percent pay more than 60 percent.[63]

Upper-income taxpayers are also the biggest spenders. By hitting them as hard as he is, Obama is ensuring that they won't be lured into spending by his stimulus proposals but will realize that they just presage the tax increases down the road.

Upper-income taxpayers must feel a bit like hogs at the Chicago stockyards—being fattened with stimulus spending so they can be slaughtered with tax increases two years down the road . . . all to make a nice breakfast for the federal government.

CLASS WARFARE BECOMES GOVERNMENT POLICY

More and more, President Barack Obama is turning American politics into a pitched battle between those who pay taxes and those who live off them.

It's the tax payers vs. the tax eaters.

Under the guise of a stimulus package to bring the economy out of its recession, the Obama administration is reworking the fundamental politics of our country, passing out checks like heroin to create a constituency addicted to public handouts, and concentrating the tax burden of paying for it all on a smaller and smaller number of Americans. A larger percentage of the American population is paying no income taxes at all and few other levies, making them unlikely to complain when taxes are raised on those who do. At the same time, they're getting checks from Washington as part of a concerted effort to build a constituency that supports big government and big handouts.

The social consensus that used to underlie public policy making in the United States has melted down. In the past, when we voted to embark on new spending, we understood that we'd all have to share the burden. And we accepted that. We all agreed that the rich should pay more and the poor less, but we knew we'd all have to shoulder some of the freight. To a great degree, we followed the Marxist maxim "From each according to his abilities and to each according to his needs." But everyone had to contribute something!

Even before Obama took office, this basic construct had begun to fracture. On the day he became president, 43 million American households—roughly a third of all households in the country—were paying no federal income taxes at all.[64] In fact, most of those people got checks *from* the government.

But when Obama's tax program is fully implemented, a majority of Americans will be exempt from paying any federal income taxes. And, instead of a tax bill most of them will get checks from Washington every year.

Under the guise of cutting taxes and "making work pay," Obama is effectively putting a majority of Americans on welfare.

This isn't entirely new, of course. The government has long handed out checks to large segments of our population. Economists call these payments "cash transfers." At first these checks targeted specific groups of people, mainly the elderly and the disabled—those who had paid into the Social Security system all their working lives. Veterans who had served our country in the military received pensions and other payments. Others who got government checks include those who were especially needy, such as unemployed single mothers trying to raise small children and people whose incomes were so low they need food stamps to maintain an adequate diet.

Washington also showered its largesse on us by granting tax deductions (which cut our taxable income) or credits (which cut our actual tax bill). If we gave to charity, paid a home mortgage, or shelled out money for local taxes, we got to deduct the payments on our income tax returns. But the rule was always the same: you could reduce only the taxes that you had actually paid. If you made a charitable contribution but earned so little that you didn't have to pay any income taxes, you got no tax benefit from your generosity. You couldn't go below zero taxes.

But then in 1986, in the days of Ronald Reagan, Washington developed a new policy: the refundable tax credit.

Reagan wanted people who worked full-time and couldn't work their way out of poverty to be able to get a hand up. He distinguished this hand up from the handouts given to welfare mothers who did not work. To the Gipper and his Republican followers, those who worked deserved our compassion more than those who didn't.

So Reagan decided that everyone who worked full-time but whose household size was such that they were still impoverished on payday, would get a credit against their income taxes—even if that meant that they didn't pay any taxes.

But even a full exemption from taxes wasn't enough for many of the workers Reagan wanted to help. They made so little that even being relieved of the need to pay income taxes didn't make enough difference to get them out of poverty. So Reagan decided to make the tax credit "refundable."

Of course, it was a "refund" in name only. Those who got the assistance weren't really getting back money they paid. They were getting these "refund" checks even though they hadn't paid any taxes to begin with.

This was called the Earned Income Tax Credit. Congress loved the EITC, and under President Clinton it expanded it dramatically. In 1993–1994, Clinton—who had pledged to "end welfare as we know it" during his campaign—persuaded the Democratic Congress to beef up the EITC and offer its benefits to people making as much as $25,000 a year or more. If their families were sufficiently large that even this income meant they lived in poverty, they would get a refund. No longer would anyone go to work at a full-time job and come home poor!

As a result, more than 20 million Americans now receive EITC payments averaging more than $1,900 each.[65]

In 2000, George W. Bush was elected president—swept into office in part by a popular mandate to cut taxes. But during the campaign he had been roughed up by his Democratic opponent, Vice President Al Gore, who said that Bush would only cut taxes for the rich while doing nothing to help the middle class. Gore noted that Ronald Reagan, the ultimate Republican tax cutter, had actually increased income taxes on the middle class, raising the bottom-bracket income tax rate from 11 percent to 15 percent as he was cutting the top levy from 50 percent all the way down to 28 percent.[66]

Gore warned that Republicans only wanted to cut taxes for the rich and would do nothing to help the average person.

But Bush had gotten elected as a "compassionate conservative"; he was determined to help the poor and middle class, as well as the rich, with his tax cuts. Between 2001 and 2003, the Bush administration instituted a federal tax cut for all taxpayers. Among other changes, the lowest income tax rate was lowered from 15 percent to 10 percent, the 27 percent rate went to 25 percent, the 30 percent rate went to 28 percent, the 35 percent rate went to 33 percent, and the top marginal tax rate went from 39.6 percent to 35 percent.[67]

Still Democrats pressed for more tax cuts for the bottom of the spectrum. How, they asked, can we help those who earn so little that they pay no income tax at all? By definition, tax cuts would offer them no assistance. Unless Bush made an effort to help them, his tax cuts could still be skewered by partisan opponents as a giveaway to the rich.

So President Bush and Congress passed a refundable tax credit of $1,000 per child for every taxpayer who earned less than $55,000 ($110,000 for a couple) and had children under the age of eighteen living at home.[68] And if he or she paid no taxes because his or her income was too low, he or she would *receive* a check. Ninety percent of the parents in the United States are eligible for the Child Tax Credit; in 2005, it led to $14.6 billion in payments or credits to families.[69]

With the refundable tax credit, Bush was able to argue that a fair share of his tax cuts were going to the poor and the lower middle class, not just to the wealthy. But in passing the credit and making it "refundable," Bush extended the concept of the tax credit in a potentially dangerous way. Now those who paid no taxes would get a check based not on their particular economic circumstances, as those who benefited from the Earned Income Tax Credit did, but simply because they had children. The EITC is really a form of negative income tax—money paid to adjust for differences in income. But the Child Tax Credit was something altogether different. It was really the start of a new form of national welfare: money people got through the tax system as an entitlement simply because they had children.

Now Obama has taken the refundable tax credit one step further, giving everyone who earns less than $190,000 a tax credit of $400 (or $800 for couples.) And if they don't pay enough in taxes to use up the $400 credit, they will receive a check for the balance. If they pay no taxes at all, they will receive a $400 check in the mail.[70]

President Obama has led the United States across an important line in the sand. No longer will we hand out checks to people just because they've paid into the Social Security system or served the country in the military. You don't even need to be part of the working poor or a parent to get a check. You just have to exist and make less than $200,000. The aid encompasses us all: we have all gone on welfare.

Obama's refundable tax credit is a permanent part of the tax code, an entitlement we'll have to honor year after year. And it is the way of such things that they never go down—only up.

Obama's tax cuts also crossed another key line in the sand: they exempted a voting majority of Americans from having to pay any federal income tax at all.

After Bush got through with the tax code, the share of federal income taxes paid by the poorest half of the country dropped by a quarter.[71] Today, the poorest half of the nation pays only 3 percent of the national income taxes.[72]

THE POOREST PAY LESS AND LESS IN TAXES: PERCENTAGE OF FEDERAL INCOME TAXES PAID BY THE BOTTOM HALF OF TAXPAYERS

(Those earning less than $32,000 in 2008)

1980	7%
1985	7%
1990	6%
1995	5%
2000	4%
2006	3%

Source: Internal Revenue Service.

Now that Obama has passed his refundable tax credit, the bottom half of the nation will probably pay no federal income taxes at all—zero, nada, zip.

Unfortunately, in the future, we can look forward to a majority of American voters having a vested interest in maintaining the Obama tax policies so that they continue to pay no taxes at all, while the burden on those who do pay taxes continues to grow exponentially.

The political ramifications of this policy will be enormous. Tax eaters will strongly outnumber tax payers, and those who are paying for our government will have little or no voice in what the government does.

But, of course, that's not all: Because of the growth in refundable tax credits, the lower middle class and poor actually *make money* from the tax system. The Heritage Foundation reports that the poorest 20 percent of the country not only pay no income taxes, but they get so much money back that they have an "effective" income tax rate of minus 5.9 percent.[73] The second quintile from the bottom also has a negative tax rate, although slightly smaller, of minus 1.1 percent.[74] Once Obama's tax package is factored in, the bottom half will not only pay no taxes but will actually receive checks from Washington.

But this isn't the only shift in the tectonic plates of national income and tax policies. As the poor get to pay less and less in taxes and receive more and more in entitlements, the richest Americans will have to pay a greater and greater share of the national tax burden.

Though we'd all agree that the rich should pay a larger share of their income in taxes than the middle class or the poor, the new economics of income and taxation skew the tax payments so drastically toward upper-income families that fewer and fewer people are paying more and more of the taxes.

In 1980, the richest 1 percent of America paid 19 percent of all federal income taxes.[75] By 2006, their share had risen to 40 percent.[76]

And it wasn't only the very rich who assumed a vastly disproportionate share of the nation's finances. The top quarter of Americans paid 73 percent of income taxes in 1980, but by 2006 their share of income taxes paid rose to 86 percent.[77]

SOAKING THE "RICH": PERCENTAGE OF FEDERAL INCOME TAXES PAID BY . . .

	Top 1% (above $389,000)	Top 25% (above $65,000)
1980	19%	73%
1985	22%	74%
1990	25%	77%
1995	30%	80%
2000	37%	84%
2006	40%	86%

Source: Gerald Prante, "Summary of the Latest Federal Income Tax Data," TaxFoundation .org, July 18, 2008, www.taxfoundation.org/news/show/250.html.

Of course, there's no need to weep for the rich. The past thirty years have seen an incredible concentration of wealth at the very top of our social pyramid. Since 1980, the share of total national income that went to the top 1 percent of our population has almost tripled, from 8 percent to 22 percent.[78] At the same time, the proportion earned by the poorest half dropped from 18 percent in 1980 to 13 percent today.[79]

THE RICH GET RICHER AND THE POOR GET POORER: PERCENTAGE OF NATIONAL INCOME THAT WENT TO . . .

Year	The Richest 1%	The Poorest 50%
1980	8%	18%
1985	10%	17%
1990	14%	15%
1995	15%	15%
2000	21%	13%
2005	22%	13%

Source: Gerald Prante, "Summary of the Latest Federal Income Tax Data," TaxFoundation.org, July 18, 2008, www.taxfoundation.org/news/show/250.html.

So there are really three classes of taxpayers in the United States:

1. The tax payers: The top 25 percent, who pay 86 percent of federal income taxes
2. The tax neutrals: The middle 25 percent, who pay the rest
3. The tax eaters: The bottom 50 percent, who pay no income taxes and get refundable tax credit checks from the government

Politically, only a distinct minority—the top 25 percent or, really, the top 1 percent of the country—face any significant tax liability. Giving the lie to Benjamin Franklin's lament that the only two things you can't avoid are "death and taxes," the bulk of the American population escapes most of the tax burden—and half get away without paying income taxes entirely.

During Obama's presidential campaign, he promised to cut taxes for 95 percent of all Americans.[80] Many were inclined to dismiss his suggestions as political pandering and unrealistic promises. But he meant it. His goal is to cut the taxpaying proportion of the American population to a minority, leaving an electoral majority that is immune to antitax rhetoric.

What will be the impact of this brave new world of tax policy? What might happen as Obama's policies unfold and more and more Americans end up paying no taxes?

Inevitably, taxes will fade as an issue in American politics. Most people won't have to pay them. The mass political base of middle-class taxpayers will disappear. Concern about taxes will be the political province only of the outvoted rich.

The antitax movements of the late 1970s and early 1980s, which culminated in the Reagan Revolution of 1980, were based on the outrage of the Joe the Plumbers of an earlier age. The blue-collar worker burdened with high taxes—which he suspected were going to pay welfare mothers who were being paid for not working—formed an infantry that stormed the nation's political system and demanded cuts in taxes. The Silent Majority of the Nixon years became the Reagan Democrats of the 1980s—the dominant political forces of their eras. Turning their backs on their liberal past, these workers, often contradicting their union's policy, broke with the Democratic Party and embraced Reagan's dogma that the government was the problem, not the solution to, America's ills.

But no more.

Obama and the Left have come to realize that the Achilles' heel of the antitax movement is its reliance on middle-income voters to win tax cuts that will go largely to upper-income taxpayers. Obama was the first to capitalize on this insight, getting elected on an overt plan to make the rich pay higher taxes while cutting levies for the vast bulk of the population.

By dividing taxpayers by class, Obama nullified the Reagan strategy. But it was the Clinton and Bush tax cuts, which so reduced the tax burden on the middle class that antitax rhetoric meant nothing to them, that made his victory possible.

Obama is passing further tax cuts on the middle class and higher tax "refunds" for the nontaxpaying poor, dramatically increasing the political isolation of the real taxpayers in America. Before he moves to raise taxes on upper-income Americans, though, he wants first to neuter them politically. By driving a fissure between the middle class, who don't pay much in federal income taxes, and the richest 25 percent, who pay almost all the taxes, he renders those who have to pay the taxes politically helpless.

And that is Obama's strategy for the future—the indefinite future: to finance the American government by raising taxes on the politically impotent rich. Hit them hard at the tax office, and then outvote them on election day.

The 25 percent of Americans who pay 86 percent of the income taxes (to say nothing of the 1 percent who pay 40 percent) will be like New York City's benighted landlords. Outvoted by their tenants, they're forced by state law to conduct their business under draconian rent controls, which so limit their incomes that many just walk away from their properties. Likewise, taxpayers could become a hostage class, subject to the political impulses and inclinations of those who don't share their tax burden.

No politician will come to their aid, since their collective voting strength isn't sufficient to win any election—not to mention the fact that any politician suspected of coddling the rich at the expense of the bulk of the voters who pay no taxes, and the sizable minority who reap benefits through "refundable" tax credits would be slated for extinction.

In the meantime, the majority continue to receive refundable tax checks in even larger amounts. It is their job to eat the tax money, not to generate it.

Of course, there's a political fallacy in Obama's worldview. The richest taxpayers may be impotent politically due to their small numbers, but they're not impotent economically. The top 20 percent of earners account for 46 percent of all consumer spending.[81] They're the ones who *spend* money. If Obama declares war on them, as he appears to be doing, he cannot recover economically without them. It's to them that he must look to make sure the American people start doing everything they're not doing right now: buying stock, paying taxes, consuming goods and services. Without their participation, the economy has no hope of recovery.

Obama cannot succeed by waging war on the rich. It didn't work when FDR tried it, and it cannot work now.

OBAMA: FOLLOWING THE LESSONS
OF FDR'S SECOND TERM

As he prepared to become president in the days between his election and the inauguration, Obama and his aides made it known that he was focusing, with special attention, on two figures from our history: Abraham Lincoln and FDR. With luck, he learned important lessons from Lincoln, who has so many to teach.

But he appears to have learned some more dangerous lessons from the story of how Franklin D. Roosevelt handled the economy during his second term—the years from 1937 until 1941, when the depression seemed to drag on with no end in sight.

To understand Obama's political strategy—so that we can defeat it—we need to learn how FDR faced a crisis very similar to that which engulfs us now. Unfortunately, Obama's tactics suggest much of the same emphasis on class warfare and special interests that characterized Roosevelt's second term.

FDR deserves his heroic reputation as an American icon. He brought us Social Security, the minimum wage, securities regulation, and widespread unionization and, of course, saved us in World War II.

But the most important brick in the wall of respect that has been erected to him was that he cured the Depression. In reality, he did no such thing.

When Roosevelt first took office in March 1933, the nation's banking structure was in a state of collapse and chaos. Most banks either had failed or were teetering on the brink. Long lines formed outside many banks, as anxious people clamored to reclaim their life savings.

FDR handled the situation brilliantly, closing all the banks and then gradually reopening them—one by one—assuring the public that he had determined that they were sound. In his inaugural address of 1933, he denounced "nameless, unreasoning, unjustified terror which paralyzes needed efforts to convert retreat into advance." [82]

The effect was electrifying. The crowds no longer beseiged the banks, and the system was restored.

In his first hundred days in office, FDR bombarded Congress with pro-posals to catalyze recovery. For the farms, he proposed to limit production to raise prices. For business, he sought to stop deflation and increase wages.

For the unemployed, he created the Civilian Conservation Corps, to put them to work in rural areas protecting our national resources. Elsewhere, he spent prodigiously on public works to offer short-term employment.

Ironically, in view of his subsequent lurch to the left, Roosevelt's first hundred days were a model of conservatism. Raymond Moley, the FDR aide who founded the "Brain Trust" that advised Roosevelt and remained its most important member during Roosevelt's first term, wrote in 1939 that "it cannot be emphasized too strongly that the policies which vanquished the bank crisis were thoroughly conservative. . . . Those who conceived and executed them were intent upon rallying confidence first, of the conservative business and banking leaders of the country and, then, through them, of the public generally." [83]

Even when the hundred days were over, Roosevelt maintained a brisk pace of national legislation to end the Depression and (as the Democratic Party theme song put it) make America a place where "Happy Days Are Here Again."

But FDR had only limited success with his bold, innovative programs. When he took office, unemployment stood at a shocking 23 percent. But by the end of his first term, it remained stubbornly high at 13 percent. There were still 10 million people for whom Roosevelt couldn't create jobs.

Roosevelt had put Keynesian economics to the test—and reached the limits of what it could do.

There is actually substantial evidence that FDR's policies extended and deepened the depression. Amity Shlaes, a senior fellow at the Council on Foreign Relations and a syndicated columnist for Bloomberg, writes in her excellent, must-read book *The Forgotten Man* that "both Hoover and Roosevelt misstepped in a number of ways." [84]

She writes that Roosevelt "created regulatory, aid, and relief agencies based on the premise that recovery could be achieved only through a large military-style effort." [85] But, she notes, Roosevelt's interventions created massive uncertainty and left potential investors wondering what would happen next. The National Recovery Administration (NRA), the centerpiece of his program, tried to raise wages and promote unionization. Its bureaucrats "frightened away capital . . . and discouraged employers from hiring workers." [86]

"Another problem," Shlaes continues, "was that laws like that which created the NRA . . . were so broad that no one knew how they would be interpreted. The resulting hesitation in itself arrested growth." [87]

So how did FDR get elected four times? Shlaes ascribes his political success to the fact that he "systematized interest-group politics . . . to include many constituencies—labor, senior citizens, farmers, union workers. The president made groups where only individual citizens or isolated cranks had stood before, ministered to those groups, and was rewarded with their votes." [88]

Unable to restore prosperity, FDR switched strategies as his 1936 reelection campaign approached. Rather than hinge his case to the nation on his record in eradicating the depression, he focused instead on class warfare, attacking the "economic royalists" who had led us into the depression. "I should like to have it said of my first administration that in it the forces of selfishness and of lust for power met their match," he declared. "I would like to have it said of my second administration that in it these forces met their master." [89]

By channeling the nation's anger about the economic mismanagement and greed that had caused the depression, FDR was able to distract voters from the grim fact that the depression had not been cured by his four years of Keynesian policies.

Instead of economic recovery, he focused on building his support among three key constituency groups: labor, farmers, and the elderly. Piecing together an electoral coalition from these special interests, he managed to assure himself of a solid and ongoing majority.

The elderly were given Social Security, which offered—for the first time—the assurance of pensions in old age. The farmers were given the Agricultural Adjustment Act, which set limits on production and paid them to keep down crop yields, first stabilizing and then inflating agricultural prices. Unions were given the Wagner Act, which made it easy to form a labor organization, guaranteed the right to strike, and established a procedure of secret ballot in representation elections.

Barack Obama knows his history well. If his economic stimulus plan fails—and the economy continues to tank—he can fall back on class divisions to get reelected.

By continuously hammering on sensationalist topics such as extravagant executive compensation, bonuses for employees of bailed-out companies, and the disproportionate earnings of the rich, he hopes to keep alive the spirit of anger and division—and keep his job.

But Obama misjudges the meaning of class in the United States. In Europe, where the heritage of Marxism is stronger, class divisions are seen as more permanent. Upward mobility has been lacking—historically thwarted in earlier times by class structure and prejudices and, these days, by the lack of economic growth.

In Europe, class lines have become rigid over the centuries; each class has developed a narrative to glorify its place in the social order. Americans see class divisions aspirationally, looking forward to the day when they can move up. Denied the easy prospect of upward mobility, the European worker is likely to feel envy and resentment, not ambition, toward the gentry.

Can Obama cash in on class resentments in the United States that mirror European politics? Is the American Dream dead?

The answer is a decisive NO! The dream is far from dead. Upward mobility in the United States continues, as it has historically.

Obama and liberals like to cite data showing that the top 20 percent of earners in the United States are making more, while the bottom 20 percent are making proportionately less. But the fact is that the makeup of that bottom 20 percent is changing constantly, as new immigrants, both legal and illegal, come in and find their footing on the lowest rung on the economic ladder. Meanwhile, those who were once in the bottom 20 percent continue their steady upward climb.

One recent study by the Congressional Joint Economic Committee analyzed those who were in the bottom 20 percent in 1979. By 1988, it found, "more of them had reached the top income quintile (14.7 percent) than had remained at the bottom (14.2 percent)."[90] "In other words," the committee concluded, "a member of the bottom income bracket in 1979 would have a better chance of moving to the top income bracket by 1988 than [of] remaining in the bottom bracket."[91] And 86 percent of those who were among the bottom 20 percent in income in 1979 rose out of this category in the ensuing nine years.

More typical of the traditional attitude of Americans toward class is the philosophy of John F. Kennedy, whose economic program was aimed at encouraging growth through tax cuts. "A rising tide," he said, "lifts all boats."[92]

This theory of shared outcomes has often been derided by liberals as "trickle-down economics"—as a theory that hopes the success of the rich will flow down to everyone else. The liberals have a point: In the past two decades, the income gains of the top 1 percent have not flowed down to the rest of the country very well. Every quintile in America experienced a growth in income in the past decade (after inflation), but the growth of the bottom four quintiles was minor compared to that at the top.

But if trickle-down doesn't always work, irrigation does. The real key is to adopt policies that encourage the downward flow of wealth, as Bill Clinton did. The Earned Income Tax Credit, welfare reform, day care, college scholarships, and the like do exactly that.

And while the bottom 20 percent, taken as a whole, have had only small increases in their collective income, the congressional study makes it clear that there is a new bottom twenty percent each year as the formerly poor move up and new immigrants come in at the bottom. This churning, not a stagnant class structure, is typical of America.

But Obama's approach is not to trickle down or irrigate, and certainly not to let a rising tide lift all boats. His policy is to undermine the wealthiest Americans by saddling them with heavy taxes, limiting their deductions, and undertaking a campaign of national vilification to subject them to universal obloquy. This approach won't help the economy—and in the process it could sabotage both our economic growth and his own political career.

HOW OBAMA IS MAKING THINGS WORSE

Each week, President Obama seems to come up with another idea of how to transform the American economic system. He seems to be in a desperate hurry to churn out these proposals while he still controls Congress and before the continuing economic recession undermines his popularity.

Yet each time he makes a new proposal he changes the ground rules of the American economic system, introducing a new element of uncertainty into business decisions. It was exactly this kind of inconsistency and unpredictability that caused the Roosevelt recession of 1937–1939. Back then, businessmen didn't know what the rules would be the next month, much less the next year. As a result, they prudently refrained from spending and investing, stymieing economic growth and recovery.

The same thing is happening now. In March 2009 alone, Obama proposed a major shift in the regulation of nonbank institutions such as hedge funds, brokerage houses, and insurance companies. He and Timothy Geithner, his Treasury secretary, spoke of the importance of regulating companies that are "too big to fail"—whose collapse would cause general economic mayhem. They implied that the federal government should be allowed to decide, on a case-by-case basis, which institutions fall into this category and be able to change the categorization whenever they feel the circumstances warrant.

How can a business operate when it doesn't know whether it's about to come under the government's regulatory control? Will Obama's bill pass? And if it does, what will it provide? A sound business procedure would be to make no long-term commitments to economic projects until these regulatory issues are resolved. The result would be paralysis at just the moment when we need these very businesses to take risks and move ahead—especially in the purchase of the so-called toxic assets held by our banking system.

The Obama plan injects a further element of uncertainty in that no business will really know if it is "too big to fail" and, hence, subject to another round of regulatory scrutiny. And what about the future? At what level of growth will a firm's success be punished with such a designation? And what will that mean?

All these factors tend to freeze economic activity as businesspeople wait for the regulatory gavel to fall.

In late March, President Obama appointed a task force, headed by former Federal Reserve chairman Paul Volcker, to recommend sweeping changes in the tax code. The panel was charged with the mandate of making its recommendations by December 2009. The very breadth of Volcker's assignment implies that huge changes are in the offing, potentially affecting every aspect of business and personal activity—adding to the uncertainty that is already paralyzing corporate and individual economic decisions.

What businessperson in his or her right mind would embark on a major investment without knowing what the tax consequences will be? And how many people would feel comfortable deciding to buy a home or making an investment without knowing whether they'll be able to deduct the mortgage or depreciate the investment?

The price of Obama's spasmodic efforts at reform will be paralysis of just the sort that prolonged the Great Depression in the 1930s.

The possibility of new rules about labor union organizing is another area that creates uncertainty. Later in this book we'll discuss Obama's card-check unionization proposal and his demand for compulsory arbitration to resolve impasses in labor contract negotiations. Any business contemplating expansion in the United States has to wonder whether Obama's proposals will lead to unionization of its new factory or workplace. Just as the Wagner Act, passed by FDR in the mid-1930s, raised the likelihood of a new, unionized environment for business, so do the Obama proposals—another source of uncertainty that could lead to the postponement of business decisions and short- and intermediate-term stagnation.

Finally, who knows what the president will come up with tomorrow? What new proposals will he make, and what will their impact be? The president cannot expect to change every aspect of the regulatory environment and the relationship between the economy and the government without curtailing exactly the kind of spending and investing that he most needs to help the economy.

Obviously, Obama is motivated by political realities; he's trying to act while he still has control over all the levers of power. But we must all realize that by indulging him and permitting these far-reaching changes, we are only lengthening and deepening the current crisis.

Some of Obama's proposals are necessary. We do need to regulate non-bank financial institutions; it is absurd that we scrutinize (though inadequately) the activities of banks but not of brokerage houses. But to every government action there is a season. And this should be a time of stability, a time for business expansion and investment to be encouraged, not undercut. There will be time for change once the crisis has passed.

Unless, like Rahm Emanuel, you believe that "no serious crisis should go to waste."

THE EUROPEAN IDEA IN OBAMA'S HEAD

With his emphasis on principles such as income redistribution, increased spending, and heavy taxation of the rich, Barack Obama is marching to the beat of a different drummer—a European drummer. These are the concepts that animate the social democracies of the Continent; they are foreign to the American traditions of democracy, independence, and limited government.

The economist Jeremy Rifkin echoes many of Obama's ideas in his new book, *The European Dream*. He tells us that the American Dream is defunct and that its natural successor is the new European model. Rifkin discusses the differences between American and European attitudes toward income redistribution.

> Americans . . . are, for the most part, unwilling to commit our tax money to the task [of income redistribution]. . . . Europeans . . . are far more willing to entertain the idea of government intervening to redress [income] inequities.[93]

In Europe, Rifkin goes on to explain,

> there is a belief that market forces, if left to their own devices, are often unfair and, therefore, need to be tamed. Government redistribution, in the form of transfers and payments to those less fortunate, is considered an appropriate antidote to unrestrained market capitalism. That is why, in Europe, the notion of creating social democracy—a mixed system that balances market forces with government assistance—has flourished since World War II.[94]

It is exactly this concept of a social democracy that seems to form the central element in President Obama's thinking. Certainly his evocation of class consciousness clearly imitates the European model.

Europeans, for example, have no problem with taxing the rich. Their marginal tax rates—the percent of income of the richest people that the government takes—are significantly higher than they have historically been in the United States.

But after Obama passes his tax program, the top rate in the United States will rise to about 49 percent. And when he passes his program to eliminate the cap on the Social Security tax, it will soar into the low 60s (counting state and local taxes) bypassing all the European nations listed above!

The European bias against the rich is so ingrained that French president

HOW MUCH DOES GOVERNMENT TAKE?
TOP MARGINAL TAX RATES, 2007

(Counts all state and local payroll and income taxes)

Netherlands	52%
France	50%
Japan	48%
Germany	48%
United States	43%
United Kingdom	41%

David Gauthier-Villars, "Sarkozy's Bete Noire: Tax on Rich," *Wall Street Journal*, March 18, 2009, http://online.wsj.com/article/SB123731_536163259491.html.

Nicolas Sarkozy recently spoke of the need to "reconcile France with the idea of success."[95]

Part of Americans' traditional love affair with success—and Europeans' empathy with poverty—comes from their differences over what causes people to move up or down the career ladder. Rifkin quotes the Pew Global Attitudes Project's observation that "two-thirds of Americans believe that success is not outside their control. . . . Asked why people are wealthy, 64 percent of Americans say [it is] because of personal drive, willingness to take risks, and hard work and initiative."[96]

And why do others fail? When asked that question, 64 percent of Americans cited a lack of thrift, 53 percent ascribed the failure (at least in part) to a lack of effort, and a like percentage said that failure was due to a lack of ability.[97]

But Rifkin notes that "in Europe, a majority in every country—with the exception of the U.K., Czech Republic, and Slovakia—'believe that forces outside of an individual's personal control determine success.'" In all, 71 percent of American respondents "believe that the poor have a chance to escape from poverty." Only 40 percent of Europeans polled agreed.[98]

Obama's emphasis on income redistribution and his determination to use the tax code to promote it may earn the ire of Joe the Plumber, but it draws applause from Europe.

The fact is that Europe desperately needs Obama. When François Mitterrand, a Socialist, became president of France in 1981, he nationalized a broad swath of French businesses and industries and embarked on a vision of achieving socialism in France. Predictably, French capital fled to Margaret Thatcher's Britain and Ronald Reagan's United States, where free markets and low taxes predominated. Stung by the resulting one-country depression, Mitterrand had to reverse field only two years into his term and reprivatize most of the companies the government had taken over.

Europe's Left learned its lesson: it is virtually impossible to launch socialism in one country when there are competing models nearby. So it began to focus on integrating all of the continent's economies into the European Union (EU) and moving it toward socialism. The ethos of eight-week vacations, paid pregnancy leaves, abridgement of the right to fire workers, and a host of other leftist policies gained broad currency throughout the EU.

But one problem remained: the United States was not on board. Stubbornly pursuing free-market and minimal-government policies, Washington benefited from a massive outflow of capital and jobs from Europe to the United States as employers and the wealthy fled the high taxes and intrusive regulation of the European Union.

Now that Obama is bringing U.S. tax policy (and soon regulatory policies) into sync with those of the European Union, the socialists are euphoric. Their problem is solved. They can go ahead building their continental utopia without having to trim their sails for fear of competition from across the ocean.

The European goal Obama seems to be pursuing runs distinctly counter to the traditional American Dream. Jeremy Rifkin adroitly emphasizes the differences:

> The European Dream emphasizes community relationships over individual autonomy, cultural diversity over assimilation, quality of life over the accumulation of wealth, sustainable development over unlimited material growth, deep play over unrelenting toil, universal human rights and the rights of nature over property rights, and global cooperation over the unilateral exercise of power.[99]

Follow Rifkin's list, and you will see Obama's program as it takes shape:

OBAMA'S EUROPEAN DREAM

"Community relationships over individual autonomy"

- Obama wants to require businesses to offer health insurance.
- He wants to include labor and environmental standards in international trade agreements.
- He would require businesses to enroll all workers automatically in any 401(k) program they offer.

"Cultural diversity over assimilation"

- He supports bilingual education and opposes designating English as the official language.

"Quality of life over the accumulation of wealth"

- He would increase taxes on capital gains and income taxes on the rich.
- He would expand family and medical leave to smaller businesses.
- He included $50 million for the National Endowment for the Arts in the stimulus package.

"Deep play over unrelenting toil"

- He supports check cards for union elections, making it easier to form unions.
- He believes that taxes on high income deter "toil."

"Universal human rights and the rights of nature over property rights"

- He supports a cap-and-trade carbon tax.
- He opposes the use of enhanced interrogation techniques for terror suspects.
- He advocates stronger government regulation of business.
- He has mandated unemployment benefits—normally available only for those laid off—for anyone who willingly quits his job for "family-related" reasons.

> **"Global cooperation over the unilateral exercise of power"**
>
> - He opposed the Iraq War unless it got UN approval.
>
> - He supports global standards on financial industry regulation.
>
> - He backs global cap-and-trade taxes on carbon emissions.

By raising taxes on the wealthy and using the money to fund government spending and tax reductions for the middle class and the poor, Obama is leading the United States very close to the European model of social democracy.

His goals belie the power of the markets and undercut our work ethic. The individual drive to work hard, make money, and move up is not the European ideal—and it is not Obama's either.

To understand where the European philosophy leads, consider the reduction in the work week. Led by the Socialist Party, France cut its workweek to thirty-five hours in order to share job opportunities and reduce unemployment. Rifkin noted that "the French experiment is particularly interesting because it defies the American logic that hard work and long hours on the job are indispensable to achieving productivity gains and a better quality of life for working people." [100]

It's all well and good for labor unions to win shorter workweeks. Most Americans figure that this means that you get overtime faster and get more of it. Not in France. There, it is *illegal* for an employee to work more than 180 extra hours per *year* (that's about 3.5 hours per week) without a collective bargaining agreement. Illegal! Not only don't you get rewarded for doing extra work in France, you can actually be punished for it!

This is socialism at its worst.

Has it ever occurred to the European socialists that some people like to work? That "deep play" is not preferable to hard work? That taking a vacation may be well and good but that the sense of accomplishment and fulfillment that comes from creating something with our hands and brains affords a more lasting pleasure?

And in this universal society of human rights, don't we have a right to work, to create, to apply ourselves—even if it drags on for more than 180 extra hours a year?

The dumbing down and mediocrity that underscore this kind of social-ism are hard to take. They run counter to every fiber of the American spirit. But they are the logical extension of where Obama wants to take us when he imposes tax rates that are prohibitive and discourage us all from working hard.

As if that weren't enough, Charles Murray, the W. H. Brady Scholar at the American Enterprise Institute, has articulated an even greater divide between European and American attitudes—and a greater challenge to those who want to keep our side of the Atlantic filled with our traditional approaches to work, family, and life.

Noting the rapid decline in European birthrates, Murray has predicted that "the European model can't continue to work much longer. Europe's catastrophically low birth rates and soaring immigration from cultures with alien values will see to that." [101]

He points out that these low birthrates, well below those necessary simply to maintain Europe's current population, exist in countries "pro-viding generous child allowance, free day-care centers, and long maternity leaves." [102]

Similarly, despite the fact that European jobs are "most carefully pro-tected by government regulation and mandated benefits are the most lav-ish," Murray points out that to Europeans the concept of work "is most often seen as a necessary evil, least often seen as a vocation and where the proportions of people who say they love their jobs are the lowest." [103]

Instead of having children and reveling in their work, Murray says, Eu-ropeans are having a "great time with their current sex partner and new BMW and the vacation home in Majorca, and [see] no voids in their lives that need filling." [104]

Citing Europeans' "self-absorption," he says they increasingly see work as "something that interferes with the higher good of leisure." He posits that much of the Europeans' low birthrate stems from their asking that if leisure is "the purpose of life, why have a child? What good are they really?" [105]

Murray views Obama's desire to move us closer to the European social-ist model as a threat to the American way of life. He warns that "irreversible damage [may] be done to the American project over the next few years. The drift toward the European model . . . is going to be stopped only when we are all talking again about why America is exceptional, and why it is so important that America remain exceptional." [106]

He argues that we must again see:

> the American project for what it is: a different way for people to live together, unique among the nations of the earth, and immeasurably precious. . . . Historically, Americans have been different as a people, even peculiar, and everyone around the world has recognized it. I'm thinking of qualities such as American optimism even when there doesn't seem to be any good reason for it. That's quite uncommon among the peoples of the world. There is the striking lack of class envy in America—by and large, Americans celebrate others' success instead of resenting it. That's just about unique, certainly compared to European countries, and something that drives European intellectuals crazy. And then there is perhaps the most important symptom of all, the signature of American exceptionalism—the assumption by most Americans that they are in control of their own destinies. It is hard to think of a more inspiring quality for a population to possess, and the American population still possesses it to an astonishing degree. No other country comes close. [107]

It's hard to imagine a better way to describe what we may lose in the leveling, bureaucratizing, and narcotizing of America that Obama seems bent on pursuing—all disguised as an economic recovery program.

The idea that work is just an interruption of our leisure time—and that we value leisure over work—runs counter to how most Americans live their lives. In his poem "When Earth's Last Picture Is Painted," the English poet Rudyard Kipling articulated best what we do think:

> . . . And no one shall work for money.
> And no one shall work for fame.
> But each for the joy of working,
> Each by his own separate star.
> To draw the thing as he sees it.
> For the God of things as they are.

ACTION AGENDA

Once you recognize how Barack Obama is trying to change our country, it's easy to fall into passivity and depression. Right now, he seems invulnerable. He has huge majorities in Congress. He can always find a few weak Republican senators—such as Maine's Olympia Snowe and Susan Collins—to defect and give him what he wants.

But Obama has a big weakness—the coming elections of 2010. Then, as happens every two years, the entire House of Representatives and one-third of the Senate will be up for reelection. That will be our chance to take back our country and rescue it from socialism.

The Democrats play a game with us. They run moderate candidates in swing districts and states. These candidates preach the virtues of a balanced budget, a strong military, and tough protections against terrorism. Some are even pro-life or side with the Right on cultural issues. Their moderation attracts swing voters, and they frequently defeat their Republican opponents. But when they hit Washington, they meekly vote the way they're instructed by House speaker Nancy Pelosi and Senate majority leader Harry Reid. They shelve their moderation and become foot soldiers in the war to bring socialism to America.

We have to expose their game. But we can't wait until 2010 to do it. Obama is changing America in important ways right now, and to let him continue his fundamental alterations in our economy, government, and even lifestyle is unthinkable.

These moderate Democrats are Obama's Achilles' heel. They are the weak links in his congressional majority. They won election as moderates, and they vote any way their leaders tell them to—and right now, that means that they are voting as socialists.

Never in history has Congress been more partisan than it is right now. It has never until now, for example, followed the model of the New York State Legislature. The New York lawmakers have a tradition they call a "short roll call": to save time, rather than call the name of every legislator, they just ask the majority leader and minority leader how they vote and then ask if any member wants to vote differently from his leader. Usually, nobody does.

The U.S. Congress has always held itself to a higher standard of independence. Members of Congress—even junior members—have never been shy about breaking ranks, and party whips traditionally have a difficult time keeping them in line.

Today, however, they might as well be using the short roll call in Washington. Few members vote differently from what their party leader wishes.

To derail Obama's rush toward socialism, we need to bring incredible pressure on the moderate swing members of Congress.

Why have these normally independent members become such automatons? It's not that they're less bright or more inclined to follow the dictates of Gilbert and Sullivan in their play *H.M.S. Pinafore:*

> I grew so rich that I was sent
> by a pocket borough into Parliament
> I always voted at my party's call
> And I never thought of thinking for myself at all.

There's one reason that these congressmen and senators are toeing the party line more faithfully than ever before: because the party increasingly controls their campaign money. No longer do candidates get most of their funds from loyal constituents back home. Instead, prominent donors from around the nation and PACs allied with the party give contributions to whomever the party leaders designate. Speaker Pelosi and Majority Leader Reid can turn the spigot on or off at will. And no one dares to cross them.

But if we call attention to the hypocrisy of these Democratic senators and congressmen—who campaign as moderates and vote as extreme leftists—we can make the cost of their party-line behavior too steep to bear and begin to fan the flames of independence and moderation.

But we need to focus our energies on the weakest links in the chain.

In 2010, the following Democratic senators will be up for reelection. It's up to us to expose their socialist votes, pressure them to change course, and defeat them in 2010:

Blanche Lincoln of Arkansas
Barbara Boxer of California
Michael Bennet of Colorado
Christopher Dodd of Connecticut

Daniel Inouye of Hawaii
Roland Burris of Illinois
Evan Bayh of Indiana
Barbara Mikulski of Maryland
Harry Reid of Nevada
Kirsten Gillibrand of New York
Charles Schumer of New York
Byron Dorgan of North Dakota
Ron Wyden of Oregon
Patrick Leahy of Vermont
Patty Murray of Washington
Russell Feingold of Wisconsin

And here are the so-called moderate House Democrats who cave in to pressure, voting time and again to pass ultraliberal programs. It's time to make them an endangered species!

PERCENTAGE OF TIME THEY VOTED ALONG WITH PARTY LEADERS

		2007	2008
NJ	John Adler		98.6
NY	Michael A. Arcuri	96	96
GA	John Barrow		92.9
IL	Melissa L. Bean		93.3
AR	Marion Berry	94	96
OH	John A. Boccieri		95.2
OK	Dan Boren	79	91
IA	Leonard Boswell	93	98
FL	Allen Boyd	91	92
CA	Dennis Cardoza	94	97
PA	Christopher Carney		88.4
KY	Ben Chandler	93	93
TN	Jim Cooper	88	92

		2007	2008
CA	Jim Costa	92	94
PA	Kathy Dahlkemper		96.6
TN	Lincoln Davis	87	93
TX	Chet Edwards	92	97
TN	Bart Gordon	88	93
FL	Alan Grayson		98.6
AL	Parker Griffith		88.4
IL	Deborah Halvorson		95.3
CA	Jane Harman	95	98
NM	Martin T. Heinrich		98.6
IN	Baron Hill		88.7
PA	Tim Holden	92	95
MD	Frank M. Kratovil, Jr.		89
NY	Daniel B. Maffei		99.3
MA	Ed Markey		98.6
GA	Jim Marshall		91.7
UT	Jim Matheson		92.3
NC	Mike McIntyre	86	89
NY	Michael E. McMahon		98.6
CA	Jerry McNerney	91	93
KY	Charlie Melancon	86	93
ME	Michael Michaud	96	94
KS	Dennis Moore	95	97
PA	Patrick Murphy	87	95
VA	Glenn C. Nye III		90.3
VA	Tom Perriello		92.5
MI	Gary Peters		98.6
MN	Collin C. Peterson	87	91
ND	Earl Pomeroy	93	97
CO	John T. Salazar	93	96
CA	Loretta Sanchez	99	96
SD	Stephanie Herseth Sandlin	89	91
MI	Mark Schauer		98.6
CA	Adam Schiff	98	98
OH	Zachary T. Space		95.9

		2007	2008
TN	John Tanner	85	95
NM	Harry Teague		91.1
CA	Mike Thompson	96	95
MN	Timothy J. Walz	94	96
SC	Joe Wilson	91	97

At www.dickmorris.com, we'll be tracking how Obama's program fares in Congress—and we'll be asking supporters to direct their comments, letters, petitions, and donations at specific targets to stop this congressional move to the left. Log on and get involved!

2

THE BANK BAILOUT
THAT BOMBED

As a result of massive government intervention and huge outlays of tax-payer money, the major banks and financial institutions are still afloat. But they might as well be dead as far as the economy is concerned. They've become floating mausoleums, closed to outsiders, making few if any loans, and trying hard to stay alive and out of trouble.

Their inability to lend is a catastrophe for the economy. And as you read this chapter, you'll see that Barack Obama is likely to make things worse by using the current crisis as an excuse to nationalize the banks—the linchpin of his plan for a socialist economy.

The crisis began in March 2008, when Bear Stearns, the brokerage house that had pioneered the securitization of mortgages, failed. Uncle Sam stepped in, injected capital, and forced it into a marriage with J.P. Morgan Chase. On September 15, 2008, Lehman Brothers failed, and in a fit of free-market bravado, the Bush administration let it go into bankruptcy. Chaos and panic gripped the financial markets. After that, the Federal Reserve, the Treasury Department, and the Bush administration resolved not to permit any more catastrophes.

In September and October 2008, we learned that more and more of America's leading financial institutions were insolvent and faced imminent collapse. All of the big banks, brokerage houses, and insurance companies tottered on the brink of bankruptcy so Bush pumped in money.

So twenty financial institutions divided up most of the initial $350 billion of government spending under the Troubled Assets Relief Program (TARP). By March 2009, almost $700 billion had been spent. As of this writing, 495 banks and other financial institutions have received money; they are now subject to the regulations the government will impose on them.

But the media's relentless focus on the major TARP recipients has obscured one important fact: that almost every U.S. bank is on the dole. It's sobering but true: most banks in America have their hands in this particular till.

Here's the list of the main welfare recipients. For a full list, go to Appendix A. Check to see if your bank is on the list. We think you ought to know, don't you?

THE TOP TWENTY PANHANDLERS IN AMERICA

Main recipients of TARP money as of March 2009

AIG	$70 billion
Citigroup	$45 billion
Bank of America (including Merrill Lynch)	$45 billion
JPMorgan Chase	$25 billion
Wells Fargo (including Wachovia)	$25 billion
General Motors	$14 billion
Morgan Stanley	$10 billion
Goldman Sachs	$10 billion
PNC Financial	$ 7.6 billion
US Bankcorp	$ 6.5 billion
Chrysler	$ 5.5 billion
GMAC	$ 5.0 billion
Sun Trust	$ 4.9 billion
Capital One	$ 3.6 billion
Regions Financial	$ 3.5 billion
Fifth Third Bankcorp	$ 3.4 billion
American Express	$ 3.4 billion

BB&T	$ 3.1 billion
Bank of NY Mellon	$ 3.0 billion
Key Corp	$ 2.5 billion

Source: http://www.propublica.org/special/show-me-the-tarp-money.

Even when banks want to give back the TARP money to escape federal regulation, they're finding that the Treasury discourages them. Washington wants to pass out the money as broadly as possible so that it can use the funds as a lever to control the banks.

TARP stopped any institution from disappearing beneath the waves, but it has done nothing to restore consumer lending and liquidity in our economy. In the wake of the massive TARP spending, the banks have been saved, but our economy has not. The U.S. financial system is like a patient in ICU whose surgery went well but who may die anyway.

TARP may have forestalled bank bankruptcies, but the fact is that the American people still can't get loans. In the first few months of 2009, the twenty largest banks to get government funds not only failed to increase their lending to consumers and businesses—they actually cut it slightly! Though they're now wallowing in federal funds, the Treasury Department said that the banks that got TARP aid cut their mortgage and business loans by 1 percent and also reduced their credit card lending. Sixty percent of the banks said they had tightened their lending standards on credit cards and other consumer loans during the quarter.[108]

Typical of the banks' reaction to the taxpayer bailout largesse was that of John C. Hope III, the chairman of the board of Whitney National Bank in New Orleans. In a comment that recalls Marie Antoinette's suggestion to the starving people of France ("Let them eat cake!"), Hope told a gathering of Wall Street analysts what he was going to do with his $300 million bailout. The *New York Times* reported on the scene:

> "Make more loans?" he asked rhetorically—as if the very notion was ridiculous. Stuffily he intoned, "We're not going to change our business model or our credit policies to accommodate the needs of the public sector as they see it to have us make more loans."[109]

This from a man whose bank's "business model" was so sound that it needed taxpayers to cough up $300 million to keep it in business!

WHERE IS THE MONEY?

So where did all the money go? What happened to the massive bailout cash if it hasn't been lent to consumers or businesses?

It's sitting in a vault at the Federal Reserve Board! Most banks used the bailout money to correct their balance sheets and reassure investors that they weren't about to tank but never actually took most of the money. Their ruse didn't work, of course. For the most part their stock prices tanked anyway, and the bankers were content to let the cash sit at the Fed. No need to alter their business models!

And the Federal Reserve Board, ever accommodating, decided to start paying interest on the TARP reserves the banks left in its vault! (As if to create an incentive *not* to help the economy by lending it out!)

In March 2009, according to reports from the Fed, a total of $800 billion in reserves owned by banks was still sitting in its vaults, happily earning interest and doing nothing to help our economy. How big is this pile of unlent money? So big that it equals all the currency in circulation in the United States at the moment. For every dollar in wallets, purses, and cash registers in the United States, there is another dollar lounging in the Fed's vault!

And what was the Fed's solution? To put more money into the vault. As we write this, the Fed has decided to pump another trillion dollars into the system—hoping it won't just sit in the vault next to the $800 billion already there.

WHY WON'T BANKS LEND?

As Christopher Boyd wrote in the *Orlando Business Journal:* "To borrow a line from Bill Clinton's 1992 presidential campaign, 'It's the economy, stupid.' " [110]

Now that the banks have gulped down the $350 billion in the initial bailout package (as of March 11, 2009), why aren't they lending?

Craig Polejes, president of the Florida Bank of Commerce in Orlando, says, "It's unreasonable to expect banks to loan money to companies that aren't making money."[111] With consumers losing their homes and jobs while businesses see the red ink of the recession adding up on their balance sheets, the banks won't risk their money.

And the lesson of the stunning failures that impelled the bailout in the first place isn't lost on a generation of managers of financial institutions: *Don't stick your neck out. Rein in risky investments. Play it safe and conservative.*

Which is, of course, precisely the opposite of what the Fed, the Treasury, and Congress had in mind when they approved the bailout. But this Catch-22—banks won't lend while the economy is bad, and the economy won't improve until banks lend—shows no signs of letting up in the near future.

Until the inevitable happens, that is, and the government takes over the banks. The futility of waiting for terrified, trembling bankers to make new loans will become more and more apparent until government takeover is the only remedy.

And who can shed the sneaking suspicion that Obama has always wanted it that way?

OBAMA'S SOLUTION

For now, Obama vehemently denies wanting to nationalize the banks. Instead, he, his Treasury Department, and the Federal Reserve have trotted out one scheme after another to rekindle lending, all to no avail. In the meantime, when you read between the lines of federal regulatory policy, it is evident that Obama not only wants to take over the banks, but is stacking the deck so that the financial institutions fall into his grasp.

But Obama can't come out and admit that he wants nationalization, so his latest plan is to lend money to hedge funds and other investors on very favorable terms if they agree to use the money to buy securities based on auto loans, credit card debt, and other consumer financing. These loans would go to banks, but also to nonbank lenders that regularly dole out funds for college costs, cars, and mortgage loans.

In other words, the hedge funds will tell the banks and other credit institutions just what Fannie Mae told the mortgage lenders that started the whole financial crisis in the first place: "Go ahead, lend money, even if you have doubts about whether the loans will ever be repaid. Don't worry. As soon as you make the loan, we'll buy it with the money the Fed is lending us. That way, even if the borrower defaults, it won't be your problem."

This sleight-of-hand finance is just like the dodgy practices that got us into this fix. And, perhaps for that reason, the new program, called TALF (Term Asset-Backed Securities Loan Facility), is off to what the *Wall Street Journal* charitably describes as "a slow start." As the *Journal* has reported, though the government is preparing to make loans up to $200 billion (and possibly to expand it to $1 trillion) so far only three deals, worth a combined $5 billion, have been cut up.[112]

Michael Ferolli, a J.P. Morgan economist, says that to call the new plan "stillborn would be too harsh, but it [TALF] is off to a rough start."[113] The *Journal* reports that "a month ago, bankers say, they thought they would be selling at least ten deals in the first round of the program. Most of these have been put on hold."[114]

What's the problem? When the Fed is making buyout money available to hedge funds, the threat of making bad loans wouldn't seem to be much of a risk. So what's the reason for the holdup?

It's the administration's own policies.

As the *Journal* says, "one reason for the slow start: the outcry over bonuses paid by AIG, the troubled insurer that received federal money. Some investors are concerned that they too could be exposed to a political storm should they take too much money from the taxpayer-funded program."[115]

When these investors see the names and bonuses of executives at AIG being published and their homes deluged with angry protestors, their reaction is to steer clear from taking tax money in any form. So every time Obama lets loose with a new volley of populist rhetoric, condemning corporate bonuses at the same firms that are receiving federal help, he shoots himself—or, rather, us—in the foot. The more he protests and condemns the bonuses and threatens to tax them away, the more he deters the very partners he needs to get the economy rolling again.

The deterrent effect of shifting federal policies, political posturing, and changing—and punitive—tax legislation is huge. Investors don't know what the rules are since they keep shifting. They're perpetually worried that a business-as-usual decision, easy in more normal times, will land them on the front page of newspapers throughout the country. It's like the situation Voltaire described in *Candide*, where the Romanian army officers shoot every tenth soldier "in order to encourage the others."

The second prong of Obama's pathetically inadequate response to the lack of bank lending is to seek to take "toxic assets" off the banks' books. (For those who enjoy pain, the following narrative explains how these assets came to festoon bank balance sheets in the first place.)

HOW THE CATASTROPHE STARTED

Thirteen Steps to Doom

Step 1   Under the Clinton administration, Congress calls for Fannie Mae and Freddie Mac to encourage more mortgage loans to low and middle income families. In 1996, Secretary of Housing and Urban Development (HUD) Henry Cisneros sets a quota requiring that 42 percent of Freddie or Fannie loan purchases or insurance be for families in the low or middle income bracket. In 2000, his successor, Andrew Cuomo, raises it to 50 percent.

Step 2   Fannie and Freddie step up their program to buy low-income mortgages and encourage lenders to issue them. To meet the Clinton administration quotas, they waive the requirements for down payments and income verification.

Step 3   Hustlers like Countrywide Financial take advantage of the opportunity and issue subprime mortgages they know cannot be repaid. They lend mortgages that cover the entire property value—no down payment needed—as well as some of the early years' interest payments and the brokers' and bankers' and lawyers' fees. Often this practice leads to a loan that exceeds the value of the property. After three years, typically, these special loans for interest will lapse and the family will have to pay the full mortgage debt. But to many families that seems like a distant, far-off threat—especially when they're looking at a nice new house.

(continued on next page)

Step 4   Fannie and Freddie buy these subprime loans, as Congress and HUD want them to do. They and other financial institutions then bundle their good and bad loans together (in a process called "securitization") and sell Wall Street investors a share of the package.

Step 5   Eager to get in on the mortgage boom, banks, brokerage houses, pension funds, and other investors flock to buy these securitized mortgages.

Step 6   To permit them to lend out more money based on these mortgage assets (called "leverage"), the banks get insurance firms such as AIG to insure the securitized mortgages. With insurance, the bond rating firms give a triple-A rating, which lets the financial institution lend as much as ten times the value of the mortgage assets.

Step 7   Eager to squeeze even more leverage out of these mortgage-backed securities, the financial institutions get other banks around the world to insure them by buying credit default swaps. With this extra backing, the financial institutions holding the mortgage-backed securities can lend many additional multiples of loans based on these assets. Credit default swaps increased from $900 billion in 1999 to $60 trillion in 2007.[116]

Step 8   With a glut of both new and existing homes on the market, real estate prices stop increasing and begin to level off.

Step 9   After three years, families holding subprime mortgages get hit with big interest rate increases, which they can't afford, and they start to default on the loans. The creditors consider foreclosing, but with real estate prices stagnant, the loan is often worth more than the house—so even taking the property entirely wouldn't pay off the debt.

Step 10   With so many homes in default, real estate prices drop and more home owners find that their mortgage outstrips their property's value. Banks have to count these loans as losses on their balance sheets.

Step 11 As the underlying mortgages go bad, the mortgage-backed securities that are based on them also go into the red. Banks call on insurance companies and holders of credit default swaps to make good on their insurance.

Step 12 The balance sheets of banks all over the world turn negative; insurance companies are unable to pay out on their policies insuring the mortgage-backed securities. These now-toxic assets drive the portfolios of major financial institutions into the red.

Step 13 Faced with huge losses and negative balance sheets, banks stop lending. Credit dries up, companies go bankrupt, and layoffs pile up. The recession begins.

The problem, of course, is how to remove these toxic assets from the banks' balance sheets. The easiest option would be for home values to increase so they become nontoxic, but the recession's unemployment and deepening economic impact rule that out.

That's why the Federal Reserve, the Treasury, and Congress applied first aid to stop the bleeding by pouring $700 billion of TARP funds into these financial institutions to make their balance sheets look better. This is the money most of these banks and brokerage houses chose to keep in the Fed's vault, rather than spending it as it was intended.

But better balance sheets didn't bring liquidity. Aware that these banks were being propped up by TARP, investors stayed away from buying their stocks and bonds. Unable to raise capital, the banks never reopened their lending windows. So TARP stopped the banks from failing but didn't do much to get the economy rolling.

All of which leaves Obama with two options:

1. Get the government and private investors to partner in buying up the toxic assets to get them off the bank balance sheets, or
2. Nationalize the banks and have the Treasury do it.

The hope that underpins both approaches, of course, is that the economy will recover, so that homes' values will rise and their prices will become high enough to pay off the mortgages. It is inevitable that this will happen at some point, but it could take a lot of waiting around. If the loans that are in default are on the bank balance sheets in the interim, the banks won't lend money. But if they are wiped off and the Treasury or outside investors hold the debt while waiting for the value of the underlying properties to appreciate, the banks will be free to lend again. At least that's how it should work in theory.

Obama says he's betting on a public-private partnership to buy up toxic assets at a fraction of their book value and hold them until the economy turns around. Then the plan would call for them to be sold them on the open market, with the private investors and the taxpayers sharing the gains. If the plan backfires and the assets never fetch a decent price, the investors and the government will share the loss between them.

The big problem is how to induce investors to share the risk and the outlay with the government. As Treasury secretary Timothy Geithner told the *Wall Street Journal*, "government cannot do this [clean up the bank assets] alone." Geithner notes, correctly, that "the best way to get through this [crisis] is if we can work with the markets. We don't want the government to assume all the risk. We want the private sector to work with us." [117]

The problem, as the *Journal* noted, is that Geithner's plea for private participation comes "at a time when Wall Street moneymakers are being vilified by the public and politicians." [118]

Just as with the TALF program, Obama's plan to rescue banks will be destroyed by his own populist rhetoric. When the president jumped in with both feet and decried the bonuses paid to AIG executives, calling for congressional or Treasury action to get the money back, he may have scored political points. But in doing so he sent a chill through the financial markets—a chill that makes it unlikely that they'll participate in any bank rescue effort. After all, if they do join in and their risk taking is rewarded, can't you see the Democrats demanding caps on their bonuses? Won't the government seek a larger share of the winnings—especially if the taxpayers are still left with some amount outstanding—rather than allow those rich, evil investors to make millions or even billions of dollars of profit?

The lesson of AIG is: what the government wants, the government gets. By voting a special tax on AIG bonuses, the House of Representatives showed that, in today's Washington, populism trumps good sense. Whether out of conviction or fear, legislators are willing to flay investors if that's what it takes to appease the public's bloodlust.

Since no investor wants to be the next one on the guillotine, the wisest course is to stay out of any bank rescue scheme. And, most likely, the investors will do just that.

To lure them in, Geithner has a backup plan: give away the store. His proposal for a public-private "partnership" is simple: the taxpayers take all the risk, and the private investors make all the money.

Joseph E. Stiglitz, a Democrat who was chairman of the Council of Economic Advisers under Clinton from 1995 to 1997—and who won the Nobel Prize in 2001—is an unlikely critic of Obama's proposal, but he has it about right. He says Geithner's proposal is a "win-win-lose proposal: the banks win, investors win—and taxpayers lose."[119] He notes that "the government would provide 92 percent of the money to buy [bank] assets, but would stand to receive only 50 percent of any gains." And the government would "absorb almost all of the losses. Some partnership!"[120]

But such public largesse creates its own problems. The end result is likely to be that the taxpayers will be stuck holding a rather large bag of debts that will produce no money—as investors walk away with tens or hundreds of millions—or even billions—of dollars.

But those private investors have watched the decapitation of AIG and General Motors. They know that once House Banking chairman Barney Frank (D-MA) learns how much they made, all hell will break loose. Even though it's his plan, Obama will lead the chorus of outrage—and Congress will respond by passing one of its 90 percent tax bills. The public anger will force them to do so.

So a lot of investors—the smart ones—will stay away.

If the Geithner plan fails, which it will, Obama will be faced with the second option: nationalization. If the feds take over the banks, they can lend money directly to consumers and businesses, just as they now do for many student loans and loans from the Small Business Administration.

Ultimately, as Obama's war on wealth continues, it's likely that he'll nationalize the banks. The more he demonizes those who get big bonuses and castigates the greed of the firms that made the mistaken investments, the more he will sap their confidence, stoke their fears, and deter them from buying up toxic assets or from new lending.

Any lingering doubt about Obama's intentions toward the financial sector should have been dispelled on March 24, 2009, when the *Washington Post* reported that "the Obama Administration is considering asking Congress to give the Treasury Secretary unprecedented powers to initiate the seizure of non-bank financial companies, such as large insurers, investment firms and hedge funds, whose collapse would damage the broader economy." [121]

At present, the government has the right to seize banks but not other financial institutions. The power the administration seeks is, literally, the ability to impose—unilaterally and without legislative approval—a socialist economy on the United States. It comes as close as anything we have seen to a legislative equivalent of the Bolshevik Revolution.

As the *Post* noted, "giving the Treasury Secretary authority over a broader range of companies would mark a significant shift from the existing model of financial regulation, which relies on independent agencies that are shielded from the political process." [122] What an understatement!

One of the proposals the administration is reportedly considering could "impose greater requirements on company boards to tie executive compensation more closely to corporate performance and to take other steps to ensure that compensation was aligned with the financial interest of the company," [123] the *New York Times* reported.

This intrusive regulation would affect not only companies that receive federal funds, but all financial-sector companies! The *Times* specifically noted that "the new rules will cover all financial institutions, including those not now covered by any pay rules because they are not receiving federal bailout money. Officials say the rules could also be applied more broadly to publicly traded companies, which already report about some executive pay practices to the Securities and Exchange Commission." [124]

Even speculation that the administration is considering limits on executive pay amounts to a declaration of war against the private sector. The fact that Obama's people leaked the story—whether or not Congress approved it—is enough to indicate that they wanted it out there.

And they leaked it during the same week that the administration was seeking private-sector cooperation in buying up the banks' toxic assets.

Does President Obama truly believe he can lecture and castigate Wall

Street on Mondays, Wednesdays, and Fridays and still get its cooperation on the days in between?

Doesn't he understand that when he ignites a public furor over AIG bonuses and then incites Congress to pass a punitive tax, he sends shivers down the spines of every other successful corporate executive? Does he seriously believe that Wall Street investors won't worry that their winnings, should they join the Treasury as partners in risky investments, would be subject to public abuse, publicity, and confiscatory taxation?

Of course he realizes that his rhetoric makes it unlikely that his program will succeed. He obviously knows the entire concept of a public-private partnership is impossible in a climate of waging class warfare, taxing the rich, and heaping contempt on anyone who makes money. The president is bright; he understands that you can't shake hands with your right while you launch a roundhouse swing with your left.

So why does Obama persist in his aggressive rhetoric? Why does he continue to treat Wall Street as something out of Dante's *Inferno*?

Because he wants the public-private partnerships to fail—and he plans to use that failure to justify his nationalization of the banks. We believe that's his real goal.

His intent to force a nationalization of banks is obvious in the way he is regulating banks. He is adopting rules that literally force a government takeover. Here's how it works:

OBAMA'S PLAN FOR GOVERNMENT TAKEOVER OF BANKS

Step 1   Get all banks and financial institutions to take TARP money

Step 2   Even if they want to give the money back, don't let them.

Step 3   Because they're getting government money, make them obey federal regulations

Step 4   Make all banks pass a "stress test," allegedly to assure their financial solvency.

(*continued on next page*)

Step 5	After administering the stress test, make banks raise more capital, again, supposedly to assure solvency.
Step 6	When the banks can't raise more capital by selling more stock, make them swap the preferred stock they gave the government in return for TARP money for common stock. This exchange lets them wipe the debt to the government off their balance sheets, but it gives the feds stock that entitles them to vote on company management (which preferred stock does not).
Step 7	Use the voting power of the common stock to dictate how to run the banks.
Step 8	Use the leverage of the banks to control the economy
PRESTO	SOCIALISM!

WHAT WILL HAPPEN IF OBAMA DOES NATIONALIZE THE BANKS?

In all likelihood, the federal government would be able to clean up the bank balance sheets a lot faster than the bankers can. The federal bureaucrats aren't wed to any of the loans; their reputation isn't involved one way or the other. They can write off debts more ruthlessly than the bankers can and can then auction them off at bargain-basement prices to bottom-feeders willing to wait for values to improve.

As many economists have pointed out, there would be little difference between outright nationalization and the current situation.

In return for the TARP bailout, the U.S. government has acquired stock in the banks it has helped. But it has been careful to buy only "preferred" shares and warrants, not common stock. ("Preferred" means that the holder gets first crack at any dividends but doesn't get to vote on bank management). By buying preferred shares, the government was trying to keep the banks in private hands (although Washington's leverage doubtless entitles it to push the banks around however it likes). The feds were also trying not to dilute the holdings of the current common-stock holders, to avoid hurting the value of their shares.

Of course, then the prices of bank stocks crashed anyway. Even so, nationalizing the banks would involve wiping out their investments. These beleaguered stockholders are, undoubtedly, hoping that the banks, like the South, will "rise again," that their shares will be worth more than Confederate money. But nationalization would kill off their fantasy permanently, incurring an important political cost.

Moreover, the federal government realizes that once it nationalizes one bank, the value of all the other shares is likely to crash, out of fears that their bank might be next.

Even so, one top economist, Nouriel Roubini, who predicted our current crisis years ago, points out that "the debate on bank nationalization is borderline surreal, with the U.S. government having already committed—between guarantees, investment, recapitalization, and liquidity provision—about $9 trillion of government financial resources to the financial system (and having already spent $2 trillion of this staggering $9 trillion figure)." [125]

"Thus," he adds, "the U.S. financial system is de facto nationalized. The only issue is whether banks and financial institutions should be nationalized de jure." [126]

Former Federal Reserve chairman Alan Greenspan says, "It may be necessary to temporarily nationalize some banks in order to facilitate a swift and orderly restructuring." [127] (But the current Fed chairman, Ben Bernanke, said on February 25, 2009, that the U.S. government isn't planning "anything like" a nationalization of banks, which would wipe out the stockholders. [128])

Roubini says he's not opposed to the idea of nationalization, as long as "you take the banks over, you clean them up, and you sell them in rapid order to the private sector." If it's "clear that it's only temporary," he could support nationalization. "No one's in favor," he says, "of a permanent government takeover of the financial system." [129]

Oh, no? Has he met Barack Obama and Barney Frank?

Roubini and others have called for a short-term nationalization he euphemistically calls "temporary receivership," [130] along the lines of what Sweden did in the 1990s, when its banking system got into trouble.

Sweden had its own banking mess in 1992. As the *New York Times* describes it, "after years of imprudent regulation, short-sighted economic policy, and the end of its property boom, [Sweden's] banking system was . . . insolvent." [131]

To address the crisis, Sweden acted boldly and quickly. It swooped in and nationalized its banks, forcing them to write down their losses. It spent $18.3 billion, in today's dollars, to rescue its banks, the equivalent of 4 percent of its GDP. (The $700 billion TARP bailout represents about 5 percent of U.S. GDP.) [132]

But the case of Sweden is notable because its government was willing to accept big political pain in return for its action. It forced the banks to admit which loans were bad and made them write them off (rather than keep them on their balance sheets, praying that things would start looking up). Then the government took over the properties that were in default, presumably evicting people from their homes and forcing businesses to close if they weren't paying off their debts.

By seizing the properties, Sweden was able to sell them off and make back a good share of the money it had to put up. Then, when the bank balance sheets were finally cleaned up, Sweden resold the banks to new private owners and made back more of its money.

In the end, the taxpayers of Sweden got more than half their money back. The shareholders lost everything, but their stock values had been close to zero anyway. And today the Swedish banking system is weathering the current financial storm rather well, having had its shakeout seventeen years ago.

By contrast, the government of Japan dithered for years, refusing to make banks write off bad loans and keeping banks in private hands. Many blame Japan's decade-long recession on the government's failure to follow the Swedes' example.

What Roubini and other proponents of nationalization are trying to avoid is creating a host of paralyzed banks that exist in name only, prevented by the toxic assets on their balance sheets from actively assisting the economy through new lending. Right now, he says, we are stuck in a nevernever land of "zombie banks" that remain in private hands, too strong to die and too weak to lend.

Roubini even worries that, by forcing sales of some banks to others, we may inadvertently have created even larger zombie banks. "We started," he says, "with banks that were too big to fail." But when the feds arranged that series of shotgun marriages—in which J.P. Morgan took over Bear Stearns and Washington Mutual, the Bank of America bought Countrywide and then Merrill Lynch, and Wells Fargo merged with Wachovia—the resulting conglomerates were just overgrown zombies. "It doesn't work!" Roubini insists. "You can't take two zombie banks, put them together, and make a strong bank. It's like having two drunks trying to keep each other standing." [133]

Instead, he says, the solution is to nationalize the banks, clean up their balance sheets, and then break them up and sell them, creating "three or four regional or national banks" out of each one. Ultimately, he says, this will make the banks "stronger." [134]

But that approach leaves one major factor to chance: Once Obama got his hands on the banks, would he clean them up and sell them off as the Swedes did? Or would he use them as tools to manage an increasingly socialist economy?

From the current, modest pressure the U.S. government is putting on banks—using the leverage the TARP program provides—we can see how eager it is to exercise an increasing degree of control. Right now, the liberals are lashing out at corporate bonuses, demanding greater consumer lending, and trying to influence credit policies.

In Obama's mortgage rescue plan, for example, banks that receive TARP money are obliged to participate in the loan restructuring program the president has proposed. (More on the rescue plan in the next chapter.) And Obama used his TARP muscle to get Chrysler bond holders to accept 29 cents on the dollar. If the feds are using their TARP leverage this aggressively, imagine what they'd do if they owned the banks!

It's easy to see the government demanding more affirmative action in bank hiring, less redlining of impoverished neighborhoods, more emphasis on minority businesses in lending, and the curtailing of lending to companies that employ foreigners or outsource or hire illegal immigrants. It's exactly this kind of meddling that led Fannie Mae and Freddie Mac to go so disastrously wrong! Politicians, egged on by their constituents, can't help themselves.

And once the politicians give themselves this kind of power over the banks and financial institutions of this nation, can you really imagine them giving it up that easily? Can you envision the bureaucrats who are hired to oversee the nationalized banks relinquishing their sinecures this quickly?

Forget about it. They'd have to be pried out of their cold, dead hands.

THE DAY THE DECLARATION OF INDEPENDENCE WAS REPEALED

It's not just that Barack Obama wants to nationalize the backbone of our nation's system of private enterprise, the financial institutions of America. He also wants to *inter*nationalize a power that was once considered a core element of our national sovereignty: the right to regulate these financial institutions.

At the G-20 summit in London on April 2, 2009, President Obama pledged U.S. support for a "framework of internationally agreed high standards" in the regulation of financial institutions.[135] In the name of "greater consistency and systematic cooperation between countries," he agreed to submit our regulatory organs—such as the SEC and the Federal Reserve—to oversight by a newly created international Financial Stability Board (FSB), which would "collaborate with the IMF (International Monetary Fund)."[136] Here's what the international regulators could do:

THE POWER OBAMA IS GIVING INTERNATIONAL REGULATORS OVER OUR ECONOMY

- "provide early warning of macroeconomic and financial risks"
- "reshape our regulatory systems so that our authorities are able to identify and take account of macro-prudent risks
- "extend regulation and oversight to all systemically important financial institutions, instruments, and markets . . . including hedge funds
- "implement tough new principles on pay and compensation and to support sustainable compensation schemes and the corporate social responsibility of all firms."[137]

That's not a typo. The last item speaks of regulating the "pay and compensation" and "corporate social responsibility" of "*all*" firms." All. Every one. As in: the entire economy!

Meet Mario Draghi, our new boss. He is the head of the Financial Stability Forum, on which the new board is to be based. He is the governor of the Banca d'Italia. The IMF and the Financial Stability Forum—and now the FSB—will be headed by Europeans. Traditionally, the United States has controlled the World Bank, while Europe got the IMF. Now Draghi and the other European central bankers will have tremendous power over the United States and its financial institutions.

This is the price Obama and the leaders of the world are making us pay for being the nation where the global financial crisis began: we are no longer our own masters.

ACTION AGENDA

The stakes in the outcome of the bank rescue plan dwarf those involved in even the president's big-spending stimulus package and the supplemental appropriations we discussed earlier. The risk of those plans is that they could force us to endure a painful cycle of inflation and recession while saddling future generations with high bills for interest and debt repayment.

But the risks and dangers involved in nationalizing the banks would be of a different order of magnitude. If the bank bailout leads to nationalization and the politicians don't follow Sweden's lead and return them to private ownership as soon as possible, the Obama administration will effectively have transformed the United States into a socialist democracy. Businesses that need operating cash to grow will have to go hat in hand to government-owned banks for loans. And the politicians making the decisions will attach whatever conditions they like to these loans (as, indeed, they're already doing with the TARP loans).

Soon Washington will be telling bankers to give preference to certain types of loans over others. Sometimes the politicians will make the mistake of betting on the wrong horse economically (as Japan did in the 1990s, when it steered investment toward companies developing big mainframe computers and away from laptops). Other times, they will substitute short-term, populist economic demands for long-term investments. And they will always be subject to the temptation to appoint somebody like Rod Blagojevich (the corrupt ex-governor of Illinois) to run the program, allowing the lending to be guided by hidden motives.

In any event, our elected officials aren't bankers—they're politicians. They're bound to get it wrong. And they'll end up costing our nation billions of dollars in lost assets.

(Some may ask, *But isn't that exactly what the privately owned banks just did?* The answer is: yes. But they did so after giving us sixty years of solid prosperity and economic growth, with few interruptions, because for the most part they heeded the demands of the marketplace. In the process, they left the world's state-driven economies in the dust.)

The stakes couldn't be higher.

That means that it's our job to be vigilant. We have to be alive to any effort to keep the banks under federal control. Nationalization could be acceptable if it is short term. But the minute we see any sign that Washington wants to hang on to the banks indefinitely—and that's a real threat—we need to take a strong stand against it.

How are we supposed to do this? The simple answer is to elect men and women to Congress who don't want the government to own the banks. Whatever both parties may claim about their fiscal responsibility, the only ones who can be reliably counted upon to keep American business in the hands of the private sector are the Republicans.

In the short term, nationalization of the banks may be inevitable. But to allow this takeover to occur under Democrats would be to invite a plunge into a socialism that could take decades to reverse. Remember that old Washington motto: "The only things that are permanent are those which are temporary."

This reality makes the election of 2010 the most important off-year election since 1974 (when voters swarmed to replace Nixonian members of Congress in the wake of Watergate). The safety of our free-enterprise economy may well hang in the balance.

3

OBAMA'S MORTGAGE PLAN THAT WON'T HELP YOU

Falling behind on your mortgage? Facing foreclosure? Lost your job? Worried about losing your house, too? Facing a personal catastrophe?

Don't look to the Obama administration's mortgage rescue plan for help—unless you're one of the lucky few who manage to qualify under its arcane provisions.

Oh, the plan says you can get help to avoid foreclosure . . . unless:

1. You've lost your job
2. You owe more than your house is worth
3. You're already in default

In other words, if you need help, you won't get it.

Announcing his mortgage program in February 2009, Obama was quite expansive, claiming that it would help "up to five million homeowners who have seen the value of their homes decline to refinance their mortgages." [138] He also said it would "assist up to four million home owners to modify subprime mortgage loans so that payments would be no more than 31 percent of household income." [139]

But the fine print sent quite a different message. The reality is, those who most need assistance will be left out in the cold by Obama's plan.

About 27 percent of the 52 million home owners in the United States with a mortgage are now "under water"—that is, the amount of their mortgage loan is greater than the value of the property that secures it.[140] Obama wouldn't be much help to most of these 13.8 million families.[141] His plan allows people to refinance or get help only if the total amount of their mortgage debt is less than their home's value or no more than 5 percent above it.[142]

As *MSN Money* puts it, many homeowners today "owe so much more than their houses are worth that a lender would do better by foreclosing." [143]

Most of the subprime borrowers fall into this category. The whole point of subprime lending was to help home buyers get loans without having to make a down payment—a system designed to encourage low-income families to buy homes. Indeed, Fannie Mae and Freddie Mac explicitly encouraged these potential buyers to take the plunge by offering to buy up their mortgages as soon as the ink was dry.

Now, however, Obama is suddenly looking askance at these very same borrowers, who merely did what Washington wanted them to do: buy a home with no money down.

When you buy a house without making a down payment, the mortgage debt is, by definition, equal to the value of the property. As soon as a recession causes the home to decline in value, it automatically puts such a home "under water"—and thus ineligible for Obama's so-called mortgage rescue plan.

And what about those who have lost their jobs in the recession? In order for an applicant to qualify for reduced mortgage payments (through a cut in the rate, a federal subsidy, or a prolongation of the period of the mortgage), Obama's program requires that the applicant be able to afford the new mortgage. Its definition of affordability is that the borrower have to pay no more than 31 percent of his income each month to service the debt.

If you can't pay the freight—because you lost your job or for any other reason—you're out of luck. As Nicolas Retsinas, the director of the Joint Center for Housing Studies at Harvard, notes, "You can modify all the loans you want, you can try to refinance loans, but if you don't have money coming in through your pay [like a] weekly paycheck, you can't pay anything." [144] That's simple enough that it shouldn't take a Harvard professor to explain it—yet it seems lost on the Harvard-educated Barack Obama.

Just to make sure anyone who is jobless doesn't sneak in under the wire, Obama requires applicants for relief to "provide their most recent tax return and two pay stubs as well as an 'affidavit of financial hardship' to qualify for the loan modification program. In the affidavit, applicants will have to cite the reasons behind their financial woes. . . . The government will then take steps to verify the information." [145]

But what about those who are behind on their mortgage payments but not yet in foreclosure? The rules of the new program are a bit vague here. The plan provides that "only homeowners in good standing" can qualify for the loans. [146] You don't have to be behind on your payments. If you can show that you're "at risk of imminent default" you are eligible." [147]

So an applicant for relief must walk a fine line: he must be "in good standing"—which, presumably, excludes those actually in foreclosure— yet at "imminent risk" of default. So if you happen to be in between these markers and don't owe more than your house is worth, you're eligible for Obama's help.

Or maybe not.

As it turns out, only home owners whose mortgages are insured or owned by Fannie Mae or Freddie Mac are eligible for Obama's plan. "Fannie and Freddie own or insure about half of the nation's $12 trillion in mortgages. Pension funds, hedge funds, insurance companies and other private investors hold the other half mainly through mortgage-backed securities." [148]

Oh, and another thing: the program is voluntary. Banks and other lenders don't need to participate. Indeed, many *won't* participate—because they don't give a damn what happens to the mortgage loans they made. Most of those original mortgage deals are long gone, sold on the secondary mortgage market and then chopped up and securitized and sold on Wall Street. Why should they worry?

Obama is hoping to entice the banks to participate by offering a $1,000 cash payment to those who service the mortgages for each modified loan and "as much as $1,000 annually for three years when the borrower stays current." [149] Home owners themselves are "eligible for $1,000 annually for five years for remaining current"—although the money will go not to them directly but to pay down the principal on their mortgage.[150]

So . . .

WHO WILL GET HELP UNDER OBAMA'S MORTGAGE RESCUE PLAN

if your lender wants to participate and

if your loan is insured, or owned by Freddie or Fannie and

if you have a job and

if your loan isn't worth more than your home and

if you are a borrower "in good standing"

. . . then you can get your loan modified.

Right?

Not so fast. There are a few other caveats: The property must be owner-occupied. In fact, it must be the homeowner's *primary* residence. The mortgage must predate January 1, 2009. It can't be investor-owned, vacant, or condemned. And the loan can't be for more than $759,750.

If you can squeeze through these eligibility standards, you may be in luck. Then you can have your mortgage reduced, through matching government and private funding, so that the payments come to 31 percent of your monthly income.

Even so, a lot of mortgage-servicing companies feel they don't have the power to reconfigure mortgage loans without the assent of the investors who might own a piece of the loan (who could number in the thousands if the mortgage was part of a syndication). So the loan-servicing companies are asking Congress to pass a law allowing them to restructure mortgages without explicit permission from the investors.

With all that in mind, then, how many people will really qualify for Obama's so-called Homeowner Stability Initiative? Not a whole lot.

In practice, if those who have gotten in over their heads on their mortgages are to find any real relief, it'll have to come through the bankruptcy courts. One bill that's making its way through Congress would allow bankruptcy court judges to modify mortgages without securing approval from the lender or the company that services the loan. This "cramdown" legislation offers the only real relief to families holding mortgages they cannot pay.

Opponents of that bill say it'll raise the cost of borrowing, leading banks to consider more mortgages to be in default. But housing advocates say, correctly, that "mortgage lenders and investors won't get serious about reworking unaffordable mortgages—through the administration's new plan or any other—without the threat of bankruptcy judges changing terms if investors and lenders won't consider modifying loans voluntarily." [151]

The latest indications from Congress are that this bill may be in trouble. The Republicans oppose it (they're wrong on this one) but so do a lot of Democrats. Why? Because they are all in hock to the mortgage lenders who have showered them with campaign contributions.

So Obama's rescue plan won't help most homeowners who need it and the Congress looks unlikely to pass the only way to get them real relief because the special interests won't let it do so.

Obama, of course, knows the shortcomings of his plan. He realizes, obviously, that there are huge gaps. He hinted as much when he cautioned that his plan "will not save every home" [152]—another memorable understatement.

So why won't he take more dramatic steps to end the crisis? During the campaign, he repeatedly bemoaned the pain families must feel at losing their homes, his words dripping with empathy. After the Iraq War turned around, those very foreclosures became the single most important issue in his campaign. So why doesn't he propose a real solution?

Because he's caught in the classic liberal Democrat predicament. If he steps in, buys the mortgages, and then cuts a good deal with the families, letting them stay in their homes without facing foreclosure or eviction, he could alleviate all the current pain. But it would come at a steep price.

What happens if the family breadwinner loses his or her job in the interim? Or has already lost the job? Is the federal government going to throw families out of their homes? Not very likely.

And then, when the economy improves and home values rebound, what if the current occupants refuse to buy back their homes at a reasonable market price? How are the taxpayers to recoup their money? Again, Washington would face the prospect of throwing people out of their homes.

The minute the liberal Democrats forced Fannie and Freddie to buy and insure mortgage loans to people who probably couldn't pay them, they set up the ultimate problem: In a democracy, how can the government evict people from their homes?

The answer is, of course, that it won't. As a result, taking over these mortgages now would mean setting up a kind of permanent government housing project for these families, keeping them in their homes at a substantial subsidy rather than evicting them and getting a fair market price for the property. These subsidized houses could sit out there for decades, a permanent drain on the economy; one can only imagine how hard some enterprising heirs might fight to hang onto those deal-of-the-century homes, trying to prolong the subsidy for generations to come.

By offering such a phony mortgage plan, Obama has, in effect, punted on the problem, letting the bankruptcy courts sort out the bad loans on a case-by-case basis. Let the judicial system order people out of their homes; the government's not about to get its hands dirty.

That's what judges are for.

4

OBAMA'S HEALTH CARE CATASTROPHE

When Barack Obama talks about health care reform, it seems as if all the news is good news. His program, he tells us, will cover 47 million people who now don't have insurance. It will lower costs for the rest of us by $2,500 annually. It will improve the quality and efficiency of the care we get. It will focus particularly on chronic illnesses to improve the management of our treatment. It will restore American competitiveness by lowering the cost of health care.

And, increasingly, Obama is fond of linking health care reform to the rescue of the economy (never let a good crisis go to waste!).

As CNN reported, in one speech "President Obama pledged . . . to cure Americans from what he called 'the crushing cost of health care,' saying the country could not afford to put health-care reform on hold. 'This is a cost,' he noted, 'that now causes a bankruptcy in America every thirty seconds.' He said that it would cause 1.5 million Americans to lose their homes." [153]

President Obama is right to complain about the high cost of health care, which now consumes 16 percent of our GDP. When Bill Clinton urged reform in 1993, it ate up 12 percent of the GDP—and he warned of disaster if it rose to 14 percent.

But Obama hasn't explained how he's going to cover 47 million more people and reduce the cost of health care at the same time.

Let us do the honors.

He won't tell you this, but the silent centerpiece of Obama's program is his plan to ration health care, giving it to some and denying it to others.

The bad news is, rationing health care is the only thing that makes his program possible.

You can't expand medical care just by spending more money. It has to be delivered by a special group of people—doctors and nurses. And there just aren't enough to go around. We barely have enough to offer health care services as it is. To stretch them even thinner—thin enough to cover 47 million more people—would be impossible.

As the *Wall Street Journal* notes, Obama's "focus only on extending health-care coverage ignores the serious shortage of primary-care physicians. Physicians are increasingly going into specialties and the ranks of generalists, the essential first line diagnosticians and caregivers, are shrinking. Without more physicians, those receiving the extended insurance will not be able to find health-care providers." [154]

Though the number of doctors in the United States rose sharply in the past decades, it has actually been leveling off, with only a slight increase, in recent years. The increase in the doctor population averages about 1 percent per year, not even enough even to keep up with U.S. population growth. And certainly not enough to care for a 20 percent increase in their workload—as projected by Obama's plan to cover 47 million new people.

The nurse population, meanwhile, has not risen at all. In a March 2008 report, Dr. Peter Buerhaus of the Vanderbilt University School of Nursing predicted that the shortage of registered nurses in the United States could reach as high as 500,000 by 2025. [155]

If doctors and nurses can barely meet the needs of the 253 million Americans who have insurance or government coverage, how will they deal with the unmet medical needs of the 47 million uninsured Americans whom Obama plans to cover? Where are all those doctors and nurses going to come from?

According to classical economics, when too many people want a service and there are too few professionals to deliver it, the price rises and those who can afford care get it; those who can't are left out.

That's what liberals say is happening today. Those who are fortunate enough to have insurance, either through the workplace or through government programs, get the care they need and the others miss out.

ACTIVE PHYSICIANS AND NURSES IN THE UNITED STATES

Physicians

2006	800,586
2005	790,128
2004	780,662
2003	774,849

Nurses

2006	2,421,000
2005	2,417,150

Source: Statistical Abstract of the United States.

If you are over sixty-five, you're eligible for Medicare and most of your health care costs are covered. If you are poor, you are entitled to Medicaid, with similarly extensive coverage. If your employer is enrolled in an insurance plan, you're covered as well. If you're a child whose parents earn too much for Medicaid but less than about $50,000 a year, you can get coverage through the State Child Health Insurance Program (SCHIP).

All told, 70 percent of Americans with health coverage get it through their employers.[156] But 47 million don't have coverage.

Who are the uninsured?

• Around one-quarter are eligible for Medicaid but haven't applied. They generally aren't sick. When they need care, they enroll in Medicaid and get it.

• Another sixth are illegal immigrants. Although Obama says he won't cover them, he will speed their path to legal status and thus to coverage.

Who are the rest? They are mainly working-age adults who are not impoverished but don't have coverage through their jobs.

Obama has already extended coverage to more children under the SCHIP program and to unemployed adults under the COBRA program. The feds pay two-thirds of the cost of insurance for anyone who is unemployed for nine months.

But how will Obama extend coverage beyond its current limits? Though he hasn't specified the details of his program, its broad outlines are visible. To cover those without insurance, Obama will require all employers either to pay for insurance or to give money to a federal program to buy it for them. He will also launch a new federal government insurance program offering benefits comparable to those given members of Congress. Consumers or employers could switch from their current plans, if they wished, to enroll in the new federal program.

That's the good news.

The bad news is that adequate medical care for the additional 47 million people is going to mean worse care for the rest of us.

The issue isn't money. Obama estimates the cost of his health care program at about $600 billion over ten years. That's surely a lowball estimate; cost calculations on medical care always are. But he can and will raise the extra money.

How? Despite pledging not to tax employer-paid health benefits during the campaign—and attacking McCain for proposing it—he might reverse field and institute such a tax. As of this writing, he is promising to fund at least half of his program by curtailing tax deductions for state and local taxes, charitable donations, or mortgages for those making more than $200,000 per year. But the charities are kicking up a fuss, and he may have to backtrack.

One way or another, he'll probably come up with the money. Democrats are good at that.

But it isn't money that is the problem—it's the supply of doctors and nurses. You can't just *buy* good medical care. It takes years to train doctors and nurses to deliver it. Even if Obama were to start now, massively recruiting future doctors and nurses, it would take at least five to ten years to build the workforce he needs.

The *New York Times* reports that Massachusetts has adopted a variant of the plan Obama is likely to propose—and impose—is facing just such a shortage of medical personnel:

> The experience of Massachusetts is instructive. Under a far-reaching 2006 law, the state succeeded in reducing the number of uninsured. But many who gained coverage have been struggling to find primary care doctors, and the average waiting time for routine office visits has increased.
>
> "Some of the newly insured patients still rely on hospital emergency rooms for nonemergency care," said Erica L. Drazen, a health policy analyst at Computer Sciences Corporation.
>
> The ratio of primary care doctors to population is higher in Massachusetts than in other states.

You can spend more money on health care, but that won't buy you an instant enlargement in the number of doctors to provide it.[157]

And Obama's cuts in the cost of health care will inevitably involve limiting compensation, at least for doctors and perhaps for nurses too. The tighter the limits, the lower the cost—but the fewer people who will enter the professions. So cost limitations are likely to worsen the supply shortage.

The answer, then, has to be rationing—government control over who gets what service. Since the problem isn't how to pay for the service but how to find the medical personnel to deliver it, Americans won't be able to opt out and pay for the services themselves. Rationing means being told what tests, procedures, operations, treatments, medicines, therapy, and so forth you're able to get and which ones you're not. These decisions, of course, will be made not by your doctor or nurse but by bureaucrats—people who've never met you but who will literally determine whether you live or die.

If you read between the lines of Obama's happy pronouncements on health care, you can see that he is leading toward rationing.

Mindful of the mistakes Bill and Hillary Clinton made in 1993, Obama always goes out of his way to say that if you're happy with your insurance, you can keep it and not be affected by his changes. But then he goes on to say that he'll cut the cost of your premiums by $2,500, presumably by implementing the standardization and management procedures described above.

Obama won't control your insurance company. He'll just control the

BREAKING THE OBAMA CODE
ON MEDICAL RATIONING

WHAT OBAMA'S CAMPAIGN PROMISED

"A study by the Rand Corporation found that if most hospitals and doctors' offices adopted electronic health records, up to $77 billion of savings would be realized each year through improvements such as reduced hospital stays, avoidance of duplicative and unnecessary testing, more appropriate drug utilization, and other efficiencies." [158]

WHAT HE MEANS

Federal bureaucrats will decide who gets what test, who gets to take what medication, who gets what treatment, how long you can stay in the hospital and other "efficiencies."

WHAT OBAMA'S CAMPAIGN PROMISED

"Barack Obama will accelerate efforts to develop and disseminate best practices, and align reimbursement with provision of high quality health care." [159]

WHAT HE MEANS

You won't be able to be reimbursed by your insurance company unless you do it our way, prescribe only the medicines we sign off on, treat the illness the way we want, and give only the tests we accept. And the emphasis, of course, will be on inexpensive care—not good care.

WHAT OBAMA'S CAMPAIGN PROMISED

"Most medical records are still stored on paper, which makes them difficult to use to coordinate care, measure quality, or reduce medical errors. Obama will invest $10 billion a year over the next five years to move the U.S. health care system to broad adoption of standards-based electronic health information systems, including electronic health records. [He] will also phase in requirements for full implementation of health IT and commit the necessary federal resources." [160] He made good on the promise in the stimulus bill, which included the allocation of the necessary funds.

money. And it will be his bureaucrats, not your insurance company, who will make the key decisions and lay out the guidelines. Of course, Obama will leave it to your insurance company and its managed care people to break the bad news to you. Government won't do that. It'll be too busy pulling the strings behind the scenes—setting the standards, designing the protocols, making up the requirements, and deciding how the money will be spent.

HOW WILL RATIONING WORK?

Rationally.

If you're old and near death, the system will not allow you a full spectrum of medical services, tests, medications, or options. If you die somewhat prematurely as a result, that's an unfortunate by-product of the needs of the system. After all, there are younger people who need the care more than you do, and there's not enough to go around.

You won't always get to see a doctor. Often you'll have to make do with a nurse-practitioner. A particularly brutal form of triage will be used to decide who can most benefit from what sort of care.

The victims will be the elderly, the sickest, and those who smoke or otherwise inflict harm upon themselves.

The beneficiaries will be the young, the poor, the newly legalized illegal immigrants, and others of Obama's constituency.

How do we know? That's how it works in Canada.

THE CANADIAN EXPERIENCE

Canada has the same kind of government-provided health care that Obama is suggesting for the United States. It looks like a different system, but it's not really. In Canada, the government pays for all medical care. Under

Obama, the government will work through private insurance companies, as well as its own insurance plan, to deliver health care. But there's not much difference.

Obama would offer insurance to everyone, making employers write policies for their workers or pay an equivalent amount into a fund to give them insurance. The federal government would subsidize anyone who couldn't afford insurance.

But under Obama's plan, as in Canada, the central government will decide what the insurance can and cannot cover. The all-important utilization controls will reside in Washington or, as in Canada, in the various state capitals.

The reason the systems are parallel is that the problems are the same. Each country's government is trying to cover everybody without enough medical personnel to go around. So the resulting rationing (aka "efficiency") puts patients at the mercy of their local bureaucrats.

And here's the key point: in Canada, you can't spend your own money to get good health care. It's illegal. In a recent article, Brett Skinner, the director of health and pharmaceutical policy research at the Fraser Institute, notes that "Canadian patients . . . are worse off than uninsured Americans, the latter of whom are at least legally allowed to use their own money or credit to buy health care. Canadian patients who want to escape the delays in the public system are also barred from paying privately for health care services. In practical terms, Canadian patients are unable to buy quicker access or better care than the government health program provides."[161]

When the bureaucracy says *no*, it means *no*. It doesn't mean you need a second opinion. Or that you can pay for the procedure yourself. It means you can't get a CT scan or MRI—not if the government says *no*.

Skinner's recent article on the Canadian health care system, published in *The American*, found that "while Americans spend 55 percent more than Canadians for health care as a percentage of their national economy,"[162]

- The United States has 327 percent more MRI units and 183 percent more CT scanners per capita than Canada.[163]

- Doctors in the United States perform twice as many inpatient surgical procedures than Canadian doctors.[164]

- And there are 14 percent more physicians and 19 percent more nurses in the United States, per capita, than in Canada.[165]

The study found that the Canadian health care system is a disaster:

OBAMA'S GOAL:
TO BRING THE CANADIAN SYSTEM HERE

- The average waiting between the time patients first saw their family physician and the time they actually got treated is now 18.3 weeks. In 1993, it was 9.3 weeks. Is it reasonable to have to wait four months for treatment?

- Less than half—44 percent—of all new drugs approved by the Canadian government in 2004 were covered by the government insurance program in October 2007. To get them? A one-year wait, on average!

- 1.7 million Canadians—about 5 percent of the population—couldn't access a family physician in 2007.

- Four years ago, the average waiting time for nonurgent cardiac surgery (which can become urgent in a hurry) in Manitoba was nineteen days. Today it's seventy-seven days.[166]

When government bureaucrats ration health care, the results can be a disaster. Take the grim story of colon cancer in Canada. Colorectal cancer rates are much higher in Canada (6.7 per 100,000)[167] than in the United States (4.8 per 100,000.)[168] And although 41 percent of cases in Canada prove fatal,[169] only 34 percent in the United States lead to death.[170]

Even though colorectal cancer is the second leading cause of death in Canada, the drug Avastin—the standard treatment in the United States—is not available to patients in Canada through the government health system. "What is going on in Canada is shameful," says Barry D. Stein, president of the Colorectal Cancer Association of Canada. "This treatment, which was finally approved last year in Canada and which was long overdue, is not reaching patients who are desperately in need of . . . a treatment which is the standard of care in the treatment of the disease."[171]

In British Columbia, parts of Quebec, and parts of New Brunswick, the drug is available for free. But in other provinces, patients have to pay $36,000 for a six-month treatment.[172]

A second drug for colorectal cancer, Erbitux, which the government approved at the same time as Avastin, has not even been launched in Canada— because the bureaucrats at the Patented Medicine Prices Review Board can't agree on a price. And two provinces, Ontario and Alberta, are not even paying for a third drug—Oxaliplatin—one of the most standard treatments. To get the care, patients must rely on a "compassionate care" program that the drug manufacturer has set up.

Here are some horror stories about Canadian health care:

SORDID TALES FROM ABOVE THE BORDER

The Failures of the Canadian Health System

Sylvia de Vries, a fifty-one-year-old corporate communications manager from Windsor, Ontario, couldn't get approval for ovarian cancer surgery from the government bureaucrats. She crossed the border to Pontiac, Michigan, where an American surgeon removed a forty-pound (18-kilogram), foot-long (35-centimeter) tumor from her body. The Toronto *Globe and Mail* reported that "had she waited two weeks, she would have faced potential multiorgan failure, rendering her unstable for surgery."[173]

"**Lindsay McCreith** was suffering from headaches and seizures, yet faced a four and a half month wait for an MRI scan in January of 2006. Deciding that the wait was untenable, Mr. McCreith did what a lot of Canadians do: He went south, and paid for an MRI scan across the border in Buffalo. The MRI revealed a malignant brain tumor. Ontario's government system still refused to provide timely treatment, offering instead a months-long wait for surgery. In the end, Mr. McCreith returned to Buffalo and paid for surgery that may have saved his life."[174]

"**Shona Holmes**, of Ontario, began losing her vision and experienced headaches, anxiety attacks, extreme fatigue and weight gain [in 2005]. Despite an MRI scan showing a brain tumor, Ms. Holmes was told she would have to wait months to see a specialist. In June, her vision deteriorating rapidly, Ms. Holmes went to the Mayo Clinic in Arizona, where she found that immediate surgery was required to prevent permanent vision loss and potentially death. Again, the government system in Ontario required more appointments and more tests along with more wait times. Ms. Holmes returned to the Mayo Clinic and paid for her surgery."[175]

"In Alberta, Canada, **Bill Murray** waited in pain for more than a year to see a specialist for his arthritic hip. The specialist recommended a 'Birmingham' hip resurfacing surgery (a state-of-the-art procedure that gives better results than basic hip replacement) as the best medical option. But government bureaucrats determined that Mr. Murray, who was fifty-seven, was 'too old' to enjoy the benefits of this procedure and said no. In the end, he was also denied the opportunity to pay for the procedure himself in Alberta."[176]

Brian Sinclair, a forty-five-year-old double amputee, died after a thirty-four-hour wait in a Manitoba, Canada, hospital emergency room during which he never saw a doctor or nurse. He was suffering from a bladder infection made worse by a blocked catheter. The medical examiner ruled that the death would have been preventable had he been seen in time. He registered at the triage area and then was forgotten about. He was discovered, dead, in a wheelchair by a security guard thirty-four hours later.[177]

To improve services, the Canadian health care system has set certain goals or benchmarks. It is hoping—hoping!—that it can cut the wait for radiation therapy to four to eight weeks.[178] If only cancer were understanding enough to wait.

It's not like that in the United States. To begin with, all elderly and poor people are covered through Medicare and Medicaid. If they don't get adequate care, it's not because of money. And anyone who lacks insurance or government coverage can always get treatment in an emergency room if their condition requires it. The reason hospitals are teetering on the verge of bankruptcy is that they have to spend so much money treating people who have no insurance. While some may be denied care here or there, lack of coverage isn't the massive, systemwide problem it is in Canada.

The net effect is that cancer death rates in Canada are 16 percent higher than in the United States.[179] And heart disease deaths are 5 percent higher.[180]

Why is the Canadian health care system set up this way? Because the government is trying to offer everything to anyone—and ending up giving too little to everyone. Just as in America, there aren't enough human resources—doctors and nurses—to go around. Even though we have more medical personnel per capita in the United States than Canada does, it's still not enough to give everybody full coverage.

Ken Lee of the Conservative Party of Manitoba summarizes the defects in the Canadian system:

> Canada's model of universal health care is failing. With unlimited demand for free services and a virtual monopoly delivering limited health services, the result has been an unsustainable level of public spending (up to 43 percent of gross government revenue is devoted to health care) and increasing rationing of services in the form of waiting lists. The monopoly that delivers health care is dominated by public sector unions that resist alternative forms of service delivery, rendering reform difficult. Bureaucrats determine what services are provided, what drugs can be prescribed, and what procedures can be offered. There is no accountability to the patient. The patient does not necessarily come first; unfortunately, the system comes first.[181]

So the Canadians, like Obama, want to achieve the ideal of full medical care for everybody. But because they are doing nothing to increase the number of doctors and nurses (and, indeed, disincentivize going into those professions), they can't deliver.

Neither can Obama.

So we face a choice, as Canada did. We can create a system in which everyone is entitled to everything but the shortage of resources empowers the bureaucrats to limit and control access to services so nobody gets adequate care. Or we can approach health care from the other end—the supply side. We can grant real incentives to encourage young people to go into medicine. We can offer lucrative careers, free of government limitations, and grant special scholarships to those willing to work in underserved areas and to practice general medicine or pediatrics. We can grow our resources and then expand our coverage.

And why won't Obama follow this prudent course? Because it will take time and by then he is worried that he will lose his political control over Congress and his popularity with the public. Striking while he still has the power may destroy the health care system, but at least he'll get it passed.

It's not just wrong to pretend we can extend medical coverage to everyone by legislative fiat without generating more doctors and more nurses—it's false, and it's cynical. Even more money won't solve the problem. Greater financing won't create more doctors or nurses out of whole cloth. That's the lesson we must learn from the example of Canada.

We all work to support our families. It's why we get up in the morning. But if the government tells us that no matter how well we do, how hard we work, how much we succeed, we cannot guarantee our family good medical care—or at least the best available—we will lose a key part of our incentive to work and produce. We surrender control over our own destiny, vesting it in bureaucrats who use statistics instead of human concern to shape their decisions.

This is the brave new world Barack Obama calls "health care reform." He says he'll cover everyone. He'll end up covering no one.

ACTION AGENDA

In 1993, Bill and Hillary Clinton tried to extend full health care coverage to everyone. Like Barack Obama, they used the rhetoric of compassion for the uninsured but covered up what the real-world consequences of their program would be.

They made one big mistake: They said they would change the health insurance structure in a bid to save costs by eliminating the middlemen and brokers. In doing so, they threatened to change everybody's health care. That scared people—and public sentiment turned against the Clintons on the issue.

Learning from their mistakes, President Obama is anxious to reassure Americans that he won't change health care coverage for anyone who has it now and is happy with it. But that's not true. When he says he'll cut the cost of our coverage by $2,500, he means that he'll introduce the kind of rationing they have in Canada. He will force our insurance carriers to give us the bad news, but it's the government that will have called the shots. Obama will never use the word "rationing." Indeed, he'll disingenuously deny that he intends it. He'll call it "efficiency" instead. But his proposal will force rationing of health care whether he admits it or not.

We can't let that happen. We must mobilize and defeat Obama's health care proposals. We need to get out the story about medical rationing and what that has led to in Canada. We can't let him win this fight.

Once everyone is covered, it will be impossible to roll the plan back. The die will have been cast, and we will no longer be able to guarantee our loved ones the care they need in their hour of greatest need.

At www.dickmorris.com, we'll be helping lead the battle to stop Obama from destroying our health care system. This is priority number one for us. Log on to the site, give us your e-mail address, and we'll help you get involved in the fight.

We've been down this socialized medicine road before. And we can't let them win this time.

5

OBAMA'S BLUEPRINT FOR POLITICAL DOMINATION

To implement and sustain an agenda as aggressive and far-reaching as President Obama has proposed, it will take a permanent political upheaval in this country, not just one victory in one election. Obama knows that if he can't use his presidency to realign America's political parties and power centers to make them friendly to his socialist agenda, he will soon become a footnote in history—a man who attempted bold changes but failed or who passed them only to see them repealed when he lost power.

His election in 2008 opened the door to the changes he wants to make. But to keep them on the books, he must win election after election, winning two terms, keeping a leftist Congress in power, and ensuring that his successor does not reverse his policies.

To do this, he has a four-part plan to create a national political realignment:

1. Grant legal status and then citizenship to as many now-illegal immigrants as possible, so that they'll vote Democratic far into the future.
2. Control the 2010 census, using it to overcount poor people, minorities, and other Democratic constituencies.

3. Change the rules of union elections to expand—vastly—the proportion of the labor force who belong to Democratic-controlled unions.

4. Use the powers of the Federal Communications Commission to muzzle conservative talk radio.

To defeat Obama's program—or repeal it once it passes—we must stop each of these efforts to change our political system. Let's begin with his plan to change, forever, the composition of the U.S. electorate.

IMMIGRATION: THE DEMOCRATIC POLITICAL PLOY

One key to Obama's plan for a permanent liberal majority is to enfranchise large numbers of people who came to this country illegally in order to win their loyalty at the polls.

He knows that the political support of the Latino population is the jump ball that will determine political dominance for a generation.

In recent years, Hispanics' political allegiance has shifted back and forth depending on how each party cultivated their votes. In the 2000 election, Latinos voted for Gore by thirty points. But in 2004, after four years of assiduous cultivation by George W. Bush, they split more evenly, supporting the Democratic challenger, John Kerry, by only ten points.

But then, when Bush introduced an immigration reform plan that conservative Republicans killed in Congress, Latinos' loyalties veered sharply back to the Democrats. In 2008, they resumed their habits of 2000 and backed Obama by more than two to one (even though McCain, the Republican candidate, had sponsored the immigration reform bill).

In congressional races, the newly Democratic Latino voters were key. In largely Hispanic districts in New Mexico and Arizona, for example, where Republicans held a 9–2 edge in House seats just three years ago, Democrats have now have the advantage by eight to three.[182]

And in other elections for Congress throughout the nation, Hispanic voters helped put Democrats over the top.

Obama is determined to keep and exploit this political advantage. He understands, after all, that Latinos are going to be an increasingly dominant force in our politics.

LATINO POPULATION GROWTH

	Population, in Millions	% of U.S. Population
1970	9.6	4.7%
1980	14.6	6.4
1990	22.4	9.0
2000	35.3	12.5
2010 (projected)	47.8	15.5
2020 (projected)	59.7	17.8

Source: "Hispanic Population in United States: 1970–2050," U.S. Census Bureau, www .census.gov/population/www/socdemo/hispanic/files/Projections.csv.

And if Obama can put the 12 to 15 million immigrants who are here il-legally on a path to lawful status and then to citizenship, he can increase the Latino voting presence materially—while winning the loyalty of Hispanic-American voters.

So Obama is determined to pass immigration reform. He has said that he's "very committed" to changing the law and has asked that legislation be "drawn up over the next several months." [183] Though he doubtless realizes that it will be harder to act during a time of high unemployment—when American citizens are competing with illegal immigrants for jobs—he knows he must act while he commands the political arena, with such deci-sive majorities in Congress.

There appear to be three basic ways in which Obama will expand the ranks of Latino voters in the United States:

1. By legislating an amnesty program for those already here
2. By providing incentives for more to come
3. By easing the path to naturalization and citizenship once they have gotten amnesty

Of course, these ideas will come with a lot of window dressing, includ-ing proposals to strengthen border enforcement and stop illegal immigration. But the incentives Obama is proposing will encourage many to leap the fence and come anyway. He's counting on it.

Congress being Congress, most of the debate on Obama's immigration reform legislation, when he submits it, will focus on the details of his amnesty provision. He's certain to follow at least the Bush approach of earned amnesty. Obama has offered us some clues as to his thinking on the subject: in a speech in Los Angeles this spring, he said that "illegal residents who have been in the United States a long time and have put down roots should have a mechanism for achieving legal status. They would have to learn English, pay a significant fine and go to the back of the line of those applying for legal entry." [184]

By focusing on "illegal residents who have been in the United States a long time and have put down roots," Obama means that he'll reward those who have successfully dodged the INS for five years. In return for their hiding out from our laws, he'll grant them eventual citizenship.

Whatever the final details of his legislative proposals are, the important thing is not the hurdles he'll ask illegals to jump to acquire legal status. They'll do whatever he asks. The real question is what incentives he'll put in place to encourage more and more people to come here, legally or illegally. The lures on this side of the border do far more to determine the flow of immigration than any other factor. And Obama is determined to roll out big prizes for coming here.

Although he claims that his health care plan won't cover illegal immigrants, we already know he's willing to turn an illegal immigrant into a legal one at the drop of a hat.

And the rewards for immigrants who have achieved legal status will be enormous! Obama plans to extend health care coverage to legal immigrants (even if they have just barely achieved this status through complying with his amnesty provisions). This coverage, of course, would extend to their families as well. Legal immigrants are now eligible for food stamps, disability insurance, and a host of other benefits. Obama will probably agree with Democratic proposals to guarantee in-state tuition at colleges to legal immigrants. He will incentivize leaping the fence—and in doing so he'll lure millions more Latinos to come here, all in the hope of getting their votes.

And once they come here illegally and then, through amnesty, get legal status, Obama will speed their path to citizenship and the ballot box. As he told a Spanish-speaking radio audience, "We're going to start by really trying to work on how to improve the current system so that people who want to be naturalized, who want to become citizens . . . that they are able to do it; that it's cheaper, that it's faster, that they have an easier time in terms of sponsoring family members." [185]

Why? Because Obama wants their votes. He needs them to keep his socialist agenda from being repealed.

ACTION AGENDA

Republicans must not surrender the Latino vote to Obama.

The president will probably succeed in persuading his top-heavy Democratic majorities in Congress to pass his amnesty proposals for illegal immigrants. But that doesn't have to mean the end of the Republican Party. Those newly enfranchised Latinos can become loyal Republicans!

Hispanic Americans, particularly Mexican Americans, are often very conservative. One-third now vote Republican. Of the 45 million Latinos in the United States, 15 million are evangelical Protestants who favor the Republican values agenda. They are pro-life and voted overwhelmingly for Bush in 2004.

As the Latinos move up the social and economic ladder, they will inevitably vote more Republican. Only if the GOP convinces them that there's no room for them in the party will they stay outside.

That would never happen, you're thinking. Not so fast: once upon a time, that's exactly what the Republican Party did to black voters. Before the 1930s, those blacks who could vote overwhelmingly backed the Republicans—the party of Lincoln, the Great Emancipator. To these African American voters, the Democrats were the party of former slaveholders in the racist South. In the 1930s and 1940s, however, Franklin Roosevelt and, particularly, Harry Truman made important inroads into the black vote. Truman based his comeback victory in 1948 in large part on pushing antilynching laws and integrating the armed forces. But Eisenhower, a Republican, carried the black vote in 1952 and 1956.

It was only when John F. Kennedy telephoned the wife of Dr. Martin

Luther King, Jr., as the civil rights leader languished in a Georgia prison cell, that blacks began to consider his candidacy. Even so, Kennedy edged Nixon out among black voters by only a small margin in 1960.

Then the GOP blew it. Even though a larger percentage of congressional Republicans backed civil rights legislation than did Democrats, in 1964 the party's presidential candidate, Barry Goldwater, voted against the landmark Civil Rights Act, which ended racial discrimination. His vote, and President Johnson's success in passing the legislation, assured the Democrats of 90 percent of the black vote in 1964. And they have gotten it ever since.

If the Republican Party wishes to avoid extinction—given the swelling numbers of Hispanic voters—it has to be more Latino-friendly, dropping attempts to force English-only initiatives and to curb schooling for illegal immigrants' children. In 2008, the Republican Party convinced Latinos that it didn't have their interests at heart. The party must avoid repeating that terrible mistake, lest it become irreversible.

COOKING THE CENSUS

When the U.S. Constitution was written, slaveholders in the southern states worried that the increasing population growth in the North would leave them politically impotent, unable to protect their right to enslave other human beings. So they adopted a provision that each slave—who had no rights and was considered property—would still be counted in the census as five-eighths of a person.

This outrageous provision, which the South made a precondition for approving the Constitution, gave the slaveholders extra votes in the House of Representatives and the Electoral College and helped keep proslavery presidents in office until 1860.

Now President Obama is hoping to use the census to give cities, liberals, and minorities extra representation—just like the slaveholders got in colonial times. This time, they will do so by counting not slaves, but people who may not exist.

For years, Democrats have watched in anguish as their congressional power eroded because people left the Democratic Northeast to flock to Republican states in the South and the West. This massive shift in national population, of course, has created a transfer of House seats, and therefore of electoral votes to the new states where these folks settled. (The Electoral College vote of each state is the sum of its House and Senate delegations.)

In a bid to arrest the decline, Democrats have long argued that census counts are false because the poor, immigrants, and inner-city residents are not fully counted. Part of the blame falls on the poor themselves, who, it is said, often don't cooperate with visits from census takers out of fear of the police or immigration authorities. Others blame high crime in urban areas, claiming that census takers are reluctant to go into these areas and residents are shy about opening their doors to strangers.

So the Democrats have long sought to use statistical sampling procedures to ramp up the counts of inner-city populations. Republicans have rejected their proposals, and the Supreme Court has ruled against some of their sampling plans in the past. (Since the census is specifically mandated in the Constitution, the Court has ample jurisdiction.)

The census of 2010, which will be the first conducted by a Democratic administration in thirty years, will not only determine the distribution of House seats at the federal level, it will also shape the distribution of state legislative seats throughout the nation. And these are especially important, since it will be the state legislatures, elected under new lines based on the new census, that will draw the legislative districts for the federal House of Representatives, largely determining its partisan balance.

A good census could give either party a decade of political power.

For example, under the Clinton administration, census takers refused to count Mormon missionaries who live permanently in Utah but serve overseas. As a result, Republican Utah lost a fourth congressional seat. (Under proposals to give the District of Columbia a vote in the House— undoubtedly a Democrat—Utah would get its extra seat, almost certain to be Republican.)

Everyone expects Obama to try to manipulate the census to increase Democratic representation. But the administration showed its hand prematurely when the president nominated New Hampshire Republican Senator Judd Gregg to be his secretary of commerce. Gregg withdrew his name when he realized that he couldn't let himself become a bipartisan fig leaf to camouflage Obama's ultra-left program.

Before Gregg pulled out, though, minority groups around the nation protested his selection. Why? Because the Census Bureau is part of the Department of Commerce. The Georgia talk-show host Martha Zoller, writing in *Human Events*, describes how even "before the ink was dry on the announcement of Sen. Judd Gregg as Commerce Secretary, the Congressional Black Caucus and Latino groups were complaining that a Republican could not be in control of the census." [186]

Gregg, who is opposed to sampling, had voted against funding increases for the Census Bureau. As chairman of the Senate Appropriations Subcommittee, which oversees the Commerce Department, Gregg had opposed a 1999 Clinton administration request for emergency funds for the 2000 census; in 1995, he had voted to abolish the Department of Commerce. [187]

These past positions made liberals suspect that Gregg couldn't be counted on to cook the books and give them a biased census. So the Obama administration let it be known that its chief of staff, Rahm Emanuel, would be in charge of the census and would have the power of oversight. The appointment of Emanuel—the former head of the House Democratic campaign committee—to oversee the census signaled Obama's intention to do all he can to manipulate the figures to give the Democrats a good, even if inaccurate, count.

Larry Sabato, the director of the Center for Politics at the University of Virginia, puts it well. "The last thing the census needs," he says, "is for any hard-bitten partisan (either a Karl Rove or a Rahm Emanuel) to manipulate these critical numbers. Many federal funding formulas depend on them, as well as the whole fabric of federal and state representation." [188]

Sabato adds, "I've always remembered what Joseph Stalin said: 'Those who cast the votes decide nothing. Those who count the votes decide everything.'" [189]

On April 2, 2009, Obama nominated Robert M. Groves to be the census director. Groves is a long time advocate of the use of sampling in the census counts. The Associated Press noted that "when he was the [census] bureau's associate director, Goves recommended that the 1990 census be statistically adjusted to make up for an undercount of roughly 5 million people, many of them minorities in dense urban ares who tend to vote for Democrats." [190]

At the time, Bush's commerce secretary, Robert Mosbacher, overruled Groves and called the proposed statistical adjustment "political tampering."

But now, when Groves tries his political tricks, there won't be anyone there to stop him.

ACTION AGENDA

There is no doubt that Obama will attempt to manipulate the 2010 census for partisan advantage. The question is: What can we do about it?

In this case, plenty. The Supreme Court has already established its jurisdiction over the census, citing the fact that it is a constitutional, not a legislative, requirement. In the past, the Court has resisted efforts to use "sampling" in making the final count. But each census poses its own particular issues—and we can't stand by and trust that Obama will adjudicate them fairly.

So it's almost inevitable that any attempt he makes to manipulate the census will be challenged in court. But that will require a lot of funding— and support for collecting evidence and for preparing the challenges. Through www.dickmorris.com, we'll keep you posted on where and when you can help this process along.

We can't let Obama steal the census.

PUSHING UNIONIZATION

Labor unions, long diminishing as an industrial force, have resurrected their political punch in the past decade. Their donations and manpower are vital to the Democratic Party and have made up a large part of the offensive that returned their party to power last year.

Now it's time for payback.

From its high point in the 1940s, when 30 percent of all American workers belonged to a labor union, the percentage of the workforce that's unionized has dropped to only 12 percent. And union membership has shifted away from blue-collar industrial unions and toward government workers' organizations, such as those representing teachers, police, firefighters, and hospital workers. Labor representation of private-sector workers has fallen dramatically.

With the growth of foreign competition, particularly in manufacturing, union membership is likely to decline further—unless labor leaders can induce more workers to organize and vote to be represented by a union.

Thus far, despite years of trying, they have largely failed to expand the union base. Now they're trying to change the rules to do so.

What makes this a political issue, not just a business problem, is the tendency of union members to follow their leadership into the Democratic camp. If, by slanting the election procedures, Obama can increase the proportion of the workforce in labor unions, he can do a great deal to assure himself of the decade of political supremacy he covets.

And since labor unions donate huge sums to the Democratic Party and its candidates, anything that swells union coffers—as an expanding membership would do—would be a big financial help to Obama's allies.

So Obama isn't just pushing unionization as a way to pay labor back for its political and financial support; his deeper plan is to increase the number of union workers so that he can add them to his political machine and be able to count on their votes and their union's contributions.

On April 2, 2008, during his campaign for president, Obama told an AFL-CIO convention that "we're ready to play offense for organized labor. It's time we had a president who didn't choke saying the word 'union.' A president who strengthens our unions by letting them do what they do best: organize our workers." [191]

Of course, there's a problem with all this: Most workers don't *want* to join unions. So the labor bigwigs have figured out a way to coerce them into doing so—the union card-check system.

Under current law, workers in a company can sign cards asking the National Labor Relations Board (NLRB) to hold an election to decide whether or not to unionize. If a majority of the workers sign the cards, the NLRB holds an election, by secret ballot, to determine the answer.

And, most often, the union winds up losing the election, even though a majority of the workforce signed cards asking for the election. Why would workers who oppose a union sign the cards? Normally they wouldn't. But the labor organizers bring incredible pressure on them to sign, often visiting them at home, harassing them on the job, and pestering them for signatures. So obviously the union must be getting some of those who actually oppose unionization to sign cards calling for a vote.

Brian Wilson of Fox News reported on one small auto parts plant in Fort Wayne, Indiana, that "got a first hand lesson on card-check. The employer acquiesced on card-check and the union got the votes it needed. Afterward, the truth came out as employees complained about the aggressive harassing and coercive tactics used by union organizers. The company appealed and a secret vote was held, and the workers voted *not* to unionize." [192]

Under the card-check bill, labor organizers wouldn't have to put up with the inconvenience of an election—certainly not one by secret ballot. The law provides that unionization will be decided not by secret ballot but by whether they can get a majority of workers to sign pledge cards—even those signed by twisted arms. (The law would allow an election only if 30 percent of the workers explicitly ask for one.)

Obama has specifically pledged to back the card-check bill, saying "I will make it the law of the land when I'm president of the United States." [193] But the potential for forcing employees to sign the cards to request a union is enormous.

Of course, coercion is a two-way street. Plenty of employers threaten their workers in order to deter them from supporting a union. John T. Palter, writing in the *Dallas Morning News*, points out that "some employers abuse the current system. It is, for example, notoriously easy, and relatively inexpensive, for an organization to terminate anyone they suspect of starting a union." [194] One good aspect of the card-check bill is that it strengthens worker protections, a badly needed step.

But employer coercion can go only so far with a secret ballot. When the boss doesn't know who voted for a union, he can't retaliate easily. But to eliminate the secret ballot—indeed to eliminate the ballot at all—would invite coercion from both sides.

In any event, as Palter notes, employer coercion isn't "why unions are on the decline. The globalization of business operations, the decline of traditionally unionized industries, the increase in workplace safety and rising standards of living have all taken much bigger tolls on union membership than employer abuses." [195] And many of the traditional goals of unions— safe workplaces and limitations on hours—are now policed by the government, making unions less necessary. But the unions are using the excuse that there is coercion by employers to pass the card check bill so they can do their own coercing. The poor workers in the middle!

The card-check bill would also require that, once a union is formed, the company negotiate a contract with it. In the event that the two parties can't come to an agreement, it provides for a government-appointed arbitrator to establish one by fiat. Since most of these arbitrators would probably be prounion (appointed by the Obama administration), the unions won't negotiate in good faith but will just sit back and wait for the arbitrator to make the decision in their favor.

The arbitration provision essentially puts the government right in the middle of the formulation of the contract—an inappropriate position. After all, it's not the government, but the company and the workers, who will have to live with the outcome.

The obituaries of failed American businesses attest to how often union demands have forced companies to close their doors, laying off all their workers. With low-cost foreign labor so readily available and few barriers standing in the way of foreign trade, American workers need to remember that moving labor offshore is an increasingly attractive alternative for many businesses. For an arbitrator to impose a deal, without giving the boss a chance to tell the union that he'll shut down if the terms aren't altered, is self-defeating for the workers involved.

ACTION AGENDA

When he was a Republican, Pennsylvania's senator Arlen Specter announced he was going to vote against card-check, saying that "the problems of the recession make this a particularly bad time to enact" the bill.[196] His statement seemed to doom the legislation since it would give the Republicans (who are united in opposition) enough votes to sustain a filibuster. But now that Specter is a Democrat, there's no way of knowing if he will succumb to pressure from Obama and Senate majority leader Harry Reid.

The *Wall Street Journal* reported that "Senator Specter said he would reconsider the bill if other efforts to amend the National Labor Relations Act to increase labor's clout are unsuccessful."[197] The *Journal* noted that "one change [Specter] supports is shortening the time frame in which union elections are held."[198] There is also speculation that Specter would back the requirement that an arbitrator be named if collective bargaining should fail to produce a union contract.

And, of course, now that Specter is serving a new master, all bets may be off.

The unions, of course, won't take the legislation's defeat lying down.

This bill is their top priority for the Obama administration—the key to their future success—and they won't take no for an answer.

And labor has the clout to make its feelings known in the Democratic Party—because Democrats are increasingly dependent on union donations to support their campaigns.

We need to put maximum pressure on the moderate Democratic senators to kill this dangerous bill.

MUZZLING TALK RADIO

In our book *Fleeced*, published in June 2008, we warned that "there may be a more devilish and fiendish plot afoot to cripple talk radio than the simple reinstatement of the Fairness Doctrine." [199]

Unfortunately, we were right. The liberals, led by Obama, are intent on killing talk radio. But they are too clever to use the Fairness Doctrine to do so. Instead, as we predicted, they're using the basic Federal Communications Commission (FCC) law to demand "diversity," "localism," and "public interest" programming in radio.

"*Diversity*" comes in through an amendment to the FCC statute introduced by assistant Senate majority leader Dick Durbin (D-IL), which passed the Senate on a party-line vote and is pending in the House. Durbin's amendment would require the FCC to "take actions to encourage and promote diversity in communication media ownership and to ensure that broadcast station licenses are used in the public interest." [200]

Durbin defines "diversity" as relating "primarily to gender, race, and other characteristics . . . in media ownership." [201] But Republican senator James Inhofe of Oklahoma may have a more accurate description: "I certainly can't tell you what 'diversity in communication media ownership' means. Federal agencies love this kind of language [in a statute] because it gives them greater leeway to interpret it however they like and impose their will upon the industry they regulate." [202]

In the hands of an FCC whose majority is Democratic, it could well give the agency a lever to oust conservative owners and reissue the broadcast license to a more "diverse" set. (There are two members of the FCC from each party—required by statute—and a fifth appointed by the president. So Obama now controls the FCC.)

"Localism," as Brian C. Anderson noted in a *Los Angeles Times* op-ed piece, would "impose greater 'local accountability' on broadcasters—that is, it would force stations to carry more local programming."[203]

Since the most popular conservative talk-show hosts—like Rush Limbaugh, Sean Hannity, Mark Levin, and Neal Boortz—are nationally syndicated, requiring stations to book local programming would mean cutting into these radio giants' airtime.

Anderson warns that "localism . . . also could require stations to set up permanent community advisory boards (including 'underserved community segments') that would have to be regularly consulted on 'community needs and issues.' "[204]

The FCC proposal, first made in January 2009, required that the "permanent advisory boards" be

> comprised of local officials and other community leaders to periodically advise them [radio station owners and managers] of local needs and issues and seek comment on the matter. . . . To ensure that these discussions include representatives of all community elements, these boards would be made up of leaders of various segments of the community, including underserved groups.[205]

Anderson calls localism "wildly impractical" and asks, "Would liberals sit on the board of a conservative station broadcasting in an urban area? Or would, say, an Islamic community leader sit on the board of a Christian station that broadcast in an area with a large Muslim population?"[206]

These community advisory boards would likely have enormous power. Stations would be obliged to listen to their input, since their very broadcast licenses could be imperiled if they don't. Indeed, Obama has urged that radio stations be required to renew their licenses every two years as opposed to every eight under current law, giving them an even shorter leash. Because radio stations operate on the public airwaves, they cannot broadcast without an FCC license to do so.

Of course, if people in a given community wanted more local programming, they could vote with their fingers and turn their radio dials to stations that offer it. The very popularity of the nationally syndicated shows indicates that they don't.

The *Public Interest* requirement would give the new community advisory boards the role of judging how well a station met the criterion, further reinforcing their power during the all-important licensing process.

To muzzle conservative talk radio, Obama has appointed Julius Genachowski as the new chairman of the FCC. Media reform groups, the ones that are trying to destroy conservative talk radio, are reportedly "joyous" over his appointment.[207]

Genachowski crafted Obama's blueprint for destroying talk radio—his Technology and Innovation Plan—during the campaign. As the plan noted, "Barack Obama believes that the nation's rules ensuring diversity of media ownership are critical to the public interest. Unfortunately, over the past several years, the Federal Communications Commission has promoted the concept of consolidation over diversity."[208]

Josh Silver, the director of the media reform group Free Press, said that under Genachowski's "leadership, the FCC's compass would point toward the 'public interest.' "[209] As Genachowski defines it, that is.

Congressional Democrats are lining up behind these changes. Not only did Durbin's amendment pass the Senate, but House speaker Nancy Pelosi spoke all the code words recently when she said that we need to "take actions to encourage and promote diversity in communication media ownership and to ensure that broadcast station licenses are used in the public interest."[210]

So, while conservatives have been directing their fire at the possibility of a restoration of the Fairness Doctrine (which required equal time for opposing points of view), the Obama administration has been aiming at even more fundamental changes in station policy, management—and even ownership.

The new effort to gut conservative talk radio stems from a report by the Center for American Progress, headed by former Clinton chief of staff and Obama transition leader John Podesta, entitled "The Structural Imbalance of Political Talk Radio."

The report said that "any effort to encourage more responsive and balanced radio programming will first require steps to increase localism and diversify radio station ownership to better meet local and community needs."[211] He suggested three ways to restore "balance" to the airwaves:

THE LIBERAL PLAN TO KILL TALK RADIO

- "Restore local and national caps on the ownership of commercial radio stations.

- "Ensure greater local accountability over radio licensing.

- "Require commercial owners who fail to abide by enforceable public interest obligations to pay a fee to support public broadcasting."[212]

Defending himself from conservative criticism, Senator Durbin noted that the requirement for "diversity in [station] ownership . . . is not a new rule. It's been around for sixty years. The other part of the Durbin amendment said that broadcast licensees had to operate in the public interest. That's also been on the books for almost fifty years."[213]

But Durbin's amendment requires the FCC to take " 'affirmative actions' to ensure that radio station ownership is diverse and that broadcasting licenses are issued strictly in the public interest."[214]

Senator Inhofe explains where the Durbin amendment might lead:

What is most concerning to me is the enforcement procedure for breaches of localism and diversity promotion regulations. The revocation of broadcaster licenses is a real possibility, which at the very least will threaten the willingness of broadcasters to appeal to conservative listeners. Senator Durbin's amendment requires affirmative action on the part of the FCC. . . . It doesn't stipulate what actions . . . but instead leaves the enforcement mechanism up to the determination of the FCC, which will likely be emboldened by the affirmative language of the amendment. I find this to be extremely dangerous, and so too should everyone who tunes in to talk radio. New regulations coupled with the threat of license revocation completely undermine the free market of the broadcast industry.[215]

ACTION AGENDA

The new liberal approach to muzzling talk radio is dangerous—especially because if it is enacted, it could become permanent. By taking away radio frequencies from their current owners and reassigning them to minority owners or liberals, the administration may be able to change decisively what we hear over the airwaves.

At the very least, the regulations could prompt stations to turn to music—no controversy there. But it's more likely that the Obama administration, through FCC fiat, would force radio stations to change owners, managers, and ideological orientation.

Imagine if comparable changes were forced on the print media. Any such move would be recognized as a gross violation of the First Amendment, sending up howls of justifiable protest. What if a Republican president ousted the owner and editorial staff of the *New York Times* and insisted on putting in conservatives (who represent the business community in New York) instead?

But the justification that radio uses "public airwaves" shields this action from First Amendment scrutiny—and permits the administration to gut talk radio behind closed doors.

We must fight this change with everything we have. Once the stations change ownership, it will be almost impossible to change them back!

It should be enough for us to demonstrate our loyalty to certain stations and their programming by listening to them every day. But in the strange world of Barack Obama, this demonstration of fealty may not be enough to assure the FCC that the community supports its station. Instead, a group of left-wing advisers could sabotage a radio station's ownership and mount a coup to topple it. They might even find a way to profit from the change in ownership!

We must work with our talk-show hosts to demonstrate our commitment to our radio stations and the programming they offer. We are sure that Sean and Rush will tell us when the stations that carry their programs have license renewal procedures pending. We should hold demonstrations in the streets to show our support for continuing the current ownership and format. We need to deluge the FCC with letters, e-mails, and petitions in support of the local programming and station ownership.

Otherwise, we could wake up one day and find that our talk radio has been replaced by dead air.

6

OBAMA SENDS MESSAGE
The War on Terror Is Over

In his first few months in office, President Obama has sent a clear message to both Americans and our enemies: the war on terror is over. On a host of fronts, he has pulled back and is pulling out. It's as if 9/11 never happened.

But terrorists *did* attack the United States that day. And they still have us in their sights. The fact that a president of the United States is disarming us—unilaterally—in the war on terror is a catastrophe in the making!

If Obama's policies are wrong, the people he has appointed to top jobs at the departments of Justice and Homeland Security are worse! They have won fame and celebrity by criticizing aggressive actions to stop terrorism. They specialize not in making *us* safer but making *the terrorists* safer.

OBAMA'S WAR ON THE WAR ON TERROR

In his first few months in office, Obama has:

- Dropped the death penalty and declined to prosecute the mastermind behind the USS *Cole* bombing. May the seventeen sailors who died in that attack—a precursor of 9/11—rest in peace!

- Closed all overseas CIA interrogation centers.

- Banned the use of waterboarding in any terror investigation, no matter the circumstances or even the imminence of the threat.

- Appointed an attorney general and Justice Department officials who are on record as opposed to the use of enhanced interrogation techniques in terror investigations.

- Announced the closing of the Guantánamo prison for terrorists.

- Granted Al-Arabiya television his first news organization interview.

- Chosen Fatah Party leader and Palestinian Authority president Mahmoud Abbas as the first foreign leader he would contact by telephone.

- Donated $900 million for Gaza reconstruction—much of which will end up under Hamas control.

- Raised no objection when Pakistan ceded control of the entire mountain area (the Swat Valley) on the Afghan-Pakistani border to the Taliban, pledging to allow it to govern the land under Shariah law. Predictably, the Taliban then used the Swat as a staging area to invade Pakistan.

- Made no protest when Yemen released more than one hundred al-Qaeda terrorists from its prisons.

- Dissolved the Homeland Security Council, a White House group of cabinet officers and staff founded after 9/11 to focus on domestic anti-terror precautions and protections. Obama has folded the council's operation back into the National Security Council (NSC), the umbrella group charged with conducting foreign policy. Since the NSC is concerned primarily with outward-looking foreign policy questions, it is unlikely to look inward and take full account of our homeland security needs.

- Chosen as his Homeland Security director Arizona governor Janet Napolitano, an expert on Mexican border issues but not on terrorism or homeland security! As CBS News has noted, Napolitano "avoid[ed] the terms 'terrorism' or '9/11' in remarks prepared for her first congressional testimony since taking office, signaling a sharp change in tone from her predecessors."[216] Instead, she speaks of terrorism as a "manmade" disaster.

(*continued on next page*)

- Failed to utter a peep of protest when Sheik Sharif Ahmed of the Union of Islamic Courts (UIC) became the new president of Somalia, a key strategic nation because of its geographic position on the horn of Africa. The Bush administration recognized the UIC as a terrorist group.

On his first day in office, Obama reversed the Freedom of Information Act (FOIA) policy of the Bush Justice Department and pledged "an unprecedented level of openness in government."[217] He ordered the new FOIA guidelines to be written with a "presumption in favor of disclosure,"[218] even though such disclosure would give important information to terrorists.

Nothing better exemplifies how Obama has turned things upside down than the administration's decision to drop the charges against Abd al-Rahim al-Nashiri, whom the Pentagon had charged with "organizing and directing"[219] the bombing of the USS *Cole*, an attack in which seventeen sailors were killed and thirty-nine injured. On February 5, 2009, Susan J. Crawford, the top authority over the parajudicial commissions Bush had created to try Guantánamo prisoners, dropped the charges against al-Nashiri in order to comply with Obama's executive order requiring a review of all detention policies and procedures at Guantánamo.[220] The United States had sought a delay in the Guantánamo trial, scheduled for February 7, 2009, but the judge had refused to grant it.[221] So, rather than proceed to try him, the Obama administration decided it was more important to complete the review than to proceed with the trial.

According to U.S. intelligence, al-Nashiri was the leader of the al-Qaeda network's operations in the Persian Gulf and was involved in plots against Western targets in the United Arab Emirates, Saudi Arabia, the Strait of Gibraltar, Morocco, and Qatar. He also fought with the Taliban in Afghanistan and in Chechnya.[222]

News media reports of the dropping of al-Nashiri's charges focused not on the mayhem he had committed in killing the sailors and damaging the *Cole* but rather on the fact that he was one of three prisoners the Bush administration has admitted it waterboarded to get information. The other two are Khalid Sheikh Mohammed, the mastermind of the 9/11 attacks, and Abu Zubaydah, an al-Qaeda operative tied to 9/11.

What inverted priorities! Waterboarding may have been essential in learning, from Khalid Sheikh Mohammed, of al-Qaeda's plans to blow up the Brooklyn Bridge and of its efforts to explode a dirty bomb in the United States. And waterboarding of al-Nashiri was likely important in rounding up all the *Cole* terrorists. (Waterboarding, by the way, is not the inhuman nightmare many have portrayed it as being. Among other things, it was a long-established hazing ritual at the Virginia Military Institute. General George C. Marshall, the World War II chief of staff and Harry S Truman's secretary of state, was waterboarded when he entered V.M.I.) To drop charges against a terrorist who killed seventeen service people simply because he was waterboarded is incomprehensible.

Obama has, of course, prohibited the use of waterboarding regardless of the circumstances. Asked at a press conference on April 29, 2009, about interrogations of terrorists, he said that waterboarding was a "shortcut" and that there were other ways to get the information. But what if there aren't? And what if the terror attack is just around the corner and there is no time for another way to learn the details? Would Obama literally consign hundreds or thousands of Americans to death so as to avoid waterboarding a terrorist who is neither a U.S. citizen or even a legal resident?

Yes he would!

Also outrageous is Obama's silence on the February 16, 2009, decision of the Pakistani government to let the Taliban govern the Swat valley and neighboring areas in northwest Pakistan using Shariah law. The decision, which effectively concedes to the Taliban exactly the kind of protected zone it had in Afghanistan—the zone where the 9/11 plot was hatched—is a giveaway to the terrorists.

As Reuters has noted, "critics are . . . saying the deal will encourage Taliban militants fighting elsewhere in both Pakistan and Afghanistan."[223]

The British newspaper *The Guardian* quotes Khadim Hussain of the Aryana Institute for Regional Research and Advocacy, a think tank in Islamabad, as describing the deal as "a surrender to the Taliban."[224] The paper also quotes Javed Iqbal, a retired Pakistani judge, as saying that "it means that there is not one law in the country. It will disintegrate this way. If you concede to this, you will go on conceding."[225]

The *Times of India* says that Pakistan was trying to find a "good" Taliban. "According to certain strategists, in Pakistan as well as in the US," the newspaper explained, "the Taliban can be broadly drawn into two categories—one, the socially ultra-conservative Islamists, who demand the rule of Shariah in areas where they dominate, and, two, the global jihadis. It's being suggested that the world can do business with the former, if only to isolate and eliminate the latter, the bad ones."[226]

But the newspaper points out that many experts say that "any kind of Talibanism is dangerous."[227]

> They point out that, good or bad, all Talibs who demand the enforcement of Shariah invoke a variant of Islam that also calls for Islamic domination by global jihad. Besides, to accept the "good" Taliban theory is to write off the rights of Muslim women, allow public stoning and summary executions.
>
> These experts feel that this romantic project to isolate and eliminate the worst of the worst, is a slippery slope that would amount to conceding ground to Islamic forces that, sooner or later, and at a time of their choice, would seek to impose their ultra conservatism on the world by jihad.[228]

When the hard-line cleric Sufi Muhammad, who negotiated the deal for the Taliban, returned to the Swat valley, the Associated Press reports, he "received a hero's welcome there by crowds shouting 'Long live Islam!' "[229] Of course he did.

NATO, which has 55,000 troops fighting in Afghanistan, was less than pleased with the decision. The truce "is certainly reason for concern," noted NATO spokesman James Appathurai. "We should all be concerned by a situation in which extremists would have a safe haven . . . it is clear that the [Swat valley] region is suffering very badly from extremists and we would not want it to get worse."[230]

Yet President Obama said and did nothing to change the situation. All Secretary of State Clinton would say was that "the agreement still needed to be 'thoroughly understood.' "[231] The Obama administration seems unwilling even to criticize the Taliban in public. Apparently surrender is just fine with it.

Now, exploiting its gains, the Taliban is increasingly posing a serious military threat to the Pakistani government. That it would do so was, of course, predictable. Once the Pakistani government gave them, in effect, a safe haven near the Afghan border, their further military advance was inevitable.

Yet even more disturbing than President Obama's policies are the people he has appointed to administer them.

Let's begin with Eric Holder, Jr., the new U.S. attorney general. Holder was instrumental in persuading President Clinton to pardon a group of FALN terrorists in 2000. The *Los Angeles Times* reports that Holder "repeatedly pushed some of his subordinates at the Clinton Justice Department to drop their opposition to a controversial 1999 grant of clemency to 16 members of two violent Puerto Rican nationalist organizations."[232] The paper notes that "angry lawmakers demanded to know why the Justice Department had not sided with the FBI, federal prosecutors, and other law enforcement officials who were vehemently opposed to the grants [of clemency]."[233]

The *Times* reported that Holder "instructed his staff . . . to effectively replace the [Justice] Department's original report recommending against any commutations . . . with one that favored clemency for at least half of the prisoners."[234]

Later, the pardon attorney at the Clinton Justice Department, Roger Adams, commented on the incident. "I remember this [episode] well," he said, "because it was such a big deal to consider clemency for a group of people convicted of such heinous crimes."[235] Adams said he told Holder of his "strong opposition to any clemency in several internal memos and a draft report recommending denial."[236] But Holder would not take no for an answer. What makes the whole episode even more reprehensible is that the terrorists had not even applied for pardons. Clinton and Holder simply decided to respond to pressure from outside groups that were advocating their release.

The sixteen FALN members pardoned at Holder's urging had been convicted of bank robbery, possession of explosives, and participating in a seditious conspiracy. As the *Times* reports, "Overall, the two groups had been linked by the FBI to more than 130 bombings, several armed robberies, six slayings, and hundreds of injuries."[237]

Joseph Connor—the son of Frank Connor, who was murdered at the age of thirty-three in the FALN bombing of Fraunces Tavern in 1975—testified before the Senate Judiciary Committee to protest Holder's nomination as attorney general. In his testimony he noted that the FALN pardons had been condemned at the time by the U.S. Senate by a vote of 95–2!

Connor's eloquent testimony also brings us face-to-face with the aftermath of terrorism:

> These terrorists took away my father's life; never allowing him to see his sons play sports in high school, never allowing him the pride in seeing his boys graduate high school and college, or meet his daughters-in- law. They took from him the joy of being father and a grandfather. They took from my mother the promise of growing old with her first love.[238]

And Connor poses some questions for Holder.

QUESTIONS HOLDER HAS YET TO ANSWER:

- Why did Holder ignore the recommendations of the FBI, the Bureau of Prisons, the former pardon attorney, prosecutors, and even his own Justice Department and champion the release of self-proclaimed terrorists?

- Why does Holder continue to hide behind executive privilege when posed direct questions on the issue—even as he was about to become part of what was being billed as the "most transparent administration in American history"?

- Why did Holder fail to contact victims or their families but meet with supporters of the terrorists?

- Why did Holder provide advice to the terrorists by coming up with the idea that they renounce violence in order to get clemency?

- Why did Holder make the unprecedented decision to allow the terrorists to make conference calls between prisons?

- Why did Holder fail to require them to provide information to resolve unsolved crimes as a condition for the pardon?[239]

Of course, the real reason Clinton and Holder granted the commutations to the FALN terrorists was to promote Hillary's candidacy for the

Senate in New York State, the home to the largest concentration of Puerto Ricans in the nation. To warm their reception for this newcomer to New York State, President Clinton was determined to grant the commutations that were being demanded by some of the ultra-left leaders of the New York Puerto Rican community.

But appointing Holder as attorney general is only part of a pattern of Obama designations that send a clear message to those trying to protect us against terrorist attacks: that they—not the terrorists they are investigating—are in the Justice Department's sights.

The worst new appointee is Dawn Johnsen, the new head of the Office of Legal Counsel (OLC). It is the OLC that advises a president on what he can and cannot legally do in terrorist investigations. In a 2008 article entitled "What's a President to Do? Interpreting the Constitution in the Wake of Bush Administration Abuses," Johnsen signaled how far backward she would lean over to protect terror suspects' rights.

Hey, Dawn, how about us American citizens?

The *National Review*'s Andrew McCarthy argues that Johnsen views the War on Terror "as something President Bush started after 9/11 rather than a years-long jihadist provocation to which the United States finally responded." He notes that "this framework would make it impossible to prosecute as war crimes such pre-9/11 atrocities as the bombings of the USS *Cole* and the embassies in East Africa." [240]

Johnsen dismisses President Bush's justification of warrantless surveillance of al-Qaeda communications into and out of the country as an "extreme and implausible Commander-In-Chief theory." [241] As McCarthy notes, however, "in fact, the practice was strongly supported by federal court precedent and has been reaffirmed by the appellate court Congress created specifically to consider such issues." Amazingly, McCarthy quotes Johnsen as saying that "job applicants to the Justice Department who have been passed over by the Bush Administration for holding leftist political views should get 'special consideration' in Department of Justice hiring." [242]

Meanwhile, in moving to close the Guantánamo prison, President Obama has raised the specter that 250 of the most hardened terrorists in the world will be released. (For a fuller discussion of this issue, see the chapter on Guantánamo in our previous book, *Fleeced*.)

One early—and chilling—example of the kinds of men Obama considers fit for release is Binyam Mohamed, an Ethiopian-born British resident who was freed from Guantánamo in the first few weeks of the Obama presidency and sent home to the United Kingdom where he will face no charges.

THE TERRORIST OBAMA FREED: BINYAM MOHAMED

- He was arrested while accompanying Jose Padilla into the United States. Padilla and Mohamed had visited an al-Qaeda training camp, where they met with Khalid Sheikh Mohammed, the mastermind of 9/11, who tasked them with making and detonating a dirty bomb in an American city.

- He trained at al-Qaeda camps, where he specialized in firearms and explosives.

- He was paid by al-Qaeda to travel to the United States to implement plans to blow up high-rise apartment buildings here.

- He attempted to enter the United States in 2002 but was turned away because his passport was forged.

Mohamed's case attracted a lot of publicity when his lawyers alleged that he had been tortured in U.S. custody. Yet now, regardless of his record of crimes against the United States, Obama is letting him go!

He is practically inviting this hardened terrorist to resume his efforts to kill us.

And if Obama isn't keeping terrorists locked up, why should anybody else? Just two weeks after Obama's inauguration, Yemen freed 170 men whom "it had arrested on suspicion of having ties to al-Qaeda."[243] The release came right after al-Qaeda had announced that Yemen would be its ongoing base of terrorist activities throughout the Arabian Peninsula. Apparently, Yemen wanted to help out its hometown industry!

Of course, Yemen wasn't entirely irresponsible in releasing these men. They were freed only "after signing pledges not to engage in terrorism."[244] These were the same kind of pledges Holder got the FALN terrorists to sign—the kind that aren't worth the paper they're written on. And, as if that weren't enough, news reports reassured us that "local tribal leaders are also expected to guarantee the good behavior of the men." [245]

Wow. What a relief.

Yemen hadn't released the men before because, during the Bush administration, it was concerned that doing so might "increase [Bush's] reluctance to release Yemeni detainees from the Guantánamo Bay detention facility." [246] Yet under Obama it apparently felt so such trepidation.

Roughly 40 percent of the remaining detainees at Guantánamo Bay are Yemenis.

They'll fit in nicely with their al-Qaeda colleagues in Yemen!

These stories are horrific enough, but they raise a more fundamental question: Is Obama out of his mind? Why would a president, charged with protecting us, let terrorists go? Why would he appoint the kinds of people he has to the Justice Department?

Let's remember where Obama comes from. Before he was elected to the Illinois State Senate, his only real job was teaching constitutional law. He has to get up to speed on economics—he's not doing too well so far— and foreign policy. But when it comes to constitutional law, he's right in his element.

Obama believes that the Constitution applies equally to the prosecution of criminal defendants and to the gathering of intelligence. He believes you have to get your information in ways that won't prevent it from being introduced as evidence in a criminal trial.

Who disagrees with this position? President Bush, to be sure—but also President Bill Clinton and even his attorney general Janet Reno. They all recognized that intelligence-gathering activities are not and should not be subject to the Fourth, Fifth, and Sixth Amendments, which protect us against searches and seizures and other intrusive investigatory tactics. They believed that if you weren't going to use the information in court to try to lock somebody up, you didn't need to jump through the constitutional hoops in gathering the evidence.

Barack Obama disagrees. And when it comes to applying his point of view, he's an absolutist about it.

Of course, he'll learn. He will come to realize that his constitutional philosophy is leaving us unprotected. Unfortunately, that might not happen until we get hit again.

ACTION AGENDA

As President Obama dismantles the war on terror, the burden shifts to us, the American people, to be more vigilant than ever. In this unilateral disarmament, he has one crucial accomplice: the news media. The liberal press has always regarded 9/11 as a diversion exploited by the right wing to keep political power. They act as if it had never happened. In our previous book, *Fleeced,* we describe how the media minimizes the risk from terrorists, even going to the lengths of biasing its reporting of thwarted attacks so as to understate their likelihood of having succeeded.

We have to watch every move Obama makes—and sound the alarm each time. Only by speaking out when the mainstream media will not can we keep alive the sense of urgency and danger that accurately reflect the times in which we live.

We will likely be hit again. We cannot dismantle our defenses without exposing our people to grave danger. President Obama will come to regret his backsliding on this issue. We can only hope he does so before more lives are lost. He certainly doesn't seem to get it yet.

7

THE UNITED STATES SENDS AID TO HAMAS . . . YES, HAMAS!

The terrorist group Hamas is dedicated to spreading worldwide jihad and to the destruction of Israel. The group reigns supreme in the Gaza Strip, showering Israel with rockets every day as it preaches its doctrine of hate and violence. These days, that's not news. But what is news—and qualifies as a catastrophe—is that the Obama administration is giving Hamas almost $1 billion in aid—money that is coming straight from the pockets of you, the American taxpayer!

Of course, this aid doesn't go *directly* to Hamas, which the State Department lists as an Iranian front. Instead, it's channeled through the group's old partner, the United Nations Relief and Works Agency (UNRWA). The U.S. contribution makes up the largest portion of a $4.5 billion package of aid to the West Bank and Gaza, voted by the international community to rebuild Gaza in the wake of the Israeli invasion.[247]

But Hamas controls UNRWA. It has so infiltrated the UN that the agency has effectively become a front group for Hamas. The terrorist group pulls its strings.

Make no mistake: When we give money to UNRWA, we're giving a check directly to Hamas.

Caroline Glick, the deputy managing editor of the *Jerusalem Post* and one of the most astute observers of the Israeli/Middle East scene, minces no words on the connection.

"UNRWA openly collaborates with Hamas," she notes. "Its workers double as Hamas combatants. Its refugee camps and schools are used as Hamas training bases and missile launch sites. Its mosques are used as recruiting grounds. And . . . the UN agency is also willing to act as Hamas's surrogate." [248]

Indeed, Peter Hansen, the commissioner-general of UNRWA, concedes that he has terrorists on his payroll. As he told the Canadian Broadcasting Corporation in October 2008, "I am sure that there are Hamas members on the UNRWA payroll and I don't see that as a crime." [249]

The links between UNRWA and Hamas are chilling.

HAMAS AND THE UNITED NATIONS: PERFECT TOGETHER

- February 2002: A member of the Palestinian terrorist faction known as Tanzim, Alaa Muhammad Ali Hassan, confesses during interrogation to perpetrating a sniper shooting from a UNRWA school in a refugee camp near the city of Nablus. Hassan also revealed that terrorists were using UNRWA school facilities to build bombs intended for terrorist attacks.

- August 2002: A Hamas member and ambulance driver named Nidal Nazzal confesses that he used an UNRWA ambulance to transport weapons and explosives while working for UNRWA, and to exploiting the freedom of movement he enjoyed to transmit messages among Hamas members in various Palestinian towns.

- September 2002: Nahd Attala, a UNRWA official in Gaza, reveals that he had used his UNRWA car to transport armed Fatah members heading off on a mission to carry out a missile attack against Jewish settlements. Nahd also used an UNRWA car to carry a twelve-kilogram explosive charge for his brother-in-law, a Fatah member.

- December 2002: UNRWA facilities in the West Bank and Gaza were reportedly used as meeting places and weapons dumps by Palestinian terrorists.

- September 2003: Three UNRWA employees were found guilty of terrorist activities (including firebombing a public bus) by an Israeli court. After the trial, Israel detained at least sixteen other UNRWA staffers for security infractions.

- May 2004: Armed Palestinians were captured on film using UNRWA medical vehicles to transport terrorists in Gaza.

- May 2008: The headmaster of an UNRWA boys' school in Gaza, Awad al-Qiq, was killed in an Israeli rocket attack. Al-Qiq led a dual life: Beyond his work at the Rafah Prep Boys' School, he was also chief rocket maker for Islamic Jihad. The Islamic Jihad identified him as "chief leader of the engineering [i.e., bomb-making] unit." Jihadi imagery was found in his home, and at his funeral the flag of the Islamic Jihad was draped over his body. The Jihad marked his death by firing rockets at Israel.[250]

According to Congressman Mark Kirk (R-IL), in December 2007 UNRWA confirmed that it gave money to families of suicide bombers.[251]

In 2002, Israeli troops entered UNRWA camps after repeated terrorist attacks. Arlene Kushner, a reporter for the Israel Resource News Agency, reports that the troops "discovered there small-arms factories, explosive laboratories, and suicide bombing cells."[252]

Kushner also reports that "So pervasive is this situation in the camps that Hamas has gained control of the UNRWA workers' union. In the Gaza Strip, the 2003 elections for union representatives saw Hamas-affiliated candidates gain substantial majorities in all union sectors, securing control of all seats in the teachers' sector. Moreover, Hamas candidates fully constitute the union's executive committee."[253]

How, then, are we supposed to reconcile our hard-earned position as leaders of the international war on terrorism with the fact that we provide 30 percent of the budget for UNRWA, with its hand-in-glove policy with terrorists? (The European Union contributes 55 percent of UNRWA's budget. Canada contributes 5 percent.)[254]

Recently, UNRWA showed its true colors by delivering a letter to U.S. Senator John Kerry during a trip to Gaza—a letter that came from the Hamas foreign ministry!

During the recent Israeli invasion of Gaza, UNRWA served as a regular megaphone for Hamas propaganda. For example, on January 7, 2009, Christopher Gunness, a spokesman for UNRWA, told the Democracy Now radio program that the Israelis had attacked a UNRWA school in Gaza. At first he said that there were "thirty confirmed fatalities and fifty-five injured, including fifteen critically." Later he said that ten more people had died during the night. The victims, he said, "came—frightened, terrified, vulnerable—to our center. They were coming to what they thought was a neutral United Nations shelter, and then the rest is history—forty people killed." [255]

The only problem with Gunness's story is that it never happened. Three civilians and between eight and ten Hamas gunmen were killed *near* the school when an Israeli military unit was attacked by a Hamas cell. No shell ever hit the school, and no one in the school was injured. As the *Jerusalem Post* reported, the "UN issued a revised report . . . admitting that as the result of a 'clerical error' it was mistaken when it reported that the compound itself was shelled." Gunness later denied ever saying that the shell had hit the school. [256]

The UNRWA uses its Web site to appeal for funds, listing banks that will receive funds from contributors—funds that are supposed to go toward rebuilding in Gaza. As Claudia Rosett has noted in *Forbes*, however, "One of [the banks] is the state-owned Commercial Bank of Syria, headquartered in Damascus. . . . for the past five years this bank has been under sanctions by the U.S. Treasury as an institution of "primary money-laundering concern." [257]

In 2004, the Treasury Department enacted sanctions against the Commercial Bank of Syria, charging that it had laundered money from the United Nations' deeply corrupt oil-for-food program in Iraq. The department also noted that the bank had handled many other transactions "that may be indicative of terrorist financing and money laundering," including two accounts "that reference a reputed financier for Usama bin Laden." [258]

In 2006, Under-Secretary of the Treasury Stuart Levey alleged, terrorists had used the bank to transfer substantial funds. "As a state-owned entity with inadequate money laundering and terrorist financing controls, the Commercial Bank of Syria poses a significant risk of being used to further the Syrian Government's continuing support for international terrorist groups," Levey said. The clients included the terrorist groups Hezbollah, Palestinian Islamic Jihad, the Popular Front for the Liberation of Palestine, and Hamas.[259]

Yet, despite UNRWA's terrible record of collaboration with Hamas, the United States is proceeding to ask its taxpayers to shell out for the so-called relief agency.

In announcing the U.S. contribution, Secretary of State Hillary Clinton went to great pains to say that "we have worked with the Palestinian Authority to install safeguards that will ensure that our funding is used only where, and for whom, it is intended, and does not end up in the wrong hands"—that is, in the hands of Hamas.[260] But since the funds will be under the control of UNRWA, it's hard to see how they can possibly be kept in the right hands!

Indeed, even if the Palestinian Authority—rather than Hamas—controls the funds, that can hardly be a solution, as the PA's hands are far from clean. Reporting on one recent Arab League conference, Jonathan D. Halevi of the Jerusalem Center for Public Affairs noted that "a considerable portion of the aid raised for the Palestinian Authority" at the meeting would go "to support terrorists held in Israeli jails and their families."[261] The Palestinian Authority pays $200 per month to families of prisoners held in Israeli jails for terrorist attacks, to a total of $40 million per year. The aid continues even after their release. Halevi observes, "This aid serves as a form of social security for current and former prisoners and sends a message that their terrorist activities are officially sanctioned by the Palestinian Authority."[262]

UNRWA has been in business for fifty-seven years, providing food, medicine, and social services to Palestinian refugees. But as the Jewish Policy Center notes, "it is directly providing financial and material support to the Hamas terrorist organization."[263]

UNRWA employs 23,000 local Palestinians in its relief work. Only one hundred of its staff members are international UN personnel from other countries. Its local-friendly hiring policy separates UNRWA from the policies of the UN High Commission on Refugees and UNICEF (United Nations International Children's Fund), which do not employ local people who are also the recipients of agency services.[264]

At the very least, UNRWA relieves Hamas of the need to spend any of its money on providing services for the Gaza Strip, which it rules. UNRWA takes care of feeding, clothing, housing, and providing education and medical care in the Gaza—allowing Hamas to spend all its money on making war against Israel.

But Yoni Fighel, a former Israeli military governor in the Palestinian territories, says that UNRWA goes much further. He says that "UNRWA workers are permitted to openly affiliate with terrorist groups." He notes that "as long as UNRWA employees are members of Fatah, Hamas, or PFLP [Popular Front for the Liberation of Palestine], they are going to pursue the interests of their party within the framework of their job. . . . Who's going to check up on them to see that they don't? UNRWA? They are UNRWA."[265]

Perhaps UNRWA's most direct involvement with terrorism is through the schools it owns and operates in Gaza. The schools' faculty is notoriously pro-terrorist. For example, Suheil al-Hindi, a UNRWA teachers' representative, spoke approvingly of suicide bombings in Gaza in 2003. "Instead of a condemnation," one report noted, "al-Hindi received a promotion and was subsequently elected to the UNRWA's clerks union."[266]

SHINING GRADUATES: TERRORISTS WHO GOT THEIR EDUCATION AT THE UNRWA SCHOOLS

- Said Sayyam, the Hamas minister of interior and civil affairs, was a teacher in the UNRWA Gaza schools for twenty-three years and headed the teachers' union.
- Former Hamas prime minister Ismail Haniyeh is among those who graduated from the UNRWA secondary school, graduating at the top of his class.
- At least forty-six terrorist operatives were students in UNRWA schools, including Ibrahim Maqadama, who helped create the military structure of Hamas.[267]

The Jewish Policy Center also reports that "there have also been widespread reports of terrorism from UNRWA-supervised facilities, including sniper attacks from UNRWA-run schools, bomb and arms factories in UNRWA camps, the transport of terrorists to their target zones in UNRWA ambulances, and even UNRWA employees directly tied to terrorist attacks against civilians." [268]

According to reports in the *New York Times* and other venues, UNRWA has "allowed terrorist groups to use their schools as 'summer camps' [for] 25,000 Palestinian children." But instead of horseback riding and swimming, these kids spent their summer receiving "paramilitary training, including instructions on how to prepare Molotov cocktails and roadside bombs." [269]

This is contemporary education—courtesy of the United Nations.

And when these bomb makers get it wrong—as they did when the homes of six Palestinian families on UNRWA's registry were "destroyed during bomb-making activities, UNRWA concluded there was not enough evidence to deny them benefits under the terrorist exclusion law." [270]

But a report from the Global Research in International Affairs Center raises an even more troubling issue: Does UNRWA want to solve the Palestinian refugee problem, or does it want to perpetuate it?

As the center points out, "UNRWA's job is to keep Palestinian refugees in suspended animation—and at low living standards—until they achieve the goal set for them by . . . Hamas: Israel's extinction. In the meantime, their suffering and anger is maintained as a weapon to encourage them toward violence and intransigence." [271]

The center notes that "UNRWA schools become hotbeds of anti-Western, anti-American, and anti-Semitic indoctrination, recruiting offices for terrorist groups. UNRWA's services are dominated by radicals who staff and subsidize radical groups while intimidating anyone from voicing a different line. UNRWA facilities are used to store and transport weapons, actually serving as military bases." [272]

In fact, the hypocrisy runs deeper. As the center points out, UNRWA is "the exact opposite of other refugee relief operations." Whereas other such agencies seek to resettle refugees, UNRWA is "dedicated to blocking resettlement" to keep alive the "thirst for revenge that inspires violence." [273]

There can be no doubt that the $900 million in new U.S. aid to

UNRWA—to say nothing of the more than $4 billion from the international community—will end up helping Hamas. Whether simply by repairing and governing Gaza while Hamas turns its attention to rocket launchings into Israel or through direct training, indoctrination, and sheltering of terrorists, UNRWA is a key to the survival of Hamas in the Middle East.

Whatever the intentions of its founders, UNRWA is no longer an impartial organization. Any belief that U.S. funds channeled through it will not reach Hamas terrorists is a dangerous delusion. The U.S. government should be commended by all nations for its work to close the flow of charitable contributions to terrorist organizations around the world. Yet whatever cash flow it has stopped in those efforts is dwarfed by the nearly $1 billion it will now be giving in aid to UNRWA—and thus, in effect, to Hamas!

For a nation that takes great pride in its claims of unwavering support for Israel and peace in the Middle East—not to mention its hard-won stance against terrorism—this is a devastating blow to our credibility.

ACTION AGENDA

It's one thing for Barack Obama to spend and spend in the United States in a misguided attempt to revive the economy. It's quite another when the aid is going to Gaza. We can't sit back and let the fig leaf of UN involvement deter us from opposing foreign aid for terrorists.

The most vulnerable figure in the mix is Obama's secretary of state, Hillary Clinton. As senator from New York and a once and likely future presidential candidate, Hillary has always played to the Jewish community. In fact, when she ran for senator in 2000, she dug up the fact that her step-grandfather was Jewish—a discovery of a branch of the family tree that came just in time to appeal to the fifth of the New York electorate that is Jewish. (Funny that she never raised her latter-day claim of Jewish ancestry in Arkansas!)

But now Hillary is taking long and loud criticism from Jewish groups such as the Zionist Organization of America for her aid proposals for Gaza. We need to keep up the heat. Write her, email her, tell her you don't approve of your tax money going to Hamas—either directly or through the United Nations.

Hillary can be reached at:

Secretary of State Hillary Clinton
U.S. Department of State
2201 C Street NW
Washington, DC 20520
202-647-4000

E-mail address: Go to www.secretary.state.gov and click on "Contact Us" and then on "E-Mail a Question/Comment."

II

HOW CONGRESS CAUSES CATASTROPHE

8

CHRISTOPHER DODD AND CHARLES RANGEL
From Idealistic Reformers to Privileged Insiders

Charlie Rangel and Chris Dodd have a lot in common. They're both long-time Democratic members of Congress from northeastern states. They were both elected to Congress as idealistic, charismatic young reformers. They have both served on the Hill for more than three decades. And they have both risen to become powerful committee chairman—Rangel chairing the House Ways and Means Committee and Dodd chairing the Senate Banking Committee.

Unfortunately, they now share something else. Both have also evolved into cynical caricatures of the ultimate Washington political insider: greedy, self-serving darlings of the special interests, hypocrites flouting the rules and getting rich on their influence and political connections.

They think they're entitled. Entitled to do whatever they want. Entitled to special favors because of who they are. Entitled to line their pockets.

Well, they're not.

It's time to send them packing.

They're a disappointment to the people who elected them, and they don't deserve the privilege of serving in Congress.

FIRST, THEY WERE IDEALISTS

In 1970, Charlie Rangel was elected to Congress, defeating the illustrious and iconic Harlem politician and civil rights leader Adam Clayton Powell, Jr. Running as a reform candidate—and criticizing Powell for his failure even to show up in Congress—Rangel won by only 150 votes. He quickly became a voice for the low-income and downtrodden members of his constituency.

A few years later, in 1974, Chris Dodd was elected to the House of Representatives, part of a new generation of congressional reformers known as "the Watergate class." These young challengers were supposed to be different—a new wave of honest, dedicated politicians who were chosen to purge the political system of the unethical excesses of the Nixon administration.

How time does change things! Now Dodd and Rangel are twin poster boys for everything that is wrong in Washington.

They weren't always that way. Both men say they felt a calling to public service that was developed while serving their country in a foreign land. Rangel was only twenty years old when he fought in the Korean War; he was awarded the Purple Heart and the Bronze Star after he was wounded by shrapnel and forced to lead forty members of his troop behind Communist enemy lines. In his memoir, *And I Haven't Had A Bad Day Since*, Rangel described how his terrifying experiences in the Army changed his life, leading him to consider wider horizons. On his return home, he finished high school, college, and law school and became an assistant U.S. attorney.

Dodd took a different and less difficult road but one that was just as influential on his decision about what to do with his life. From 1966 to 1968, Dodd served in the Peace Corps in a small town in the Dominican Republic, an experience he later described as "life-changing." During a two-year stint, he helped people in a remote village build a school and improve their infrastructure and community. He told National Public Radio, "I came back from that experience determined that, one way or another, I wanted to be involved in the public life of my country." [274] In 1969, on his return to the United States at the height of the Vietnam War, Dodd joined the Army Reserve. In 1972, at the age of twenty-eight, he graduated from law school, spent about a year and a half in private practice, and then ran for the Connecticut House of Representatives seat that he would hold for three terms. In 1980, he was elected to the Senate.

WATCHING THE CONSEQUENCES OF CORRUPTION . . .

It wasn't just the Peace Corps that inspired Dodd to enter politics. There was another big factor. While Dodd was living in the Dominican Republic, his father, then–Connecticut senator Thomas Dodd, was serving his third term in the U.S. Senate. In 1967, Thomas Dodd was formally censured by the Senate for taking $116,083 in campaign money ($782,183.62 in 2009 dollars) for his personal use and for accepting other illegal gifts.[275] Chris Dodd was far from home when it happened, but he could not have escaped the family's sorrow over his father's downfall. Though Thomas Dodd avoided impeachment and remained in the Senate for several more years, he was a broken man, with few friends and no influence. Returning home, he lost the race for his own party's nomination to the Senate in 1970. Even after the Democratic Party abandoned him, Dodd refused to give up and ran as an independent. Chris Dodd served as campaign manager for his father's final, unsuccessful Senate race.

Dodd's understanding of his father's painful humiliation in the Senate and his stunning rejection by the voters seems to have left him with a visceral need to exonerate his father and probably contributed to his decision to enter politics. For the next thirty years he would try, with some success, to rehabilitate his father's name and legacy. According to Chris Dodd's older brother, Thomas Jr., his father is always on his brother's mind. "He said to me once, 'Every time I walk on the Senate floor, I feel that he's vindicated.' "[276]

. . . BUT NOT LEARNING FROM THEM

One thing Dodd didn't learn from his father's tragic fall from power was to beware of friends bearing gifts. For years, other people have paid down payments, expenses, and mortgages on homes where he resided and that he claimed to own. Some of these benefactors had business with the federal government, which created, at the very least, an appearance of impropriety. Bur Dodd saw nothing wrong with that. He thought it was just a "courtesy."

And that kind of courtesy is something Chris Dodd has come to expect. As a senator for twenty-nine years, he's grown accustomed to the "courtesies"—small and large—that are provided to him. Dodd's comments over the years suggest he thinks they're no big deal. Most of us, on the other hand, might think otherwise and would describe the "courtesies" as special treatment he received solely because of his elected position.

The same might be said of Congressman Rangel. As a young lawyer in Harlem, he watched as one of the most respected leaders in his community, Adam Clayton Powell, Jr., was unseated in the House while under investigation for misusing $40,000 in public funds. Powell was a legend in his district. Elected in 1947, he had challenged racial discrimination in Congress, often inviting his constituents to join him in the House Dining Room, which was informally segregated and open to white members only. Powell became chairman of the House Education and Labor Committee and worked with Presidents Kennedy and Johnson to pass legislation creating the school lunch and student loan programs, increasing the minimum wage, increasing aid to education, and almost fifty other landmark bills.

But despite his charisma, commitment, and success, Powell lost the support of his colleagues and his constituents after accusations about misuse of government funds and long, unexplained absences from Congress. After he lost a libel lawsuit in New York, he was found in contempt and spent most of his time in Florida and Bimini in an effort to evade a subpoena. Eventually, he was expelled from the House during its investigation of him— a much more serious fate than the one suffered by Senator Dodd in the same year. Although Powell was reinstated almost two years later, his loss to Rangel a few months later spelled the end of his political career.

But Rangel, like Dodd, seems not to have internalized either the moral or political dangers of public corruption. He now stands accused of using his position as chairman of the House Ways and Means Committee to solicit money from corporations (including AIG) to fund the Charles B. Rangel Center for Public Service at the City College of New York; of failing to report $75,000 in rental income from his vacation villa in the Dominican Republic; of living in four rent-stabilized apartments in New York City in violation of the rent stabilization laws and at below-market rates; of failing to disclose the sale of a home in D.C.; of committing discrepancies in reporting the value of property he owns in Florida; of improperly using the

House garage to store his old Mercedes-Benz; and of paying his son more than $80,000 in campaign funds to design a web site that has been ridiculed for its ridiculous design and independently valued as worth about $100.

It is a sad story: Today, these two reformers, these two idealists, are both subjects of Ethics Committee investigations.

They have one more thing in common: both are favorites of the American International Group. AIG, of course, has a great interest in the work of Rangel's House committee, which writes tax legislation, and in Dodd's Senate committee, which controls banking and insurance legislation. Now, with AIG as the international symbol of everything that's wrong with corporate America, their cozy relationships with that corporate pariah are contributing to their own deserved demise.

CHRIS DODD AND "OPM"—OTHER PEOPLE'S MONEY

From the time he entered Congress, Chris Dodd quietly depended on other people's money to pay for his houses and some of his living expenses. It doesn't seem to have troubled him that most adults actually pay for their own homes with their own money. That's the way we do it in America. We don't ask others to contribute to improving our standard of living. We don't look around and wonder who would be the best person to make our down payment. But that notion was apparently completely foreign to Dodd. Nor did it seem to cross his mind that there was something wrong with the specter of a member of Congress, a senator, asking for handouts from people who potentially had interests before Congress that could affect their livelihood. He wanted a nice place to live—apparently nicer than he felt he could afford on his own—and somehow, miraculously, others stepped forward to donate to that most worthy cause.

Time after time, Dodd's patrons were willing to fork over substantial amounts of money to purchase and maintain various houses for him. His first housing benefactor was a Washington, D.C., club owner named Sanford Bomstein, who was a longtime personal banker and fund raiser for Dodd's father. Later he turned to Edward R. Downe, Jr., a charming and generous New York entrepreneur who ultimately pled guilty to federal criminal charges arising out of his blatant insider trading.

Downe was a high-profile player on the New York political and social scene. In the early 1980s, he frequently hosted political fund-raisers and cocktail parties for prominent Democratic politicians at his sumptuous apartment on Fifth Avenue and Sixty-fourth Street in New York City. The duplex apartment on Central Park, graced with modern art and antique furniture, was a regular setting for his political soirees. Several times a month, he would invite people from his wide circle of friends to meet rising political stars. In 1986, he married the automobile heiress Charlotte Ford, the elder daughter of Henry Ford II. He and his wife then lived in twin apartments in New York City and separate mansions at the beach in Southampton. The one place they never seemed to spend much time in was Washington, D.C.

Finally, after Downe's criminal convictions made him radioactive on any joint public documents with Dodd, a business associate and close friend of Downe, who received millions in federal contracts—stepped up and went in with him on a house in Ireland for Dodd.

With a little help from his friends, Dodd got a free ride for years. Then he turned around and made a profit on it, selling the D.C. property and buying out the Ireland estate.

Why would he do this? Because he could. Wasn't he entitled? After all, he was a congressman and then a U.S. senator. And since he'd worked full-time in the real world for less than two years before he was elected to the House, he hadn't had much time to build a suitable nest egg to buy a place of his own. So what's a congressman to do? Live in a rented apartment in Washington? Not Chris Dodd! Instead he knocked on the door of rich friends— twice in Washington and once in Ireland. Rich friends who might have had some interest in what Congress or the federal government do. And who were only too happy to help the needy senator.

Given the private pain and sorrow and the public humiliation that Chris Dodd and his family must have endured during his father's scandal, it's astonishing to realize how soon after his own election Dodd brazenly accepted the financial help of a former crony of his father to pay for a house in D.C. for himself. The ordeal Dodd's father went through wasn't just a minor embarrassment, it was historic: only five other members of the Senate had ever been censured. After sixteen months, the Senate committee investigating the elder Dodd unanimously recommended censure, saying that his conduct was "contrary to good morals, derogates from the public trust expected of a Senator, and tends to bring the Senate into dishonor and disrepute."[277]

The charges were serious. The committee report accused Thomas Dodd of:

- Accepting $8,000 ($53,905 in 2009 dollars) in cash from the International Latex Corporation, in violation of the prohibition on corporate contributions

- Double billing the Senate and private groups for travel expenses for thirteen trips

- Accepting the free use of three cars paid for by a constituent for almost two years

- Diverting $116,083 ($782,183.62 in 2009 dollars) in campaign funds raised at testimonial dinners to his personal use between 1961 and 1965, including $50,000 used to renovate a summer home[278]

According to the renowned columnists Drew Pearson and Jack Anderson, who first publicly exposed the broad range of Thomas Dodd's unethical conduct, the Senate also ignored or failed to follow up on other credible evidence of wrongdoing, including his "backdoor law practice, payroll padding, payroll maneuvering, favors to gift-bearing lobbyists, [and] accepting free automobiles and airplane travel from those doing business with the government."[279] Pearson and Anderson's sources were two employees and two former employees of Dodd, who secretly copied four thousand documents from Dodd's office and provided them to Pearson and Anderson.

For example, according to the journalists, a former employee of Latex International had told them that the former head of the company had paid Dodd $8,000 in cash to get his support in seeking an ambassadorship but had then changed his testimony before the Senate.[280] Another witness, Sanford Bomstein, also reversed himself, testifying that the money raised at the Dodd testimonial had clearly been intended to be a personal gift to Dodd, even though Bomstein had previously signed a report that said just the opposite.[281]

Despite the voluminous evidence against him, Thomas Dodd did not go quietly. He denied all wrongdoing and at times pointed a finger back at his accusers. Dodd unsuccessfully accused his own employees of forging thirty-nine checks written to a D.C. liquor store. He sued former employees for invasion of privacy (he lost) and in a number of cases tried to blame his own improper spending of campaign funds on them! It was not a pretty picture.

Surprisingly, Thomas Dodd never actually denied he had received the money in question. His unusual defense was that the donors to the testimonial receptions actually thought they were making tax-free gifts to him, not political contributions to his campaign. This was contradicted by the text in the written invitations and the understanding of most of the organizers.

Apparently Senator Thomas Dodd had large debts—including an overdue tax bill of about $13,000 (about $89,000 in 2009 dollars). To put it into perspective, consider that the annual salary for senators from 1955 to 1965 was $22,000.[282] In 1965, it increased to $30,000.[283] So in 1963 and 1964 Dodd owed more than half of his annual salary in back taxes.

According to Pearson and Anderson, Dodd was frantically trying to raise money to pay back his personal creditors—as well as the IRS—and was willing to trade political favors for some of the loans he received. Pearson and Anderson described his relationship with one local businessman:

> There is an interesting story involving the friendship between Sen. Tom Dodd and Sanford Bomstein who loaned $5,000 to Dodd in 1958 and raised $12,804 for him at a D. C. reception in 1963, part of which was used to pay Bomstein back.
>
> Bomstein is a former cigar-store owner in Bridgeport, Conn., who moved to Washington to conduct four swinging nightclubs and restaurants. . . . where the teenage swingers congregate. It is the most popular rock 'n roll rendezvous in downtown Washington.
>
> Bomstein has also been president of the Food and Beverage Association of the District of Columbia and as such was active in appearing before Congressional committees on behalf of liquor dealers. He has wanted to

keep the drinking age in the District of Columbia at 18 instead of 21, an age which brings teenagers flocking into the District of Columbia from adjacent Maryland and Virginia on weekends.

Shortly before Bomstein helped raise $12,804 at the 1963 D.C. reception for Dodd, the Senator from Connecticut was being pressed by Internal Revenue on a previous income tax payment. He owed the government $13,500 and Internal Revenue notified him that it had waited for payment as long as it could. If there was further delay, IRS agents threatened to open his books.[284]

Pearson and Anderson further described the symbiotic Dodd-Bomstein connection:

Dodd's Juvenile Delinquency Subcommittee had been investigating the sale of liquor to teenagers in the District of Columbia. . . . After Dodd became chairman of the Juvenile Delinquency Subcommittee, the investigation into D.C. nightclubs was suddenly halted. So it's not surprising that Bomstein was happy to help raise money for Dodd.[285]

In June 1967, after the investigating committee's unanimous ruling, the U.S. Senate voted to censure Senator Thomas Dodd by a vote of 94–5. Only four of his colleagues joined him in voting against the measure.

But that was not the end of the Dodd family relationship with Mr. Bomstein.

THE DODD HOUSE ON E STREET

When Chris Dodd came to Washington with his first wife, Susan Mooney Dodd, they bought a town house at 508 E Street, SE.

But there was something unusual about the Dodds' acquisition of the house on E Street. A review of the transaction on the D.C. land records shows that the Dodds had two surprising partners in the sale. Guess who? A blast from the past. The names of Sanford Bomstein and his wife, Doris Bomstein, appear on the deed filed on the property records in Washington.

RELEASE OF DODDS AND BOMSTEINS RE ORIGINAL SALE

Grantor

GREEN, WALTER
HOLCOMB, GERARD F

Grantee

BOMSTEIN, DORIS
BOMSTEIN, SANFORD
DODD, SUSAN
DODD, CHRISTOPHER J

Legal Description(s)

Land Record:

Square   Lot

0845   0017

Related Document Information

N/A

Property Address

WASHINGTON

0508 E ST SE
DC

1985 DEED OF SALE BY DODDS AND BOMSTEINS TO ROACH:

Grantor

BOMSTEIN, DORIS
BOMSTEIN, STANFORD
DODD, SUSAN M
DODD, CHRISTOPHER J

Grantee

ROACH, SEAN

What was Chris Dodd thinking? Only a few years after his father had been mortified by the censure by his Senate colleagues—effectively destroyed both personally and politically—his son involved himself in a financial deal with a man who had shown just how far he would go to suck up to a politician who might help him. Bomstein had been a key player in the evidence in the Dodd case. There were published reports about Bomstein's loans, fund-raising, and interest in federal legislation before Tom Dodd's subcommittee.

With all that baggage in tow, wouldn't anyone in Chris Dodd's position run away screaming from Bomstein? Even without it, any reasonable member of Congress would turn down a handout from the likes of Bomstein—out of ethics, caution, or common sense. Yet somehow Chris Dodd ended up in partnership with Mr. and Mrs. Bomstein.

Dodd has disclosed no particulars about this unconventional arrangement with his father's former chum, who had a keen interest in congressional actions about the drinking age in D.C. He recently told the *Hartford Courant* that he had "received help in the down payment from a family friend who had been tangled in a campaign-finance scandal with Dodd's father."[286] That appears to be the first time that Dodd admitted that he was given financial help on his first D.C. house.

In fact, Dodd was not legally required to disclose any information about his personal residences in the annual financial disclosures filed in the House and Senate. That's one of the serious loopholes in the disclosure requirements for members of Congress: they can keep their personal residence real estate transactions to themselves and don't have to account for them. That's a big mistake. The logic behind it seems to be that a home is not a business investment and need not be disclosed. But the people of Connecticut had a right to know that Chris Dodd was accepting the largesse of a character like Sanford Bomstein. Dodd's conduct regarding this and another property in D.C. show just how badly reform is needed in that area. All members of Congress should be required to disclose information about their ownership and partners in any property, regardless of whether they live in it.

Still Dodd went ahead with the dubious partnership, confident that he could keep it quiet—and for more than thirty years no one reported on it. We don't know exactly how the Bomstein deal was structured, but from what we know about Dodd's subsequent property partnerships, it's fair to assume that Bomstein didn't make any money for the "help" he gave Dodd.

NO DOWN(E) PAYMENT

By 1986, it was time for Dodd to move on. Maybe he wanted a nicer place. Maybe Bomstein wanted to get out of the town house deal. We may never find out what happened. In any event, several months after the release on the E Street property was filed, Dodd moved into yet another unconventional financial partnership. On May 2, 1986, Senator Chris Dodd and his friend and benefactor, the businessman Edward R. Downe, Jr., jointly purchased a $180,000, two-bedroom, two-bath condominium apartment in an elegant prewar building at 2153 California Avenue in the tony Kalorama Park area of Washington, D.C. According to information recently disclosed by Senator Dodd, he approached Ed Downe about a joint investment:

> "We were friends. I was single at the time. He was single at the time," Dodd said. "*It would have been expensive for me to do it on my own*. It wasn't the only reason, but [I asked] him if he wanted to kind of go in on it with me." Downe, who had made a fortune in publishing before amassing a vast collection of American art, agreed to cover half the down payment, half the monthly condo fees and half the $128,000 mortgage on the condominium, records released by Dodd show.[287] [emphasis added]

Once more Dodd was living off other people's money. Why? Because "it would have been expensive to do it on my own."[288]

QUESTION: What do most people do when they can't afford to buy a house? When it would be expensive to do it on their own?

ANSWER: They don't buy it. They suck it up and find a place they can afford.

Unless they're a senator, in which case they get other people to pay for it.

Dodd apparently turned to the right person for his handout. According to the *New York Times*, "Mr. Downe doled out loans and gifts almost willy-nilly, sometimes getting himself into binds. . . . Friends confirm that Mr. Downe did spray around a lot of his own money. Almost anyone with a hard-luck case would get a loan, not always repaying it." [289]

It seems that Downe was made for Dodd! He didn't deny his influential friend's request to pick up half the tab for his D.C. home. Dodd now claims that he and Downe had an agreement that allowed Downe to use the apartment in D.C. whenever he was in Washington. Dodd mentioned that they were both divorced at the time, suggesting that they liked to go out together. But anyone who has ever known Downe or seen him in his own setting, would seriously doubt that Downe would have ever wanted to crash at Dodd's apartment. The penthouse at the Ritz-Carlton or the Four Seasons would have been more his style. And Downe's carefree bachelor days with Dodd hardly overlapped the purchase of the apartment. Downe married Charlotte Ford just four months later. With their twin apartments on Sutton Place in Manhattan and their twin mansions in Southampton, the Downe-Fords didn't need Dodd's hospitality. And given his Democratic politics and involvement in the New York City art world and social and philanthropic scene, the Reagan-Bush Washington of the late 1980s probably wasn't high on Downe's travel list. So Dodd would have had the run of the apartment.

What's truly amazing is that Dodd seems not to have seen any problem with such an unorthodox arrangement—a U.S. senator living off a successful businessman who had serious financial interests that were regulated by the federal government. Downe was a wealthy entrepreneur who, in 1985, began to sit on the boards of both the investment banking firm Bear Sterns and the Kidde Corporation. Dodd has been a recipient of big bucks from Bear Sterns, receiving more than $350,000 since 1989.[290] In the summer of 1992, Downe pled guilty to federal charges stemming from insider trading based on the confidential information that he had access to as a director. He was accused of regularly passing along information he learned in board meetings to a large number of family and friends, who also traded on his advice.

Dodd claims he "contacted" the Senate Ethics Committee before he made the deal with Downe and was told that he did not have to disclose it. That is correct—again, by Senate rules, Dodd had no obligation to disclose the details of his personal residence—but that's not the same as saying that the Ethics Committee affirmatively approved the Dodd-Downe deal. (That would be hard to imagine, even for that useless, self-serving body.) And Dodd certainly knew himself that this was not an appropriate deal to make. Regardless of whether the exact language of the rules required him to disclose the transaction, he should have done so. His partner in the property was not a spouse or relative but a well-connected businessman. He should have disclosed it. Even Chris Dodd could figure that out. (By the way, did Dodd also contact the House Ethics Committee before he made the deal with Bomstein on his first house?)

A few years after the purchase, Downe told Dodd he was under federal investigation for insider trading. Once he learned that, Dodd claims, he terminated the financial relationship. He told the *Hartford Courant:*

> "Having a relationship financially—it was obviously not something that I thought was appropriate," Dodd said. "So we severed the relationship financially; did not sever the friendship." Downe also continued to contribute to Dodd's political campaigns.[291]

Dodd claims that in 1990, he took out a new mortgage for $180,000 and paid Downe $41,000 for his share of the expenses.[292] End of story.

His salary in 1986, when he purchased half of the D.C. apartment valued at $180,000, was only $75,000. He also had $194,000 in mortgages on his home in charming East Haddam, Connecticut (which weren't subject to disclosure either).[293] That's $284,000 in mortgage debt. Assuming that Dodd was making a take-home salary of $50,000, he couldn't have had much left after paying the mortgages, condo fees, insurance, and taxes.

Downe, of course, made nothing on the four-year investment. Dodd, on the other hand, later sold the property for a substantial profit—but doesn't seem to have shared it with Downe.

But Dodd gave as good as he got, maybe even better. Years later, he managed to save Downe from the consequences of what turned out to be major crimes. That was worth a lot more than anything Downe could have given Dodd.

DEED FOR DODD AND DOWNE PURCHASE OF D.C. APT.

General Information

Document #: 8600017618

Filing Date: 5/2/1986

Instrument Type: DEED

Roll: 164

Comment:

# of Pages: 4

Book Type: LAND

Filing Time:

Consideration Amt: $0.00

Frame: 725

Grantor

CALIFORNIA HOUSE PARTNER

Grantee

DODD CHRISTOPHER J

DOWNE, EDWARD R JR

CONVEYANCE TO DODD BY DOWNE

Document #: 9000008756

Filing Date: 2/13/1990

Instrument Type: DEED

Roll: 513

Comment:

# of Pages: 2

Book Type: LAND

Filing Time:

Consideration Amt: $0.00

Frame: 192

Grantor

DOWNE, CHARLOTTE

DOWNE, EDWARD R JR

Grantee

DODD, CHRISTOPHER J

Legal Description(s)

Land Record:

Square

2528

Lot

2187

0308

Source: D.C. Property Records

DODD GETS DOWNE A PRESIDENTIAL PARDON

After Downe pleaded guilty to wire fraud and tax evasion related to his insider trading, he was sentenced to 3,000 hours of community service. After reaching a settlement with the SEC on the insider trading charges, he was fined $11 million. He was forced to sell his Southampton home, his Florida condominium, and his art collection. Although he was permitted to keep his apartment in Manhattan, it will revert to the government on his death.

The charges against him were serious: according to the SEC, Downe "had exploited insider trading information and set up offshore bank accounts to hide millions of dollars of illegal profits for himself and members of his wealthy social circle."[294] Apparently, the information Downe picked up at his board of directors meetings was passed on to family and friends over drinks at his Southampton home and clubs, during poker games, and at other social events. The SEC estimated that Downe and his pals made in the neighborhood of $23 million in profit from the scam.

Downe could have been subject to serious jail time for his crimes. But Chris Dodd personally wrote to the sentencing judge in defense of his friend—and eight years later he also sent a personal letter to President Clinton seeking a pardon for his insider trading crimes. On January 19, 2001, the day before he left office, Clinton issued the pardon.

Dodd emphasized Downe's remorse and good character: "The example[s] of Ed's private goodness [are] extensive," Dodd said, "but they all share one thing in common—they were all done quietly to help people, average people in need."[295]

Did Dodd consider himself one of those average people in need who had benefited from Downe's goodness? Whether he did or not, he certainly managed to help Downe in return. It's no easy thing to get a prized presidential pardon. But an analysis of all of Bill Clinton's controversial last-minute pardons indicates that there was one common denominator in those selected: personal access to the president or his counsel to make the case and circumvent the justice department.[296] As the *New York Times* reported, Downe's last-minute pardon application "bypassed the Justice Department" and "has been criticized by lawyers at the Securities and Exchange Commission.[297]

For someone in a position like Downe's, Chris Dodd was a fortuitous friend to have. Dodd had been appointed chairman of the Democratic National Committee by Bill Clinton; he enjoyed easy access to the president and the White House. He'd spent years raising money for Clinton. Access was no problem. He could help Downe's application get a hearing—no need to go to through regular channels Not only the S.E.C., but the Justice Department was blind-sided by the unexpected and blatantly political pardon.

As the *Times* wrote in an editorial about the controversial pardon:

> Politics rather than a careful weighing of the merits also appears to have been the deciding factor in Mr. Clinton's pardon of Edward Downe Jr. . . . Prosecutors in Ms. White's office learned of the pardon decision last Friday—too late to effectively register their objections.[298]

It was the ultimate favor for Downe.

IRELAND: ANOTHER FREE RIDE

There is a magical place in western Ireland called Innishnee. Though only about an hour and a half away from the city of Galway, this small Connemara island is light-years away from anything urban or contemporary. As you drive out there, the landscape suddenly changes from the predictable Galway suburbs to dramatically beautiful scenes of rural county Galway, where mountains and lakes are bathed in golden sun and mauve shadows line the road to picturesque Roundstone, the closest mainland town to Innishnee.

A small bridge only about twenty to thirty feet long connects Roundstone to Innishnee, where unpaved roads that are wide enough for only a single car or two cows cross the small island. There's not much traffic, but when two cars approach each other, local custom obliges one driver to back up to the nearest driveway to let the oncoming car pass by—even if that driveway is half a mile behind. Farmers slowly walking along the road with their cows also herd them into driveways to let the occasional car pass, even as the cows try to stick their large heads into the car windows.

It is a quiet, beautiful place where time has stood still. There are no

McMansions, no stores, and virtually nothing to compete with the unparalleled views.

On the southernmost tip of the island, atop a crest overlooking the water on three sides with mountains in the background, is a spectacular piece of property of almost eleven acres, with a pristine 1,700-square-foot dormered white house at its highest point. The sheer size of the property dwarfs all other plots on that end of the island. From the high point where the house stands, the property continues across a shallow inlet to ethereal mountains which are part of the plot. With the property extending on both sides of the water, the beautiful view is protected from the intrusion of any new buildings that would spoil the enchanted setting. To the right is the dramatic Bertaghboy Bay, which flows out to the Atlantic Ocean. Behind the house, at a much lower point, the bay separates Innishnee and Roundstone.

It is this unique house and exquisite property that Chris Dodd bought with the help of yet another friend in 1994.

Dodd told the *Hartford Courant* that he first saw the stunning vacation property in the late 1980s and learned several years later learned that it was for sale. But, once again, while Dodd wanted to buy the property, he couldn't afford it. It's a common problem: How many of us have seen a beautiful house in a gorgeous setting in a foreign country and dreamed of buying it?

The difference is, the rest of us usually come to our senses and realize we can't afford such a thing—and would hardly ever use such a distant vacation home anyway.

But not Chris Dodd. He wanted it and was determined to make it work. So what did he do?

He found yet another friend to pay for it—and to give him exclusive use of the property. Dodd has admitted that he couldn't afford to buy the place on his own: "It would have been tight" to purchase it solo, he says.[299] So who to turn to?

By 1994, Downe could no longer help: his felony convictions had made him radioactive. Even if he had had the financial resources to help out, Dodd couldn't afford to share another deed with a convicted felon. So what could he do? Pay for the property himself? No way.

But he lucked out again. This time, an acquaintance agreed to pay for two-thirds of the property, leaving him responsible for only one-third.

And guess who that acquaintance was? An old college friend of Downe.

According to Kevin Rennie of the *Hartford Courant*, William "Bucky" Kessinger was a college friend of Downe and his partner in a Missouri real estate firm. Indeed, it was Downe who introduced Kessinger to Dodd.[300] Talk about six degrees of separation! And there's more: when the property was sold to Dodd and Kessinger, Downe was right there with them to witness the transaction and he actually signed the deed.[301] Isn't that what friends are for?

But what was Downe really doing there? Was he involved in the purchase of the property? Did he own part of it? Wait a minute. Was Kessinger actually a stand-in for Downe? Don't start thinking that Kessinger was just a straw man standing in for Downe. Dodd has stated categorically that he wasn't. So apparently that's that.

According to Dodd, Kessinger thought that property in Ireland was a good investment. Unfortunately for Kessinger, he was apparently unaware of the rules of engagement when buying real estate with Dodd. It's Dodd who makes the money; it's the partner who spends it. So the professional real estate maven seems to have been the only landowner in Ireland who lost out on the incredible Irish property boom of the last decade—the largest increase in property values in the history of Ireland. Because when Dodd eventually bought him out, the price did not in any way reflect the meteoric rise in Irish property prices.

The original cost of the property was $160,000. But the new partners didn't split the selling price evenly. Instead, Dodd bought only a third of the property and Kessinger two-thirds. Dodd claims to have paid $12,000 for his investment. But wouldn't it have made more sense for them to buy the property in equal shares? Dodd told the *Hartford Courant* that he can't remember why they did it this way. Really, who can remember every detail? Is it that important that Dodd only had to pay only $12,000 to get such a spectacular property? What's the big deal?[302]

Hey, wait a minute, you may be thinking. *Just why did Dodd and Kessinger divide that property in thirds? Wouldn't that make more sense if there were three investors, not two?* Perish the thought that Downe was in for the other third. Just because Downe had a history of chipping in on Dodd's homes doesn't mean he did so in Ireland. And just because he was there at the closing doesn't mean he was an investor. And just because it was his partner who bought the property with Dodd doesn't make him a partner, too. And just because another business associate of Downe's tried to influence the local zoning board to approve renovations to the property doesn't mean anything, does it? Surely it's all just a coincidence. Dodd himself says that Downe had no ownership interest in the property; he merely visited from time to time.

In describing how he first saw the property, Dodd has made it seem as if he somehow just landed there in the late eighties, but as Kevin Rennie reports, Downe has been known in the Roundstone-Innishnee area for some time; in fact, it may have been he who introduced Dodd to it.:

> Someone might also have noticed that of all the affluent seaside towns in all the world, it's the one where Dodd has a home that Downe and current wife, Mary, have in the past few years been sponsors of local events. Dodd and the Downes have even been sponsors of the same horsey Champion of Champions event in tony Roundstone.[303]

Given that Dodd says he talks to Downe every day, it's hard to believe that Downe *wouldn't* have mentioned the area to him. Rennie has also discovered other connections Downe may have had with the property: even as Dodd was just contemplating purchasing the property, another associate of Downe was trying to get county approval for renovations there:

> In 1993, Irish planning officials were slow in approving renovations to the property Dodd wanted to purchase. A Galway businessman, John W. M. Moore, tried to hurry them up, writing a letter reminding the bureaucrat in charge that Dodd "was an excellent friend of Galway's" as it tried to replace hundreds of jobs lost when Digital, the computer company, closed a facility.
>
> Moore, by remarkable coincidence, was involved in Crystal Brands of Ireland, a crystal exporting company that also employed Downe, who is identified as a "network manager" on a Dun and Bradstreet document.[304]

What a small world!

• • •

In 2002, one year after Downe was pardoned by Clinton, Dodd and his second wife, Jackie M. Clegg, purchased Kessinger's share of the property so that they would own the Innishnee property outright. Despite the rise in the value of Irish properties at that time, Kessinger made only $20,000 more than his original sale price in 1995.

The Innishnee purchase had appreciated by only 18 percent during the time Kessinger was part owner—a surprisingly poor investment, especially for such an experienced real estate businessman. "According to the Irish Department of Environment, Heritage and Local Government," the *Hartford Courant* reports, "the price of existing homes throughout Ireland increased about 150 percent during those years."[305]

Kevin Rennie compares the price Dodd paid to buy Kessinger out with other properties in the area:

> Two years after the [housing] bubble exploded, homes smaller than Dodd's and on smaller pieces of property than his are on the market for several times the maximum $250,000 Dodd has declared his is worth each year on his Senate disclosure forms since 2002.
>
> Waterfront properties on the "Irish Riviera" don't often come on the market. In today's dire real estate market, a 750-square-foot, two-bedroom townhouse in nearby Roundstone is for sale for $750,000. A 900-square foot, three-bedroom semi-detached house, boasting of a view of Innishnee, the island where Dodd's house stands high above Bertaghboy Bay, is offered for $700,000.[306]

So Dodd seems to have bought out Kessinger's share at considerably below market price. He defended his purchase by showing the *Hartford Courant* an appraisal made a year before the sale went through that valued it at $190,000. At a time when smaller houses on lesser pieces of property were selling for three times the amount that Dodd paid, it's hard to find a rational explanation for the appraisal Dodd's property received; we'll leave it to your imagination.

Dodd told the *Courant* that it was incorrect to assume that prices all over Ireland had risen. He speculated that Innishnee properties hadn't gone up because the bridge had been in bad repair for years and couldn't handle heavy loads."[307] *Say what?* Hey Chris, don't you remember that the bridge was fully replaced in 2001, the year before your appraisal? Dodd even seems to be puzzled at the ongoing interest in his ownership of the Irish property. HINT TO CHRIS: Maybe it has something to do with the price you paid (or didn't pay)?

Without even seeing the outside of the house, anyone looking at the Dodd property today would would laugh at the idea that it's worth no more than $250,000, as Dodd reports on his financial disclosure statement. Besides the beautiful setting and immense piece of land surrounded by water, the house is charming and the land is well kept. Stone walls in perfect condition surround the property; discreet signs indicate the name of the security company. A locked red iron gate keeps visitors at bay. Tranquil and isolated in its setting, it is only a five-minute ride to Roundstone, a lively fishing village that attracts many Dubliners for summer and weekend homes. Roundstone has restaurants and shops and is a lively center for horse and pony races, sailing, and art shows in the summer. The Dodd "cottage" is no little thatched-roof hut in the middle of nowhere. It's a substantial home in a much desired area, on property that's hard to equal.

Yet when it comes to characterizing the purchase, Dodd seems to be in a dream world. In discussing his various properties and silent partners with the *Courant*, he said, "These were pretty transparent. They've been reported widely in the press, particularly the Irish cottage," Dodd said. "It's fairly routine and non-controversial in my mind."[308]

"Fairly routine and non-controversial"? Not exactly, Chris. Don't you read the newspapers? "Pretty transparent"? Is he kidding? There was nothing transparent at all about his ownership. In his Senate disclosure forms for the years 1995 through 2002, Dodd never divulged the name of his fellow owner who held the other two-thirds interest in the Innishnee property. Nor did he ever reveal his partner's name in any other forum. He didn't even follow the directions on the disclosure form and list the address of the property. He simply called it "Galway cottage." Maybe he didn't want anyone to find out any details about it. Because the only way any information about the ownership of the Innishnee property would be somewhat transparent was if you traveled to Dublin and visited the office of the land registry. Even there the mortgage documents weren't available to the public—but the name of his partner, William Kessinger, was. Traveling thousands of miles to find the name but no other information is Dodd's idea of "pretty transparent"? The purchase and sale of this property was anything but.

One thing that definitely was not transparent was the fact that the firm owned by Dodd's partner in the Irish house, Bucky Kessinger, received federal contracts while he and Dodd owned the house together. Did Dodd check with the Ethics Committee on that, too? Because regardless of whether Dodd helped him or not—and there is no evidence that he did—it certainly doesn't look good for a U.S. senator to partner with a man whose business received federal funds. Especially with the kind of amazing deal Dodd got on the real estate. And especially if Kessinger was also a partner of Ed Downe, as reported in the *Hartford Courant*.

Bucky Kessinger's business, Kessinger Hunter, a Kansas real estate broker and development firm, leased federal property. According to records of the Office of Management and Budget, the firm received $1,371,343 in federal contracts from 2000–2003. (Records before 2000 are not available.) The sale of Kesinger's share of the Irish property went through in January 2003, the last year Kessinger Hunter received money under a federal contract. But in that year the amount received almost doubled.

Contracts to KESSINGER/HUNTER & COMPANY (FY 2000–2008)
Summary

Total dollars: **$1,371,343**
Total number of contractors: **1**
Total number of transactions: **20**
Source: OMB Watch, http://www.fedspending.org/fpds/fpds.php?
parent_id=176507&sortby=u&detail=-1&datype=T&reptype=
r&database=fpds&fiscal_year=&submit=GO.

But by the time Dodd bought Kessinger out, Kessinger/Hunter had begun to look at much bigger horizons—which would eventually involve more that $85 million in federal contracts and require a bill passed by Congress to make the deal happen.

As early as 2002, Kessinger/Hunter expressed interest in developing a 9000-acre piece of land, near Kansas City, Kansas, that had previously been the site of the Sunflower Army Ammunition Plant.[309] Kessinger/Hunter partnered with the International Risk Group and created a new entity, Sunflower Redevelopment, LLC, which proposed a clean-up and development of the former ammunition plant site. There were lots of complications, but eventually Sunshine worked out a deal that would give it title to the property, which it would clean up and develop into residential, retail, and university space. Sunshine sought federal funds from the Department of Defense to do the cleanup, but it turned out that it would need Congressional permission to directly transfer title to the land to a private developer.

On June 23, 2005, the Senate approved an amendment to the Defense Department Authorization bill, S. 2400. The amendment passed on a voice vote by unanimous consent. There is no evidence that Chris Dodd recused himself on the bill, which would help his old partner. Nor did Dodd recuse himself when the full authorization bill, including the special amendment for Sunshine, passed.

Dodd should, at the very least, have recused himself from both those votes. Here he was voting to help his partner in the Irish land deal to the tune of $85 million. But he evidently didn't see anything wrong with voting for a bill that would benefit Kessinger and possibly Downe.

What are friends for?

So, Dodd's Irish property dealing weren't really so transparent, were they?

In 2003, when he bought out Kessinger at a bargain-basement price, Dodd's Senate personal financial disclosure form, as posted on www .opensecrets.org, did not include the page that provides for details of all transactions, describing all sales and purchases of real property. But that year, for the first time, the "Galway cottage" is listed as a joint asset with his wife. There are no details about the 2003 sale. And the disclosure of the value of the property has stayed consistently the same for the last fifteen years—between $100,000 and $250,000.

It may be the only place in Ireland that didn't have an increase in value.

When Dodd ran for president, his disclosure form indicated, for the first time, that the value of between $100–$250,000 was based on the value at the time of sale. The form requires the value of the asset at the time filed, not the time reported, but Dodd has ignored that since 2002.

Once again, Dodd had made a great deal. He got someone (whoever . . .) to pay two-thirds of the expenses while he had full use of the property. And then he bought it for a song.

By the time he purchased the house in Ireland in 1994, he owned the apartment in D.C., with a $180,000 mortgage, as well as his waterfront home in East Haddam, on the bank of the Connecticut River, with mortgages of $148,000 (1985), $46,000 (1987), and $50,000 (1993). So once he bought his one-third interest in the Irish property, Dodd had outstanding mortgage obligations of $433,000—without counting taxes, insurance, upkeep, and so on. And this at a time when his Senate salary was $133,600.

Dodd's account of the purchase ends on a truly bizarre note, which raises even more questions. Dodd says that he paid Kessinger $127,000 for his share. But then he says that he *voluntarily* paid even more, giving Kessinger a "gift" of more than $50,000. Why would he do that?

> Dodd said he also used his own money to pay off the existing mortgage—including Kessinger's share—which amounted to a gift to Kessinger of more than $50,000. *"Candidly, our thinking was at the time, Jackie and I: Let's be more conservative on this in case anybody should ever raise a question about whether or not this is somehow an enrichment or taking advantage of the situation."* [310]

Whenever a politician starts a sentence with the word "candidly," it should raise a bright red flag. Would anyone in his right mind actually voluntarily overpay his share of a mortgage by $50,000? Not likely. Dodd now says he paid Kessinger a total of $177,000 for his two-thirds interest in a house that was appraised at $190,000. You do the math. What a generous guy he is. It sounds kind of crazy, doesn't it? Unless there was more to the story. We'll stay tuned.

But—hypothetically speaking—if the Ireland property was originally bought for $160,000 and Dodd owned one third of it, his share would come to about $53,000—pretty close to the extra amount he generously paid to Kessinger. Imagine, still hypothetically, that he didn't pay a nickel for the house but Kessinger (or Downe) put up all the money and, of course, let the senator have sole use and possession of the property. Wouldn't it make sense—hypothetically speaking that is—for Dodd to pay back Kessinger not just his two thirds but also the original $53,000 that Dodd—hypothetically—didn't actually pay when he bought the house?

But for once Dodd was prescient. Questions have indeed been raised about whether there was "somehow" an enrichment or taking advantage of the situation. It sure looks like it. But while questions have been raised, the answers have not been at all credible—even with the extra $50,000. Or especially with the extra $50,000.

But Dodd's questionable housing practices didn't end there.

COUNTRYWIDE FINANCIAL

In the summer of 2008, Portfolio.com reported that Countrywide Financial had given a "VIP" mortgage deal to Senator Chris Dodd and his wife, Jackie Clegg, on two 2003 mortgages totaling $528,000 for their Connecticut and Washington, D.C., homes. Countrywide apparently operated a program called "Friends of Angelo," named after former Countrywide president Angelo Mozilo, which provided special benefits to celebrities who might be important to the bank in the future. *Portfolio.com* reported that the VIPs got a much better deal because Countrywide often reduced their points and gave them a better interest rate.[311]

Many people blame Countrywide for starting the current global meltdown with its extensive marketing of subprime and initial low interest loans that led to hundreds of thousands of defaults. Many of the loans were then sold to Fannie Mae and Freddie Mac, which were taken over by the U.S. government last fall because of the huge number of defaulted loans that caused the agencies to fail.

Dodd immediately insisted he knew nothing about any special treatment, but later claimed that although he did know that he and his wife were part of a VIP program, he thought it was just a "courtesy." And, obviously, such "courtesies" were normal occurrences.

But a former Countrywide loan officer disputes Dodd's account. According to the *Wall Street Journal*:

Former Countrywide Financial loan officer Robert Feinberg says Mr. Dodd knowingly saved thousands of dollars on his refinancing of two properties in 2003 as part of a special program the California mortgage company had for the influential. He also says he has internal company documents that prove Mr. Dodd knew he was getting preferential treatment as a friend of Angelo Mozilo, Countrywide's then-CEO.

That a "Friends of Angelo" program existed is not in dispute. It was crucial to the boom that Countrywide enjoyed before its fortunes turned. While most of the company was aggressively lending to risky borrowers and off-loading those mortgages in bulk to Fannie Mae and Freddie Mac, Mr. Feinberg's department was charged with making sure those who could influence Fannie and Freddie's appetite for risk were sufficiently buttered up. As a Banking Committee bigshot, Mr. Dodd was perfectly placed to be buttered. . . .

Mr. Feinberg, who oversaw "Friends of Angelo" from 2000 to 2004, . . . told us that as the loan officer in charge he was supposed to make sure that the "VIP" clients knew at every step of the process that they were getting a special deal because they were "Friends of Angelo."

"People are referred into that department as 'very important people.' You're told that your loan is priced from Angelo. As the 'Friends of Angelo department,' [the department] has to give them a sense of importance and explain the reduction of fees and the rate as a result of being a 'Friend of Angelo,' " he says.

As to Mr. Dodd, Mr. Feinberg says he spoke to the Senator once or twice and mostly to his wife and that like other FOAs Mr. Dodd got 'a float down,' which means that even after he had a preferred rate, when the prevailing rate dropped just before the closing, his rate was reduced again. Regular borrowers would pay extra for a last-minute adjustment, but not FOAs. 'They were aware of it because they were notified and when they went to the closing they would see it,' Mr. Feinberg says, adding that he 'always let people in the program know that they were getting a very good deal because they were 'Friends of Angelo.' All of this matters because Mr. Dodd was one of those encouraging Fannie and Freddie to plunge into 'affordable housing' loans made by companies like Countrywide.

One indicator of his influence is the [amount] in campaign contributions—more than to any other politician—that Fan and Fred have given him since 1989, according to the Center for Responsive Politics. These contributions are legal. But favors like those Mr. Dodd is alleged to have received may not be. Mr. Feinberg says he went public with his story because when he heard Senator Dodd on TV talking about predatory lending, he felt it was "hypocritical" and he says, "I just thought, 'This is wrong.'"[312]

Countrywide contributed more than $100,000 in campaign contributions to Dodd, second only to then Senator Barack Obama. The company was not alone in feeling that Dodd was crucial to erecting the house of single cards of subprime mortgage deals that ultimately collapsed. Fannie Mae and Freddie Mac, who purchased the subprime mortgages and disseminated them all over Wall Street, also gave Dodd special favors, this time in the form of campaign contributions. Dodd proved useful to Fannie and Freddie, killing any attempt to rein them in. Here's a list of the top recipients of contributions from Fannie Mae and Freddie Mac. Notice who is number one:

TOP RECIPIENTS OF FANNIE MAE AND FREDDIE MAC CAMPAIGN CONTRIBUTIONS, 1989–2008

Name	Office	Party/State	Total
1. Dodd, Christopher J	S	D-CT	$133,900
2. Kerry, John	S	D-MA	$111,000
3. Obama, Barack	S	D-IL	$105,849
4. Clinton, Hillary	S	D-NY	$75,550
5. Kanjorski, Paul E	H	D-PA	$65,500

Source: Center For Responsive Politics

That Chris Dodd is a popular guy, isn't he?

Since last summer, the Senate Ethics Committee, chaired by Senator Barbara Boxer, has been investigating whether Dodd knowingly received an illegal gift. But those folks don't move too fast, so don't expect a resolution any time soon. And Boxer is a Democrat, so don't expect her to roll on one of her own.

QUESTION: How many regular people got a 'courtesy' on their mortgages?

AIG

Dodd's missteps have not been limited to his personal housing transactions. By April 2008, AIG had become the universal symbol of the excesses and greed that caused the global financial meltdown. After receiving a total of $182 billion in federal bailout money, the company did not seem to get either the need for cutting back on their extravagant business practices or the rage that was simmering against them across the country.

Shortly after the company received its first $75 billion in federal bailout funds, reports of lavish corporate outings at expensive resorts began to be reported in U.S. media outlets. Anger against AIG for continuing its profligate ways exploded, reaching its peak when a Connecticut bus tour was organized to visit and protest at the homes of AIG employees.

The final straw came when it was revealed that AIG had doled out more than $100 million in huge bonuses to its executives after it accepted the federal bailout money. When it became apparent that Congress had authorized the payment of these bonuses, the public demanded to know who was behind the approval.

Turns out it was none other than Chris Dodd, chairman of the Senate Banking Committee.

When the first reports of this appeared in the media, Dodd vehemently denied having anything to do with it. But later Dodd changed his story. He said that after checking, he realized that he had "reluctantly" agreed to make the change when the secretary of the treasury asked him to do it. (After a thorough investigation, he was surprised to find out the culprit was himself!)

Of course, as chairman of the Banking Committee, Dodd could have said no. He couldn't have been forced to do it. But he didn't—he went right along with the Obama administration.

Dodd's been slammed in the media ever since. It didn't help that reports surfaced a few days later showing that AIG executives had emailed employees and urged them to contribute to Dodd because he was about to become chairman of the Senate Banking Committee and would oversee any legislation that related to AIG. Within three days, the AIG folks rounded up $160,000. Dodd is the top recipient of AIG donations, with a total of $281,038—almost three times as large as New York's Senator Chuck Schumer, who was in second place.

TOP RECIPIENTS OF AIG CONTRIBUTIONS

Name	Total Contributions
Dodd, Chris (D-CT)	$281,038
Schumer, Charles E (D-NY)	$111,875
Obama, Barack (D-IL)	$110,332
McCain, John (R-AZ)	$99,249
Baucus, Max (D-MT)	$90,000
Kerry, John (D-MA)	$85,000
Johnson, Nancy L (R-CT)	$75,400
Sununu, John E (R-NH)	$69,049
Clinton, Hillary (D-NY)	$61,515
Lieberman, Joe (I-CT)	$57,900
Rangel, Charles B (D-NY)	$53,000

Source: Center For Responsive Politics, http://www.opensecrets.org/orgs/recips.php?id=D000000123&type=P&state=&sort=A&cycle=A.

Things weren't going well for the Connecticut Senator. The AIG story was everywhere. But then it got even worse: It turned out that Dodd's wife, Jackie M. Clegg, had been appointed to the Board of Directors of IPC Holdings, an offshore company based in Bermuda and controlled by AIG. Between 2000 and 2004 she was paid more than $12,000 a year.[313]

Dodd just can't get away from AIG, can he?

But actually, he's a favorite of all of the financial institutions, not just AIG. Here's a chart showing the major contributions he's received, with those from the financial sector in bold:

TOP CONTRIBUTORS TO DODD 2008

Contributor	Total
Citigroup Inc	$316,494
United Technologies	$264,400
SAC Capital Partners	$248,500
American International Group	$223,478
Royal Bank of Scotland	$218,500
Bear Stearns	$201,000
Goldman Sachs	$180,200
Credit Suisse Group	$157,050
Morgan Stanley	$156,600
JPMorgan Chase & Co	$134,050
Merrill Lynch	$132,950
Lehman Brothers	$122,300
Hartford Financial Services	$117,150
KPMG LLP	$116,650
General Electric	$113,000
UBS AG	$110,800
St Paul Travelers Companies	$107,100
Travelers Companies	$104,700
Deloitte Touche Tohmatsu	$103,000
The Hartford	$94, 550

Those banks and insurance companies sure do like Senator Dodd, don't they?

THE THOMAS DODD RESEARCH CENTER

On October 16, 1995, the president of the United States, Bill Clinton, flew on Air Force One to Storrs, Connecticut, for the dedication and opening of the Thomas Dodd Research Center at the University of Connecticut.

The Dodd Center will be the repository for Senator Thomas Dodd's papers, as well as those of his son, former governor Rowland, and former senator Prescott Bush, the father and grandfather of the presidents Bush.

At the festivities for the opening, no one ever mentioned the sad ending to Dodd's career when he was censured by the Senate for taking campaign money for his personal use.

The Center was funded by $8 million from the state of Connecticut and $1 million raised by Senator Dodd. Those who privately contributed to this public building and research center have not been disclosed. So we have no idea who made contributions and whether they have any business with the federal government. The names should have been disclosed. Why should private contributions to a public university be kept secret? Someone obviously decided that the names would not be revealed.

Don't you wonder why?

But one familiar name appears on the Center's Board of Advisers: Ed Downe.

Wherever you find Chris Dodd, Ed Downe is not far behind. He and his family have continued to contribute the maximum allowable contribution to all his campaigns. He describes himself as an "Independent Investor."

WHAT'S WRONG WITH CHRIS DODD

Chris Dodd is the epitome of the Washington insider politician who is tone deaf to everything except the Beltway conventional wisdom.

He's been there for so long, he's part of the problem.

He expects handouts

He doesn't understand what the big deal is about the many homes he's bought with the help of generous partners. Partners who do business with the federal government.

He doesn't get why his amendment to benefit A.I.G. is inciting people.

In fact, he just doesn't get it.

ACTION AGENDA

If you think there's any problems with any of Chris Dodd's housing transactions, including the Countrywide mortgages, call Barbara Boxer's office. She's the chairman of the Committee on Ethics. The Committee that does nothing.

The Capital switchboard number is 202-224-3121. Just ask for her office and let them know what you think.

CHARLIE RANGEL AND AIG

Charlie Rangel is a hypocrite. A big one.

When it was first announced that AIG executives had been awarded outrageous bonuses even despite their company's despicable performance and congressional Democrats were proposing to wipe out the bonuses out by levying special taxes on them, it was, unexpectedly, Charlie Rangel, the head of the Ways and Means Committee, who demurred. The taxing power, he said, should not be used as a political weapon.

But then, suddenly, Rangel changed his mind. He not only supported but sponsored the bill to impose a 90 percent tax on the bonuses paid to AIG and other employees of banks that received TARP bailout money.

Once Rangel saw which way the wind was blowing and got his marching orders from Pelosi and company, he was suddenly transformed into a populist avenger, ravaging everything in his path.

With his change of heart, he's become outraged, furious, blaming those who received the bonuses of "getting away with murder"[314] and destroying communities. During the debate on the House floor, his rage was in full force: "Are these guys going to get away with what they have done to our communities, what they have done to our homes, what they have done to our pride, what they have done to our country and what they have done for the world?"[315] Rangel asked.

But Rangel's first reaction—to oppose the tax—reflects his long and cozy relationship with the Wall Street and mortgage crowd. He's taken plenty of campaign money from them over the years. Here's a look at his top donors in 2008:

TOP DONORS TO CHARLES RANGEL IN 2008

Contributor	Total
AXA	$62,100
Citigroup	$61,950
Credit Suisse Group	$56,800
Metlife	$50,500
JPMorgan Chase & Co.	$50,200
American Express	$37,800
New York Life Insurance	$30,900
Johnson & Johnson	$27,900
Rudin Management	$27,600
Bank of New York Mellon	$25,000

Source: "Top Contributors Charles B. Rangel, 2007–2008," OpenSecrets.org, www
.opensecrets.org/politicians/contrib.php?cycle=2008&cid=N00000964.

You'll notice that six of his top ten donors—those in boldface—are from the financial and banking field. He's a real favorite of the Wall Street guys. Could it have something to do with his writing the tax code as chairman of the House Ways and Means Committee? These folks want access. Could that be why Rangel was number one on Citigroup's list of recipients, receiving more than any other member of Congress? Or why he was number one on Credit Suisse's list, too? And JPMorgan Chase as well? Only one House member received more than he did from AIG. This is nothing new. Throughout Charlie Rangel's career, the banks have been contributing to him big time. Here's a look at the total since 1989:

TOP DONORS TO CHARLES RANGEL SINCE 1989

Contributor	Total
Citigroup	$182,600
New York Life Insurance	$170,750

Contributor	Total
Metlife	$141,097
Goldman Sachs	**$113,100**
JPMorgan Chase & Co	**$107,650**
General Electric	$102,000
Philip Morris	$99,478
AFLAC	$96,000
Credit Suisse Group	**$90,300**
American Federation of Teachers	$86,300
American Federation of State, County, and Municipal Employees	$82,000

Source: "Top Contributors, Charles B. Rangel," OpenSecrets.org, www.opensecrets.org/politicians/contrib.php?cid=N00000964&cycle=Career.

But now Rangel has no use for his old friends with deep pockets. He has even criticized those in the Obama administration who permitted the bonuses, calling them "out of touch"[316] Speaking on New York 1 television, Rangel said that Obama's economic team had blown it:

Someone screwed up—period. With all due respect to [Tim] Geithner and [Henry] Paulson, they come out of Wall Street and Goldman Sachs. They don't know what pain is.... So getting a $6 million bonus is just natural to them. They don't know shame, they don't know how to apologize. They never feel the awkwardness of seeing the people who've lost their lives economically as a result of their greed.[317]

Hmmm. Could Charlie have actually forgotten that he'd gone knocking on AIG's big door last year looking for a $10 million handout for a school to be named after him? Isn't that kind of like a bonus? Is getting a $10 million donation to feed your ego somehow less offensive than a $10 million bonus for anything else? And what about about the $5 million donation he had gotten for his school from a foundation controlled by Maurice Greenberg, the former CEO of AIG? How is that any different than a bonus?

Or could it actually be even worse—if published reports are true, that it was tied to a *quid pro quo* for legislation favorable to AIG?

THE CHARLES B. RANGEL CENTER FOR PUBLIC SERVICE

What is it about Washington that makes normally sensible men act crazy when they decide they want to build a monument to themselves or to their family?

Rangel seems to have become infected with this disease—at least when it comes to his decision to raise funds to pay for a school to glorify his name. After due consideration, Rangel decided who would help pay for his project: we would.

In 2007, Rangel submitted an earmark for $1.9 million to fund the Charles B. Rangel Center for Public Service at City University of New York.[318] Now, that takes nerve! Using your power as a congressman to appropriate federal tax money to finance your favorite egotistical project.

Some of the congressman's colleagues in the House were not amused by Rangel's self-celebrating earmark. Congressman John Campbell challenged Rangel: "You don't agree with me or see any problem with us, as members, spending taxpayer funds in the creation of things named after ourselves while we're still here?"[319]

"I would have a problem if *you* did it," Rangel replied, "because I don't think that *you've* been around long enough that having your name on something to inspire a building like this in a school."

Rangel refused to see anything wrong with the project. "I cannot think of anything I am more proud of," he said.[320]

CBS News quoted from promotional brochures for the Center, which promised:

> a new "Charles B. Rangel Center for Public Service," the "Rangel Conference Center," "a well-furnished office for Charles Rangel," and the "Charles Rangel Library" for his papers and memorabilia. It's kind of like a presidential library, but without a president. In fact, the brochure says Rangel's library will be as important as the Clinton and Carter libraries.[321]

Really, Charlie? That's how you see yourself?

As the debate on the earmark was ending, Congressman Campbell summed up Rangel's hubris: "We call it the 'Monument to Me,' because . . . Congressman Rangel is creating a monument to himself."[322]

Perhaps Rangel became so obsessed with the monument to himself that he lost sight of what was acceptable conduct for a congressman.

It should go without saying that no member of Congress should be permitted to sponsor an earmark for—that is, *spend the taxpayers' money on*—a personal project.

But when the taxpayers' money was not enough to fund Rangel's Monument to Me, the chairman of the Ways and Means Committee decided to hit up his good buddies at AIG and other corporations for big donations.

THE CONGRESSMAN AND AIG

As mentioned above, Charlie Rangel wasn't always so critical of AIG. The company had provided campaign money to him over the years and he and its former CEO, Maurice Greenberg, had become friends. In fact, according to published reports, Greenberg had helped to steer a $5 million contribution from a foundation to Rangel for his eponymous Center.

But Rangel wanted more. And so did City University, which, according to the *New York Times*, was hoping to get a $10 million contribution from AIG.[323] A meeting was set up, and Rangel made a pitch for a contribution. It's what happened next that has raised questions.

One of the attendees at the meeting wrote to Rangel and asked for his support on a tax measure that would be worth millions to AIG, a tax measure that Rangel had opposed in the past. And guess what? He changed his position. Rangel claims that he had decided to change his mind about the bill well before he ever received the AIG letter.

Of course.

You see the problem: The chairman of the Ways and Means Committee, who has almost unilateral power over tax legislation, is meeting with a company that wants a tax break. And the purpose of the meeting is for Charlie to beg for money. It doesn't look good, does it?

Not surprisingly, AIG made assurances that its request had nothing to do with Rangel's own bid for $10 million for his center.

Of course not.

Because if a legislator does something as a *quid pro quo*, it is a crime. And neither Rangel nor AIG would ever want to get involved in such a thing.

Probably squeamish about the appearance of such a deal, AIG never donated the $10 million. But Rangel must still have been grateful for the $5
million AIG's former chairman Greenberg had steered his way.

Rangel got into even more trouble over his aggressive fund raising tactics. *The New York Times* reported that Rangel had used his congressional
stationery indicating that he was Chairman of the Ways and Means Committee to solicit funds for foundations. According to the *Times*:

> one was sent to an administrator at the Starr Foundation, where Mr. Green-
> berg serves as the chairman. The foundation did not make a donation in
> 2006. . . . In March 2007, two months after Mr. Rangel had been elevated
> to Ways and Means chairman, he wrote a letter directly to Mr. Greenberg,
> using his Congressional stationery. By the end of the year, Mr. Greenberg
> had pledged $5 million, by far the largest contribution to a project that has
> raised $11 million to date.[324]

After widespread reports of Rangel's practice of using his congressional imprimatur to solicit funds appeared in the media, Rangel initially defended the practice, declaring it legal. But he then changed his position and
asked the House Ethics Committee to investigate the matter. That was in
July 2008—and so far there's been no finding by that committee.

Don't hold your breath.

What is it about building a Monument to Me that makes our elected officials go begging to the nearest corporate donor?

Bill Clinton, for example, spent his last years in office hitting up every
last rich guy and Middle East leader for contributions to his library. What's
wrong with that? Well, first, he was raising money directly from the White
House while he still had the power to do major favors. And then he arro-
gantly did it in secret and defiantly refused to release the names. It doesn't
inspire confidence in our system, does it? When Clinton granted a last-minute pardon to the fugitive Mark Rich that circumvented the Justice Department mechanism, there was widespread suspicion that it was bought and
paid for by Denise Rich's $450,000 contribution to the library (as well as
gifts of furniture and campaign contributions to Hillary).

And Charlie Rangel isn't the only man on the Hill with his very own Monument to Me. Senators Richard Shelby (R-AL) and Thad Cochran (R-MS) have also gotten earmarks for projects bearing their names while they still serve in the Senate. This practice is both tasteless and disgraceful.

Right now, there's frantic fund-raising going on to build—albeit from private money—a new Edward M. Kennedy Institute of the Senate in Boston. According to the *Boston Globe:*

> Drug companies, hospitals, and insurance firms have helped to amass $20 million to finance a nonprofit educational institute in Boston that will honor Senator Edward M. Kennedy.... The biggest donation has been $5 million from Amgen Inc., a national biotechnology drug firm based in California that depends heavily on federal healthcare policies and Medicare prescription drug reimbursements for its profits.... The Service Employees International Union gave $2.5 million, and the United Brotherhood of Carpenters and Joiners of America pledged $1 million. The Novartis US Foundation gave $250,000, and Blue Cross and Blue Shield of Massachusetts gave $200,000.[325]

QUESTION: What do all of these groups have in common?

ANSWER: They all are regulated (at least partially) by the federal government, seek money from it, and/or seek legislation in Congress.

QUESTION: Who's the chairman of the Labor, Health and Education Committee that makes decisions on all health care–related bills?

ANSWER: The one and only Senator Kennedy.

That's the problem.

Though Senator Kennedy himself has not been involved in the fund-raising, his son, Ted Kennedy Jr. represented him at a fund-raising dinner. Those who are making the fund-raising calls told the *Globe* that there were no ethical issues with the fund-raising efforts, since the senator himself had no role in overseeing it. They also indicated that they intended to reach out to the financial and entertainment industries for contributions, too.

But segregating the senator is not enough. If any of his family members and staff are attending the fund-raisers and speaking to possible donors, there's at least the appearance of an ethical problem, isn't there?

There should be a broad prohibition against any public official doing any private fund-raising for something that relates to him or his family, whether it's named after him or not. Public officials shouldn't be able to raise money from any person or entity that has business before Congress.

It's that simple.

RANGEL AND THE OIL COMPANY TAX BREAK

But the AIG solicitation isn't the only source of concern over Charlie Rangel's questionable mix of tax policies and personal solicitations.

It seems that Rangel had personally sought another contribution to his new school. This time he met with Eugene M. Isenberg, the chief executive officer of Nabors Industries, a petroleum exploration company that had moved its drilling operations offshore after 9/11 to avoid federal taxes. Although Rangel had been publicly critical of the company in 2004, by the time Isenberg pledged $1 million for his school in 2007, Rangel was firmly in support of the valuable tax loophole that Isenberg was seeking to keep.[326]

It's not just that Rangel changed his mind. The circumstances and context of his meetings with Isenberg were appalling. On the very morning that the Ways and Means Committee would consider the bill that would benefit Nabors, Rangel met with Isenberg to discuss his contribution to the school. After the discussion was finished, the pair moved across the room to meet with Nabors's lobbyist. It was then that Rangel made a commitment to oppose the bill that had passed the Senate that would eliminate the loophole. Several days later, a check for $100,000 arrived at the City University.

That kind of conduct, suggestive of a *quid pro quo,* would seem to cross the kind of basic ethical line that most people would recognize. But Charlie Rangel seems to have vaulted way over that line time after time. Here are some of the violations he has been accused of:

New York State's rent stabilization law controls the rent landlords can charge for primary residences in certain buildings. To be eligible for a stabilized rent, the apartment must be your primary residence.

But as the *New York Times* disclosed, Charlie Rangel has four of them, all in the same building. He gets these 2500 square feet of Manhattan apartment at half price.

One of his four rent-stabilized apartments was used as a district office, which he paid for with taxpayer money. His landlord, eager to curry favor with him, hasn't challenged his reduced rent.

And for several years Rangel had a fifth primary residence. He got a homestead exemption on his property taxes for a house in Washington, saying that this too was his primary residence and that he paid taxes there—neither of which is true.

Asked about these shenanigans, Rangel retorted angrily that where he lived was nobody's business.[327]

Rangel bought a vacation villa in the Dominican Republic and forgot to report $75,000 in rental income from the property on his taxes. Now, remember, as chairman of the Ways and Means Committee, this is the man who writes the nation's tax laws. How could he forget such a thing?

Unbelievably, he has blamed his failure to report these taxes, at least in part, on language problems, because the residents of the Dominican Republic speak Spanish. Then again, so does half of Rangel's district. If anyone could have found a translator, presumably it was Charlie Rangel.

All of these issues are now before the House Ethics Committee for investigation. But given the record of that august body, we're none too hopeful. In July 2008, Speaker Pelosi pledged that the matters would be dealt with quickly. It's April 2009 as we write this—and still nothing has happened.

Like Chris Dodd, Charlie Rangel has gotten exceptional housing at a cut rate. And, like Dodd, he has depended on AIG and the big banks and investment companies to fund his campaigns while masquerading as a populist attacking them. Both of their futures are before their respective Ethics

Committees. But, more than that, it will be up to the voters to determine their fates.

ACTION AGENDA

If you have a problem with Rangel's conduct, let Nancy Pelosi know about it and demand that he be removed as chairman of the Ways and Means committee. She can be reached at: 202-224-3121.

9

THERE IS NOTHING LIKE A NAME
Ted Kennedy, Jr., the Senator's Son

Some people may insinuate that I am looking to trade on my family name. This is definitely not the case.

—TED KENNEDY, JR., April 2004

Apparently Caroline Kennedy isn't the only member of the Kennedy family who's tried to capitalize on her famous last name. Even before her disastrous attempt to be appointed as Hillary Clinton's successor in the Senate, her cousin, Ted Kennedy, Jr., was one big step ahead of her. For years, Kennedy Jr. has been boldly exploiting both his name and his intimate relationship with the most influential member of the U.S. Senate when it comes to health care and organized labor: his father, Senator Ted Kennedy.

Those twin pillars of special interests—the health care establishment and labor unions—have been the foundation of Ted Kennedy, Jr.'s, phenomenal success in the last decade. And his father has been all too willing to help out in making the family connection into a lucrative business for his son.

Despite his righteous denials, public reports and anecdotal information indicate that Ted Kennedy, Jr., actually does privately trade on his famous family name.

Now that his father is set to be the quarterback on health care reform, Ted Kennedy, Jr., is positioned to be in the right place at the right time. His "health care advisory" firm, the Marwood Group, is busily offering its services to hedge funds and other interested groups in the United States and overseas.

What does Marwood offer? Advice and information on what to expect from Washington on health care reform and any and all issues that relate to the health care industry.

What makes Marwood so well equipped to sell this advice?

At the very least, the perception that its information comes straight from the chairman of the committee that will determine every single detail of health care reform. Beyond that, the perception that paying Ted Kennedy, Jr.'s, firm might give you unparalleled access to Senator Ted Kennedy, Sr.

Needless to say, most hedge funds (and lots of other businesses) would jump at the opportunity to have the inside scoop on which businesses will benefit and which will suffer because of the radical changes that are currently being considered for the health care system. Any clues, about the regulation of drugs, medical devices, nursing homes, hospitals, insurance companies, the biotech industry, and so on can mean a gain or loss to those industries and to the hedge funds that invest in them. An early heads-up can lead to immediate trading—buying, selling, shorting. That kind of information is a gold mine.

And Ted Kennedy, Jr., understands that completely. While there is nothing illegal about Kennedy Jr.'s activities and no evidence of any leaking of insider information by Senator Kennedy, the health care industry is desperate for any information and advice, and he knows it.

MAKING THE MOST OF FAMILY TIES

Looking back, it seems rather obvious: sometime around 2000, Ted Kennedy, Jr., apparently decided to begin to commercialize his unique and very valuable family contact in the Senate. Why not? It's a cardinal rule of business: you use what you have.

To get the ball rolling, Kennedy Jr.'s firm, the Marwood Group, hung out its shingle and registered to lobby in Washington for the four years from 2001 to 2004. Not surprisingly, all of its clients came from a single sector of the economy: health care. For almost half that period, starting in June 2001, Kennedy's father was the chairman of the Senate Committee on Health, Education, Labor and Pensions. That turned out to be extremely helpful to Ted Jr.

Whether you agree with Ted Kennedy or not, he has been a consistent champion of universal health care for more than twenty years and an influential voice for children, the elderly, consumers, and those without their own lobbyist in Washington.

His son, however, has followed a different agenda.

Ted Kennedy, Jr., went to Washington for one reason: to make money. He wasn't there to be a devoted public servant or a tireless advocate for the poor and the downtrodden. He paid little heed to the familiar Kennedy family mantra about the importance of service to our nation and its people. To be clear: Ted Kennedy, Jr.'s, firm was not working on legislation to protect consumer interests or the public interest. Far from it: the Marwood Group was a lobbyist for big health care businesses—whose interests were, in many cases, directly adverse to those of consumers.

And what was Ted Jr.'s unique selling proposition? Well, how many other lobbying firms can deliver the chairman of the Committee on Health, Education, Labor and Pensions to a meeting?

Take a look at who paid them. One of the firm's first clients was the mega-pharmaceutical company Bristol-Myers Squibb (BMS). That's a pretty big fish to land for a new firm with no track record. Then again, if your father is the Senate's leader in health care, chairs one of the key committees, and has access to information about what's going on about congressional interest in the regulation of drugs, it's a good investment for any drug company.

And BMS needed all the help it could get. The company had an urgent issue before Congress that was worth literally billions of dollars. To protect its profits, BMS was pulling out all the stops to try to pull off a major legislative feat.

When BMS hired Ted Jr.'s firm in 2001, it was engaged in a monumental lobbying effort to try to extend the patent on its runaway success drug, Glucophage, which was designed to control adult-onset diabetes. Although

BMS's patent was due to run out in late 2001, the company was trying to benefit from a possible loophole in the patent law that might allow it to extend the patent for three more years and prevent other companies from selling a less expensive generic alternative. The loophole was a long shot, and the clock was ticking: the firm had only a few months to convince Congress to grant it the extension and keep its competitors from knocking down its doors.

To say this was worth a lot to BMS would be a prodigious understatement: In the year 2000 alone, sales of Glucophage amounted to *more than $3 billion!*[328]

If other companies were allowed to compete against BMS with low-priced generics, that $3 billion would be out the window. Of course, the company spent little time worrying about the drug's burdensome price to consumers, who had filled 25 million Glucophage prescriptions in 2000.[329] That wasn't its concern.

But someone at BMS *should* have been focusing on it. According to the public interest lobbying organization Congress Watch, extending the patent and continuing BMS's exclusive right to produce the drug would cost consumers millions of dollars. Congress Watch dramatically described the potential financial effect, based on a formula created by the FDA:

> Every minute that generic versions of Glucophage are not available adds an additional $1,000 to consumers' prescription drug bills. Every hour costs consumers an additional $61,540. Every day costs consumers nearly $1.5 million extra. The six-month costs to consumers are $269 million. And the three-and-a-half year costs to consumers, should BMS succeed in its attempt to extend the Glucophage patent, would be $1.9 billion.[330]

In the fight to maintain total control over selling the drug, money was no object for BMS. In 2001, the company spent $4.9 million on lobbying to try to get the Glucophage patent extended.[331] Before Marwood arrived on the scene, BMS had relied on the most prominent and influential lobbying firms in town to try to convince Congress to buy their position. So why did it suddenly hire an inexperienced little firm late in the year?

In part because, by late 2001, BMS wanted to sit down with Senator Ted

Kennedy, who had assumed the chairmanship of the health committee that June. Where was the best place to go for that? To Marwood, of course. And that's what BMS did. According to the *Washington Post*:

> The manufacturer, which spent $2.6 million on lobbying during the first six months of this year, retained Republican Haley Barbour and Democrat Thomas Boggs to contact key lawmakers. *Bristol-Myers also arranged for a meeting between company President Peter Dolan and Sen. Edward M. Kennedy (D-Mass.) through the senator's son, Ted Kennedy Jr., a lobbyist.*[332] [emphasis added]

Actually, Ted Kennedy, Jr., never registered to lobby for BMS, but others in his firm did. It's not clear why Ted Jr. didn't register himself. Maybe he wanted to avoid public scrutiny of this eyebrow-raising transaction, in which the son of a senator was paid $20,000 for merely arranging a meeting for his father with the head of a corporation lobbying for special-interest legislation—a new low in lobbying annals, even by Washington's extremely low standards. Even if he wasn't registered, though, it's reasonable to conclude that Kennedy Jr. was the one who did the key "work"—arranging the meeting between the BMS president and his father that was so crucial to BMS.

And Ted Kennedy, Jr., wonders why some people believe he trades on his famous name?

The BMS fee was a good one, considering the fact that it likely involved only a few minutes of time. After all, how long can it take to call your father and ask him to meet with one of your clients? For this, Marwood was paid $20,000 in 2001—a paltry amount to BMS but a full one-quarter of the Marwood Group's lobbying fees for its first year. Not bad for just scheduling a meeting.

Surprisingly, though, in its 2001 lobbying disclosure form Marwood claimed it had made no contacts with the House of Representatives, the Senate, or any federal agency. No contacts with the federal government? So how did BMS manage to get that meeting with the elder Kennedy? And what *was* it paying Marwood to do? You don't hire a registered Washington lobbying firm if it isn't going to do any lobbying for you.

What's also interesting about Marwood's 2001 disclosure form is that it doesn't admit to any involvement in the BMS patent issue. Under the section that requires a lobbying firm to describe the specific issues it lobbied on for BMS, Marwood wrote:

> Provide advice re: grassroots program and work with provider team to help identify emerging biotechnologies and products.[333]

Say what?

"*Grassroots* program"? What were they going to do—organize spontaneous community opposition to lower prescription prices on Glucophage? And "identify emerging biotechnologies"? Are they kidding?

How about "use your family position to sell a meeting with your father and the president of BMS to try and help BMS hold on to its billion-dollar patent"? How about "help us hang on to our pharmaceutical patents"?

Every other lobbying firm that BMS hired in 2001 listed specific bills and/or issues it had been hired to lobby for or against. Most of them related to the extension of the Glucophage patent. And significantly, BMS itself did not list "emerging biotechnologies and products" in its meticulous twenty-nine-page year-end disclosure of the issues it had lobbied on in 2001.

Marwood listed two lobbyists on its BMS disclosure form—yet those lobbyists apparently never lobbied for BMS or contacted anyone on behalf of the drug company, if we're to believe its statement that it never contacted Congress or any federal agency. So why were they listed as lobbyists? One of them was Ted Kennedy, Jr.'s, partner in forming the firm, John Moore, a former political operative in New York governor George Pataki's administration. What did they do for BMS? If they weren't contacting any federal officials, why did they file a lobbying disclosure form?

Yet there were no inquiries made about any of these dubious disclosures. Why? Sadly, that's business as usual in Washington. Congress has never wanted to regulate lobbyists, and it ignores even the most patently ridiculous filings. At that time, although the filings were public, they weren't available online, and few people would have bothered to make the trip to Washington to sift through them.

One has to ask why Marwood was initially hired by BMS. It certainly wasn't because of the firm's political skills and lobbying expertise—as a brand-new firm, it hadn't developed any. But then again, it didn't *need* any. It was apparently hired for a simple, raw political reason: to pay the son of a senator to arrange for a private meeting of great importance to a company with a matter of great economic concern. BMS had already hired many of the top-tier lobbyists in Washington; it didn't need the lobbying services of the new kids on the block.

To understand the breadth of lobbying done by BMS at the time it hired Marwood, here's a list of BMS's lobbying expenditures in 2001:

2001 ITEMIZED LOBBYING EXPENSES FOR BRISTOL-MYERS SQUIBB

Firms Hired	Total Reported by Filer	Reported Contract Expenses (Included in Total Reported by Filer)
Bristol-Myers Squibb	$4,860,000	—
Bristol-Myers Squibb	—	$4,860,000
Timmons & Co.	—	$320,000
Patton Boggs LLP	—	$260,000
Barbour, Griffith & Rogers	—	$200,000
Bergner, Bockorny et al.	—	$120,000
Public Strategies	—	$80,000
Gorlin Group	—	$80,000
Hogan & Hartson	—	$80,000
BKSH & Associates	—	$60,000
Capitol Health Group	—	$60,000
FoxKiser	—	$60,000
Bennett, Turner & Coleman	—	$40,000
Williams & Jensen	—	$40,000
Steelman Health Strategies	—	$40,000
Anders, Jeffrey M.	—	$28,000
Marwood Group	—	**$20,000**

Firms Hired	Total Reported by Filer	Reported Contract Expenses (Included in Total Reported by Filer)
Richard F. Hohlt	—	$20,000
Gibson, Dunn & Crutcher	—	$20,000
Loeffler Group	—	$0
Total		$1,528,000

Source: "2001 Itemized Lobbying Expenses for Bristol-Myers Squibb," Center for Responsive Politics, www.opensecrets.org/lobby/clientsum.php?lname=Bristol-Myers+Squibb&year=2008.

BMS was spending more than $6 million to lobby Congress and federal agencies that year. Did it really need to pay an extra $20,000 to Marwood?

One wonders exactly what each of those lobbying groups was paid to do for BMS—especially the other firms that were paid only $20,000. Did they, too, set up special meetings for BMS? Whatever anyone else did for the pharmaceutical giant, it's obvious that Marwood wasn't hired to be the key substantive lobbyist for BMS.

After that short, helpful stint in 2001, BMS didn't re-up with Marwood. But in 2003, when BMS needed help with the Senate Labor, Health, and Education Appropriations bill, guess who they turned to? The one firm that had a unique connection to the Senate Health, Education, Labor and Pensions committee: Marwood. This time it paid the firm $80,000—in part for its help on an appropriation to permit Medicare reimbursement for myocardial profusion imaging. BMS knew a good thing when it saw it! This time Marwood disclosed that it had contacted the Senate to lobby for BMS. Wonder which senator it called first?

Marwood attracted two other clients in its first year. One was the Advanced Medical Technology Association, a huge trade association that represents manufacturers of medical devices (such as Medtronics), medical software, equipment, and supplies. According to Marwood's 2001 lobbying disclosure form, it was hired to:

Inform policy makers about Advanced Medical Technology and its membership.

This is not a joke.

Apparently, Advanced Medical spent $40,000 in order to have the Marwood Group introduce it to the very same federal agencies it had been lobbying for years on its own and through hired firms. To give you an idea of the scope of its lobbying practice, Advanced Medical spent more than $7 million in the two years before it hired Marwood. So why would it need to hire this young firm to tell the agencies about itself and its membership? Hmm . . .

Once again, the disclosure lists a number of "lobbyists"—but claims that it never contacted members of the House or Senate in the course of its work for Advanced Medical.

Do you see the pattern that's emerging here? Did Ted Kennedy, Jr., set up two meetings with his father in exchange for that $40,000 fee? What else could the firm have done for the money that one of Advanced Medical's other lobbying firms couldn't have done? Whatever services Marwood performed, Advanced Medical shelled out roughly $160,000 to the firm over a three-year period.

Advanced Medical has hired firms to lobby on health care issues, including Medicare and Medicaid reimbursement and appeals and legislation regarding medical devices, and on federal budget matters. Guess who is extremely influential on all those issues?

Advanced Medical is no stranger to Senator Kennedy's office. Its current executive vice president is David Nexon—who served as a senior policy adviser on health care for the senator before joining Advanced Medical Technology. After Nexon took over in 2005, Advanced hired another Kennedy Jr.–related lobbying firm, WayPoint Advisors, paying the firm $40,000 each year for the next two years to work on legislation dealing with medical devices and Medicare lab fees.

All told, Advanced Medical paid Marwood and WayPoint $200,000.

Here's a list of Marwood's federal lobbying clients, and their fees, from 2001 to 2004.

THE MARWOOD GROUP

2004 Total Lobbying Income: $490,000

Client	Total
Advanced Medical Technology Association	$40,000
Ascension Health	$80,000
Bristol-Myers Squibb	$80,000
Catholic Healthcare West	$40,000
Dubuis Health System	$50,000
Mpm Capital	$80,000
Omrix	$80,000
Synergy Research Group	$40,000
Trizetto Group	$0

2003 Total Lobbying Income: $260,000

Client	Total
Ascension Health	$40,000
B. Braun Medical	$60,000
Bristol-Myers Squibb	$80,000
Catholic Healthcare West	$40,000
Trizetto Group	$40,000

2002 Total Lobbying Income: $260,000

Client	Total
Advanced Medical Technology Association	$80,000
Ascension Health	$0
Catholic Healthcare West	$40,000
Oxford Health Plans	$80,000
Trizetto Group	$40,000

2001 Total Lobbying Income: $80,000

Client	Total
Advanced Medical Technology Association	$20,000
Bristol-Myers Squibb	$20,000
Trizetto Group	$40,000

Source: "2004 Total Lobbying Income," Center for Responsive Politics, www.opensecrets.org/lobby/firmsum.php?lname=Marwood+Group&year=2004.

According to federal lobbying disclosure records, after 2004 Marwood no longer participated in federal lobbying. That year, several unflattering stories were published detailing the unheard-of commissions—running into the millions of dollars—that Ted Kennedy, Jr., had received from labor unions and the City of Boston, with some help from his father. The Kennedys must have been anxious to avoid further stories of the kind.

Yet the fact is that although Marwood had officially closed down its lobbying operations in 2004, it hadn't gone out of business. Marwood's clients simply migrated to another Kennedy Jr.–related entity, Waypoint Advisors.

When Waypoint filed its first lobbying disclosure in mid-2005, it listed the same address, phone number, and lobbyist—and, coincidentally, the same clients—as Marwood. So why did Waypoint suddenly take the place of Marwood? Was it to distract attention from the connection between health care lobbying work and Ted Kennedy, Jr.?

By the end of the year, Waypoint Advisors had moved to a new address, listed a new phone number, and disclosed several new lobbyists.

Here's a list of Waypoint's lobbying clients for 2005 and 2006:

WAYPOINT ADVISORS, LLC

2005 Total Lobbying Income: $280,000

Client	Total
Advanced Medical Technology Association	$40,000
Alkermes	$0

Client	Total
Ascension Health	$80,000
Bristol-Myers Squibb	$80,000
Catholic Health East	$0
Dubuis Health System	$80,000
Trizetto Group	$0

2006 Total Lobbying Income: $380,000

Client	Total
Advanced Medical Technology Association	$40,000
Alkermes	$80,000
Ascension Health	$80,000
Bristol-Myers Squibb	$80,000
Catholic Health East	$0
Catholic Healthcare West	$0
Dubuis Health System	$80,000
GlobeImmune	$20,000
Trizetto Group	$0

Source: Center for Responsive Politics, www.opensecrets.org.

Anything about those lists look familiar? Did you notice that Waypoint's clients are the same firms that used to retain Marwood? Just as it had once turned to Marwood for help on Medicare reimbursements, now BMS looked to Waypoint to handle the issue—and added the Prescription Drug Access Program to its wish list.

All these issues, of course, involved matters before Senator Ted Kennedy's committee.

In 2006, pushed by Senators McCain and Obama, Congress began seriously exploring lobbying reforms—including a ban on lobbying by spouses and immediate family. Press reports began to focus on spouses who lobbied. It was a kind of scrutiny the Kennedys couldn't have welcomed; the writing was on the wall.

For whatever reason, Waypoint Advisors closed down its lobbying business at the end of 2006. But it still maintains a Washington office and can be reached at the phone number originally listed for the Marwood Group. What it does is anyone's guess.

Before the new reforms took effect in 2007, it was neither illegal nor a violation of the Senate ethics rules for a family member of a senator to be a lobbyist. It certainly should have been. Think about it: in some situations, paying a family lobbyist could be a way to funnel money to a senator. It's unlikely that any such thing happened here, but at the very least Ted Kennedy, Jr.'s, Marwood/Waypoint business created an appearance of impropriety. On an even more basic level, it just doesn't look good for the family of an elected official to benefit financially because of his ability to set up meetings in the Senate. If they can get paid five figures for setting up meetings, what else might they be tempted to offer for sale?

But things have substantially changed. The wide-ranging lobbying reforms Congress passed in 2006 included a ban on lobbying of a senator by a spouse or immediate family.

The new rules prohibit all "official contacts" between a senator or his personal, committee, or leadership staff and any spouse or immediate family member. That would make it hard for someone like Ted Kennedy, Jr., to "contact" his father about his clients' concerns. And it would make it impossible for any of his business entities to market their unique selling proposition: access to power.

These reforms were serious. Legislators also passed a Sense of the Senate stating that: "lobbyists should not use a family relationship to gain special advantage over other lobbyists." This meant one thing: it was time for Ted Kennedy, Jr.'s, firms to get out of the lobbying business. The days of family members profiting because their spouses or parents are influential senators are over.

Amen.

So now that his firm has been officially forced out of the public lobbying business, what does Ted Kennedy, Jr., do now?

It's hard to tell exactly, since Marwood doesn't have to disclose its clients or its business.

The Marwood Group goes out of its way to suggest that it has little to do with government relations. The company's current Web site—which is blocked to outsiders except for a very simple home page—describes it as a "healthcare advisory and financial services firm headquartered in New York

City with offices in Washington, DC and London." [334] That wording seems designed to leave the impression that Marwood is merely an investment firm that happens to do business with New York, D.C., and London locals.

But *Business Week* described the firm in a slightly different way in an entry updated as of 2008:

> The Marwood Group LLC is a business development and government re-lations consulting firm. The firm offers strategic marketing, joint-venture assistance, and government relations advisory services to healthcare service providers, pharmaceutical, bio-technology, medical devices, and financial service institutions and organizations. [335]

What's the difference? Well, according to *Business Week*, Marwood is an organization with a professional interest in what is happening in Washington.

Once it stopped registering as a lobbying firm, Marwood—and later Waypoint—had no obligation to disclose their clients. So we don't have any idea whom the firm now represents.

We do know that Marwood (and Waypoint) still maintains a Washington, D.C., office. The company's sparse Web site description suggests that the firm provides "asset management," "healthcare research," and health-care sales." But a series of news reports provided some insight into what Ted Kennedy, Jr., has been doing since his days helping out BMS.

Since Ted Jr.'s firm focuses on health care and private investments, most of his clients are still extremely interested in access to credible intelligence on new legislation that might affect the health care industry and the private equity field. And the younger Kennedy can still be helpful in this regard—because information is what it's all about.

As Jeff Young of *The Hill* noted in writing about the Marwood Group:

> If the currency of Washington is information, investment firms and lobby shops use the same coinage. Employees of investment firms and lobbying operations both seek to gain advance knowledge of legislation or federal regulations that could have a big impact on business.
>
> Though Marwood and Health Policy Source serve different markets—

investors versus lobbying clients—and have different motives—targeting investment dollars versus influencing public policy—they each perform similar services in the political intelligence realm and provide specialized, inside information to clients that pay dearly for it.[336]

For all practical purposes, the fact that Ted Kennedy, Jr.'s, firm is no longer a registered lobbying organization may not be what matters. He has unique access to the only person besides President Obama who will decide which provisions will be in the health care reform package that will come before Congress. This is the number one concern of the universe of pharmaceutical companies, hospitals, doctors, nurses, insurance companies, nursing homes, hedge funds, investors, and labor unions—all of whom want to know what's going on behind the scenes in the great battle for health care reform.

Whether or not he's a lobbyist, Ted Jr. is still a player in the Washington information game.

HITTING UP THE LABOR UNION PENSION FUNDS

In 2004, *Forbes* reported that Kennedy was soliciting labor union pension funds from pals of his father to invest in a private fund he was marketing:

> Edward M. Kennedy Jr. is quite the rainmaker. In less than two years the scion of the stalwart U.S. senator from Massachusetts has raised $100 million for the $325 million Intercontinental Real Estate Fund III, tapping the pension boards of the labor unions that have supported dad for years. Kennedy's Marwood Group will collect $1.2 million in fees over three years for his efforts.[337]

But here's the strange thing: The $1.2 million Kennedy Jr. made for getting the union's pension board to invest with the Intercontinental Real Estate Fund III didn't come from Intercontinental. It was charged to the unions!

Why would a union pay Kennedy's marketing fee in exchange for the privilege of investing its pension money? Wouldn't it make more sense for

Intercontinental—which had hired the marketers and gotten the money—
to pay that fee? A lot of union people asked the same question. After all,
pension funds don't normally pay for the marketing expenses of companies
that pitch them to get them to invest.

One of the board members of a teachers' pension fund invested in Intercontinental raised the issue:

> The $10 billion Chicago Teachers' Pension Fund, wooed by the younger
> Kennedy, spent months mulling whether to invest $35 million with Inter-
> continental. Jacob Silver, a 13-year veteran of the Chicago pension board,
> learned about Intercontinental over dinner with Kennedy at an Orlando
> conference last summer. Other Chicago trustees met with Kennedy, and in
> November Intercontinental made a formal proposal to the Chicago fund's
> board. The board's lawyer, Joseph Burns, noticed the marketing fee in the
> offering documents and alerted the board via e-mail. "It took a lot of nerve
> even to ask us for the money," says Silver. "Intercontinental hired him [Ken-
> nedy]—we didn't." He adds that the pension fund had never before been
> asked to pay extra for a fund's marketing costs.[338]

The Chicago board refused to pay the fee.

After all, the fee was backward. The company that's soliciting the investment should pay for the marketing, not the pension fund that contributes
its money.

So why did Kennedy Jr. hit up the union for the money?

Taking a page from the Bill Clinton playbook, Kennedy did it because
he could.

With Senator Edward Kennedy's power in labor circles—and his chairmanship of the labor committee—most unions wouldn't want to say no.
And who knows how many gave in and paid up?

When the dispute became public, Kennedy defended himself against
suggestions that he was trading on his family name. He suggested that he
viewed his work as a "public service," insisting "I am committed to building my company and providing the highest-quality service to my friends in
organized labor."[339]

Public service? Is he kidding? What kind of public service is it to take millions of dollars from working people's pensions to line your own pockets? Especially when the entire transaction is predicated on your relationship to your father? Remember, those "friends" Ted Jr. referred to are the same folks who are always looking for votes from their other good friend, Senator Ted Kennedy, chairman of the Senate committee on Health, Education, Labor and—what was that again? Oh, yes, and *Pensions.*

Do you see what's wrong with this picture? The son of a senator who's in a position to influence all legislation regarding unions and pensions is hitting up pension funds from the very unions who want favors from his father? And hitting them up for a controversial and unorthodox fee?

Do the unions have to worry that they might not get what they want— or even might see retaliation—if they don't succumb to the demands for enormous fees to come from the pensions of their workers?

It gets worse. The teachers' union incident wasn't an isolated one. In Senator Kennedy's home state of Massachusetts, the state's Pension Reserves Investment Management Board approved a $10 million investment in another Intercontinental fund marketed by Ted Kennedy, Jr. The pension board was chaired by the state's treasurer, Timothy Cahill. According to the *Boston Globe,* Senator Kennedy invited Cahill and a deputy, Doug Rubin, to a special barbecue dinner at his Hyannis Port oceanfront home.[340] Cahill told the *Globe* the pension issue was never discussed at the Kennedy party.

Of course not.

And Rubin says they didn't even know that Kennedy was involved in the deal.

Of course not.

Rubin even disputes the $200,000 fee Kennedy Jr. billed the State of Massachusetts, claiming that Kennedy had nothing to do with the deal.[341]

What's going on there? It's impossible to say.

Can't Ted Kennedy, Jr., find something to do that doesn't involve his father?

These days, Kennedy is still involved in private financing, including other health care ventures. And he's a prominent speaker at business conferences predicting what will happen on specific health care issues before the federal government—including the business ramifications of health care reform.

Once again, he's taking advantage of his closeness to the core of power on health care issues. And no doubt he's figured out ways to turn his position to his financial advantage.

It's a powerful position indeed. Information on the specifics of the health care plan in each sector of the industry can change markets, make or lose millions, and lead to big fees.

Ted Kennedy, Jr., has figured it all out.

It's all in a name.

10

STEALTH LOBBYISTS
The Former Congressional Leaders Who Secretly Influence Federal Policies and Spending

Please don't call them lobbyists. You might upset them.

They're *not* lobbyists! Not at all.

They call themselves something entirely different: "strategic advisers," for instance, or "policy advisers." Sometimes they're just "government relations consultants." But they're definitely not lobbyists.

Why would you even think such a thing? Simply because they work for lobbying firms to help get legislation passed in Congress?

Here's a helpful translation of this novel insider Washingtonspeak:

Terms like "strategic advisers," "policy advisers," and "government relations consultants" refer to the well-heeled people—usually high-level former government officials or relatives of powerful lawmakers or former presidential campaign gurus—who charge exorbitant fees to corporations, foreign governments and other foreign interests, labor unions, trade associations—and anyone else who will secretly pay them—to try to pass (or kill) special-interest legislation or get money for favorite projects.

Think that sounds a lot like what a lobbyist does? You're right. If it walks like a duck, talks like a duck, and acts like a duck, it's a duck. And if it acts like a lobbyist, is paid like a lobbyist, and works for a lobbying firm or to influence legislation, it's a lobbyist.

Except, of course, in Washington.

The lobbyists who wrote the legislation to regulate lobbying actually managed to protect their little game by carving out several rather ridiculous exceptions to the definition of a lobbyist. For example, if you don't actually call or write to a member of Congress or the Executive Branch or their staff to get legislation passed, you're not a lobbyist—even if you push for that legislation in plenty of other ways. You can be paid to offer advice on whether specific legislation should be passed or killed; sit with your client and draft legislation; prepare a list of talking points; create a list of all of the people who should be contacted to further the legislation; organize *other* people and groups to contact legislators; make appointments with key staff and legislators; speak to reporters about the merits of your client's position; track the progress of the bills; even draft revisions to bills and amendments.

None of that counts as lobbying. Not in Washington.

That's what happens when the goats are put in charge of guarding the garbage.

The "advisers" who thrive under these rules righteously claim that they're not lobbyists. In fact, they're *stealth lobbyists*—working to get legislation passed while these regulations shield them from the reporting and disclosure requirements of all other lobbyists, subverting the entire purpose of lobbying disclosure requirements.

It's time to out them.

They need to be treated like any other lobbyists—regardless of what professional name they give to their work.

They need to disclose what they're doing and how much they're paid.

Think about it: Why do we require quarterly and annual lobbying disclosure? So that we can monitor several things: who's trying to influence the people we elected to represent us; how much they're being paid to wield their influence over the legislative process; and what it is they're trying to achieve. But as inadequate as the lobbying disclosure requirements are—and they certainly are—the stealth lobbyists get around even those minimal legal requirements.

They've figured out how to game the system, and they've made it legal. For example, you're technically not a lobbyist if you devote less than 20 percent of your total working time on a client's matters to lobbying activities. In other words, you can engage in covered lobbying activities all you like—as long as you do so for only 19 percent of the time spent on the client's work.

Should serious regulation of lobbyists depend on the amount of time they spend on lobbying? If you're engaged in lobbying activities at all, you're a lobbyist and you should be regulated like one. End of story.

Why did the lobbying industry push for this crazy distinction? For one simple reason: because registered lobbyists are required to disclose what they are working on, who hired them, and how much they're being paid.

Unlike lobbyists, "strategic advisers" and "government relations consultants" keep their work secret. For them—and their clients—that's a big plus. Many corporate clients would prefer that no one know about the millions they spend to defeat health care reforms, for example, or to get an earmark passed that will benefit their business. That's where "strategic advisers" come in handy: as stealth lobbyists, they're very effective in producing results for their clients while keeping things conveniently under the radar.

Another reason these lobbyists want to avoid being regulated is the legal prohibition on lobbying for two years after leaving government service. Under our current lobbying regulations, former senators, cabinet members, and assistant secretaries, to mention just a few, are forbidden to lobby their colleagues for two years after leaving their influential government jobs. That's a sensible provision, designed to prevent government officials from cutting last-minute deals before leaving office in exchange for future work or favors and to prevent even the perception of conflicts of interest. But the folks in Washington have figured a way around it: under today's loose standards, all a departing official needs to do is join a lobbying firm and call himself an "adviser." Like cockroaches that develop immunity to every new roach spray, lobbyists find their way out of the regulatory scheme without missing a step.

Who are these clever stealth lobbyists? You'll recognize many of them. They're former everythings: senators, congressmen, even a former president (Bill Clinton is one stealth lobbyist who doesn't hesitate to pick up the phone and call Democratic leaders to push the programs that are important to groups that are paying him). Some are relatives of prominent politicians, such as Ted Kennedy, Jr. Others are close former presidential campaign operatives who want to preserve the option of joining the executive branch at a later date. Senate majority leaders are especially popular stealth lobbyists. Of the last four Senate majority leaders, three are stealth lobbyists: Tom Daschle, George Mitchell, and Trent Lott. The fourth, Bob Dole, is a full-fledged registered lobbyist. All four now work for lobbying firms. While it's not illegal, these "advisers" should all have to disclose their clients and the issues that they "advise" them about getting through Congress.

Former House leaders are doing well under this system, too—among them former majority leaders Richard Gephart and Dick Armey, both registered lobbyists.

It's obvious that leadership positions in Congress are good training spots for both lobbyists and stealth lobbyists. That's where they develop their skills—and, apparently, find their future clients. The ones they don't want us finding out about.

There are now 15,150 registered lobbyists in Washington. D.C. Among them, they were paid $3.24 billion in 2008.[342] They're a fast-growing population. But we have no idea exactly how many stealth lobbyists are out there or exactly how much they were paid. All we know is that they're out there doing their quiet and influential work and getting paid well—quite well—for their time.

That stealth technology really works!

Take a look at a few of our former congressional leaders:

TOM DASCHLE: STEALTH LOBBYIST PAR EXCELLENCE

Former Senate majority leader Tom Daschle is the quintessential stealth lobbyist. After his defeat in 2004, he joined the powerful Washington law firm and lobbying organization, Alston & Bird.

Daschle claims he's not a lobbyist. In fact, he's stated publicly that lobbying is "beneath" him.[243] The thing is, he's not a lawyer, either. So what's he doing working at a firm that only does lobbying and legal representation?

Take a guess.

He's a special adviser to Alston & Bird's public policy group. He was lured to the firm, in part, by another former Senate majority leader, Bob Dole, who sought him out after he lost his Senate seat. These former majority leaders sure stick together.

At the time, Dole apparently envisioned a hands-on lobbying role just like his own for Daschle. Because when Daschle joined the lobbying firm in 2005, Dole told the *Washington Post:* "He's got a lot of friends in the Senate, and I've got a lot of friends in the Senate, and, combined, who knows—we might have 51," Dole joked. "It's going to work fine. You need some flexibility and diversity. I don't think any successful firm is all Democrat or all Republican." [344]

Dole was obviously referring to the likelihood that the well-connected new bipartisan duo would be lobbying together to round up the fifty-one votes that would be needed to pass or kill a client's bill, amendment, or earmark. That's called lobbying. What else would he be expecting Daschle to do?

As another former Senate majority leader turned lobbyist, Trent Lott, explained it, "You can't be advising people on how to deal with Congress without, in effect, at least indirectly influencing Congress." [345]

And that's what Daschle does. He helps clients figure out the best way to influence Congress, directly or indirectly. There's a word for that: *lobbying.*

As the *Washington Post* observed about the former senator's new role: "Daschle is merely the latest high-profile former lawmaker to jump to the lucrative world of lobbying and law firm work in what has become an increasing trend." [346]

It seems as if everyone knew that Daschle was a lobbyist—except Daschle himself.

Oh, and one other important official: Barack Obama.

Obama had promised that he would neither appoint former lobbyists nor permit political appointees to work on contracts or regulations that related to their previous employment. Yet as soon as he became president-elect, Obama made Tom Daschle his first cabinet appointment, tapping him to be secretary of health and human services. Apparently all Daschle had to do was label himself an "adviser" and deny he was a "lobbyist," and that was enough to convince Obama.

But even Daschle couldn't sincerely claim there would be no conflict of interest because of the breadth of his former clients and the firm's and his own affiliations that relate to health care. First of all, Daschle had been a board member of the Mayo Clinic, an organization with major financial and programmatic interests in federal health care policy. Second, and more important, Daschle's employer, Alston + Bird, received more than $4.7 million in lobbying fees in 2008 from health care interests, including drug companies, nursing homes, nurses, clinical laboratories, and insurance companies. Finally, Daschle had been paid big bucks for speeches paid by health giants such as UnitedHealth Group.

Why didn't anyone on Obama's team raise a concern about Daschle's work for Alston & Bird? His status within the firm was no secret. His role as an important part of its "health care and legislative policy team" was highly touted by the firm. Here's how its Web site describes Daschle's role:

> Our health care legislative and policy team has the significant advantage of including two former U.S. Senate Majority Leaders—Senators Bob Dole and Tom Daschle—both resident in our Washington office and champions of many health care issues in their Senate Finance Committee and leadership roles. We have authoritative knowledge of the legislative and administrative policies and processes, and we work with the key decision-makers who impact health care providers, manufacturers, distributors, retailers and trade associations. We are dedicated policy professionals with proven success.[347]

Did the Obama folks really think there'd be no conflict of interest when Daschle's employer, Alston & Bird—and maybe Daschle himself—represented every possible aspect of health care? The firm's health care clients included:

- Nursing home coalitions that receive reimbursements from HHS and that depend on Medicare rates set by the agency

- Pharmacies that also receive federal reimbursements on prescription drugs

- Insurance companies, hospitals, doctors, and nurses, who will be seriously affected by the massive health care reform touted by Obama

It's a manifestation of Obama's hypocrisy that he actually nominated Daschle and planned to elevate him to be the White House health czar—

with an unprecedented office in the White House as well as at HHS. Why? Because, given Alston & Bird's portfolio of clients, it's hard to imagine that Daschle didn't spend most of his time there working on health care issues.

As the list of Alston & Bird's lobbying clients below indicates, $4.75 million—60 percent—of the firm's roughly $8 million in lobbying fees in 2008 were paid by clients with health care interests.

Even by Washington standards, that's enormous. And, trust us, those folks weren't looking for an "adviser" to give a PowerPoint presentation on how the committee system works, or to tell them who the key players are in the Senate, or to give some general lecture on health care reform. They were looking for success and influence. That's why they went to Alston & Bird in the first place.

And Alston & Bird very much understands what its clients want. The firm is proud of the fact that it counts such former congressional leaders among its members, publicly promoting their experience in Congress. Here's another candid description of their work on the firm's Web site:

> Distinguished attorneys and advisors with lifetimes of experience in how Washington works are the core of the Legislative and Public Policy Group, an esteemed collection of experts in the field which includes two former U.S. Senate Majority Leaders: Senator Bob Dole (R-KS) and Senator Tom Daschle (D-SD). . . . Senator Dole, the 1996 Republican candidate for president and former Senate Majority Leader who . . . has an enormous reservoir of knowledge and expertise—based on more than forty years at the pinnacle of political life in Washington—that has proven to be invaluable to Alston & Bird's clients . . .
>
> Senator Daschle brings extensive knowledge of public policy, trade and international issues. He also has keen insight into the areas of energy, financial services, telecommunications, health care and taxation.
>
> Senator Tom Daschle is a Special Public Policy Advisor in Alston & Bird's Washington, D.C. office, and is a member of the Legislative and Public Policy Group. As a non-attorney, Senator Daschle focuses his services on advising the firm's clients on issues related to all aspects of public policy with a particular emphasis on issues related to financial services, health care, energy, telecommunications and taxes. . . .
>
> With more than 25 years of service in the House of Representatives and

the Senate and 10 years as Senate Democratic Leader, Senator Daschle has played an instrumental role in the development of U.S. legislative and regulatory policy.[348]

If Daschle isn't a lobbyist, why would Alston & Bird promote his position in the firm's "legislative practice" so aggressively?

And Alston & Bird is involved in high-stakes legislation. To get a sense of the kind of legislative activity the firm engages in, look at some of the health care "successes" it describes on its site:

Representing clients with public policy concerns demands firsthand knowledge of the policy-making process and those in the position of making policy decisions. Alston & Bird has a proven track record of achieving policy success, as well as protecting the interest of clients. The following are a few recent examples of ways in which we delivered successfully for our clients:

- Secured authority for vaccine administration reimbursement for a Medicare Part D vaccine
- Protected numerous at-risk clients from billions of dollars in proposed payment reductions in recent Medicare legislation
- Developed strategy for a privately held company with annual revenues upward of $2 billion that sought new indications for approved medical imaging contrast agents and explored regulatory pathways for combination drug-device products that would deliver contrast agents
- Secured increased payment of more than $400 million for certain clients that provide Medicare services to beneficiaries with chronic health conditions
- Garnered positive legislative changes for two out of only three health care providers in a bill that extracted $50 billion in payment decreases to other health care providers[349]

These "successes" were no minor achievements. They involved highly complicated issues that required not just "policy advice" but knowledge, skill, and—most of all—connections. But wouldn't any such assignment create a conflict of interest for Daschle?

Did the Obama people ignore this glaring potential conflict of interest, or did they just not get it? It's hard to imagine that they failed to understand the problem.

To get a sense of just how pervasive the health care business is at the firm, here's a breakdown of the lobbying fees paid to Alston & Bird in 2008:

ALSTON & BIRD

2008 Total Lobbying Income: $8,080,000
Health Care Interests: $4,735,000

Client	Total	Sector
Abriesbott Laborato	$90,000	Health care
Administrative Tax Practice Coalition	$40,000	
Airtricity	$50,000	
Alliance for Quality Nursing Home Care	$270,000	Health care
American & Efird	$10,000	
American Association of Nurse Anesthetists	$120,000	Health care
American Clinical Laboratory Association	$90,000	Health care
American College of Gastroenterology	$200,000	Health care
American Hospital Association	$80,000	Health care
American Hospital Association	$0	Health care
American Orthotic & Prosthetic Association	$140,000	Health care
American Public Gas Association	$30,000	
American Public Transportation Association	$40,000	
Anthem Inc.	$0	Health care
Anthem Inc.	$0	Health care
APCO Worldwide	$10,000	
Assurant Inc.	$0	Health care
AT&T Inc.	$240,000	
Baker Tilly	$150,000	
Bayer Corp.	$120,000	Health care
Bose Corp.	$0	
Bracco Diagnostics	$0	Health care
Celgene Corp.	$50,000	Health care

Client	Total	Sector
CH Boehringer Sohn	$10,000	Health care
Checkfree Corp.	$20,000	
Chemed Corp.	$20,000	Health care
Cheyenne International	$60,000	
Cltn Against Domain Name Abuse	$120,000	
Cltn of Full Service Community Hospitals	$240,000	Health care
Covenant Health System	$50,000	Health care
CSL	$170,000	Health care
CVS/Caremark Corp.	$210,000	Health care
Deripaska, Oleg	$0	
Donohoe Companies	$40,000	
E on Climate & Renewables	$0	
Educap	$10,000	
Employee Deferred Compensation Fairness Coalition	$0	
Endo Pharmaceuticals	$0	Health care
Erickson Retirement Communities	$20,000	
Fidelity National Information Services	$110,000	
Fresenius Medical Care	$160,000	Health care
Fundamental Health	$90,000	Health care
Generic Pharmaceutical Association	$190,000	Health care
Genomic Health	$0	Health care
Giner	$40,000	Health care
Goodroe Healthcare Solutions	$0	Health care
Governor's Ethanol Coalition	$0	
Greenlight Capital	$30,000	
GUS	$230,000	
Health Management Association	$120,000	Health care
HealthSouth Corp.	$440,000	Health care
Horizon Wind Energy	$120,000	
Humana	$0	Health care
Integra Realty Resources	$30,000	
Interlease	$40,000	
Jer Partners	$240,000	
Kansas City Area Transit Authority	$0	

Client	Total	Sector
Kendall-Jackson Wine Estates	$20,000	
Kestrel Enterprises	$60,000	
Lackawanna County Board of Commissioners	$60,000	
LHC Group	$180,000	Health care
Lifescan	$120,000	Health care
Marine Polymer Technologies	$0	
Marmon-Herrington Co.	$0	
Mesa Power	$80,000	
Mylan Laboratories	$200,000	Health care
North American Carbon Capture & Storage Association	$0	
National Association for Home Care	$210,000	Health care
National Association of Behavioral Health	$180,000	Health care
National Electrical Manufacturers Association	$480,000	
National Geographic Education Fund	$40,000	
National Retail Federation	$105,000	
Physician Sales & Service	$0	Health care
Polymer Group	$0	
Porterfield & Lowenthal	$10,000	
Potomac Counsel	$40,000	
Prostrakan Inc.	$15,000	Health care
Renal Leadership Council	$330,000	Health care
Robinson Manufacturing	$0	
Roche Group	$120,000	Health care
Roho Group	$200,000	Health care
RoundPoint Capital Group	$30,000	
Rupari Food Services Inc.	$0	
S. Rothschild & Co.	$10,000	
Servipronto de El Salvador	$0	
Shared Health	$30,000	Health care
Silicon Graphics	$40,000	
St George Healthcare Center	$0	Health care
Syngenta Corp.	$0	
Tennessee Hospitals Association	$80,000	Health care

Client	Total	Sector
Treadwell Corp.	$40,000	
UC Group	$150,000	
US Exchange Holdings	$0	
US Oncology	$20,000	Health care
Vestas American Wind Technology	$210,000	
Viant Health Payment Solutions	$270,000	Health care
Virgin Galactic	$0	
Vision Service Plan	$200,000	Health care
Who Says?	$10,000	

Source: Center for Responsive Politics and lobbying disclosure documents.

Daschle's nomination was quickly withdrawn—but not because of his stealth-lobbying experience. Rather, it was because of his failure to declare $182,000 in income. But his financial disclosure form does provide an interesting window into the lucrative world of stealth lobbyists. For a complete view of his disclosure, see http://pfds.opensecrets.org/N00004583_2008_Nom.pdf.

According to Daschle's January 2009 report, during the previous two years he received $2.1 million in wages from Alston & Bird—*for part-time work!* And he sure must have delivered, because during the same time period he was also paid $2,108,760 by InterMedia, a private equity firm that supplied the $182,000 car and driver that caused his tax problems. It's not clear what he did for InterMedia, but it certainly paid well.

But that's not all. Daschle was a very busy man. In addition to the $4.2 million he collected in wages, bonuses, and consultant fees, during this period he made another $491,775 in director's fees for firms such as the Freedom Forum, BP, and others. And he took in another $390,000 for speech making.

This was quite a change for Tom Daschle. In 2004, as majority leader, Daschle made around $165,000 a year. It sure pays to have "congressional leader" on your résumé!

Daschle still contends he's not a lobbyist. But are we really supposed to believe that high-paying special interests paid millions to Daschle and Alston & Bird for civics lessons on the legislative process?

That seems doubtful. What such clients want—and what Alston & Bird explicitly offers—is access to power and decision makers. If what Daschle has been doing isn't considered lobbying, it should be.

It's time for the stealth lobbyists to stand up and be counted.

GEORGE MITCHELL, FRIEND OF DUBAI

The world of stealth lobbying has also been a professional home for another former Senate majority leader: George Mitchell. The man who's become Barack Obama's special envoy to the Middle East was, until recently, the global chairman of the law and lobbying firm DLA Piper.

DLA Piper is a megafirm with 1,500 lawyers in twenty offices, including Dubai. That particular office is significant because the sheikh of Dubai retained DLA Piper to help it get rid of an embarrassing lawsuit filed against Sheikh Mohammed Bin Rashid Al Maktoum, the leader of Dubai. It was a big deal for DLA Piper. After the firm collected more than $9.5 million in fees for legal work, lobbying, and damage control on the case, the suit was finally dismissed. (For a full discussion of this tawdry case, see our previous book, *Fleeced*, pp. 159–162.)

The lawsuit was brought in Miami on behalf of parents of young boys who alleged that the government of Dubai had regularly and systematically kidnapped small boys—starting at age three—from Bangladesh and Pakistan and forced them into virtual slavery as camel jockeys (only boys of very low weight and size can race on the camels). The suit alleged that the boys were kept in squalid quarters, never sent to school or given medical care, and not even toilet-trained; they were abandoned when they were too heavy to ride the camels.

After the United Nations began to report on trafficking in children in Dubai and the United Arab Emirates and the press began to cover the story about the kidnappings, enslavement, and horrid living conditions of the young camel jockeys, the sheikh suddenly started to be concerned about the poor little boys. It was time for reforms. Suddenly robots replaced the young boys as camel jockeys and institutional housing was established for the former camel jockeys. Schooling and medical care were provided.

Once the suit was filed, DLA Piper went into high gear for the sheikh. The firm's filings with the Justice Department's Office of Foreign Agent Registration list hundreds of calls and visits made to the State Department, the National Security Council, Secretary of State Condoleezza Rice, and Senator Hillary Clinton (whose husband was a business partner of the sheikh at the time), to try to get the U.S. government to intervene in the lawsuit. The lobbying was successful; the suit was eventually dismissed after the government notified the judge of its intention to intervene.

It pays to have friends in high places.

But is Mitchell another Obama appointment that ignores the enormous potential conflict of interest that exist because of the clients at his last job—at DLA Piper?

Once again, Obama seems oblivious to the implications of such an appointment.

As for Mitchell, he claims he had no involvement in the camel jockey matter and that he was not a lobbyist for Dubai. He's also claimed he never discussed the case with the sheikh when he visited Dubai. Still, on one visit to Dubai he gratuitously defended the United Arab Emirates' "efforts to rescue the camel jockeys." [350] Was he just personally interested in this issue or was it part of the service delivered for a client? And how likely is it that the chairman of the sheikh's American law firm would not have discussed a case that was so important to the sheikh that he paid almost $10 million in legal and lobbying fees to the firm to get it to pull out all the stops to fix the problem for him?

Two months after he left the firm to take his appointment as Middle East envoy, DLA Piper's own Web site still hyped Mitchell's—as well as former secretary of defense William Cohen's and former house majority leader Dick Armey's—Middle East bona fides:

Iraq Reconstruction

* * *

DLA Piper US and The Cohen Group have formed a joint Iraq Task Force to respond to increasing client interest in Iraq's reconstruction by *advising them on opportunities and risks associated with doing business in Iraq and the Middle East generally. Both firms have significant experience in the region, as well as in other areas undergoing transition, such as Afghanistan and Kosovo, and are already actively advising clients on matters relating to Iraq.* [emphasis added]

Senator George Mitchell *enjoyed an illustrious 15-year career in the US Senate, including six years as the Senate majority leader, and has since earned an unsurpassed reputation in the field of international diplomacy as an individual with an extraordinary ability to help resolve difficult international disputes. He is widely respected by US political figures in both parties and is known and trusted by many of the world's diplomatic and political leaders.*

Congressman Dick Armey *was recognized during his 18 years in national political office for his fairness and his ability to build consensus among parties with conflicting objectives . . .*

Secretary William Cohen *has had a long and distinguished career in Washington, including eight years as a Republican congressman and 18 years as a Republican senator, before being chosen by President Bill Clinton to lead the Department of Defense. As secretary of defense from 1997–2001, Secretary Cohen oversaw US military operations on every continent and held substantive meetings with foreign leaders in over 60 countries.*[351]

Long after Mitchell left DLA Piper for the State Department, the firm's Web site still refers to him as "Chairman Emeritus." It's clear that Mitchell is still a big deal at the firm—that even his name alone carries a lot of weight.

The firm also has other clients that may cause Mitchell problems. According to Bloomberg News, DLA Piper was paid another $2.29 in lobbying fees by clients focused on or headquartered in the Middle East, including two interested in "human rights" in Iran.[352] In the past, the firm was hired by the Embassy of Turkey. In December 2008, the firm registered as a foreign agent for the United Arab Emirates.[353] Based on public disclosures, DLA Piper also represented First Kuwait General Trading and Contracting for a $240,000 fee. The Lebanon Renaissance Institute paid a whopping $530,000 fee for lobbying services on "matters re: U.S. and Lebanon relations." (The nonlobbyist George Mitchell is the son of Mary Saad, who emigrated to the United States from Lebanon when she was eighteen years old.)

DLA Piper also has offices and clients in Egypt, Abu Dhabi, Kuwait, and Oman and an affiliation with a law firm in Saudi Arabia. Could this be a problem for the new Middle East envoy?

It's something to think about.

The sheikh, Dubai, and the Embassy of Turkey were formally withdrawn as DLA Piper clients in a filing with the Justice Department just two days after Obama's inauguration, when Mitchell's new post had already been announced. Was this an attempt by Mitchell to distance himself and the firm from their longtime clients?

But DLA Piper was registered as a foreign agent for the United Arab Emirates in December 2008.

Coincidentally, Mitchell visited both Turkey and Abu Dhabi on his second trip to the Middle East, in February 2009. This was doubtless helpful to DLA Piper and its clients in the region—even though Mitchell did nothing to benefit them. Just being able to point to the enormous influence of their former partner (who might someday return) is valuable.

As a foreign envoy for the U.S. government, George Mitchell has a staggering number of potential conflicts of interests. Just look at the amazing scope of DLA Piper's lobbying client list for 2008:

DLA PIPER LOBBYING CLIENTS AND FEES, 2008

Total Lobbying Income, 2008: $11,670,000

Client	Total
Akbar Nikooie (Iran human rights)*	**$80,000**
Amazon.com	$40,000
American Council of Life Insurers	$200,000
American International Group	$0
AON Corp.	$30,000
Arnouse Digital Devices	$0

Client	Total
Assn of Pool & Spa Professionals	$30,000
Bba Aviation Services Group	$10,000
BDO International	$0
BP	$0
Bristol-Myers Squibb	$20,000
Canfor Corp.	$880,000
Cape Wind Assoc	$120,000
Career Builder.com	$60,000
Charles Schwab & Co.	$40,000
Check Free Corp.	$0
Citizens Financial Group	$280,000
Comcast Corp.	$160,000
Corradino Group	$60,000
Dewey Square Group	$0
Diageo	$720,000
DLA Piper	**$100,000**
Dubai Group (re Foreign Investment)†	**$110,000**
Dubai—Executive Office	$480,000
eBay	$10,000
Emirates Investment & Development	**$90,000**
Experian Group	$60,000
Federal Home Loan Bank of Indianapolis	$230,000
First Kuwaiti Gen Trading & Contracting	**$240,000**
Gemological Institute of America	$80,000
General Cigar Holdings	$200,000
Genesee County Drain Commissioner	**$200,000**
Ghaemi, Saied (Iran human rights)	**$150,000**
Globe Metallurgical	$430,000
Greenhunter Energy	$190,000
Home Buyers Warranty	$30,000
I Have a Dream Foundation	$0
Independent Fuel Terminal Operators Association	$120,000
Ingersoll-Rand	$0
Interactive Gaming Council	$180,000
Irving Oil	$140,000

Client	Total
JD Irving	$0
Jones Lang LaSalle	$150,000
Kerzner International Resorts	$0
Kiawah Resort Association	$180,000
Kopin Corp.	$0
Kraft Foods	$410,000
Lane Hospitality	$0
Lebanon Renaissance Institute	**$530,000**
Lehman Brothers	$70,000
Limited Brands	$30,000
Lloyd's of London	$0
Lockheed Martin	$100,000
Magna Entertainment	$90,000
Maine Veterans Homes	$60,000
Marriott International	$0
Masefield America	$40,000
Medicines Co.	$1,530,000
Merrill Lynch	$210,000
Metropolitan Health Networks	$10,000
Morgan Stanley	$50,000
National Coalition on E-Commerce & Privacy	$190,000
National Employment Opportunities Network	$160,000
National Fraternal Congress of America	$200,000
Northville Industries Corp.	$70,000
Ocean Duke Corp.	$0
Parkwood Corp.	$60,000
PGA Tour	$150,000
Professional Warranty Service Corp.	$30,000
Qualcomm	$290,000
Raytheon Co. Military Funding	**$390,000**
Recording Industry Association of America	$120,000
Rite Aid Corp.	$160,000
Sanofi-Aventis	$160,000
SleepMed	$20,000
Snoqualmie Indian Tribe	$50,000

Client	Total
Snowsports Industries America	$30,000
Staples	$0
Starwood Hotels & Resorts Worldwide	$320,000
The Interactive Gaming Council	$190,000
TiVo	$0
Tokyo Electric Power	$0
Towson University	$30,000
Tronox	$10,000
Verizon Communications	$280,000
Vista Print	$10,000

*Boldface entries are Middle East–related clients.
†May include nonlobbying work.
Sources: Center for Responsive Politics; Foreign Agent Registration, U.S. Justice Department.

The almost $12 million in lobbying fees listed above represent only a minute part of the revenues to DLA Piper. With offices all over the Middle East, the company's legal fees from businesses in that area are obviously soaring.

All of which raises a simple question: Doesn't President Obama's new special envoy have an unquestionable conflict of interest—one that violates Obama's own rules?

ANOTHER MAJORITY LEADER TURNED LOBBYIST: TRENT LOTT

In late December 2007, the Washington political world was shocked when then-senator Trent Lott announced that he was resigning from the Senate. For decades, Lott had held a series of leadership positions in the Senate, including majority leader, minority leader, and whip. Several weeks after his resignation, he announced that he was forming a lobbying firm with another former senator, John Breaux.

By resigning in early January, Lott managed to circumvent the new lobbying law that prohibited members of Congress from actively lobbying for two years after they leave office. Since he resigned from the Senate days before the new law went into effect in January 2008, Lott was required to wait for only a year before he became a registered lobbyist.

In the meantime, Lott has followed in the footsteps of his fellow Senate leaders, becoming a stealth lobbyist. Here's the list of clients who have flocked to his new firm in its first year:

BREAUX LOTT LEADERSHIP GROUP

Total Lobbying Income, 2008: $8,045,000

Client	Total
Algenol Biofuels	$210,000
Association of American Railroads*	**$600,000**
AT&T	**$600,000**
Charter Brokerage	$50,000
Chevron Corp.	$75,000
ChevronTexaco	$450,000
Coalition for Patent Fairness	$100,000
DaVita	$100,000
Delta Air Lines	**$575,000**
Entergy Corp.	$450,000
FedEx	$300,000
JM Family Enterprises	$170,000
LHC Group	$100,000
National Association for Home Care	$135,000
Nissan North America	**$500,000**
Northrup Grumman	**$500,000**
Pharmaceutical Research and Manufacturers of America	$350,000
Plains Exploration & Production Co.	**$600,000**
Raytheon Co.	$225,000
Shaw Group	$370,000
Shell Oil	**$500,000**
Southern Shrimp Alliance	$300,000
TECO Energy	$100,000

Client	Total
Tyson Foods	$225,000
United Space Alliance	$300,000

*Boldface entries are clients paying Breaux Lott $500,000 or more.
Source: Center for Responsive Politics.

What's amazing is the number of Breaux Lott clients who paid more than half a million dollars in fees in their first year of representation (indicated in the entries that are bolded in the chart above). And these are all heavy-duty clients: AT&T, Shell Oil, Delta Air Lines. Compare this, for example, with Daschle's firm: not one of Alston & Bird's clients paid the firm half a million dollars or more in a single year. And even the megalobbying firm DLA Piper had only three clients that paid half a million or more. Yet seven Breaux Lott clients paid the big bucks.

In its initial year, Breaux Lott made just as much as Alston & Bird. Next year should be even better.

The new boys in town are shaking things up.

So far, Trent Lott himself has not registered as a lobbyist, but his one-year prohibition is now up. So let's watch and see whether he becomes a publicly declared lobbyist or remains a stealth lobbyist.

BOB LIVINGSTON, THE DEFINITELY NOT STEALTH LOBBYIST

Former senators aren't the only ones raking in the big lobbying bucks. After leaving office, members of the House of Representatives are equally prone to delving into the lobbying universe.

Take Bob Livingston, the former House majority leader. He's not a stealth lobbyist. To the contrary: he's an in-your-face, way-out-there lobbyist, making deals wherever he can.

Livingston resigned from Congress after he was outed for his extramarital affairs, which were publicized right after he criticized Bill Clinton about Monica Lewinsky. (What a coincidence!) Instead of becoming speaker of the House, as he had anticipated, he became a major lobbyist.

Here's a summary of his clients and fees:

Livingston Group Lobbying Income, 1999–2008

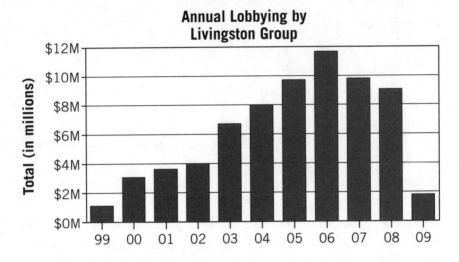

Annual Lobbying by Livingston Group

LIVINGSTON GROUP

Total Lobbying Income, 2008: $9,040,000

Client	Total
3001	$70,000
Accenture	$300,000
Anglo-American	$150,000
Apex Silver Mines Corp.	$340,000
Applied Signals Technology Corp.	$220,000
Arcadian Networks	$120,000
Ashland	$400,000
Aztec Software	$80,000
BearingPoint	$160,000
Bohannan Huston	$120,000
Boys Town	$20,000
Brunswick Corp.	$0
Case Western Reserve University	$240,000
Caspian Alliance	$0
City of Carbondale, IL	$80,000

Client	Total
City of New Orleans, LA	$130,000
Council for Democratic Iran	$340,000
Daybrook Fisheries	$10,000
Defense Solutions	$0
DMC Consultors/Morgan City Harbor	$40,000
Energy Conversion Devices	$90,000
Erickson Air-Crane	$180,000
European Aeronautic Defence and Space Company	$200,000
Federal Judges Association	$20,000
Girl Scouts of the USA	$160,000
Goodyear Tire & Rubber	$240,000
GovBiz Advantage	$20,000
Greater New Orleans	$30,000
Greater New Orleans	$10,000
Hoveround Corp.	$20,000
ICF International	$130,000
Innovative Emergency Management	$200,000
Inspec Foams	$20,000
International Shipholding Corp.	$120,000
Investment Co. Institute	$200,000
Jacobus Tenbroek Memorial Fund	$140,000
Lend Lease Corp.	$600,000
Link Plus	$160,000
Livingston Group	$40,000
Livingston Group	$70,000
Livingston Group	$200,000
Marine Desalination Systems	$0
Mayo Clinic	$120,000
Merscorp	$140,000
MWH Global	$30,000
National Capitol Concerts	$10,000
National Association of State Universities and Land-Grant Colleges	$160,000
New Orleans Business Council	$80,000
Oracle Corp.	$330,000

Client	Total
Peter D. Sahagen & Stephen Garofalo	$50,000
PKD Foundation	$70,000
Plaquemines Parish, LA	$200,000
PLM Group/ITAA	$50,000
PLM Group/Miles Automotive Group	$10,000
Port of New Orleans	$80,000
Raytheon Co.	$90,000
Rolls-Royce	$120,000
Rush System for Health	$320,000
Sasol North America	$450,000
Skadden, Arps et al.	$10,000
Southern Shrimp Alliance	$80,000
State of Florida	$70,000
Summit Communications/Eligio Cedeno	$50,000
Thomas More College	$80,000
Tulane University of Louisiana	$100,000
University of New Orleans	$50,000
U.S. Vets	$0
Verizon Communications	$210,000
Verizon Communications	$30,000
Warren L. Green & Associates	$110,000
Waterways Council	$190,000
West Jefferson Medical Center	$80,000

Livingston's client list is the best evidence of just how important leadership positions are to the lobbying industry, He's everywhere!

OBAMA CAMPAIGN GURU BECOMES "ADVISER" TO LOBBYING FIRM

Shortly after President Obama's inauguration, Matthew Nugen, former national political adviser to the Obama campaign, was hired by Ogilvy Government Relations, one of the top lobbying firms in D.C., as a "strategic adviser."

Nugen insists he's not a registered lobbyist in his new job at the mega-lobbying firm, which does nothing but lobby Congress and the administration. Instead, he says that his role will be "to help my clients interpret the thinking of the administration and what's coming down the pike."[354]

After the Democratic National Convention, Nugen was assigned to travel with then vice presidential candidate Joe Biden. (The ever-talkative Biden must have been a great source of information!)

Nugen hit the ground running. According to Politico.com, Nugen immediately began "meeting Ogilvy clients and sharing his insight into the new administration and the thinking of its senior aides and policy advisers."[355]

That's Washingtonspeak for using his contacts and friendships with former Obama campaign aides who now work in the administration to find out what's going on inside the White House—and sell that information to lobbying clients outside the White House.

That's the expanded definition of what a "strategic adviser" does.

Ogilvy has plenty of clients who might be interested in the observations of Nugen, the firm's well-connected nonlobbyist. Last year, the firm received $20 million in lobbying fees! Its clients included banks, hedge funds, and oil and pharmaceutical companies. Some of its illustrious clients, which will be seeking the support of the Obama administration, were:

OGILVY GOVERNMENT RELATIONS

Client	2008 Fee
AIG	$150,000
AIG shareholders	$90,000
Blackstone	$2,820,000
Citigroup	$320,000
Pfizer	$320,000
United Health Care	$300,000
American Petroleum Institute	$320,000
Chevron	$580,000
Credit Suisse	$140,000

Client	2008 Fee
European Airbus	$240,000
Fannie Mae	$80,000
Hedge Fund Managers	$140,000
Visa	$200,000
National Rifle Association	$380,000
Association of International Auto Manufacturers	$120,000
Poker Players Alliance	$480,000

Source: "Ogilvy Government Relations," Center for Responsive Politics, www.opensecrets .org/lobby/clientsum.php?lname=Ogilvy+Government+Relations&year=2008.

As the above indicates, Ogilvy represents plenty of banking and credit card interests, pharmaceutical firms, oil companies, hedge funds, car manufacturers, and health care clients—to name just a few.

What are they looking for in a firm like Ogilvy?

The banks are constantly seeking handouts from the government; they'll want to know what the administration is thinking. Hedge funds and private equity funds are hoping to keep Congress and Obama from taxing their investors like the rest of American workers, instead of letting them pay only 15 percent in taxes. (Did you notice how the Obama stimulus bill avoided that issue?) The French aeronautics firm Airbus is trying to make sure a huge U.S. government contract goes its way. The oil companies want to limit support for alternative energy sources. And so on.

Get the picture?

The nonlobbyists at Olgivy do. And you can bet they'll keep the information flowing.

ACTION AGENDA

The first thing we must do is press for new legislation that requires *all* employees of lobbying firms who have any contact with a client—other than secretarial staff—to register as lobbyists and disclose who they are "advising," just as the "official" lobbyists must do.

We need to know what these people are doing.

We should also require all members of Congress and all congressional staff to disclose all meetings with lobbyists and the purpose of the meeting. This can be done on a Web site established by each member and each committee.

New York's Senator Kirsten Gillibrand pledged to list her full schedule in detail on her Web site; it was an admirable promise, but some reports suggest she's now listing only public meetings. That defeats the purpose: *all* such meetings, including private conferences, should be listed.

We pay our representatives to do the people's work. We have the right to know what they're up to.

III

HOW SPECIAL INTERESTS CAUSE CATASTROPHE

11

THE SHEER CHUTZPAH OF COUNTRYWIDE FINANCIAL EXECUTIVES

In his classic best seller *The Joys of Yiddish*, Leo Rosten defined the word "chutzpah" as:

> gall, brazen nerve, effrontery, incredible "guts," presumption plus arrogance such as no other word and no other language can do justice to.[356]

Is there any better description for the astounding decision by a number of former high-level executives at Countrywide Financial to set up a new business, Private National Mortgage Acceptance Company, known as PennyMac—a joint venture with the investment management firms Black-Rock and Highfields Capital Management? PennyMac is buying "delinquent home mortgages that the government took over from other failed banks, sometimes for pennies on the dollar. They get a piece of what they can collect."[357]

PennyMac—even the name seems like a cruel insider joke. What does it stand for, **P**enny **M**ortgages **A**fter **C**ountrywide?

Countrywide Financial, of course, is the company blamed by many for the subprime mortgage crisis that detonated the current global financial meltdown. As the largest mortgage company in the United States, Countrywide lost $1.6 million in the final months of 2007 because of the huge number of mortgage defaults on its creative mortgages, which left hundreds of thousands of people unable to pay. During that same period, the company paid megamillion-dollar bonuses to its top executives.

And now the former architects of the Countrywide debacle are buying distressed mortgages from failing banks at the lowest possible prices, working out affordable deals with home owners, and making millions on them by turning around and selling the mortgages once again. But this time they're selling *performing* mortgages, which, of course, are more valuable. They can easily make the mortgages work now. Why? Because they bought them for so little money and can afford to give the borrowers a good deal. For example, PennyMac recently bought $558 million of home mortgages from the FDIC, which acquitted the notes after the collapse of the First National Bank of Nevada. PennyMac paid $42.2 million, averaging 30 to 50 cents on the dollar. It keeps 20 cents on every dollar that it initially recovers, with an increase to 40 cents down the line.[358]

So now some of the same Countrywide folks who benefited the most from the heady days of the precollapse mortgage market are now also benefiting from the traumatic downturn that Countrywide helped to create. Now, that's chutzpah.

Commenting on PennyMac, *New York Times* columnist Gail Collins put it best: "It's like Jeffrey Dahmer selling body parts to a clinic."[359]

PennyMac is headed by Stanford L. Kurland, who was president of Countrywide until September 2006. Kurland used to be the number two man at the company, second only to CEO Angelo Mozilo. Kurland is considered to be one of the architects of the creative mortgages at Countrywide. He escaped and sold $200 million worth of stock before the company crashed a few months later. He's brought along some of his old pals: David M. Walker, the former chief lending officer for Countrywide Bank, a subsidiary of Countrywide Financial, who will be the chief credit officer at PennyMac; Mark P. Suter, the former chief strategy officer for Countrywide Bank, who will be chief portfolio strategy officer at PennyMac; and Michael L. Muir, the former chief financial officer for Countrywide Bank, who will be chief capital markets officer.[360]

Kurland claims that he left Countrywide before the problems began and had nothing to do with the bad mortgages that destroyed the company. But not everyone agrees with him. As Eric Lipton notes in the *New York Times*, "lawsuits against Countrywide raise questions about Mr. Kurland's portrayal of his role. They accuse him of being at the center of a culture shift at Countrywide that started in 2003, as the company popularized a type of loan that often came with low 'teaser' interest rates and that, for some, became unaffordable when the low rate expired."[361]

The teaser rates at the beginning of a loan were sometimes even below 1 percent for adjustable-rate mortgages. According to a lawsuit filed by California attorney general Jerry Brown, "Countrywide obscured the negative effects—including rising rates, prepayment penalties and negative amortization—which would inevitably result from making minimum payments or trying to refinance. The company misrepresented or hid the fact that borrowers who obtained its home loans—including exploding adjustable rates and negatively amortizing loans—would experience dramatic increases in monthly payments."[362] Many of the defaulted mortgage loans at Countrywide began with those teaser interest rates. When the interest rates suddenly increased dramatically, the home owners were, understandably, in no position to pay.

But that was then, this is now, and the PennyMac folks don't look back. Instead, they're aggressively focused on making money on the failed mortgages they own. According to the *New York Times*, the company has telemarketers working fifteen hours a day trying to speak to the overdue home owners whose mortgages they now own. The results range from a workout to the filing of a foreclosure for those who won't play ball with them.[363] So it's a good deal for PennyMac either way.

Kurland is highly optimistic about the future profits of his new venture. One of his partners, Jonathon S. Jacobson, a cofounder of Highfields Capital Management, seems to be looking forward to more mortgage losses to scoop us. Sounding rather like a vulture, Johnson told Reuters of the bright future he foresees for PennyMac: "whole loan losses have barely begun to materialize" so far, he says, but he expects the losses to soar over the next two to three years. When that happens, "PennyMac will be extraordinarily well positioned as both a buyer and servicer of these assets."[364]

Translation: As more banks and mortgages fail, PennyMac stands to make a killing.

Kurland and his team have even boasted that PennyMac can teach the government a thing or two about how to solve the housing and financial crisis, calling their operation a "role model." [365]

Talk about chutzpah.

Too bad they weren't thinking about becoming role models when they were luring in all those people who bought untenable mortgages during their tenure at Countrywide.

12

PAY TO PLAY
No-Bid Contracts Exchanged for Campaign Cash

In many states, there seems to be a very close correlation between companies that are awarded huge no-bid contracts by governors and those that contribute big bucks to the campaigns of those same governors.

It's happening all over.

It's called pay to play, and it means just what it sounds like: if you want to play in the highly lucrative state contract system, you have to pay.

That means making campaign contributions—big ones. And, for the most part, it means corruption.

According to Craig Holman, a public interest lobbyist for *Public Citizen*, "pay-to-play" is an "act of official corruption or the appearance of public corruption. Even where there is no agreement between contractor and government official, large donations from people who win contracts raise an appearance of a problem with the public." [366]

And that appearance of a problem is spreading through statehouses all over the country.

Take a look at Pennsylvania, where Democratic governor Edward Rendell awarded a no-bid contract to advise the Pennsylvania Housing Finance Authority to David Rubin, the head of CDR Financial Products, after Rubin made $40,000 in campaign contributions to Rendell. [367]

Rubin has been in the news lately. It seems his company was awarded another no-bid contract in New Mexico—for $1.5 million, after making a $100,000 contribution to Governor Bill Richardson's campaign committees.[368]

Rendell, Richardson, and Rubin all deny any wrongdoing. But Rubin's company is under investigation by a federal grand jury in New Mexico to determine whether there was, in fact, a pay-to-play arrangement.

We've all watched the drama in Illinois, where the wacky former governor, Rod Blagojevich, allegedly tried to sell Barack Obama's old Senate seat. He also granted a $300,000 state contract to suggest minority contractors for state highway projects.[369] Guess who got that one? Roland Burris, the guy Blago named to Obama's Senate seat, perhaps because Burris had given Blagojevich $20,000 in campaign donations.[370]

And it's not just governors who are involved in these questionable contracts; the practice continues throughout the food chain of elected officials, from congressmen to attorney generals to mayors.

Several years ago, the Department of Homeland Security awarded a no-bid contract to the American Association of Airport Executives, its Transportation Security Clearinghouse division, and Daon, an Irish biotech company. Tom Ridge, the former director of Homeland Security, was a director of Daon. The contract, potentially worth hundreds of millions of dollars, assigned the groups the task of issuing secure identification cards to millions of transportation workers.

But it wasn't Ridge who pushed for the contract. It was Congressman Hal Rogers (D-KY) who sponsored an earmark for the project. Not everyone shared Rogers's glowing view of the American Association of Airline Executives. According to the *New York Times*, questions were raised by critics of the contract about "how the association, with little experience in high-technology secure identifications and biometrics, could handle such a task."[371]

How did Rogers get interested in the issue? Maybe it happened when he and his wife went on a free trip to Ireland that was cosponsored by the association and Daon. Or maybe it was on one of the many other trips Rogers and his wife took on the association's dime—trips that cost a total of almost $70,000.[372] Or maybe it was the $18,000 in campaign contributions.[373] (For more information about Rogers's many travels at the expense of special interests he befriends, see our book *Outrage*.)

After all these kindnesses, Congressman Rogers was only too happy to do a favor for a friend.

But he's not alone. Both parties participate in pay-to-play schemes.

The City of Indianapolis was trying to raise cash by selling off 1,100 properties—including police stations, maintenance buildings, and parks. The *Indianapolis Business Journal* reported that the Republican mayor of the city, Gregory A. Ballard, gave the contract to a guy who had given $25,000 to the campaigns of Indiana's Republican governor, Mitch Daniels, and who had hired a lawyer who is the mayor's "right-hand man."[374] That's what friends are for!

Sometimes you need special qualifications to get your hands on the goodies you want. Qualifications, for instance, such as being married to then–Michigan state attorney general Jennifer Granholm, now the state's governor. Her husband, Daniel Mulhern, got nearly $300,000 in no-bid "leadership training" contracts from Wayne County while Jennifer was the county's chief attorney.[375]

Want to invest $25,000? You may be too late. Before he was removed from office, you should have given the money to Rod Blagojevich. He knew how to take care of campaign contributors. As the *Chicago Tribune* reports, three-quarters of the 235 people who donated that much or more to his campaigns received special favors, such as "lucrative state contracts, coveted state board appointments, or favorable policy and regulatory actions."[376]

No-bid contracts are the latest gravy train for state and local governments throughout the country. There is no reliable estimate of the scope of the practice, but it's making negative headlines from New Mexico to South Dakota to Pennsylvania to Indiana to Illinois to Michigan.

Most government contracts are awarded only after closely monitored competitive bidding. Typically, those who want the business submit sealed bids. The public officials shepherding the process aren't supposed to confer with the bidders; they are supposed to open all the bids at the same time, and the lowest bidder gets the contract. Obviously, there have to be exceptions: federal law, for example, allows no-bid contracts where only one firm is able to do the work, in an emergency, or where one firm demonstrates that it has "a unique and innovative" concept for the work.[377]

But give a politician a fat piece of candy like a no-bid contract to dole out, and chances are good that he'll give it to his favorite—and a politician's favor usually rests on those who donate generously to his campaign.

But wait, you may be thinking, *isn't that illegal?* It depends on the transaction. If the public official specifically links the donation to his campaign to the contract, he'll wind up in prison. But if all that happens is that (first) A gives to B's campaign and then (second) B awards A a no-bid contract, it can be hard for prosecutors to prove any linkage between the two events. If both sides use winks and nods instead of words—and nobody's videotaped or recorded—the deal can be hard to prosecute.

Such pay-to-play shenanigans may not be illegal, but that doesn't mean they're not corrupt. And corruption is eating away at our faith in democracy, a catastrophe in the making.

We can't sit back and wait for public prosecutors to police our system. It's too hard to prove a corrupt arrangement in court. But we can use publicity to identify the culprits and bring them before the court of public opinion.

You'll notice that this chapter goes after both Democrats and Republicans. That's because neither party has a monopoly on corruption—and both could use a thorough housecleaning.

Let's look in greater detail at the larceny going on right under our noses:

SENATOR ROLAND BURRIS (D-IL)

For example, there's the man whom former Illinois governor Rod Blagojevich appointed to fill Obama's seat in the Senate: Roland Burris. Blago appointed Burris after federal prosecutors taped him trying to sell the seat to suitors such as Congressman Jesse Jackson, Jr., and others. Blagojevich got the right to name Burris, despite his pending prosecution, because the Illinois legislature refused to pass a bill requiring a special election to fill the seat—probably because they were worried about a Republican victory—and because it took its sweet time impeaching him and ousting him from office.

Did Burris pay for his seat? Many times over. Roland Burris, a former Illinois attorney general, has been on the giving and receiving end of dubious favors for more than a decade.

One thing about Burris is for certain: he gave as good as he got!

He gave: When he was attorney general, Burris doled out no-bid contracts like any good Chicago pol. In 1992, his office signed about $4 million in such deals for outside legal help.[378] More than half that amount—$2.25 million—went to lawyers and firms that had anted up and donated to Burris's attorney general campaign or the main Democratic fund-raising committee.[379] After leaving his seat as state attorney general, Burris kept his position as a top money source for Governor Blagojevich, hosting a fund-raiser for him and donating, through various companies, at least $20,000 to his campaigns.[380]

He gave, but he also made sure he got. As a private citizen (and generous campaign donor), Burris received more than $1 million in no-bid consulting contracts from Illinois state government agencies controlled by the governor.[381] The cushiest one was a $290,000 contract to scour the state looking for firms that might qualify for state Department of Transportation contracts under the affirmative action program.[382]

Companies from all over the United States hired Burris to arrange state business for them. A Philadelphia firm, Loop Capital Markets, received more than $750,000 in pension bond business after it hired Burris for $5,000 per month to steer projects its way.[383]

Another company, ACS Healthcare Solutions, hired Burris for $240,000 and landed an $18 million contract with the Cook County public health system to help collect unpaid bills. But ACS ran into big trouble in Las Vegas, where it was named in the indictment of a public hospital official. That led the county to pull the contract.[384]

More fortunate was Central DuPage Hospital, which hired Burris and his partner, Fred Lebed, to win "approval from state hospital regulators to build a $140 million cutting-edge cancer treatment center, even though the board had initially opposed the idea and approved building a similar facility just a few miles away."[385] But Central DuPage got the approval it sought by arguing that there "was room for more than one proton center in the Chicago region [even though] there are only five such facilities operating in the United States."[386]

Probably Burris's most suspect transaction came as he left private life to become state attorney general. His old law firm, which had no history of working for the state, gave him a "buyout" of $100,000, allegedly for work he had done before he became attorney general.[387] Once in office, Burris turned around and gave his old firm $436,000 of no-bid state legal work![388] Nothing like a nice clean quid pro quo!

Most governors try to appoint men and women who mirror their philosophy of government. Blagojevich sure found his man.

FORMER GOVERNOR ROD BLAGOJEVICH (D-IL)

Of course, Burris's activities are only the tip of the iceberg called Rod Blagojevich, whose name has become a national synonym for political corruption. Blagojevich had been a colorful regional figure for years, but he really achieved national prominence late in 2008, when FBI wiretap tapes were released that revealed him crassly evaluating how much he should get paid for appointing someone to President-elect Obama's Senate seat.

But why were the feds tapping Blago's phone in the first place? Why had they bugged his office? The wiretaps were there because Blagojevich was under investigation for his long history of selling contracts to political donors. Selling the U.S. Senate seat was just his latest ploy.

BLAGO'S CORRUPTION

- The *Chicago Tribune* reports that a former agency director for Blagojevich admitted to federal prosecutors that he "bought his job, in part, with two $25,000 donations" to the Blagojevich campaign.[389]

- A Chicago engineering firm "wrote two $25,000 checks in 2006 and, within months won $25.4 million in new state business."[390]

- A Chicago pharmacist said that "his $25,000 check to the governor's campaign was the price tag for fixing a critical state audit of his drug store."[391]

- Six months after a Chicago attorney, Myron Cherry, gave the Blagojevich campaign the second of two $25,000 checks, "the state insurance agency hired his law firm as part of a team to negotiate a multi-state legal dispute over alleged fraud by insurance companies for which his firm was paid $900,000 in legal fees."[392]

- A Chicago architectural firm gave $25,000 and got a contract to revamp the "oases" on the Illinois Thruway. Then, when the contract got mired in bureaucracy, the firm kicked in another $50,000. After that, the project went ahead smoothly.[393]

- Ali Ata, the director of the Illinois Finance Agency, pled guilty to lying to federal prosecutors when he denied that his $50,000 campaign donation was a reason for his getting the $127,000 job.[394]

- ACS State & Local Solutions donated $25,000 and got $79 million in contracts, including one for "$15 million to oversee the disbursement of child-support checks."[395]

We'll probably never know the full scope of his corruption, but what we do know makes quite a story.

And on and on. If Blagojevich had a job or a contract within his power to award, it seems, it was available in exchange for campaign contributions. The price? Twenty-five thousand dollars—not a princely sum, but a little here and a little there, and soon you're talking about real money!

GOVERNOR ED RENDELL (D-PA)

At least they caught Blagojevich. As of this writing, another governor is still in office despite awarding no-bid contracts to special friends, former colleagues, and donors. Governor Ed Rendell of Pennsylvania, a former Democratic National Committee chairman, has come under withering media criticism for giving out legal and consulting contracts without bidding, but not without demanding favors from the recipients.

There was so much pressure in the state that Rendell finally signed a bill to ban pay-to-play contracts in Pennsylvania in March 2009.

But before the well dried up, Rendell took the process of fleecing the public one big step further when he started paying money to his friends and political allies—not only without bidding but without any contract at all! And guess what? The firm that got the contractless money was the very one where Rendell had worked before he became governor!

The Ballard Spahr law firm, where Rendell worked, got $773,000 from the state Department of Transportation without a contract. Why was there no bidding? Why no contract? According to Rendell, it was an emergency: the document Ballard had to sign to get paid after it had finished the work said that it had to work without a contract "due to the extreme urgency of the work required." [396]

What was the cause of such "extreme urgency"? A flood? A tornado? Some other natural disaster? No. It was because the governor wanted to sell off the Pennsylvania Turnpike to private business and wanted his old law firm to do the lucrative legal work. As the *Philadelphia Bulletin* noted, "the turnpike is in no danger of disappearing or being unable to continue operations." [397]

Of course, the emergency no-bid provision nicely eliminated the unpleasant possibility that another firm might get the work. But that's surely just a coincidence—right, Governor?

And what lucrative work it was! Ballard's chairman, Arthur Makadon, billed the state $637.50 per hour for his services, and his partners Kenneth M. Jarin and Adrian R. King, Jr., billed it $531.25 and $403.75 an hour, respectively.[398] (By the way, Ken Jarin's wife is Robin Wiessmann, who until January 2009 controlled the Pennsylvania Department of the Treasury— the office that approved the payments to Ballard, her husband's firm. All in the family!)

In all, the Ballard firm made three quarters of a million dollars before it finally signed a contract with the state on May 24, 2007, for its future services. Since then, Ballard has billed an additional $2 million for its legal work on privatization.[399]

But that wasn't the end of it: Ballard got even more money. John Estey, a Ballard chairman and Rendell's former chief of staff, is the chairman of the Delaware River Port Authority, a state agency. DRPA has paid the Ballard firm nearly $3 million in legal fees since Rendell became governor, making it the largest outside legal contractor.[400] Before Rendell was elected, the *Philadelphia Bulletin* reported that Ballard received only $25,000 in legal work from DRPA.[401]

Why is Rendell so good to his old buddies at the Ballard firm? Nostalgia? Not likely. The generous campaign donations he gets from the firm's leaders might have more to do with it. The list of Ballard's donations to the governor is quite impressive:

MONEY GOV. RENDELL GOT FROM HIS OLD LAW FIRM

- Ballard Spahr itself gave Rendell $481,000.[402]

- Ballard Spahr chairman Arthur Makadon donated $87,500 to Rendell's campaigns.[403]

- Partner Ken Jarin donated $90,000 to Rendell. He also serves as treasurer of the Democratic Governors Association, which gave Rendell $1.5 million.[404]

- David Cohen, a former Ballard Spahr chairman, gave $80,000 to Rendell; his wife, Rhonda, gave Rendell $156,000 more. (Help me, Rhonda!)[405]

- The Philadelphia Future Political Action Committee—headquartered in Ballard Spahr's offices—donated $470,000 to Rendell. The aforementioned David Cohen is the PAC's treasurer.[406]

But these donations—totaling close to $1.4 million—may tell only part of the story. Because of Pennsylvania's two-term limit for governors, Ed Rendell is obliged to retire as governor in January 2011. Could it be that he's making a nice nest for his retirement by sending business to Ballard Spahr? Could the firm figure in his retirement plans?

Ballard wasn't the only campaign contributor who got Ed Rendell's special attention. When Boscov's, a Pennsylvania-area department store chain, went bankrupt in August 2008, Albert Boscov asked for state help in restructuring his company.[407] Citing Boscov's "reputation" as a successful businessman, Rendell came to the rescue, pumping $35 million of taxpayer money into the company.[408] Why did he do it? Was it because there were important jobs for his constituents at stake? Or was it the fact that Boscov had given him $139,000 for his campaign and that other family members had kicked in an additional $25,000?[409]

And then there's the Houston, Texas, law firm of Bailey Perrin Bailey, and its Philadelphia cocounsel Cohen, Placitella & Roth. The state of Pennsylvania hired the firms without bidding to represent it in a lawsuit against

Janssen Pharmaceuticals, a subsidiary of Johnson & Johnson. Ken Bailey donated $75,000 to Rendell's campaign and paid for $16,000 of airfare for the gubernatorial race.[410] Earlier, at another firm, Bailey had donated $25,000 to a previous Rendell campaign; Stewart Cohen, from the Philadelphia firm, gave Rendell's campaign $12,000.[411]

And don't forget the $599,000 worth of no-bid contracts Rendell awarded to the California firm DCR Financial Products, headed by David Rubin—who gave Rendell $45,000 for his campaigns.[412]

(Full disclosure: Dick worked for Rendell when he ran for governor unsuccessfully in 1990. Rendell's campaign was derailed by thousands of dollars of unpaid parking tickets he had racked up in his district attorney's car, often in front of his dry cleaner's. But Rendell seemed like an honest sort.)

GOVERNOR BILL RICHARDSON (D-NM)

When Bill Richardson pulled out as Barack Obama's nominee to head the Commerce Department, he was very hush-hush about his reasons. He simply made a broad reference to a grand jury investigation in New Mexico, saying that it might become a "distraction" from his duties at Commerce, and bowed out before anyone had time to ask questions.

But it appears that Governor Richardson may also have been in the pay-to-play game—and that he, like Ed Rendell, may have favored a California financial firm with some important New Mexico state business at a time when that firm's leader was arranging to send more than $100,000 in campaign contributions his way.[413]

On March 19, 2004, CDR Financial Products of California—the same firm that gave Ed Rendell $45,000—was approved by the State of New Mexico to advise it on complex bond swaps. Six days later, according to the *New Mexico Independent*, its chief, David Rubin, gave the Democratic Governors Association—chaired by Bill Richardson—a $10,000 donation.[414] Three months later, another firm controlled by Rubin gave $75,000 to a PAC controlled by Richardson.[415] Later that same year, Rubin gave $25,000 to another Richardson PAC, Moving America Forward.[416] As the *Independent* reports, "over the same time period CDR [Rubin's firm] pocketed more than $1 million from the state."[417]

Richardson hired Rubin and his firm to advise him on how to raise $1.5 billion for road and rail construction in his state. Rubin's firm made $1.5 million (1 percent of the deal) for this advice.[418]

In 2006, CDR and two other firms were raided by the FBI. By January 2008, they were under investigation by the Justice Department, the Internal Revenue Service, and the Securities and Exchange Commission.[419]

With this investigation pending, with FBI having raided CDR, and with the money trail leading straight to the governor, how on earth could Obama even have considered him as a potential commerce secretary?

It's bad enough that Richardson's name had surfaced in connection with a pay-to-play scandal involving bond issues. But he may really have crossed the line if it turns out, as has been alleged, that he tried to corrupt the state auditing process—the very protocol that is intended to prevent corruption in the state's bookkeeping.

From 1998 to 2003, before Richardson became governor, the firm of Meyners & Company handled a quarter of a million dollars in state auditing work. After Richardson's election, however, the firm's fortunes took a turn for the better. From 2003 to 2008, it won "nearly $7.8 million in public auditing contracts," according to the *New Mexico Independent*.[420]

How did Meyners manage to collect such a windfall of new work? Ask the head of the firm: Bill Richardson's friend Bruce Malott, who served as the treasurer of Richardson's 2002 gubernatorial primary campaign. Another principal at Malott's firm, Reta D. Jones, had served as his campaign treasurer in the 2002 general election; she filled the same position in his 2006 reelection campaign and his 2008 presidential campaign. Jones is now chair of the State Lottery Authority; Malott has been appointed to the New Mexico State Retiree Health Care Authority, the Education Retirement Board, and the New Mexico Public Accountancy Board (from which he retired at the end of 2008).[421]

In all, Malott's firm conducted almost one hundred audits of state agencies, passing out clean bills of health to nearly every one. But some of the recipients of Malott's firm's blessing were later found to have been knee deep in corruption.

For example, Meyners failed to notice that the Region III Housing Authority, a state agency it audited, was so shaky financially that it defaulted on $5 million in bonds it owed the state.[422] It also failed to notice abuses at another state housing agency—abuses so extensive that they've led to a grand jury investigation by the state attorney general. A 2006 State Investment Council report "revealed widespread misuse of the bond money [by the housing agency,] a number of questionable expenditures and transactions and an extreme lack of documentation for financial records— documentation that was never kept or was taken or destroyed," according to the New Mexico media.[423] But Malott and his firm somehow missed all that.

So buried was this apparent corruption that Bill Richardson ran for president in 2008, participated in all the debates, and was actually nominated by President Obama to be secretary of commerce before these scandals emerged. Imagine how it would have affected the country if Richardson had been confirmed—as secretary of commerce, of all things!—or even been elected president!

GOVERNOR JENNIFER GRANHOLM (D-MI)

Now that Illinois governor Rod Blagojevich has been impeached and removed from office, there's no doubt in our minds as to who the worst governor in America is. Hands down, Jennifer Granholm of Michigan gets the nod. Under her, Michigan has racked up a notable pair of firsts: in 2007, it became the first state in the nation to enter the current recession/depression, and with a February 2009 jobless rate of 12.0 percent it ranks first in unemployment nationwide.[424]

And that's not all: when she faced a huge budget shortfall, Granholm threatened to shut down state government unless she got a huge tax increase—a levy that pushed Michigan further into deficit and depression.

But it's not just her intellect that falls short. Her integrity leaves a lot to be desired also. She and her husband, the consultant Daniel Mulhern, received nearly $300,000 in no-bid contracts from Wayne County government in the months after Jennifer left as the county's corporation counsel to become Michigan attorney general.[425]

Mulhern claims that there was no ethical conflict because he "did not work for the county while Jennifer was there."[426] But the six contracts he got right after she left, and while she still had plenty of clout as the incoming state attorney general, certainly make one suspect that politics might have been at work.

A month after Jennifer left, Mulhern solicited a contract from one of Granholm's "top allies," Airport Director David Katz. He got a no-bid $7,500 gig to provide "management coaching" for the director.[427]

Even when he had to bid for a contract, Mulhern could rest content in the knowledge that even if he lost the bid, he'd still snag the contract. A few months after his wife's departure from the county government, Mulhern's firm, Pioneering Management Possibilities (PMP), bid $140,000 for a contract to train airport personnel.[428] He lost the bid. In fact, he was the highest bidder. The competing firms bid between $30,000 and $74,000. But, no matter, the airport evaluation team, headed by his reliable friend David Katz, chose PMP anyway.[429] (Katz later surfaced as the campaign manager for Granholm in her successful race for governor.)

When his wife ran for governor, Mulhern decided the PMP contract could be politically embarrassing for her and he pulled out of the project. But Mulhern's other contracts with Wayne County followed fast and furious:

- A two-day, $15,000 gig at a retreat for a hundred of the county's executive staffers.[430]

- An eight-month contract for $64,000 to put on a Leadership Development Program for forty county executive staffers.[431]

- A monthly leadership program for three top county officials costing $14,000.[432]

Nice work if you can get it!

ACTION AGENDA

It's time for change. Don't think that this kind of corruption is inevitable and can't be stopped. It can be and in a very important—and formerly corrupt—field it has been. Stopped cold.

The single most corrupt area of state and local government used to be the awarding of lucrative contracts to underwrite bond issues. The underwriters got huge fees. Historically, they had usually been selected by competitive bidding, but in the late 1980s and early '90s, more and more of these underwriters won their contracts without bidding, Increasingly, they got their contracts from the elected state comptroller or treasurer. These state officials went out of their way to avoid competitive bidding, citing the complexity of the bond issues or their urgency to justify awarding them without bidding.

Alert to the opportunity, banks, underwriters, accounting firms, and law firms that wanted in on the action poured tens of millions in campaign contributions into the coffers of candidates running for treasurer or comptroller in order to get special treatment.

But in 1993, a series of scandals led to a crackdown by the Securities and Exchange Commission (back then, it still had teeth). The SEC entered into agreements with the underwriting firms barring campaign contributions to candidates running for offices in which they would have the power to select underwriters. The SEC then codified the agreement into Rule G-37, which barred all underwriters and their employees from conducting bond business in states where they had made campaign contributions in the preceding two years. And, if they made such contributions, they couldn't underwrite bond issues in that state for two more years.

The flood of contributions and the resultant corruption immediately dried up. A study showed that "the use of negotiated bonds dropped suddenly following the banning of campaign contributions."[433] Reviewing the impact of the new rule, the study estimated that "about one-third of municipal bond issuers [had] acted corruptly" under the old negotiated system and had switched from competitive bidding "to a negotiated [bond] issue in order to gain the opportunity to realize a private gain in the form of campaign contributions."[434] The study's "rough estimate" was that state and local taxpayers saved $500 million in "real interest costs" in the year after the reform was enacted by curtailing the corruption.[435]

A private, nonpartisan civic watchdog group, Americans for Limited Government (www.getliberty.org) makes a dramatic proposal: it wants to apply the same rules to no-bid public contracts. If you get a contract from a state or local government without public bid, you can't donate to any po-

litical campaign in that state for two years. And if you have already contributed, you can't get a no-bid contract for the next two years!

Makes sense, doesn't it? In one stroke, all of the problems we've been
discussing in this chapter would go away. Nobody would pay to play!

ALG reports that "an ever growing number of states and municipalities
are enacting 'Pay To Play' laws that bar or severely limit campaign contributions by state and local contractors, their top executives, and, in some
instances, the executives' spouses and dependents."[436]

GETTING CLEAN:
STATES THAT BAR PAY-TO-PLAY

- **New Jersey:** For once the leader in ethics reform, bars contractors—
  whether no-bid or competitively bid—from contributing more than $300
  to any candidate for governor or to any state or local party committees.

- **Connecticut:** Where the state treasurer went to jail over a contributor/bond
  issue scandal; bans donations to state or local candidates from firms or
  their principals who have more than $50,000 in state contracts.

- **Hawaii:** No donations from any contractor to any candidate.

- **South Carolina:** No donations from any no-bid contractor.

- **West Virginia:** No donations from any contractor to any candidate. You
  can't even bid on a contract if you have given money.

- **Vermont:** Bans donations from contractors to the state treasurer.

- **Ohio:** No donations from firms having contracts of more than $10,000.

Keep an eye out for pay-to-play bids in your own state and yell when you
see them. Loudly—and to the media. This has to stop.

To keep abreast of developments in your state, go to the ALG Web site,
www.getliberty.org. Get involved—help ALG turn off this corruption!

13

SLOW SURRENDER
How Our Banks and Investment Firms Are Opening the Door to Shariah Law and Muslim Extremist Domination

There is a worldwide, religiously powered movement to undermine and conquer our Western and American way of life. One of the key tools of this movement is Shariah-compliant financing. It is a practice, orchestrated by Muslim extremists, that is designed to use the oil-generated wealth and economic clout of key Islamic nations to hijack our institutions, our social policies, and, ultimately, our values in the name of Islamic rule.

If this movement continues to gain in power and influence, it will, indeed, be a catastrophe for our way of life.

Meet Sheikh Muhammad Taqi Usmani. He is a prominent Islamic scholar and former justice of the Pakistani Shariah Appellate Court. In 1999, in addition to his Pakistani judicial role, Sheikh Taqi Usmani got a new day job: Dow Jones, HSBC, and many other top financial institutions hired him to advise them on where to invest hundreds of millions of dollars! And this was no short-term trial run: in March of this year, Dow Jones announced its "celebration" of the program's tenth anniversary (although Usmani recently had to resign).

Unfortunately, Usmani has a bad habit of issuing radical, troubling fatwas—legal opinions about personal and public behavior based on Islamic law that are deemed to be binding on all Muslims, regardless of where they live. Flying in the face of the oft-expressed notion that Islam is a peaceful religion, Sheikh Taqi Usmani has a different position: he urges "that Muslims living in the West conduct violent Jihad against the infidels at every opportunity." [437]

Lest there be any doubt about who those infidels he's referring to are— *he means us.* That's right: Sheikh Taqi Usmani advocates killing as many of us as possible, at every opportunity—until we all surrender. He is a man with a mission: to eradicate every religion except Islam. In his book *Islam and Modernism,* he proclaims that, in the West, the "killing is to continue until the unbelievers pay Jizyah after they are humbled or overpowered." [438] Jizyah is a tax collected from every non-Muslim adult living in a Muslim land; the tax is meant as a symbol of subjugation to the Islamic state and laws.

So the sheikh's intent is to kill as many of us as possible; to tax the rest of us; and to subject the living to Muslim rule, regardless of their own wishes.

Why? To ensure the general freedom to preach Islam? No—to show us who's boss. That *he* is. That his religion is the only religion. And that no other religions should be tolerated. It's all very clear to him: "If the purpose of killing was only to acquire permission and freedom of preaching Islam," he says, he would have called on the world to murder the infidels "until they allow for preaching Islam." But his designs are more far-reaching: "The obligation of Jizyah and along with it the mention of their subordination is a clear proof that the purpose is to smash their [other religions'] grandeur." [439]

His rant continues, chillingly: "At least in my humble knowledge there has not been a single incident in the entire history of Islam where Muslims had shown their willingness to stop Jihad just for one condition that they will be allowed to preach Islam freely. On the contrary, the aim of Muslims as declared by them in the battle of Qadsia was, 'To take out people from the rule of people [i.e., representative government] and put them under the rule of Allah.' " [440]

By the "rule of Allah," Sheikh Taqi Usmani is referring to what is often known as Shariah law, the legal framework based on Islamic principles of jurisprudence that encompasses civil and criminal actions and personal and moral behavior. The sheikh works tirelessly to spread the acceptance of Shariah law wherever possible. And he has been among the leading proponents of extending that rule beyond our churches, synagogues, and mosques to our wallets, bank accounts, and life savings.

In 1987, Sheikh Taqi Usmani was one of the issuers of a fatwa that announced a series of Islamic preconditions for Muslim investment in publicly traded stocks. This was a new concept, and in the intervening years it is one that has taken hold in the United States. And the sheikh, who does not hide his contempt for non-Muslims, has become a leader in what has become known as Shariah-compliant financing.

And, until very recently, he sat on the advisory boards of some of our major financial institutions.

Americans are uniquely vulnerable to paranoia. We have such a wonderful country that we are always worried about the potential that some new conspiracy may be lurking around the corner to destroy or change it. The historian Richard Hofstadter wrote about this phenomenon—and politicians' efforts to co-opt it—in his influential book *The Paranoid Style in American Politics*. But even paranoids have enemies—and those who want to infect our financial institutions with the virus of Shariah compliance are among our most dangerous opponents.

Shariah law is the basis of the Islamic religion. It regulates what devoted Muslims may and may not do. It prohibits eating pork and drinking alcohol. It stipulates that one must pray five times each day, always facing Mecca. It requires daytime fasting during the month of Ramadan and a visit to Mecca during one's lifetime. As such, it resembles the Talmudic law that governs Judaism in its comprehensiveness and specificity. Yet its tenets are far more ambitious, even rapacious—at least as interpreted by modern Islamic radicals.

In the late 1990s, investors from the Islamic world—who controlled vast amounts of oil money—began approaching American banks and investment firms, requesting that the companies set up special investment funds to include only industries and companies that eschew any activities prohibited by Shariah law. That way, devout Muslims could be confident that their money would not promote any activity that was inconsistent with Islamic law—such as pork farming or alcohol distribution. Eager to gratify

the every whim of these wealthy foreign investors, many of the most prominent American financial institutions set up Shariah-compliant indices so
investors in stocks and bonds could put their money only in companies that
did not engage in conduct prohibited by Shariah law. In effect—pardon the
pun—they made sure the investments would be kosher.

To guide it in deciding what company stocks and bonds to include in
the Islamic Index, Dow Jones and the other firms that have created Shariah-
compliant funds have retained a group of Shariah scholars who were fully
conversant with the intricacies of the Islamic legal code to form a Shariah
advisory board. These scholars set up criteria for Shariah-compliant investments. As Frank Gaffney, now president of the Center for Security Policy
and a former official in Ronald Reagan's Defense Department, describes it:
"The issuing company must not be involved in 'vice industries' like businesses associated with pork, alcohol, interest income–generating activities,
entertainment (such as pornography and gambling) or Western defense industries. . . . [They must be] engaged in acceptable businesses [and] must
not violate the prohibition Shariah imposes on earning or paying interest."[441] (Getting around the interest ban takes some doing, but with a few
imaginative euphemisms, even that becomes possible for these funds.)

The Shariah advisers must, of course, also examine the "financial
statements of companies in which [Shariah-complaint] investments are
being made"[442] to police their compliance with Shariah law. If they are in
violation—if they earn too much from interest or invest in any forbidden
activity—they have to be purified by donating to one or more "charities"
approved by the Shariah advisers. In addition, Shariah-compliant funds
must invest 2.5 percent of the proceeds of the investments they control in
these designated "charities."

That has led to a serious problem. Unfortunately, several of these sanctioned charities are thinly veiled fronts for terrorist organizations such as
Hamas and Hezbollah and funnel money to the families of suicide bombers
in Palestinian communities and Islamist madrassas in places such as Pakistan.[443] Gaffney notes that "three of the largest Shariah-favored charities in
the U.S. have since 9/11 been shut down by the U.S. government for providing financial support of terrorism and other pro-jihad conduct."[444]

The 2.5 percent tariff that Shariah-compliant funds must donate to
"charities" runs into billions of dollars.[445] As the flow of Shariah money

increases, it becomes a key source of financing for our enemies—often through cash provided unwittingly by devout, but peaceful, Muslims.

And when a Shariah-compliant fund makes a mistake—say, by investing in a trucking company that one day carries hogs—it must donate additional funds to charity for "purification." Alexiev explains that an investor's return from such ill-gotten gains must be "deducted and given to charity by the Shariah advisors. All of this happens before disbursement to the investor, who has no say in the matter whatsoever. Where this money goes is anybody's guess. . . . But it doesn't take a rocket scientist to figure out that a Shariah board is unlikely to contribute to the Boys Club." [446]

The Shariah advisers themselves, who determine whether investments are acceptable under Muslim law, are generally Islamist extremists. They have even coined the phrase "financial jihad" to characterize this new form of economic warfare against the "unbelievers." [447] As Alex Alexiev notes, "dozens of radical Islamists are Shariah advisors and financial institutions pay them royally. Some of them sit on as many as two dozen of these boards and make millions of dollars, at least some of which is then donated to extremist causes." [448]

Specifically, Alexiev warns that Shariah-compliance advisory boards are peopled by "radical Islamists trained and indoctrinated in the Wahhabi or Deobandi-controlled Sharia faculties in Saudi Arabia, Pakistan, and elsewhere." These men, he notes, "are the intellectual driving force behind the Wahhabi/Salafi ideology of Islamism and the leading theological enablers of extremism and terrorism." [449]

WHO SITS ON SHARIAH COMPLIANCE BOARDS?

- **Sheikh Muhammad Taqi Usmani.** The former justice of the Pakistani Shariah Appellate Court, whom we met earlier in this chapter, was "first retained in 1999 by Dow Jones to serve on its august Shariah board," Gaffney notes. "In the years since, he has added dozens of other financial institutions, including HSBC, to the list of SCF providers whom he advises." [450]

Usmani recently demonstrated his authority over Islamic investments when he declared that certain investments were not Shariah-compliant, causing market turmoil. He sits on the supervisory board of a dozen Islamic banks. Until recently he advised more than twenty-five stock funds on how to comply with Islamic laws.[451] Dow Jones terminated its association with Usmani after Gaffney's Center for Security Policy raised a fuss.

- Still on the payroll of leading American banks is **Sheikh Yusuf al-Qaradawi** of the Muslim Brotherhood. As Alexiev says, Qaradawi "has repeatedly endorsed suicide bombings against innocent civilians."[452]

- **The North American Islamic Trust** (NAIT), which, according to *Front Page* magazine, "runs a Shariah-compliant mutual fund out of Burr Ridge, Illinois." Until recently, NAIT managed a $40 million fund for Dow—even allowing it to use the name Dow Jones Islamic Fund under a licensing agreement.[453]

  But Dow had to sever its relationship with NAIT after federal agents disclosed that NAIT was "a Saudi-tied front for the pro-jihad Muslim Brotherhood that holds title to some of the most radical mosques in America. The Justice Department last year named NAIT an unindicted co-conspirator in a terror money-laundering scheme to funnel more than $12 million to Hamas suicide bombers and their families under the guise of charity. Dow has since revoked NAIT's license."[454]

Some estimates suggest that as much as $1 trillion may currently be invested around the world in funds that follow Shariah-compliance rules. As Gaffney notes, "if trends continue . . . such funds may grow to many times that amount within a few years."[455]

Shariah law authorities are now being paid by Dow Jones, Barclays, Standard & Poor's, HSBC, Citibank, Merrill Lynch, Deutsche Bank, Goldman Sachs, Morgan Stanley, UBS, and others "to determine and assure the compliance of these institutions' products with Shariah," according to the Center for Security Policy's Shariah Risk Due Diligence Project.[456]

The center cites this list of six "key drivers of this Shariah compliance finance market":

1. Specialized law firms such as King and Spalding, Patton Boggs, Gibson Dunn, and Gerstyn Savage

2. Shariah consulting firms such as Shariah Capital
3. Shariah Index Providers such as HSBC, Standard and Poor's, Dow Jones and FTSE
4. Accounting firms
5. Software providers
6. Global banking institutions such as Barclays, Merrill Lynch, UBS, Deutsche Bank, Morgan Stanley Capital, Citibank, UBS, and Goldman Sachs[457]

The Center for Security Policy outlines the requirements that are usually demanded of financial institutions engaged in Shariah-compliant financing:

1. Avoidance of interest charges
2. Shared risk between parties
3. Avoiding investments in banned industries such as defense, pork, media, banking, alcohol, and insurance
4. The appointment of Shariah advisory boards to create and oversee the adherence of investments to Shariah
5. An obligatory donation of "tainted" revenue, which must be "purified" and given to Shariah-approved charities[458]

Alex Alexiev, an expert in Shariah law, notes that the supposed goal of Shariah-compliant financing is "to make it possible for Muslims to conduct financial transactions while observing Shariah prohibitions against lending at interest (*riba*), uncertainty (*gharar*), and forbidden products and activities such as pork, alcohol, gambling, entertainment, etc."[459]

Of course, as Alexiev points out, it's almost impossible to invest money without risk or interest. So Shariah-compliant financing resorts to subterfuge:

The Shariah experts that must bless these transactions, engage in all kinds of more or less transparent legal fictions, ruses, gimmicks and deceptive techniques. Ironically, in doing that, they engage in the age-old Islamic practice of legal fictions, known as *hiyal*, which was originally designed to make it possible to do business transactions while circumventing Shariah injunctions, [which] didn't make much sense even in the early days of Islam.[460]

The first company to set up a Shariah-compliant fund was Dow Jones, which set up the world's first Islamic market index in 1999. Now there are seventy separate Islamic indexes.[461]

Investor's Business Daily has reported that "Wall Street is jumping into this hot new market [of Shariah compliant financing] oblivious to the risks not just to the bottom line, but to national security. It knows little about Shariah law and is turning to consultants to create 'ethical' products to sell."[462]

The newspaper reported that "Citibank and Goldman Sachs, for example, are creating investment vehicles that cater to Muslim investors in order to grab some of the billions in management fees in the offing. These products include Shariah-compliant bonds, mutual funds, mortgages, insurance, hedge funds and soon REITs."[463]

Dow Jones, and other mutual funds and financial advisers who set up Shariah-compliant indices, license the right to use them as an investment guide. Frank Gaffney explains that "The Dow Jones Islamic Index's first customer was a Cayman Island company, which licensed both the use of the Islamic index and the Dow Jones name to create the Dow Jones Islamic Index Portfolio."[464]

Institutional compliance with Shariah law is a slippery slope. Today it means not investing in any company that makes pork. But it also means not putting your funds into any company that makes weapons for the American or Israeli military. Tomorrow, Gaffney speculates, it might be used to require companies to have "footbaths in public institutions, prayer rooms and time off for prayers in both public and private sector establishments, latitude for cabdrivers and cashiers to decline to do business with certain customers or handle certain products, an Islamist public school in Brooklyn, etc."[465]

But beyond the money Shariah-compliant funds channel into terrorist groups, the very propagation of Shariah law as a legitimate way to regulate our society runs directly counter to our most elementary conceptions of personal freedom, equality, and social justice. Shariah law requires a lot more than a certain diet, the avoidance of pornography, and limits on interest income. Gaffney points out some of its other inconvenient requirements, which call for "beheadings, stonings, floggings and amputations for petty crimes in places like Saudi Arabia, Iran and Sudan. Indeed, it is the same Shariah law that underlies the doctrine of war called Jihad used by Islamist terrorists to impose through violent means their theocracy and legal code on the entire world." [466]

Alex Alexiev says that the main political objective of Shariah-compliant financing is "to legitimize Shariah in the West," [467] to isolate Muslim communities from mainstream society, and to "create Islamic enclaves controlled by Shariah in the middle of Western society." [468]

And in the United Kingdom, at least, the Islamic fundamentalists are closing in on their goal. British prime minister Gordon Brown recently announced his ambition to make London the Islamic finance capital of the world. Part of the effort to make London Shariah-friendly was a decision by the most senior judge in the United Kingdom that declared that the Muslim community could establish its own legal framework and use Shariah law to settle marital arguments and regulate finance. Lord Chief Justice, Lord Phillips said, "Those entering into a contractual agreement can agree that the agreement shall be governed by a law other than English law." [469] According to Phillips's decision, Muslims in the United Kingdom could use "Islamic legal principles as long as the punishments and divorce rulings comply with English Law." [470]

Even the archbishop of Canterbury, the head of the Church of England, seemed to be promoting Shariah rule when he suggested in a BBC interview that the adoption of Shariah law in Britain "seems unavoidable and, as a matter of fact, certain conditions of Shariah are already recognized in our society and under our law, so it is not as if we are bringing in an alien and rival system." [471] Incredibly, Muslims in the United Kingdom are now eligible to receive extra benefits if they have more than one wife, even though polygamy is illegal in Britain. [472]

The columnist Cal Thomas, a vigilant defender of our democratic values, explains the implications of applying Shariah law to divorce proceedings:

WOMEN UNDER SHARIAH

- Muslim women are prohibited to marry without their parents' consent—a rule that can only worsen the problem of forced marriage.

- A wedding can be held without the bride even being present, as long as her guardian consents—opening the door to widespread underage marriage.

- Muslim women are allowed to marry only men of the Muslim faith.

- A Muslim man can divorce his wife simply by repudiating her and suffers no obligation to support her or their children thereafter.

- A Muslim woman is prohibited from divorcing her husband without his consent.

- Abuse cannot be presented as grounds for a woman to divorce her husband.

- Sons are entitled to inherit twice as much as daughters.

- Divorced women must not remarry, at risk of losing custody of their children.[473]

Gaffney warns that the Islamists want to go even further. They are calling for "Shariah-compliant schools (they already have them in Britain); a push in Canada for separate Shariah courts for all matters within the Muslim community; Shariah tolerance for honor killings of women in Germany; destruction of non Shariah-compliant businesses in dedicated 'Muslim enclaves' in France; and in various countries, Shariah approved assassinations of critics of Islam and anyone leaving Islam worldwide."[474]

Where Shariah law is applied, the nightmares suggested by these draconian regulations become reality.

LIFE UNDER SHARIAH

Those living under Shariah law, especially women, are subjected to harsh penalties—even death—even when they are already victims. Consider these examples:

SHARIAH JUSTICE

- In December 2007, a British teacher in Sudan was sentenced to forty lashes and a year in jail for allowing students to name their teddy bears Mohammad. When word spread, Islamic mobs rallied and called for her death.

- In November 2007, a teenage Saudi gang-rape victim received a sentence of two hundred lashes under Shariah law "for riding in the car with her rapists."

- In 2006, "a thirty-four-year-old mother who was forcibly raped was ultimately tried and convicted of adultery, and was ordered to be stoned to death."

- The publication of cartoons in Denmark that were "deemed disrespectful of Mohammad" sparked protests, leading to demonstrations and "the killing of many people."[475]

But the real goal of those pushing for Shariah-compliant funds at major financial institutions is to build them into the investments of the huge sovereign wealth funds amassed by Islamic countries. If these powerhouses, which control up to $5 trillion in assets (even after the recent worldwide financial crisis) can submit their portfolios to Shariah-compliance experts, the power of these clerics could become huge.

Originally, Shariah-complaint financing was eschewed by the sovereign wealth funds. Perhaps more surprising, it was actually unpopular among Muslims, many of whom simply didn't trust the Shariah funds to give them good returns on their capital or even to keep their money safe. As Alexiev notes, "there is, of course, a small captive audience of devout believers that would practice it even if they were losing money, but the vast majority [of the world's Muslim investors] looks askance at Shariah Compliant Financing."[476]

He cites the example of Pakistan, where only 3.5 percent of all assets are managed in compliance with Shariah, despite an official edict—issued in 1980—promoting the concept. Alexiev notes that similar conditions prevail in most Muslim countries.[477] So to encourage Muslims to invest in

Shariah-compliant funds, it became essential for Western financial institutions to embrace the concept. "Western involvement is key because most Muslims, rich or poor, do not trust their own banks and need the West to legitimate Islamic finance."[478]

These Muslim investors found eager and willing partners in the Western banks, which, Alexiev says, "jumped into [Shariah-compliant financing] for one reason only and that is the lure of many tens of billions in transaction fees from an industry that currently has nearly a $1 trillion under management."[479]

Still, some ask if Shariah-compliant financing can really be all that bad. Shouldn't Muslims be allowed to invest in companies they believe in?

Of course—if they had a choice. And there's the rub. Devout Muslims living in the West are allowed to use regular banks in the absence of Shariah-compliant alternatives, under the Shariah doctrine of "extreme necessity." But, as Alexiev points out, "once [Shariah-compliant finance] institutions do exist, you are religiously obligated to patronize them exclusively. Thus, by allowing the spread of Shariah compliant financing in the West, we are, wittingly or not, pushing the Muslims in the hands of the Islamists."[480]

The current flirtation with Shariah-compliant financing of the world's major banks and investment houses is bad enough. But if Shariah-compliant financing ever marries the sovereign wealth funds from Muslim countries, they could constitute a massive financial power, capable of transforming Western civilization. Or destroying it.[481]

The Center for Security Policy warns that "it is very likely that Islamic banking and Sovereign Wealth Funds [from Islamic countries] are rapidly becoming one and the same phenomenon. This would mean that at some point in the near future, if not already, Sovereign Wealth Funds will become an instrument for promoting and legitimating Shariah in the West."[482]

Even after the market crashes of 2008 and 2009, Sovereign Wealth Funds have massive amounts of cash to invest. Although not all of these funds are Islamic—some are Russian and Chinese and from Western nations—many of them are.[483]

Once these funds become fully linked with Islamic sovereign wealth funds, their financial clout may well multiply dramatically. But sovereign wealth funds can't just come to American banks and ask them to invest in

Islamic causes or not to invest in any "tainted" industry. They can, however, use the premise of a Shariah-compliant financial vehicle to maintain that they are simply honoring their religion and its principles.

Giving Muslim extremists massive leverage by linking sovereign wealth funds with Shariah-compliance boards is a frightening prospect indeed. Imagine the likes of Sheikh Muhammad Taqi Usmani deciding which companies should or should not get massive investments from the sovereign wealth funds of countries such as Kuwait, Saudi Arabia, Qatar, and others.

As the global financial crisis deepens, the demand for capital—from anywhere—will become increasingly acute. If the powers controlling the sovereign wealth funds from Islamic countries demand the inclusion of Shariah-compliance provisions in any investments they make, it is hard to see our financial policy makers worrying too much about the impact of these funds on our freedom. As Gaffney puts it, "there will be a Katie-bar-the-door attitude toward funds from these sources," and the danger of widespread proliferation of Shariah-compliant financing will be even greater.[484]

Just ponder for a moment what a catastrophe that would be. In order to attract the precious money controlled by these sovereign wealth funds, companies would have to pitch their activities to appease and please the extremist Shariah-compliance officers. It would put the power to control us into the hands of those who want to destroy us.

Not only could these advisers use this massive leverage to hurt the United States, the international Jewish community, and Israel, they also could use it to destabilize our entire capitalist system (or what is left of it when Obama gets through with it).

Consider the mayhem that a few mortgage lenders visited on the American economy when they went around issuing subprime mortgages—or the destabilization that occurred when savings and loan associations promoted crony investments in the 1980s. Our financial system is highly vulnerable to just these kinds of shenanigans, and Shariah-compliant financial advisers would be only too happy to figure out how to use that exposure to their advantage.

The airplanes of 9/11 smashed the towers of the World Trade Center. But Shariah-compliant financing has the potential to go further and smash our country's fragile economic future.

ACTION AGENDA

Think there couldn't possibly be much you can do about Shariah-compliant financing? Think again! With the U.S. government moving to buy shares of stock in all the nation's major banks and financial institutions—and, likely, nationalizing many of the major banks—it is the government, *our* government, that must decide whether or not to allow Shariah-compliant funds to be established.

And, as Frank Gaffney points out, for a government-owned institution to have a Shariah-compliant fund is a clear violation of the First Amendment. It involves a state action (or an action by a bank either owned by the government or in which the government has an ownership stake of 40 percent or higher) to benefit an "establishment of religion," which is, thank God (again, pardon the pun), prohibited by the First Amendment.

Gaffney is right when he argues that the federal government cannot permit financial institutions under its control to have Shariah-compliant funds or to put Shariah law experts on its advisory boards. The fees paid to these "experts" for explicitly religious advice clearly violate the separation of church and state.

A lawsuit is being brought to force AIG—the insurance giant that the federal government bailed out in 2008 and again this year—to drop its Shariah-compliant financing program. The suit alleges that, since AIG is now controlled by the government, its Shariah programs constitute a state action that is barred by the First Amendment. With Uncle Sam owning more than 80 percent of AIG, they've got a good case.

Yerushalmi points out that AIG had to give the government "preferred stock (preferred means it has special benefits over regular shareholders) which would allow the Treasury to receive 79.9 percent of any dividends paid and to vote with the common stockholders in an amount equal to that 79.9 percent."[485] Not unreasonably, he points out that "by anyone's definition, if you control 79.9 percent of the voting rights of a company, you not only own the company, you control it. That is de facto and de jure control. The company can do nothing you don't want it to. Period."[486]

Yerushalmi concludes that "whatever AIG is doing, it is effectively acting on behalf of the U.S. government. If a private entity is really controlled by or acting in the place of government, that entity must abide by the protections in the U.S. Constitution against government violations of our civil liberties."[487] Including the First Amendment.

Yet AIG, Yerushalmi argues, "intentionally promotes Sharia-compliant businesses and insurance products, which by necessity must comply with the 1200-year-old body of Islamic law based on the Qur'an and other Islamic canon, which demands the conversion, subjugation, or destruction of the infidel West, including the United States.[488]

"To help achieve these objectives," he continues, "and with the aid of federal tax dollars, AIG employs a three-person Shariah Advisory Board, with members from Saudi Arabia, Bahrain, and Pakistan."[489]

AIG says that the role of its Shariah authority "is to review operations, supervise its development of Islamic products, and determine Shariah compliance of these products and investments."[490]

That combination violates the First Amendment.

An even more outrageous violation of the establishment clause of the First Amendment is unfolding in Minnesota, where the state is sponsoring a Shariah-compliant program to help Muslims buy homes without violating their religious prohibition against paying interest.

Under the program, the state buys a home and resells it to a Muslim home buyer. The down payment and monthly installments on the mortgage are agreed to up front at current mortgage rates. This arrangement permits the Muslim family to avoid paying interest. The state pays the interest; the family simply reimburses it, thus avoiding the religious proscription.[491]

Imagine a program for observant Orthodox Jews where the state would send in workers to turn on lights for them during the Sabbath! Or to drive them around for free so they don't have to operate a motor vehicle on Saturday. That's exactly what this Minnesota program amounts to.

What business does a state have to jump through such hoops to help members of a specific religion to purchase homes? If anything violates the wall of separation between church and state, this is it! We are grateful to www.jihadwatch.org for bringing this crazy law to public attention.

If courts are going to bar schools or government buildings from posting the Ten Commandments on their walls, they must also bar Shariah compliance by banks or financial institutions that are dominated by the federal government.

We all need to support the Center for Security Policy in its work to block Shariah from fighting our values through our top banks and insurance companies. If it can prevail in the AIG suit, it will win a test case that will fully reverse the Islamic offensive. The center is financed by public contributions in its work to protect our Constitution, secular government, and Western values. You can find it at http://www.centerforsecuritypolicy.org/index.xml.

Oh, and by the way, the governor of Minnesota is Tim Pawlenty. He is a Republican who was on the short list for vice president in 2008. These days, he's often mentioned as a candidate for the 2012 Republican presidential nomination. Why don't you drop him an e-mail and let him know what you think of Minnesota's Shariah-compliant mortgage program? His e-mail address is tim.pawlenty@state.mn.us.

He'll love hearing from you.

14

HOW BILL CLINTON GOOFED . . .COSTING YOU $60 BILLION

Which administration do you think gave away more money to Big Oil? Bush 43 or Clinton?

Bet you guessed wrong.

Because no matter how much George W. Bush and Dick Cheney worked overtime to figure out ways to funnel money to their oil company buddies, the Clinton administration—through sheer and incomprehensible incompetence—gave them more!

Sometimes it's tempting to read conspiracy theories into the actions of our government, particularly when the opposite party is in power. But there is no conspiracy theory here. Just a story of an outrageous screw-up—one that is robbing us all of cash we could all use in this struggling economy.

In fact, American taxpayers will be subsidizing the major oil and gas companies for years to come, all because of the mistakes of Bill Clinton's Department of the Interior. It's estimated that its blunder will end up funneling up to $60 billion to Big Oil![492]

Letting Big Oil grab $60 billion from the taxpayers—while we're facing the largest deficit in history—qualifies as a catastrophe in anybody's book.

The problem began when President Clinton and his interior secretary, Bruce Babbitt, decided to stimulate oil and gas exploration in the Gulf of Mexico by agreeing to reduce, or even outright eliminate, the royalty payments energy companies would normally owe the federal government for the right to drill there. The concept was to exempt them from royalties—which usually run between 12 and 16 percent of the cost of revenues—until they reached a certain volume of production, or until oil or gas prices rose above specific price levels.[493]

The basic idea was a good one. With America's energy needs skyrocketing and domestic production of oil dropping, it was only wise that our eyes turn south—to the Gulf of Mexico. Estimates of how much oil is buried under its floor run as high as 4 billion barrels—oil that modern technology has finally made it possible to recover.

So Clinton and Babbitt urged Congress to pass the Outer Continental Shelf Deepwater Royalty Relief Act of 1995, which reduced the royalties the energy companies would have to pay to drill in the gulf. Congress provided that the royalty relief would remain in effect as long as oil and gas production from gulf leases remained below a certain volume. The legislators reasoned that, since the suspension of royalties was an incentive program to encourage exploration and drilling in the gulf, it would no longer be necessary after a significant volume of energy began flowing from these leaseholds.

Astonishingly, however, Congress overlooked one key factor: it failed to include any provision tying the suspension of royalty payments to the price of energy. No problem, the Clinton people said. We'll just include the price threshold in the drilling contracts that the Interior Department issues to each energy company. New legislation to discontinue the royalty relief once prices rose, they said, was unnecessary. Famous last words.

At the time, the price issue didn't seem too urgent. After a series of significant oil and gas discoveries in the North Sea and elsewhere, energy prices were low. India and China had yet to go through their rapid development; their surge of energy appetite was in the future.

So, in 1996 and 1997, Clinton's Department of the Interior signed leases for gulf exploration and drilling with major energy companies, specifying that they would be exempt from royalty requirements unless the price of oil rose above $34 per barrel of oil and an equivalent price for natural gas.[494] After all, the Clinton administration reasoned, if prices were high, the energy companies wouldn't need relief from royalty payments. They'd be making plenty on the oil and gas they mined in the gulf.

Why didn't Clinton and Babbitt ask Congress to amend the Royalty Relief Act to require full royalty payments if the price rose above a certain level? Why did they rely on the advice of their own lawyers that it was not necessary to ask Congress? We don't know the answer, but we do know, in retrospect, that it was a huge mistake.

The program took off like a rocket. Deepwater oil production in the gulf shot up from 42 million barrels in 1996 to 348 million in 2004.[495] Natural gas production jumped almost tenfold.

But then a funny thing happened: in the *next* two years, 1998 and 1999, all the leases issued to energy companies included the royalty relief but failed to mention the provision that the relief would be reduced if prices rose![496]

By 2000, the Interior Department discovered its mistake, and the provision has been included in the leases issued since that date.[497] But the mistake had been made—and to this day no one knows why.

There has never been a credible explanation—or, for that matter, *any* explanation—of why the 1998 and 1999 contracts left out that important price threshold provision. From all that anyone can tell, some idiot may simply have forgotten to include the clause in the leases.

So when energy prices began to rise, peaking in the summer of 2008, the government began to feel the loss in revenue that flowed from the inexplicable screw-up. When the number crunchers at Interior tried to increase the royalty payments of energy companies whose leases dated back to 1998 and 1999, the leaseholders told them to go fly a kite. The reduction in royalty relief wasn't included in their contracts!

Even when oil prices rose as high as $160 a barrel in the summer of 2008 and gas prices followed suit, the lucky oil and gas companies were able to keep drilling for oil under those faulty 1998 and '99 leases—without paying one cent in royalties to the government!

By 2006, the Interior Department estimates, the government had lost out on collecting *$956 million in royalties* on those 1998 and '99 leases.[498] When the data come in for 2007 and 2008, given the huge increase in energy prices, the tab will surely be higher. By the time all the oil and gas is pumped from those gulf wells, the Interior Department estimates, it may be out $10 billion.[499]

Not surprisingly, like true politicians, the Interior Department and Congress are now demanding that the oil and gas companies be gracious enough to overlook the government's mistake and restore the royalty relief reduction clauses to those 1998 and 1999 leases.

Interior is taking the position that it didn't *have to* include the underlying language providing that it would increase royalty payments if the price of energy rose. The department says that the federal law, passed in 1995, gives it the right to raise the required payments whether or not they're specified in their leases.

Alas, the federal courts don't agree.

Patricia Minaldi, a federal district court judge in Louisiana, ruled that the Interior Department could not make the Kerr-McGee Oil and Gas Corporation, one of the beneficiaries of the 1998 and '99 leases, pay royalties just because energy prices had risen.[500]

But Judge Minaldi went further. Not only does the Interior Department not have the right to increase royalty payments for 1998 and 1999 where the leases do not give it that power, she ruled, it cannot even enforce the leases—written in other years—that explicitly provide for increases in royalty payments as the price of energy goes up! Not only will the Feds have to do without the royalties on those 1998 and 1999 leases where they forgot to include price thresholds, but they can't even demand royalties based on a price threshold at all—even when the provision was included in the contract. Why? Because in imposing the threshold price, the court held, the Interior Department had gone beyond what Congress had authorized!

Sustaining Minaldi's ruling, a federal appeals court ruled on January 12, 2008, that Kerr-McGee should not have to pay royalties on eight Gulf of Mexico leases from 1996 to 2000! The court ruled that Congress provided that the royalty reduction would be suspended only if the volume of oil and gas from the wells rose above certain thresholds—and that it was illegal for the Interior Department to demand that full royalties be paid if the price went up.[501]

Barry Russell, president of the Independent Petroleum Association of America, commented on the court ruling, saying:

The intent of Congress with the Deepwater Royalty Relief Act was to provide an incentive for companies to obtain royalty relief based on the volumes of crude oil and natural gas produced, rather than on a price threshold. [The Department of the Interior] subsequently installed a price threshold that would determine when those incentives would cease. The circuit court has now found the Interior Department's actions to be outside the scope of the law.[502]

Lawyers for the Interior Department were livid. They told the media, "If the court's interpretation of Congress's action in 1995 is correct, certain leaseholders will be able to produce massive amounts of oil and gas without paying royalties to the United States without regard to the price, perhaps amounting to one of the biggest giveaways of federal resources by Congress in modern history."[503]

That's the problem, folks. According to the *New York Times*, the Government Accountability Office—the congressional watchdog agency—estimated in January 2007 that the government would lose roughly $60 billion over twenty-five years under the court ruling.[504]

So the decision of the genius lawyers in the Clinton administration—that they could simply insert the price threshold into the Gulf drilling leases without asking Congress to approve the price threshold—turned out to be another mistake.

This time it was a $60 billion mistake!

Naturally, the politicians were furious at their own collective stupidity. Congressman Edward Markey (D-MA), who was in Congress when the original royalty exemption was passed, condemned the court decision in strong language. Speaking in 2007, he said:

At a time when oil prices are hovering close to ninety-five dollars per barrel, it is unconscionable that [the energy companies] would continue to push forward with this brazen attempt to rob the American people in broad daylight.[505]

The congressman's outrage was not diminished by the inconvenient fact that it was Congress that left the door open by passing their sloppy 1995 bill. Senator Jeff Bingaman (D-NM), the chairman of the Senate Energy

Committee, also attacked the court decision, saying that it "will result in the oil and gas industry being able to tap billions of dollars of the public's natural resources for free, with none of their resulting income shared with the American public."[506]

In July 2007, in a bid to cover itself, the House acted to undo its own incompetence by voting to impose a "conservation of resources" fee on oil and gas taken out of the gulf under the 1998–99 leases.[507] Typically, the provision was inserted in a farm bill at the last minute on its way through the House. But the Senate failed to approve the amendment—and to this day the government is still being deprived of the royalty revenue.

The new Obama administration and Congress will probably revisit the issue and seek to recoup the royalty revenues through a conservation fee. The power of the federal government to impose taxes is pretty broad, and the courts might uphold such legislation. Or they might conclude—correctly—that the law is simply a retroactive end run around the leases that have already been signed with the energy companies.

In either case, nothing Obama or the Congress can do will recoup the tens of billions of dollars that the government has already lost in royalties on gulf oil and gas—all lost because some knuckleheads on the legal staff of Clinton's Interior Department failed to ask Congress for price threshold legislation—and because others on the contract-writing staff forgot to insert the requirements into two years of leases.

It looks as though we don't always have to worry about government officials being bought off by Big Oil. Sometimes they manage to give away our money without even getting any personal favors in return!

15

TARMAC HOSTAGES
How Airlines Imprison You on the Runway

What do American Airlines, Delta Air Lines, Continental Airlines, United Airlines, and US Airways have in common?

All five airlines went to court—through their trade group, the Air Transport Association—to block you, the consumer (and their customer), from having any rights at all when you're trapped in their planes on airport runways for hours and hours at a time.

In December 2007, the Coalition for an Airplane Passengers' Bill of Rights (http://www.flyersrights.org) persuaded the New York State legislature to pass a law requiring airlines to provide passengers with "food, water, electricity, and waste removal when a flight from a New York airport waits more than three hours to take off." [508] The law provided for a fine of up to $1,000 per passenger if the airline did not comply.

Food, water, and toilets after three hours. What a radical concept!

Of course, the airlines fought this bill tooth and nail. When the legislature dismissed their objections and passed it, they went to court to block it. After a defeat in the U.S. Federal District Court, they appealed to the U.S. Circuit Court of Appeals, where a conservative panel of judges overruled the law.

Bravo! The airlines shafted their passengers once again!

As air travel increases and airport facilities fail to expand to meet the demand, the problem of lengthy tarmac delays is becoming more and more serious. In the first ten months of 2007, 1,523 flights had to wait on the runway for more than three hours to take off from U.S. airports, nearly a one-third increase over the 1,152 flights kept waiting over the same period during the previous year.[509] And there was a 40 percent increase in lost baggage.[510]

The New York State Legislature had to act because Congress has failed to do so. Comprehensive legislation to protect air passengers was passed by the House, but it died in the Senate in 2008 because of Republican opposition.

Canadians are more fortunate. A passengers' bill of rights, passed by the Canadian Parliament in June 2008, requires airlines to allow passengers to leave the plane after any delay of ninety minutes or more and to reboard the aircraft once it's ready to take off. The Canadian law obliges airlines to provide stranded travelers with meal and hotel vouchers, except when the delays are caused by bad weather.

The Canadian legislation also provides that:

HOW CANADA PROTECTS FLYERS

Passengers have a right to punctuality.

1. If a flight is delayed and the delay . . . exceeds 4 hours, the airline will provide the passenger with a meal voucher.

2. If a flight is delayed by more than 8 hours and . . . involves an overnight stay, the airline will pay for [the] hotel and airport transfers for passengers . . .

3. If the passenger is already on the aircraft when a delay occurs, the airline will offer drinks and snacks if it is safe, practical and timely to do so. If the delay exceeds 90 minutes and circumstances permit, the airline will offer passengers the option of disembarking from the aircraft until it is time to depart.[511]

In the United States, on the other hand, passengers have virtually no protection.

In February 2007, JetBlue Airways became the only airline in the United States to issue, voluntarily, its own Customer Bill of Rights. These self-imposed regulations include:

COMING CLEAN:
JETBLUE'S PASSENGER BILL OF RIGHTS

- Guaranteed customer notification of cancellations, delays, and diversions.

- A $1,000 payment for customers who are "involuntarily denied boarding."

- Free television, food and drink, access to "clean" restrooms, and, medical treatment as needed for customers whose flight is delayed three hours or more after scheduled departure.

- For delays of more than five hours, the airline pledges to "take necessary action so that customers may deplane."

- A $50 voucher for future JetBlue travel for arrival delays of one to two hours.

- A voucher for future travel—equal in amount to the full round-trip fare the passenger paid—for ground delays that lead to a delay in arrival of two hours or more past the scheduled time.[512]

If JetBlue can do it, why can't American or Delta or United or Continental?

JetBlue was prompted to act, of course, because of its dismal record on Valentine's Day, February 14, 2007, when more than a thousand passengers were stranded on nine different JetBlue flights at New York's John F. Kennedy airport due to a snowstorm. As the *New York Times* reported, "the air and toilets on the plane went foul, and the passengers, who well understood the impact of snow, were given little or no information about why they couldn't just be set free in the terminal. Roll a stairway over? Bring a bus? Allow them to walk? No? Why not?" [513]

As JetBlue's CEO, David Neeleman, said, despite the weather conditions, there was "no excuse" for the company's performance that day.

JetBlue's Bill of Rights must have heartened its frequent flyers, but things didn't necessarily improve on the other big airlines. Kate Hanni, a passenger who was stranded for eight hours on the runway on an American Airlines flight on December 29, 2007, was so outraged at the "indifference" that she said the airline showed to her that she founded the Coalition for an Airline Passengers' Bill of Rights.

The *Wall Street Journal* described the scene:

> After hours of sitting on the runway, the toilets on the American Airlines jet were overflowing. There was no water to be found and no food except for a box of pretzel bags. A pregnant woman sat crying; an unaccompanied teen sobbed. The captain walked up and down the aisle of the MD-80, trying to calm angry passengers. At one point, families with children lined up to be bused to the terminal, but a bus never came. [514]

Eventually, Hanni's flight—scheduled to run from San Francisco to Dallas—was diverted to Austin, Texas, because of thunderstorms. Finally, as the *Journal* reported, "after eight hours on the runway and twelve hours, total, on the plane, the captain told passengers he was going to an empty gate, even though he didn't have permission." [515] And why didn't he have access to the empty gate? It appears that, with thunderstorms in the region, "according to airline officials, Austin managers decided to focus on handling regular flights to other cities such as Chicago and St. Louis, hoping they could stay on schedule." [516] This "pivotal decision" meant that Hanni's flight had to sit and sit and sit on the runway. [517]

American Airlines was not totally insensitive as its plane sat on the runway. Like a hostage taker who lets women and children go, the airline "allowed about 20 local Austin and San Antonio passengers to get off rather than wait to fly to Dallas only to hop back on a connection back to Austin." [518] Their luggage, not so fortunate, had to remain on board.

As the *Journal* reported, "conditions in the . . . cabin quickly deteriorated—toilets overflowed, families ran out of baby diapers. American did not act to empty the toilet tanks until the plane had been stuck on the ground for more than five hours."[519]

Meanwhile, American was cheerfully using its four operating gates for regularly scheduled flights and the captain was telling his captives he couldn't find a gate.

Of course, American was only acting in its own self-interest. Airplane delays are cataloged by the federal government, and taking unusual measures to accommodate the stranded flight and letting the passengers off could have triggered a domino effect and caused dozens of delays, which would have looked bad for American's on-time record. But without any passenger bill of rights, the airline incurred no penalty for keeping the passengers locked for hours in a stale and sweltering airplane with no food.

While JetBlue responded to its abysmal performance by embracing a passenger bill of rights, American—and other airlines—continue to battle against any such regulation in Congress, the state legislatures, and the courts.

Of course, punishing airlines for delays and requiring that they permit passengers to deplane, get food, or use the bathroom, would worsen their on-time record. Returning to the gate could cause planes to lose their place in line for takeoff and might even run afoul of federal limits on crew workdays.

Currently, the FAA's "8/16" rule limits a pilot's total work day to sixteen hours, including a maximum of eight at the airplane's controls. The rule, of course, is designed to stop tired pilots from flying. A pilot cannot start a new flight that would push him over the eight-hour limit, but he can continue a delayed flight for up to sixteen hours. So if the plane returns to the gate and the delay would push the pilot's workday over eight hours, he may not fly the plane. If he sits on the runway, on the other hand, he can take off.

Requiring compensation for customers who are delayed for many hours; banning long tarmac delays; and obliging airlines to offer food, water, and clean restrooms to delayed passengers: such regulations would trigger a shocking entire new priority for airlines—the passenger would have to come first. Airlines might have to maintain standby crews waiting to fly if delays force a crew to go beyond their allotted work time. Air traffic control systems might have to give airplanes credit for time spent returning to the gate and keep them from losing their place in line for takeoff.

The FAA will have to adjust its rules to protect passengers.

It's about time it did!

The closest we've come to an airline passenger's bill of rights was the bill that was sponsored by Congressman James Oberstar (D-MN) and passed by the House before it was killed in the Senate. The chairman of the House Committee on Transportation and Infrastructure, Oberstar ingeniously inserted the provision into legislation extending the life of the Federal Aviation Administration (FAA), which also gave airlines $500 million in taxpayer-funded "war insurance" protecting them against disruptions in service.[520]

The U.S. Department of Transportation tried to address the issue of tarmac delays by appointing a task force to recommend improvements in how passengers are treated during such delays. While the task force urged airlines to provide for "better communication and improved preparedness to provide stranded passengers with food and water," the nonbinding "model contingency plan" did not suggest set time limits for forcing a return to the gate, nor did it call for mandatory steps to improve service to passengers who were stranded.[521]

In short, it did next to nothing. Its mealy-mouthed provisions were adopted by a vote of 34–1, the lone opponent being Kate Hanni, the head of the passenger advocacy group, who had been appointed to the commission as a sop to the public.

But Hanni was not entirely shut out. The one proconsumer recommendation the task force made was to allow airlines to be sued in state court. The doctrine of federal preemption bars state courts from hearing any cases that relate to "routes, rates, or services" provided by airlines.[522] But the DOT task force recommended that airlines be required to specify what they would do for passengers who are stuck on the tarmac in their contract of carriage with the passenger (the microprint on the back of your paper ticket). If they did so, passengers could sue for violation of contract—an action that could well be heard in state court.

In light of the possible results, the airlines have declined to endorse the task force's recommendations out of fear of what might happen if state courts should get jurisdiction.

The reason Congress won't act to protect air passengers, of course, is that its members are beholden to the airlines for campaign donations and all sorts of other favors. The airlines have ratcheted up their donations to members of Congress from $2.7 million in 2004 to $3.5 million in 2008.[523]

Here is the list of the members of Congress who have gotten the most in campaign contributions from the airlines and their PACs. Notice the first name on the list: Senator Jay Rockefeller from West Virginia. Guess what? He's the chairman of the Senate Transportation Committee!

AIRLINES: TOP PAC RECIPIENTS, 2008

Rank	Candidate	Amount
1	Jay Rockefeller (D-WV)	$37,000
2	Jerry F. Costello (D-IL)	$34,000
3	James L. Oberstar (D-MN)	$31,999
4	Ted Stevens (R-AK)	$28,568
5	Mitch McConnell (R-KY)	$25,000
6	Saxby Chambliss (R-GA)	$24,500
7	Joe Knollenberg (R-MI)	$22,498
8	Patty Murray (D-WA)	$21,499
9	Daniel K. Inouye (D-HI)	$19,000
10	John L. Mica (R-FL)	$18,000
11	Bennie G. Thompson (D-MS)	$17,998
12	Tom Petri (R-WI)	$17,500
13	Richard Durbin (D-IL)	$17,000
14	John Cornyn (R-TX)	$16,750
15	Charles B. Rangel (D-NY)	$16,000
16	Kay Bailey Hutchison (R-TX)	$15,000
17	Nick Lampson (D-TX)	$12,999
18	Jim McCrery (R-LA)	$12,500
19	Peter DeFazio (D-OR)	$12,000
20	David Scott (D-GA)	$11,300
21	Ken Salazar (D-CO)	$11,000
22	Steven C. LaTourette (R-OH)	$11,000

Rank	Candidate	Amount
23	Gordon H. Smith (R-OR)	$11,000
24	Kay Granger (R-TX)	$10,500
25	Joe Barton (R-TX)	$10,000

Source: "Airlines Top PAC Recipients," Center for Responsive Politics, www.opensecrets .org/industries/pacrecips.php?ind=T1100&cycle=2008.

But sometimes the airlines don't stop at campaign contributions; sometimes they grant special favors. For example, in the fall of 2008, right after the House and Senate voted on the TARP bailout for the nation's major financial institutions, a number of them got together to send New York Democratic congressman Charles Rangel, the chairman of the House Ways and Means Committee, and five other congressmen on a junket to the Caribbean.[524] American Airlines provided free tickets for the members—even though its gift violated House ethics rules.

ACTION AGENDA

You don't have to let the lobbyists and the airlines have the last word. You can act to force adoption of an airline passengers' bill of rights.

The Coalition for an Airline Passengers' Bill of Rights has written a model code that should be passed immediately by Congress and signed by the president. It is a real code—unlike the phony one proposed by the DOT's task force—and it would give passengers real power to force adequate service.

It requires airlines to:

1. Establish procedures to respond to all passenger complaints within twenty-four hours and with appropriate resolution within two weeks.
2. Notify passengers within ten minutes of a delay of known diversions, delays, and cancellations via airport overhead announcement, on aircraft announcement, and posting on airport television monitors.

3. Establish procedures for returning passengers to terminal gate when delays occur so that no plane sits on the tarmac for longer than three hours without connecting to a gate.

4. Provide for the essential needs of passengers during air- or ground-based delays of longer than three hours, including food, water, sanitary facilities, and access to medical attention.

5. Provide for the needs of disabled, elderly and special needs passengers by establishing procedures for assisting with the moving and retrieving of baggage, and the moving of passengers from one area of airport to another at all times by airline personnel.

6. Publish and update monthly on the company's public web site a list of chronically delayed flights, meaning those flights delayed thirty minutes or more, at least forty percent of the time, during a single month.

7. The formal implementation of a Passenger Review Committee, made up of non-airline executives and employees but rather passengers and consumers—that would have the formal ability to review and investigate complaints.

8. Make lowest fare information, schedules and itineraries, cancellation policies, and frequent flyer program requirements available in an easily accessed location and updated in real time.

9. Ensure that baggage is handled without delay or injury; if baggage is lost or misplaced, the airline shall notify customer of baggage status within twelve hours and provide compensation equal to current market value of baggage and its contents.

10. Require that these rights apply equally to all airlines code-share partners, including international partners.[525]

How odd that, in the United States of America, it should be controversial to require an airline to provide food, water, sanitary facilities, and access to medical attention for flights delayed more than three hours! But it is. Legislation to implement these recommendations was killed in the Congress last year.

The coalition, headed by Kate Hanni, is battling hard for your rights and deserves your support. Join or send a donation to them at www.flyers rights.org.

Here is a list of the members of the oversight committees in the House and the Senate. Don't wait until you're stranded to write them to demand passage of the passenger's bill of rights! (If you do wait, bring stationery on your next flight so you can write them nasty letters while you're sweltering on the ground. The airline won't provide it!)

MEMBERS OF THE COMMITTEE ON TRANSPORTATION AND INFRASTRUCTURE,

U.S. House of Representatives, 111th Congress
Majority (2165 RHOB); 202-225-4472
Minority (2163 RHOB); 202-225-9446
James L. Oberstar, Minnesota, Chairman

Democrats

Nick J. Rahall II (WV)	Michael H. Michaud (ME)
Peter A. DeFazio (OR)	Russ Carnahan (MO)
Jerry F. Costello (IL)	Grace F. Napolitano (CA)
Eleanor Holmes Norton (DC)	Daniel Lipinski (IL)
Jerrold Nadler (NY)	Mazie K. Hirono (HI)
Corrine Brown (FL)	Jason Altmire (PA)
Bob Filner (CA)	Timothy J. Walz (MN)
Eddie Bernice Johnson (TX)	Heath Shuler (NC)
Gene Taylor (MS)	Michael A. Arcuri (NY)
Elijah E. Cummings (MD)	Harry E. Mitchell (AZ)
Ellen O. Tauscher (CA)	Christopher P. Carney (PA)
Leonard L. Boswell (IA)	John J. Hall (NY)
Tim Holden (PA)	Steve Kagen (WI)
Brian Baird (WA)	Steve Cohen (TN)
Rick Larsen (WA)	Laura Richardson (CA)
Michael E. Capuano (MA)	Albio Sires (NJ)
Timothy H. Bishop (NY)	Donna F. Edwards (MD)

Solomon P. Ortiz (TX)

Phil Hare (IL)

John A. Boccieri (OH)

Mark H. Schauer (MI)

Betsy Markey (CO)

Parker Griffith (AL)

Michael E. McMahon (NY)

Thomas S. P. Perriello (VA)

Dina Titus (NV)

Harry Teague (NM)

Republicans

John L. Mica (FL) (Ranking
Republican Member)

Don Young (AK)

Thomas E. Petri (WI)

Howard Coble (NC)

John J. Duncan, Jr. (TN)

Vernon J. Ehlers (MI)

Frank A. LoBiondo (NJ)

Jerry Moran (KS)

Gary G. Miller (CA)

Henry E. Brown (SC)

Timothy V. Johnson (IL)

Todd Russell Platts (PA)

Sam Graves (MO)

Bill Shuster (PA)

John Boozman (AK)

Shelley Moore Capito (WV)

Jim Gerlach (PA)

Mario Diaz-Balart (FL)

Charles W. Dent (PA)

Connie Mack (FL)

Lynn A. Westmoreland (GA)

Jean Schmidt (OH)

Candice S. Miller (MO)

Mary Fallin (OK)

Vern Buchanan (FL)

Robert E. Latta (OH)

Brett Guthrie (KY)

Anh "Joseph" Cao (LA)

Aaron Schock (IL)

Pete Olson (TX)

U.S. SENATE COMMITTEE ON COMMERCE, SCIENCE, AND TRANSPORTATION

Democrats

Chairman John D. Rockefeller,
IV (WV)

Daniel K. Inouye (HI)

John F. Kerry (MA)

Byron L. Dorgan (ND)

Barbara Boxer (CA)

Bill Nelson (FL)

Maria Cantwell (WA)

Frank R. Lautenberg (NJ)

Mark Pryor (AR)

Claire McCaskill (MO)

Amy Klobuchar (MN)

Tom Udall (NM)

Mark Warner (VA)

Mark Begich (AK)

Republicans

Kay Bailey Hutchison (TX)
(Ranking Member)

Olympia J. Snowe (ME)

John Ensign (NV)

Jim DeMint (SC)

John Thune (SD)

Roger Wicker (MS)

Johnny Isakson (GA)

David Vitter (LA)

Sam Brownback (KS)

Mel Martinez (FL)

Mike Johanns (NE)

16

THE SILENT CATASTROPHE
Post-Traumatic Stress Disorder in Our Military

In January 2009, more American soldiers killed themselves than were slain by enemy combatants.[526] The stresses and traumas of war, unabated even by today's high-tech military environment, are taking a larger toll among our military than all the roadside bombs, ambushes, and suicide bombers combined. This quiet catastrophe has the military scrambling for answers. One senior Army official, speaking anonymously, called the phenomenon "terrifying. We don't know what is going on," he added.[527]

Twenty-four soldiers committed suicide in January 2009. That is six times the total of the previous January.[528] Colonel Kathy Platoni, the chief clinical psychologist for the Army Reserve and National Guard, cited multiple deployments, the stigma associated with seeking treatment, and, ironically, the excessive use of antidepressant medication as possible reasons for the problem. (Antidepressants have been found to increase suicide rates, particularly among people aged eighteen to twenty-four.)[529]

The past year has seen a troubling growth in the suicide rate among our men and women in uniform. CNN reported that the military suicide total for 2008 was "the highest annual level of suicides among soldiers since the Pentagon began tracking the rate 28 years ago."[530] One hundred and twenty-eight soldiers are confirmed to have committed suicide in 2008; another fifteen died from suspected suicides.[531] Marine suicides also rose from twenty-five in 2006 to thirty-three in 2007 to forty-one in 2008.[532]

One underlying factor contributing to the rise in depression and suicide among our fighting forces is that the entire military and veterans' establishment is geared to treating physical wounds—not wounds of the mind, which are less easily detected but equally dangerous.

Let's not forget that the second most significant casualty of the war in Vietnam—after the 58,000 Americans who died there—was the massive social disruption it caused in the lives of an entire generation of returning veterans.

Hundreds and hundreds of thousands—perhaps millions—of minds were shattered by the experience of fighting in Southeast Asia. An entire generation was scarred by drug abuse, alcoholism, spousal abuse, unemployment, suicide, and hopelessness because of the hell to which they were exposed during their tours of duty.

Today we face a similar problem with the 1.6 million soldiers who have fought in Iraq and Afghanistan. In the coming months they will be returning home in increasing numbers, and we must not let them down as we did those who fought for us in Vietnam. We must help them to come to grips with their experiences—to learn how to survive them, lest they be crippled by nightmares, flashbacks, delusions, depression, or worse.

Unfortunately, there is scant evidence that the VA is making the necessary adjustments to deal with this impending crisis—despite the massive increase in its funding that President Obama has proposed. Much more needs to be done to alert Congress and the administration to the horrific issues faced by returning veterans.

Though Obama and the VA seem eager to assure these vets that they will receive free health care, good homes, and, if possible, jobs, they don't appear to be giving equal emphasis to the need to help restore healthy minds.

The disaster is the post-traumatic stress disorder (PTSD) from which these returning veterans will suffer. The catastrophe is how slowly our government is coming to grips with how to treat it.

Though the military has made progress in training leaders on how to deal with depression and PTSD, Colonel Platoni says, "there is still a huge problem with leadership who shame them when they seek treatment." [533]

The macho culture of "suck it up, kid" is still very much with us.

The prevalence of PTSD has become more and more apparent as the wars in Iraq and Afghanistan have dragged on. Everyone in the military was shocked when a Pentagon study estimated that 10 percent of the returning soldiers met the military's criteria for PTSD.[534] Out of 222,620 soldiers returning from Iraq and Afghanistan that it evaluated in its recent study, the Pentagon found that 21,620 had the condition.[535] Of those diagnosed with PTSD or depression, 80 percent reported having seen combat, fired their weapon, and watched people being killed or wounded. Of those who tested negative, only half had had these searing experiences.[536]

The New England Journal of Medicine puts the rates even higher. In its study of four combat units (three Army and one Marine) returning from Iraq or Afghanistan, the *Journal* found that 17 percent of the Iraq veterans and 11 percent of those coming home from Afghanistan suffered from PTSD.[537]

But the most recent study—by the RAND Corporation, a nonprofit research organization, in April 2008—shows that, with repeated deployments, the problem is escalating sharply. RAND says that 20 percent of the veterans of both the Iraq and the Afghan wars—300,000 men and women in total—will suffer from PTSD or serious depression by the end of their tours of duty there.[538] The study also found that 19 percent report that they experienced a possible traumatic brain injury while deployed.[539] And 7 percent have both PTSD and possible traumatic brain injury.[540]

RAND estimates that it will cost $6.2 billion to treat the PTSD, depression, and traumatic brain injuries of the returning soldiers.[541] "There is a major health crisis facing those men and women who have served our nation in Iraq and Afghanistan," said Terri Tanielian, the project's coleader and a researcher at RAND. "Unless they receive appropriate and effective care for these mental health conditions, there will be long-term consequences for them and for the nation. Unfortunately, we found there are many barriers preventing them from getting the high-quality treatment they need." [542]

PTSD was first officially diagnosed in 1980 at the request of Vietnam veterans organizations. Once known as "shell shock" or combat fatigue, post-traumatic stress disorder can develop after witnessing or experiencing a traumatic event.

USA Today notes that PTSD "produces a wide range of symptoms in men and women who have experienced a traumatic event that provoked intense fear, helplessness or horror." The paper notes that soldiers "re-experience traumatic events through flashbacks, hallucinations, or nightmares. Often these are triggered by exposure to anything that reminds them of the trauma. Among the symptoms are "troubled sleep, irritability, anger, poor concentration, hypervigilance, and exaggerated responses."[543]

Those who suffer from PTSD may "feel depression, detachment or estrangement, guilt, intense anxiety and panic, and other negative emotions. They often feel they have little in common with civilian peers; issues that concern friends and family seem trivial after combat."[544] During nightmares, they may even strike their spouses or partners but remember nothing about it after waking up.

SUFFERING FROM PTSD

Jesus Bocanegra was an Army infantry scout who suffers from PTSD. "I had real bad flashbacks. I couldn't control them," Bocanegra, 23, says. "I saw the murder of children, women. It was just horrible for anyone to experience."

Bocanegra recalls calling in Apache helicopter strikes on a house by the Tigris River where he had seen crates of enemy ammunition carried in. When the gunfire ended, there was silence.

But then children's cries and screams drifted from the destroyed home, he says. "I didn't know there were kids there. . . . Those screams are the most horrible thing you can hear."

His readjustment has been difficult: his friends threw a homecoming party for him, and he got arrested for drunken driving on the way home.[545]

Lieutenant Julian Goodrum, an Army reservist, is being treated for PTSD with therapy and antianxiety drugs. A platoon leader in Iraq, he experienced isolation, depression, an inability to sleep and racing thoughts after his return home.

(continued on next page)

"It just accumulated until it overwhelmed me. I was having a breakdown and trying to get assistance," he says. "The smell of diesel would trigger things for me. Loud noises, crowds, heavy traffic give me a hard time now. I have a lot of panic. . . . You feel like you're choking."[546]

Sean Huze, a Marine corporal, doesn't have PTSD but says everyone who saw combat suffers from at least some combat stress. He says the unrelenting insurgent threat in Iraq gives no opportunity to relax, and combat numbs the senses and emotions.

"There is no 'front,' " Huze says. "You go back to the rear, at the Army base in Mosul, and you go in to get your chow, and the chow hall blows up."

Huze, thirty, says the horror often isn't felt until later. "I saw a dead child, probably three or four years old, lying on the road in Nasiriyah," he says. "It moved me less than if I saw a dead dog at the time. I didn't care. Then you come back, if you are fortunate enough, and hold your own child, and you think of the dead child you didn't care about. . . . You think about how little you cared at the time, and that hurts."

Smells bring back the horror. "A barbecue pit—throw a steak on the grill, and it smells a lot like searing flesh," he says. "You go to get your car worked on, and if anyone is welding, the smell of the burning metal is no different than burning caused by rounds fired at it. It takes you back there instantly."[547]

Allen Walsh, who was attached to a Marine unit providing force protection and chemical decontamination, says he has experienced PTSD, which he attributes to the constant threat of attack and demand for instant life-or-death decisions.

"It seemed like every day you were always pointing your weapon at somebody. It's something I have to live with," he says.

At home, he found he couldn't sleep more than three or four hours a night. When the nightmares began, he started smoking cigarettes. He'd find himself shaking and quick-tempered.

"Any little noise and I'd jump out of bed and run around the house with a gun," he says. "I'd wake up at night with cold sweats."[548]

Perhaps the most serious part of the Pentagon's recent study of Iraq and Afghanistan veterans was its finding that fewer than 40 percent of those afflicted by PTSD have sought help.

"You can't just say that I've got a hundred programs, therefore, I've done my job," said Steve Robinson, the executive director of the National Gulf War Resource Center. "This study indicates that the sickest veterans who need the most help won't go." [550]

The study documents the horrors to which Iraq soldiers are exposed. Ninety percent reported being shot at; half reported having handled a dead body. [551]

The New England Journal of Medicine study found that 95 percent of Marines and Army soldiers in Iraq had been shot at. Fifty-six percent had killed an enemy combatant. And 94 percent had seen bodies and human remains. [552] This is the stuff of nightmares and flashbacks.

"There are no clear enemy lines, non-stop pace, the war surrounds the soldier 360 degrees. The enemy can be man, woman or child. This is an extremely stressful situation," said Steve Robinson. [553]

According to Fox News, "Robinson said men and women who in the past would have died in the field have survived thanks to advanced body armor, but in many cases the soldiers are living with severe, life-altering injuries or are watching their friends grapple with them. In other cases, many of the less injured are National Guard and Reservists who are being sent back to the theater two and three times." [554]

The New England Journal of Medicine study suggested that about a quarter of returned soldiers were drinking excessively. One researcher said, "I know from walking and talking to people that more like 75 percent are indulging in excessive alcohol to self-medicate, to escape." [555]

Fox News spoke with Barbara Critchfield, a counselor at Shoemaker High School near Fort Hood in Texas, where nearly 80 percent of students

had parents deployed overseas. Now that their parents have started returning from the front, they say, their behavior is causing concern among the
students.

"Some talk about fathers, who all they want to do is drink and sleep—
we know there is PTSD," she said. "I don't know how far-reaching it is, they
might be isolated incidents, I don't know." [556]

But many of those suffering do not go for treatment.

As CNN reports, on his second day in Iraq, Staff Sergeant Georg-
Andreas Pogany saw an Iraqi body that had suffered severe trauma, and he
suffered what he considered a nervous breakdown. "I wasn't functioning.
I was having physical symptoms. I was having a behavioral reaction," he
recalled. [557]

"After struggling through the night, he said he decided to tell his supe-
rior officer out of fear that if we do go out on a patrol and I do freeze up, that
could have consequences too." Instead of receiving the help his condition
required, however, he was cautioned *not* to seek treatment. "He was told to
reconsider for the sake of his career, he said." [558]

"The message was: 'Hey, you're a coward. You're acting like a coward.' " [559]

The New England Journal of Medicine study confirmed other evidence that
those who need help most are the least likely to seek treatment. "Of those
whose responses were positive for a mental disorder, only 23 to 40 percent
sought mental health care. Those whose responses were positive for a mental disorder were twice as likely as those whose responses were negative to
report concern about possible stigmatization and other barriers to seeking
mental health care." [560]

Because of the repeated deployments to which Iraq veterans are subject, the nature of the war, and the all-volunteer military, past indicators of
PTSD may not be applicable to the Iraq War. Experts are concerned that the
incidence may be vastly greater than anyone has thought.

The prevalence of PTSD threatens to strain the financial resources of
the Veterans Administration. In 2005, the *Washington Post* reported that "In
the past five years, the number of veterans receiving compensation for . . .
PTSD has grown nearly seven times as fast as the number receiving benefits
for disabilities in general, according to a report this year by the inspector

general of the Department of Veterans Affairs. A total of 215,871 veterans received PTSD benefit payments last year at a cost of $4.3 billion, up from $1.7 billion in 1999—a jump of more than 150 percent." [561]

But the *Post* noted that this increase did not really factor in the full impact of the Iraq and Afghan wars "because the increase is largely the result of Vietnam War vets seeking treatment decades after their combat experiences." [562] When the Iraq and Afghan vets return, the impact is likely to be enormous.

Even as many soldiers don't seek treatment for PTSD, others are inclined to conclude grimly that it can never be cured. As Chris Frueh, the director of the VA clinic in Charleston, South Carolina, told the *Post*, "we have young men and women coming back from Iraq who are having PTSD and getting the message that this is a disorder they can't be treated for, and they will have to be on disability for the rest of their lives." [563]

This unjustified pessimism could lead to the creation of a permanent class of veterans who think themselves disabled and live on government pensions. Those who are granted 100 percent disability status from the Veterans Administration get about $2,300 per month. [564] And, the *Post* reports, "once veterans are declared disabled, they retain that status indefinitely." As Frueh notes, "the [Veterans] department's disability system encourages some veterans to exaggerate symptoms and prolong problems in order to maintain eligibility for benefits. . . . My concern about the policies is that they create perverse incentives to stay ill. It is very tough to get better when you are trying to demonstrate how ill you are." [565]

Frueh warned that this system sets up an "adversarial relationship" between doctors and returning soldiers over whether to assign a disability status for their PTSD. [566]

But most people agree that the more serious problem is that some patients never get the help they need—because, as Frueh told the *Post*, "they are unwilling to undergo the lengthy process of qualifying for disability benefits, which often requires them to repeatedly revisit the painful episodes they experienced." [567]

Some, like Steve Robinson, accuse the Veterans Administration of deliberately failing to diagnose PTSD in returning soldiers to avoid the cost of disability payments. Robinson said, "what they [the VA] are trying to do is figure out a way not to diagnose vets with PTSD. It's like telling a patient with cancer, 'if we tell you you don't have cancer, then you won't suffer from cancer.'" [568]

The RAND Corporation study, like both the Pentagon and *The New England Journal of Medicine* studies, found that only about half of those suffering from PTSD or major depression get help. [569]

"If PTSD and depression go untreated or are undertreated, there is a cascading set of consequences," said RAND project coleader Lisa Jaycox. "Drug use, suicide, marital problems and unemployment are some of the consequences. There will be a bigger societal impact if these service members go untreated. The consequences are not good for the individuals or society in general." [570]

Why don't returning servicemen and women seek treatment? RAND reports that "many are worried about the side effects of medication or believe that family and friends can provide more help than a mental health professional" but that "even more reported that they worried seeking care might damage their career or cause their peers to lose confidence in their abilities." [571]

RAND recommends that "the military create a system that would allow service members to receive mental health services confidentially in order to ease concerns about negative career repercussions." "We need to remove the institutional cultural barriers that discourage soldiers from seeking care," RAND project coleader Terri Tanielian said. "Just because someone is getting mental health care does not mean that they are not able to do their job. Seeking mental health treatment should be seen as a sign of strength and interest in getting better, not a weakness. People need to get help as early as possible, not only once their symptoms become severe and disabling." [572]

Unfortunately, even when the Pentagon finds that servicepeople are suffering from PTSD, it does not always refer them for counseling. A 2005 study by the Government Accountability Office found that "only about one in five Iraq and Afghanistan war veterans who screen positive for combat-related stress disorders are referred by the Pentagon for mental health treatment." [573]

Fox News reports that many current and former government officials are concerned about the ability of the Pentagon and the Veterans Administration to handle the new flood of PTSD cases.

"We are not prepared for the body count we are seeing, mental health or otherwise," said Sue Bailey, assistant secretary of defense for health affairs during the Clinton administration. "America's mood is not prepared for this."[574]

"The [Veterans Administration] is not geared up and the [Department of Defense] is not geared up," said Rick Weidman, a spokesman for Vietnam Veterans of America. "That's why some of us have been talking, and you are going to see a major front of veterans saying we need this fixed and we need this fixed now."[575]

But just as soldiers are reluctant to report psychological trauma to their officers or even to the Veterans Administration, the VA itself has a palpable bias against taking mental issues seriously.

The Pentagon, facing the deadly increase in military suicides, seems to be doing better. It has set up Defense Department Centers of Excellence for Psychological Health and Traumatic Brain Injury under the command of Army Brigadier General Loree Sutton. The centers are designed to "establish quality standards for: clinical care; education and training; prevention; [and] patient, family and community outreach."[576] They are to be staffed by behavioral health consultants and nurses and will be open 24/7. The Pentagon says that the centers "can deal with everything from routine requests for information about psychological health and traumatic brain injury, to questions about symptoms a caller is having, to helping a caller find appropriate health care resources."[577]

General Sutton's office has also launched a program called Real Warriors, in which "service members can talk about and listen to the stories of those who sought help for psychological injuries or traumatic brain injuries."[578] By focusing on "the story of real warriors facing real battles both on as well as off the battlefield, with wounds both visible and invisible," General Sutton hopes to stimulate soldiers and veterans to seek help and cope with their problems.

To show that PTSD is not some new fad, Real Warriors features the ancient Greek play *Ajax* by Sophocles, in which "a warrior who has been deployed for several years tries to kill his commanding officer, but ends up killing himself."[579]

But the Veterans Administration itself is less sensitive to PTSD. President Obama's budget request for the 2009–10 fiscal year increases Veterans Affairs spending by $15.1 billion, raising it from $97.7 billion to $112.8 billion.[580] This should be more than enough money to deal with the vast PTSD problem among returning veterans. But the priorities the Veterans Administration has identified in spending the funds show a blind spot when it comes to PTSD.

One would hope that this massive increase in spending would include lots of money for PTSD treatment. But the Veterans Administration, though lauding the extra money, made no mention of PTSD or any other psychological counseling as it recounted the benefits of the extra funding.

So where is the money going? The VA says it will be used to expand VA health care eligibility to half a million "deserving" veterans over the next five years.[581] It notes that the new budget "provides greater benefits for Veterans who are medically retired from active duty"[582] and praised its increase in educational support. The VA lauded the additional "specialty care" funded in the budget and listed "such areas as prosthetics, vision and spinal cord injury, aging, and women's health."[583] It applauded the new attention to homelessness among veterans. The VA celebrated the expansion of its services in rural areas. In fact, it listed every conceivable use of the new money—*except* for treating PTSD, suicidal tendencies, or severe depression. Those words were never mentioned!

ACTION AGENDA

The old-school Veterans Administration knows what to do about those who have lost arms or legs in combat. But it doesn't know enough about those who have suffered grievous psychological scars—despite all that we should have learned as a country from the true horrors suffered by the returning veterans of the Vietnam War. This problem needs attention before it leaves an entire generation of our veterans emotionally crippled.

Here are the people to write to:

- Obama's newly appointed secretary of veterans affairs is Eric K. Shinseki. He can be reached at the Department of Veteran Affairs: 1-800-827-1000.

- The chairman of the Senate Committee on Veterans is Daniel K. Akaka. His address is P.O. Box 50144, Honolulu, HI 96850, and his phone number is 202-224-9126.

- And, in the House, the chairman is Bob Filner. He can be reached at:

House Committee on Veterans' Affairs
335 Cannon House Office Building
Washington, DC 20515
202-225-9756

CONCLUSION

As we said in the introduction, the time for action is now!

Barack Obama may be our president, but he's not a dictator. He has a lot of tough votes ahead of him in Congress, and he needs to win them. If he wants to continue to hold on to power, he will have to bring enough of his minions back to Congress in 2010 that he'll still be calling the shots in Washington.

It's up to us to play defense against Obama's radical agenda. We need to mobilize to pressure the weak links in his congressional majority whenever crucial votes are coming up. The ultraliberals in Congress, such as Congresswoman Maxine Waters and Senator Barbara Boxer, aren't worth pressuring. They couldn't be more delighted with Obama's socialist agenda. But the moderates—or at least those who run as moderates—from the Democratic Party can be pressured. And they must be!

We suggest that you set up an e-mail club with your friends and family so that you can instantly reach out to dozens or even hundreds of people and get them to send e-mails, letters, and phone calls to these moderate Democrats, pressuring them to vote against Obama's agenda.

Scan down the list of congressmen and senators at the end of the War on Prosperity chapter. See which ones come from your district or state. Make a special point of pressuring them.

Then go to www.dickmorris.com and share your e-mail address with us. In addition to sending you our columns and newsletters, we'll keep you posted on when key votes are taking place on the issues discussed in this book—so that you, in turn, can use *your* e-mail list to get your friends and family to pressure those key members of Congress.

There will be several special elections between now and November 2010. These races—and the scheduled governors' contests in New Jersey and Virginia—will give us a real chance to send a message of discontent and opposition to the Obama agenda. By beating the Democratic candidates in these races, we can make it clear how badly his agenda contrasts with the views of the American people!

When these races come up, we'll recommend independent expenditure groups to which you can contribute, helping them target the vulnerable races and win them.

And, when 2010 comes around, we'll be working full-time on reversing the Obama majorities in Congress so as to roll back his socialist program.

This is no time for apathy or alienation or hopelessness.

It's a time for action.

The stakes literally could not be higher.

ACKNOWLEDGMENTS

We would like to begin by thanking Morgan Buehler for her wonderful and prompt research. This is our second book with her. She also worked with us on *Fleeced*. And we hope to do many more with her.

We would like to thank James McGann for his help with research on the Canadian health system and earmarks, Frank Gaffney for helping us to grasp the intricacies of the threat posed by Shariah Law, and Barry Elias for his economic wisdom and advice.

Thanks to Chuck Brooks for his patriotism and his inputs on Shariah law and terror policies and to Ken Lee of the Canadian Conservative Party for his info on the health care system there.

We also thank Maureen Maxwell, Tom Gallagher, and Irma Gallagher for all their help.

Sandy Frazier, the best book PR person around, is helping to make this book a success as she did with *Outrage* and *Fleeced*.

Cal Morgan, our editor for the past seven books (all best sellers) is doing something right and we are grateful.

Our thanks to Opensecrets.org, the web site of the Center for Responsive Politics, for making the political system transparent.

And, finally, to Jonathan Burnham, Kathy Schneider, Christine Boyd, Tina Andreadis, Kate Blum, Josh Marwell, Doug Jones, Brian Grogan, Cindy Achar, John Jusino, and Brittany Hamblin at HarperCollins, for bringing the book swiftly to print.

APPENDIX
Complete List of TARP Recipients (as of March 11, 2009)

Name	Type	Date	State	Bailout Amount (in Millions)
Citigroup	Bank	10/28/08	NY	$45,000
Bank of America (including Merrill Lynch)	Bank	10/28/08	NC	$45,000
AIG	Insurance corporation	11/25/08	NY	$40,000
AIG (second round)	Insurance corporation	3/2/09	NY	$30,000
JPMorgan Chase	Bank	10/28/08	NY	$25,000
Wells Fargo	Bank	10/28/08	CA	$25,000
General Motors	Auto company	12/29/08	MI	$14,284
Goldman Sachs	Bank	10/28/08	NY	$10,000
Morgan Stanley	Bank	10/28/08	NY	$10,000
PNC Financial Services	Bank	12/31/08	PA	$7,579.2
U.S. Bancorp	Bank	11/14/08	MN	$6,599
Chrysler	Auto company	1/2/09	MI	$5,500

Name	Type	Date	State	Bailout Amount (in Millions)
GMAC	Financial services	12/29/08	MI	$5,000
SunTrust	Bank	12/31/08	GA	$4,900
Capital One Financial Corp.	Bank	11/14/08	VA	$3,555.2
Regions Financial Corp.	Bank	11/14/08	AL	$3,500
Fifth Third Bancorp	Bank	12/31/08	OH	$3,408
American Express	Financial services	1/9/09	NY	$3,388.9
BB&T	Bank	11/14/08	NC	$3,133.6
Bank of New York Mellon	Bank	10/28/08	NY	$3,000
KeyCorp	Bank	11/14/08	OH	$2,500
CIT Group	Financial services	12/31/08	NY	$2,330
Comerica	Bank	11/14/08	TX	$2,250
State Street	Bank	10/28/08	MA	$2,000
Marshall & Ilsley	Bank	11/14/08	WI	$1,715
Northern Trust	Bank	11/14/08	IL	$1,576
Zions Bancorp	Bank	11/14/08	UT	$1,400
Huntington Bancshares	Bank	11/14/08	OH	$1,398.1
Discover Financial Services	Financial services	3/13/2009	IL	$1,224.6
Synovus Financial Corp.	Bank	12/19/08	GA	$967.9
Popular, Inc.	Bank	12/05/08	PR	$935
First Horizon National	Bank	11/14/08	TN	$866.5
M&T Bank Corporation	Bank	12/23/08	NY	$600
Associated Banc-Corp	Bank	11/21/08	WI	$525
First BanCorp	Bank	1/16/09	PR	$400
Webster Financial	Bank	11/21/08	CT	$400
City National	Bank	11/21/08	CA	$400
Fulton Financial Corp.	Bank	12/23/08	PA	$376.5
TCF Financial	Bank	11/14/08	MN	$361.2
South Financial Group	Bank	12/05/08	SC	$347
Valley National	Bank	11/14/08	NJ	$330
Wilmington Trust Corporation	Bank	12/12/08	DE	$330

Name	Type	Date	State	Bailout Amount (in Millions)
East West Bancorp	Bank	12/05/08	CA	$306.5
Sterling Financial Corp.	Bank	12/05/08	WA	$303
Susquehanna Bancshares	Bank	12/12/08	PA	$300
Citizens Republic Bancorp	Bank	12/12/08	MI	$300
Whitney Holding Corp.	Bank	12/19/08	LA	$300
UCBH Holdings	Bank	11/14/08	CA	$298.7
First Banks	Private bank	12/31/08	MO	$295.4
New York Private Bank & Trust Corp.	Private bank	1/9/09	NY	$267.3
Flagstar Bancorp	Bank	1/30/09	MI	$266.7
Cathay General Bancorp	Bank	12/05/08	CA	$258
Wintrust Financial Corp.	Bank	12/19/08	IL	$250
PrivateBancorp	Bank	1/30/09	IL	$243.8
SVB Financial Group	Bank	12/12/08	CA	$235
International Bancshares Corp.	Bank	12/23/08	TX	$216
Trustmark Corp.	Bank	11/21/08	MS	$215
Umpqua	Bank	11/14/08	OR	$214.2
Washington Federal	Bank	11/14/08	WA	$200
MB Financial	Bank	12/05/08	IL	$196
First Midwest Bancorp	Bank	12/05/08	IL	$193
First Niagara	Bank	11/21/08	NY	$184
Pacific Capital Bancorp	Bank	11/21/08	CA	$180.6
United Community Banks	Bank	12/05/08	GA	$180
Boston Private Financial Holdings	Bank	11/21/08	MA	$154
Provident Bankshares Corp.	Bank	11/14/08	MD	$151
National Penn Bancshares	Bank	12/12/08	PA	$150
Dickinson Financial Corp. II	Private bank	1/16/09	MO	$146.1
Western Alliance Bancorporation	Bank	11/21/08	NV	$140
Central Pacific Financial Corp.	Bank	1/9/09	HI	$135
CVB Financial	Bank	12/05/08	CA	$130
Sterling Bancshares	Bank	12/12/08	TX	$125.2
FirstMerit Corp.	Bank	1/9/09	OH	$125
Banner Corp.	Bank	11/21/08	WA	$124

Name	Type	Date	State	Bailout Amount (in Millions)
Signature Bank	Bank	12/12/08	NY	$120
First Merchants Corp.	Bank	2/20/09	IN	$116
1st Source Corp.	Bank	1/23/09	IN	$111
WTB Financial Corp.	Private bank	1/30/09	WA	$110
Anchor BanCorp Wisconsin	Bank	1/30/09	WI	$110
S&T Bancorp	Bank	1/16/09	PA	$108.7
Taylor Capital	Bank	11/21/08	IL	$104.8
Old National Bancorp	Bank	12/12/08	IN	$100
Park National Corporation	Bank	12/23/08	OH	$100
F.N.B. Corporation	Bank	1/9/09	PA	$100
First Busey Corporation	Bank	3/6/09	IL	$100
Pinnacle Financial	Bank	12/12/08	TN	$95
IBERIABANK Corp	Bank	12/05/08	LA	$90
Sun Bancorp	Bank	1/9/09	NJ	$89.3
Plains Capital Corp.	Private bank	12/19/08	TX	$87.6
Midwest Banc Holdings	Bank	12/05/08	IL	$84.8
Westamerica Bancorporation	Bank	2/13/09	CA	$83.7
Integra Bank Corporation	Bank	2/27/09	IN	$83.6
Sandy Spring Bancorp	Bank	12/05/08	MD	$83
Heartland Financial USA	Bank	12/19/08	IA	$81.7
Hampton Roads Bankshares	Bank	12/31/08	VA	$80.3
First Financial Bancorp	Bank	12/23/08	OH	$80
Independent Bank Corp.	Bank	1/9/09	MA	$78.2
Columbia Banking System	Bank	11/21/08	WA	$76.9
TowneBank	Bank	12/12/08	VA	$76.5
Texas Capital Bancshares	Bank	1/16/09	TX	$75
Bank of the Ozarks	Bank	12/12/08	AR	$75
WesBanco	Bank	12/05/08	WV	$75
Old Second Bancorp	Bank	1/16/09	IL	$73
First Place Financial Corp.	Bank	3/13/2009	OH	$72.9
Green Bankshares	Bank	12/23/08	TN	$72.3
Independent Bank Corporation	Bank	12/12/08	MI	$72
Virginia Commerce Bancorp	Bank	12/12/08	VA	$71

Name	Type	Date	State	Bailout Amount (in Millions)
Flushing Financial Corp.	Bank	12/19/08	NY	$70
Southwest Bancorp	Bank	12/05/08	OK	$70
Superior Bancorp	Bank	12/05/08	AL	$69
Nara Bancorp	Bank	11/21/08	CA	$67
First Financial Holdings	Bank	12/05/08	SC	$65
First Bancorp	Bank	1/9/09	NC	$65
SCBT Financial Corp	Bank	1/16/09	SC	$64.8
CoBiz Financial	Bank	12/19/08	CO	$64.4
Wilshire Bancorp	Bank	12/12/08	CA	$62.2
Union Bankshares	Bank	12/19/08	VA	$59
Lakeland Bancorp	Bank	2/6/09	NJ	$59
Great Southern Bancorp	Bank	12/05/08	MO	$58
Liberty Bancshares	Private bank	1/23/09	AR	$57.5
MainSource Financial Group	Bank	1/16/09	IN	$57
Lakeland Financial Corporation	Bank	2/27/09	IN	$56
Center Financial Corp.	Bank	12/12/08	CA	$55
WSFS Financial	Bank	1/23/09	DE	$52.6
NewBridge Bancorp	Bank	12/12/08	NC	$52.4
Ameris Bancorp	Bank	11/21/08	GA	$52
FNB United Corp.	Bank	2/13/09	NC	$51.5
BancTrust Financial Group	Bank	12/19/08	AL	$50
State Bankshares	Private bank	1/16/09	ND	$50
Seacoast Banking Corp.	Bank	12/19/08	FL	$50
Home BancShares	Bank	1/16/09	AR	$50
Fidelity Southern Corp.	Bank	12/19/08	GA	$48.2
BancPlus Corporation	Private bank	2/20/09	MS	$48
The Bancorp	Bank	12/12/08	DE	$45.2
MetroCorp Bancshares	Bank	1/16/09	TX	$45
Cadence Financial Corp.	Bank	1/9/09	MS	$44
Exchange Bank	Private bank	12/19/08	CA	$43
Southern Community Financial	Bank	12/05/08	NC	$42.8
Sterling Bancorp	Bank	12/23/08	NY	$42
First Community Bancshares	Bank	11/21/08	VA	$41.5

Name	Type	Date	State	Bailout Amount (in Millions)
PremierWest Bancorp	Bank	2/13/09	OR	$41.4
Capital Bank	Bank	12/12/08	NC	$41.3
Berkshire Hills Bancorp	Bank	12/19/08	MA	$40
Reliance Bancshares	Private bank	2/13/09	MO	$40
Heritage Commerce Corp.	Bank	11/21/08	CA	$40
Cascade Financial Corp.	Bank	11/21/08	WA	$39
Peoples Bancorp	Bank	1/30/09	OH	$39
OceanFirst Financial Corp.	Bank	1/16/09	NJ	$38.3
QCR Holdings	Bank	2/13/09	IL	$38.2
Eagle Bancorp	Bank	12/05/08	MD	$38.2
Bridgeview Bancorp	Private bank	12/19/08	IL	$38
Financial Institutions	Bank	12/23/08	NY	$37.5
First Defiance Financial Corp.	Bank	12/05/08	OH	$37
TIB Financial Corp.	Bank	12/05/08	FL	$37
State Bancorp	Bank	12/05/08	NY	$36.8
Fidelity Financial Corp.	Private bank	12/19/08	KS	$36.3
Yadkin Valley Financial Corp.	Bank	1/16/09	NC	$36
West Bancorporation	Bank	12/31/08	IA	$36
Marquette National Corp.	Private bank	12/19/08	IL	$35.5
Porter Bancorp	Bank	11/21/08	KY	$35
Enterprise Financial Services Corp.	Bank	12/19/08	MO	$35
Encore Bancshares	Bank	12/05/08	TX	$34
The Bank of Kentucky	Bank	2/13/09	KY	$34
First Market Bank	Private bank	2/6/09	VA	$33.9
First Security Group	Bank	1/9/09	TN	$33
Firstbank Corp.	Bank	1/30/09	MI	$33
Centrue Financial	Bank	1/9/09	MO	$32.7
Pulaski Financial Corp.	Bank	1/16/09	MO	$32.5
MutualFirst Financial	Bank	12/23/08	IN	$32.4
Parkvale Financial Corp.	Bank	12/23/08	PA	$31.8
Bank of North Carolina	Bank	12/05/08	NC	$31.3
Royal Bancshares of Pennsylvania	Bank	2/20/09	PA	$30.4
Hawthorn Bancshares	Bank	12/19/08	MO	$30.3

Name	Type	Date	State	Bailout Amount (in Millions)
First M&F Corp.	Bank	2/27/09	MS	$30
StellarOne Corp.	Bank	12/19/08	VA	$30
Farmers Capital Bank Corp.	Bank	1/9/09	KY	$30
First United Corp.	Bank	1/30/09	MD	$30
Tennessee Commerce Bancorp	Bank	12/19/08	TN	$30
Bancorp Rhode Island	Bank	12/19/08	RI	$30
Peapack-Gladstone Financial	Bank	1/9/09	NJ	$28.7
Colony Bankcorp	Bank	1/9/09	GA	$28
Bank of Marin Bancorp	Bank	12/05/08	CA	$28
CenterState Banks of Florida	Bank	11/21/08	FL	$27.9
Intermountain Community Bancorp	Bank	12/19/08	ID	$27
Alliance Financial Corp.	Bank	12/19/08	NY	$26.9
Citizens & Northern Corporation	Bank	1/16/09	PA	$26.4
Washington Banking Company	Bank	1/16/09	WA	$26.4
Patriot Bancshares	Private bank	12/19/08	TX	$26
HMN Financial	Bank	12/23/08	MN	$26
LNB Bancorp	Bank	12/12/08	OH	$25.2
Princeton National Bancorp	Bank	1/23/09	IL	$25.1
Peoples Bancorp of North Carolina	Bank	12/23/08	NC	$25.1
VIST Financial Corp.	Bank	12/19/08	PA	$25
Intervest Bancshares	Bank	12/23/08	NY	$25
Horizon Bancorp	Bank	12/19/08	IN	$25
Rogers Bancshares	Private bank	1/30/09	AR	$25
The First Bancorp	Bank	1/9/09	ME	$25
First California Financial Group	Bank	12/19/08	CA	$25
Shore Bancshares	Bank	1/9/09	MD	$25
HF Financial Corp.	Bank	11/21/08	SD	$25
Crescent Financial Corp.	Bank	1/9/09	NC	$24.9
National Bancshares	Private bank	2/27/09	IA	$24.7
Eastern Virginia Bankshares	Bank	1/9/09	VA	$24
Community Trust Financial Corp	Private bank	1/9/09	LA	$24
Heritage Financial	Bank	11/21/08	WA	$24

Name	Type	Date	State	Bailout Amount (in Millions)
Bridge Capital Holdings	Bank	12/23/08	CA	$23.9
Severn Bancorp	Bank	11/21/08	MD	$23.4
Park Bancorporation	Private bank	3/6/09	WI	$23.2
First Citizens Banc Corp.	Bank	1/23/09	OH	$23.2
TriState Capital Holdings	Private bank	2/27/09	PA	$23
Central Bancorp	Private bank	2/27/09	TX	$22.5
Central Community Corp.	Private bank	2/20/09	TX	$22
Wainwright Bank & Trust	Bank	12/19/08	MA	$22
Middleburg Financial Corp.	Bank	1/30/09	VA	$22
Liberty Bancshares	Private bank	2/13/09	MO	$21.9
Blue Valley Ban Corp.	Bank	12/05/08	KS	$21.8
Indiana Community Bancorp	Bank	12/12/08	IN	$21.5
BancIndependent	Private bank	3/13/2009	AL	$21.1
AmeriServ Financial	Bank	12/19/08	PA	$21
The Baraboo Bancorporation	Private bank	1/16/09	WI	$20.7
Unity Bancorp	Bank	12/05/08	NJ	$20.6
United Bancorp	Bank	1/16/09	MI	$20.6
Citizens South Banking Corp	Bank	12/12/08	NC	$20.5
BNCCORP	Private bank	1/16/09	ND	$20.1
C&F Financial Corp.	Bank	1/9/09	VA	$20
MidSouth Bancorp	Bank	1/9/09	LA	$20
First Financial Service Corp	Bank	1/9/09	KY	$20
D.L. Evans Bancorp	Private bank	2/27/09	ID	$19.9
First PacTrust Bancorp	Bank	11/21/08	CA	$19.3
Carver Bancorp	Cdfi	1/16/09	NY	$19
Bar Harbor Bankshares	Bank	1/16/09	ME	$18.8
HopFed Bancorp	Bank	12/12/08	KY	$18.4
Sovereign Bancshares	Private bank	3/13/2009	TX	$18.2
Peoples Bancorp	Private bank	2/13/09	WA	$18
Security Federal Corp.	Bank	12/19/08	SC	$18
ECB Bancorp	Bank	1/16/09	NC	$17.9
Community First	Private bank	2/27/09	TN	$17.8
Community Bankers Trust Corp.	Bank	12/19/08	VA	$17.7

Name	Type	Date	State	Bailout Amount (in Millions)
First Northern Community Bancorp	Bank	3/13/2009	CA	$17.4
Southern First Bancshares	Bank	2/27/09	MS	$17.3
Liberty Shares	Private bank	2/20/09	GA	$17.3
F&M Financial Corporation	Private bank	2/13/09	TN	$17.2
Northern States Financial Corp.	Bank	2/20/09	IL	$17.2
Guaranty Federal Bancshares	Bank	1/30/09	MO	$17
First American International Corp.	Cdfi	3/13/2009	NY	$17
F&M Financial Corporation	Private bank	2/6/09	NC	$17
Bank of Commerce	Bank	11/14/08	CA	$17
White River Bancshares Company	Private bank	2/20/09	AR	$16.8
Timberland Bancorp	Bank	12/23/08	WA	$16.6
Codorus Valley Bancorp	Bank	1/9/09	PA	$16.5
First Federal Bancshares of Arkansas	Bank	3/6/09	AR	$16.5
1st Financial Services	Bank	11/14/08	NC	$16.3
Parke Bancorp	Bank	1/30/09	NJ	$16.3
Pacific City Financial Corp.	Private bank	12/19/08	CA	$16.2
Valley Financial Corp.	Bank	12/12/08	VA	$16
MidWestOne Financial Group	Bank	2/6/09	IA	$16
Carolina Bank Holdings	Bank	1/9/09	NC	$16
Community West Bancshares	Bank	12/19/08	CA	$15.6
Stockmens Financial Corporation	Private bank	2/6/09	SD	$15.6
Tri-County Financial Corp.	Private bank	12/19/08	MD	$15.5
BankFirst Capital Corp.	Private bank	1/23/09	MS	$15.5
First Reliance Bancshares	Private bank	3/6/09	SC	$15.3
LSB Corp	Bank	12/12/08	MA	$15
Centra Financial Holdings	Private bank	1/16/09	WV	$15
State Capital Corporation	Private bank	2/13/09	MS	$15
Nicolet Bankshares	Private bank	12/23/08	WI	$15
Monarch Financial Holdings	Bank	12/19/08	VA	$14.7
Tidelands Bancshares	Bank	12/19/08	SC	$14.4
First National Corporation	Private bank	3/13/2009	VA	$13.9

Name	Type	Date	State	Bailout Amount (in Millions)
Magna Bank	Private bank	12/23/08	TN	$13.8
First Texas BHC	Private bank	3/6/09	TX	$13.5
Oak Valley Bancorp	Bank	12/05/08	CA	$13.5
LCNB Corp.	Bank	1/9/09	OH	$13.4
Morrill Bancshares	Private bank	1/16/09	KS	$13
HCSB Financial Corporation	Bank	3/6/09	SC	$12.9
Adbanc	Private bank	1/30/09	NE	$12.7
Community Financial Corp.	Bank	12/19/08	VA	$12.6
Bankers' Bank of the West	Private bank	1/30/09	CO	$12.6
Security State Bancshares	Private bank	2/20/09	MO	$12.5
PeoplesSouth Bancshares	Private bank	3/6/09	GA	$12.3
OneUnited Bank	Cdfi	12/19/08	MA	$12.1
1st Constitution Bancorp	Bank	12/23/08	NJ	$12
First Manitowoc Bancorp	Private bank	1/16/09	WI	$12
Blue Ridge Bancshares	Private bank	3/6/09	MO	$12
The Queensborough Company	Private bank	1/9/09	GA	$12
FNB Bancorp	Private bank	2/27/09	CA	$12
Plumas Bancorp	Bank	1/30/09	CA	$11.9
Medallion Bank	Private bank	2/27/09	UT	$11.8
DNB Financial Corp.	Bank	1/30/09	PA	$11.8
TCB Holding Company	Private bank	1/16/09	TX	$11.7
Pacific Coast Bankers' Bancshares	Private bank	12/23/08	CA	$11.6
Cecil Bancorp	Bank	12/23/08	MD	$11.6
First Community Corp.	Bank	11/21/08	SC	$11.4
Central Virginia Bankshares	Bank	1/30/09	VA	$11.4
Central Jersey Bancorp	Bank	12/23/08	NJ	$11.3
Southern Bancorp	Cdfi	1/16/09	AR	$11
Farmers & Merchants Bancshares	Private bank	3/6/09	TX	$11
Stonebridge Financial Corp	Private bank	1/23/09	PA	$11
Ridgestone Financial Services	Private bank	2/27/09	WI	$10.9
First Southern Bancorp	Private bank	1/30/09	FL	$10.9
BCSB Bancorp	Bank	12/23/08	MD	$10.8

Name	Type	Date	State	Bailout Amount (in Millions)
First Community Bank Corp. of America	Bank	12/23/08	FL	$10.7
Crosstown Holding Company	Private bank	1/23/09	MN	$10.7
Northwest Bancshares	Private bank	2/13/09	WA	$10.5
Katahdin Bankshares	Private bank	1/30/09	ME	$10.4
Citizens Bancorp	Private bank	12/23/08	CA	$10.4
United Bancorp of Alabama	Bank	12/23/08	AL	$10.3
North Central Bancshares	Bank	1/9/09	IA	$10.2
Midland States Bancorp	Private bank	1/23/09	IL	$10.2
First Bankers Trustshares	Private bank	1/16/09	IL	$10
NCAL Bancorp	Private bank	12/19/08	CA	$10
Mid-Wisconsin Financial Services	Private bank	2/20/09	WI	$10
Center Bancorp	Bank	1/9/09	NJ	$10
Mid Penn Bancorp	Bank	12/19/08	PA	$10
Northway Financial	Private bank	1/30/09	NH	$10
Stewardship Financial Corp.	Bank	1/30/09	NJ	$10
New Hampshire Thrift Bancshares	Bank	1/16/09	NH	$10
Blackhawk Bancorp	Private bank	3/13/2009	WI	$10
ColoEast Bankshares	Private bank	2/13/09	CO	$10
Central Bancorp	Bank	12/05/08	MA	$10
1st United Bancorp	Private bank	3/13/2009	FL	$10
First Litchfield Financial Corp.	Bank	12/12/08	CT	$10
Uwharrie Capital Corp.	Private bank	12/23/08	NC	$10
BOH Holdings	Private bank	3/6/09	TX	$10
Greer Bancshares	Private bank	1/30/09	SC	$10
Regent Bancorp	Private bank	3/6/09	FL	$10
Coastal Banking Company	Bank	12/05/08	SC	$10
Southern Missouri Bancorp	Bank	12/05/08	MO	$9.5
Moneytree Corp.	Private bank	3/13/2009	TN	$9.5
Florida Business BancGroup	Private bank	2/20/09	FL	$9.5
FCB Bancorp	Private bank	12/19/08	KY	$9.3
PSB Financial Corporation	Private bank	2/27/09	LA	$9.3

Name	Type	Date	State	Bailout Amount (in Millions)
Provident Community Bancshares	Bank	3/13/2009	SC	$9.3
Carollton Bancorp	Bank	2/13/09	MD	$9.2
Elmira Savings Bank	Bank	12/19/08	NY	$9.1
Community Partners Bancorp	Bank	1/30/09	NJ	$9
Broadway Financial Corporation	Bank	11/14/08	CA	$9
Grandsouth Bancorporation	Private bank	1/9/09	SC	$9
UBT Banchares	Private bank	1/30/09	KS	$8.9
Salisbury Bancorp	Bank	3/13/2009	CT	$8.8
Citizens First Corp.	Bank	12/19/08	KY	$8.8
Farmers Bank	Private bank	1/23/09	VA	$8.8
Equity Bancshares	Private bank	1/30/09	KS	$8.8
Georgia Commerce Bancshares	Private bank	2/6/09	GA	$8.7
United American Bank	Private bank	2/20/09	CA	$8.7
Sonoma Valley Bancorp	Private bank	2/20/09	CA	$8.7
First Western Financial	Private bank	2/6/09	CO	$8.6
Summit State Bank	Bank	12/19/08	CA	$8.5
Annapolis Bancorp	Bank	1/30/09	MD	$8.2
Syringa Bancorp	Private bank	1/16/09	ID	$8
Commonwealth Business Bank	Private bank	1/23/09	CA	$7.7
Oak Ridge Financial Services	Bank	1/30/09	NC	$7.7
Valley Commerce Bancorp	Private bank	1/30/09	CA	$7.7
Metro City Bank	Private bank	1/30/09	GA	$7.7
First Gothenburg Bancshares	Private bank	2/27/09	NE	$7.6
Country Bank Shares	Private bank	1/30/09	NE	$7.5
Centrix Bank & Trust	Private bank	2/6/09	NH	$7.5
Emclaire Financial Corp.	Bank	12/23/08	PA	$7.5
The Little Bank	Private bank	12/23/08	NC	$7.5
Citizens Bancshares	Cdfi	3/6/09	GA	$7.5
Somerset Hills Bancorp	Bank	1/16/09	NJ	$7.4
Avenue Financial Holdings	Private bank	2/27/09	TN	$7.4
First Sound Bank	Bank	12/23/08	WA	$7.4
First BancTrust Corp.	Private bank	2/20/09	IL	$7.3
Western Community Bancshares	Private bank	12/23/08	CA	$7.3

Name	Type	Date	State	Bailout Amount (in Millions)
FFW Corp.	Private bank	12/19/08	IN	$7.3
Central Federal Corp.	Bank	12/05/08	OH	$7.2
Fidelity Bancorp	Bank	12/12/08	PA	$7
Hamilton State Bancshares	Private bank	2/20/09	GA	$7
Old Line Bancshares	Bank	12/05/08	MD	$7
Central Valley Community Bancorp	Bank	1/30/09	CA	$7
Guaranty Bancorp	Private bank	2/20/09	NH	$6.9
Idaho Bancorp	Private bank	1/16/09	ID	$6.9
Western Illinois Bancshares	Private bank	12/23/08	IL	$6.9
Security California Bancorp	Private bank	1/9/09	CA	$6.8
Pierce County Bancorp	Private bank	1/23/09	WA	$6.8
Monarch Community Bancorp	Bank	2/6/09	MI	$6.8
Highlands Independent Bancshares	Private bank	3/6/09	FL	$6.7
WashingtonFirst Bank	Private bank	1/30/09	VA	$6.6
Alarion Financial Services	Private bank	1/23/09	FL	$6.5
Pacific International Bancorp	Bank	12/12/08	WA	$6.5
First Intercontinental Bank	Private bank	3/13/2009	GA	$6.4
Citizens Commerce Bancshares	Private bank	2/6/09	KY	$6.3
Moscow Bancshares	Private bank	1/23/09	TN	$6.2
Meridian Bank	Private bank	2/13/09	PA	$6.2
Peninsula Bank Holding Co.	Bank	1/30/09	CA	$6
American State Bancshares	Private bank	1/9/09	KS	$6
IBW Financial Corporation	Private bank	3/13/2009	DC	$6
Beach Business Bank	Private bank	1/30/09	CA	$6
Patapsco Bancorp	Private bank	12/19/08	MD	$6
ICB Financial	Private bank	3/6/09	CA	$6
Rising Sun Bancorp	Private bank	1/9/09	MD	$6
Howard Bancorp	Private bank	2/27/09	MD	$6
Leader Bancorp	Private bank	12/23/08	MA	$5.8
Security Business Bancorp	Private bank	1/9/09	CA	$5.8
Central Bancshares	Private bank	1/30/09	TX	$5.8
FPB Bancorp	Bank	12/05/08	FL	$5.8

Name	Type	Date	State	Bailout Amount (in Millions)
Seaside National Bank & Trust	Private bank	1/23/09	FL	$5.7
United Financial Banking Companies	Private bank	1/16/09	VA	$5.7
Liberty Financial Services	Cdfi	2/6/09	LA	$5.6
Mission Valley Bancorp	Cdfi	12/23/08	CA	$5.5
Valley Community Bank	Bank	1/9/09	CA	$5.5
First Southwest Bancorporation	Private bank	3/6/09	CO	$5.5
Legacy Bancorp	Cdfi	1/30/09	WI	$5.5
Connecticut Bank and Trust Co.	Bank	12/19/08	CT	$5.5
The Private Bank of California	Private bank	2/20/09	CA	$5.5
Midtown Bank & Trust Co.	Private bank	2/27/09	GA	$5.2
Mission Community Bancorp	Private bank	1/9/09	CA	$5.1
Southern Illinois Bancorp	Private bank	1/23/09	IL	$5
Commerce National Bank	Bank	1/9/09	CA	$5
Financial Security Corp.	Private bank	2/13/09	WY	$5
The First Bancshares	Bank	2/6/09	MS	$5
First Express of Nebraska	Private bank	2/6/09	NE	$5
Blue River Bancshares	Private bank	3/6/09	IN	$5
Germantown Capital Corporation	Private bank	3/6/09	TN	$5
Private Bancorporation	Private bank	2/27/09	MN	$5
First ULB Corp.	Private bank	1/23/09	CA	$4.9
First Menasha Bancshares	Private bank	2/13/09	WI	$4.8
BNC Financial Group	Private bank	2/27/09	CT	$4.8
Alaska Pacific Bankshares	Bank	2/6/09	AK	$4.8
Cache Valley Banking Company	Private bank	12/23/08	UT	$4.8
Monument Bank	Private bank	1/30/09	MD	$4.7
Capital Bancorp	Private bank	12/23/08	MD	$4.7
CalWest Bancorp	Private bank	1/23/09	CA	$4.7
F&M Bancshares	Private bank	1/30/09	TN	$4.6
First Priority Financial Corp.	Private bank	2/20/09	PA	$4.6
Puget Sound Bank	Private bank	1/16/09	WA	$4.5
1st Enterprise Bank	Private bank	2/13/09	CA	$4.4
Pinnacle Bank Holding Company	Private bank	3/6/09	FL	$4.4

Name	Type	Date	State	Bailout Amount (in Millions)
Northeast Bancorp	Bank	12/12/08	ME	$4.2
Pacific Coast National Bancorp	Bank	1/16/09	CA	$4.1
Pacific Commerce Bank	Bank	12/23/08	CA	$4.1
The Bank of Currituck	Private bank	2/6/09	NC	$4
Todd Bancshares	Private bank	2/6/09	KY	$4
Premier Service Bank	Private bank	2/20/09	CA	$4
California Bank of Commerce	Private bank	2/27/09	CA	$4
Santa Lucia Bancorp	Bank	12/19/08	CA	$4
Hilltop Community Bancorp	Private bank	1/30/09	NJ	$4
Carolina Trust Bank	Bank	2/6/09	NC	$4
Capital Pacific Bancorp	Private bank	12/23/08	OR	$4
Texas National Bancorporation	Private bank	1/9/09	TX	$4
Community Business Bank	Private bank	2/27/09	CA	$4
Redwood Capital Bancorp	Private bank	1/16/09	CA	$3.8
Pascack Community Bank	Private bank	2/6/09	NJ	$3.8
AMB Financial Corp.	Private bank	1/30/09	IN	$3.7
CedarStone Bank	Private bank	2/6/09	TN	$3.6
Mercantile Capital Corp.	Private bank	2/6/09	MA	$3.5
AB&T Financial Corp.	Bank	1/23/09	NC	$3.5
Madison Financial Corp.	Private bank	3/13/2009	KY	$3.4
First Bank of Charleston	Private bank	2/6/09	WV	$3.3
California Oaks State Bank	Private bank	1/23/09	CA	$3.3
Congaree Bancshares	Private bank	1/9/09	SC	$3.3
Treaty Oak Bancorp	Private bank	1/16/09	TX	$3.3
Hometown Bancorp of Alabama	Private bank	2/20/09	AL	$3.3
FPB Financial Corp.	Bank	1/23/09	LA	$3.2
Crazy Woman Creek Bancorp	Private bank	2/20/09	WY	$3.1
Lone Star Bank	Private bank	2/6/09	TX	$3.1
Sound Banking Company	Private bank	1/9/09	NC	$3.1
Catskill Hudson Bancorp	Private bank	2/27/09	NY	$3
Tennessee Valley Financial Holdings	Private bank	12/23/08	TN	$3
Bank of Commerce	Private bank	1/16/09	NC	$3

Name	Type	Date	State	Bailout Amount (in Millions)
Citizens Community Bank	Private bank	12/23/08	VA	$3
St. Johns Bancshares	Private bank	3/13/2009	MO	$3
Marine Bank & Trust Company	Private bank	3/6/09	FL	$3
PGB Holdings	Cdfi	2/6/09	IL	$3
Redwood Financial	Private bank	1/9/09	MN	$3
Santa Clara Valley Bank	Private bank	2/13/09	CA	$2.9
US Metro Bank	Private bank	2/6/09	CA	$2.9
Bank of George	Private bank	3/13/2009	NV	$2.7
Regent Capital Corporation	Private bank	2/27/09	OK	$2.7
CBB Bancorp	Private bank	2/20/09	GA	$2.6
First Resource Bank	Private bank	1/30/09	PA	$2.6
Community Investors Bancorp	Private bank	12/23/08	OH	$2.6
Goldwater Bank	Private bank	1/30/09	AZ	$2.6
Community 1st Bank	Private bank	1/16/09	CA	$2.6
AmeriBank Holding Company	Private bank	3/6/09	OK	$2.5
Green Circle Investments	Private bank	2/27/09	IA	$2.4
Columbine Capital Corp.	Private bank	2/27/09	CO	$2.3
First Choice Bank	Private bank	2/13/09	CA	$2.2
Security Bancshares of Pulaski County	Private bank	2/13/09	MO	$2.2
Ojai Community Bank	Private bank	1/30/09	CA	$2.1
Market Bancorporation	Private bank	2/20/09	MN	$2.1
Surrey Bancorp	Private bank	1/9/09	NC	$2
TCNB Financial Corp.	Private bank	12/23/08	OH	$2
Lafayette Bancorp	Private bank	2/20/09	MS	$2
Northwest Commercial Bank	Private bank	2/13/09	WA	$2
Fresno First Bank	Private bank	1/23/09	CA	$2
Hometown Bancshares	Private bank	2/13/09	KY	$1.9
Merchants and Planters Bancshares	Private bank	3/6/09	TN	$1.9
Monadnock Bancorp	Private bank	12/19/08	NH	$1.8
Seacoast Commerce Bank	Bank	12/23/08	CA	$1.8
Community Bank of the Bay	Private bank	1/16/09	CA	$1.7
Manhattan Bancorp	Bank	12/05/08	CA	$1.7

Name	Type	Date	State	Bailout Amount (in Millions)
Hyperion Bank	Private bank	2/6/09	PA	$1.6
Saigon National	Private bank	12/23/08	CA	$1.5
Regional Bankshares	Private bank	2/13/09	SC	$1.5
DeSoto County Bank	Private bank	2/13/09	MS	$1.2
Independence Bank	Private bank	1/9/09	RI	$1.1
Community Holding Company of Florida	Private bank	2/6/09	FL	$1.1
Calvert Financial Corp.	Private bank	1/23/09	MO	$1
BankGreenville	Private bank	2/13/09	SC	$1
Bern Bancshares	Private bank	2/13/09	KS	$1
Gregg Bancshares	Private bank	2/13/09	MO	$0.8
Banner County Bank Corp.	Private bank	2/6/09	NE	$0.8
First State Bank of Mobeetie	Private bank	2/27/09	TX	$0.7
Midwest Regional Bancorp	Private bank	2/13/09	MO	$0.7
Green City Bancshares	Private bank	2/27/09	MO	$0.7
Corning Savings and Loan Association	Private bank	2/13/09	AR	$0.6
Butler Point	Private bank	3/13/2009	IL	$0.6
The Victory Bank	Private bank	2/27/09	PA	$0.5
Community Bancshares of Kansas	Private bank	3/6/09	KS	$0.5
Haviland Bancshares	Private bank	3/13/2009	KS	$0.4
The Freeport State Bank	Private bank	2/6/09	KS	$0.3

NOTES

INTRODUCTION

1 In recent testimony: Bret Baier, "Terrorism Is a 'Man-Caused' Disaster?" FoxNews.com, March 17, 2009, www.foxnews.com/story/0,2933,509597,00.html.

2 $200,000 to fund: "A Sample of the 9,287 Omnibus Bill Earmarks," www.heritage.org/Research/Budget/upload/porktable.html.

3 $190,000 for the Buffalo Bill: Ibid.

4 $2,192,000 for the Center: Ibid.

5 $1,791,000 to fund Swine Odor: Ibid.

1. OBAMA'S WAR ON PROSPERITY

6 9,287 earmarks: Brian M. Riedl, "Omnibus Spending Bill: Huge Spending and 9,000 Earmarks Represent Business as Usual," Heritage.org, March 2, 2009, www.heritage.org/research/budget/wm2318.cfm.

7 $1,049,000 for control: "A Sample of the 9,287 Omnibus Bill Earmarks," www.heritage.org/Research/Budget/upload/porktable.html.

8 $200,000 to fund: Ibid.

9 $190,000 for the Buffalo Bill: Ibid.

10 $2,673,000 for the Wood Education: Ibid.

11 $300,000 to promote women's sports: Ibid.

12 $206,000 to promote "wool research": Ibid.

13 $2,192,000 for the Center for Grape: Ibid.

14 $1,791,000 for Swine Odor: Ibid.

15 $45,000 for weed removal: Ibid.

16 $469,000 for a fruit fly: Ibid.

17 $800,000 for oyster rehabilitation: Ibid.

18 $4,545,000 for wood utilization: Jim Redden, "Federal Spending Bill Paves Way for State, Regional Projects," *Portland Tribune*, March 11, 2009, www.westlinntidings.com/news/story .php?story_id=123679286085530500.

19 $75,000 to create a "totally teen zone": "A Sample of the 9,287 Omnibus Bill Earmarks."

20 $300,000 for research on migrating: "Omnibus Appropriations Act of 2009," GOP.gov, February 25, 2009, www.gop.gov/bill/111/1/hr1105.

21 $900,000 for Chicago planetarium "A Sample of the 9,287 Omnibus Bill Earmarks."

22 $190,000 to buy trolleys: "Former Member Earmarks," *USA Today*, www.usatoday.com/ news/tabledata/formermemberearmarks.txt.

23 $380,000 for lighthouse renovation: Sue Clark, "Lighthouse Earmarks: Pork or Prize?," March 15, 2009, http://lighthouse-news.com/2009/03/15/lighthouse-earmarks-pork-or-prize/.

24 $7,800,000 for sea turtle research: "Hawaii Related Projects in Omnibus Bill Will Receive $372 Million," Akaka.Senate.Gov, March 10, 2009, http://akaka.senate.gov/public/index .cfm?FuseAction=PressReleases.Home&month=3&year=2009&release_id=2579.

25 $2,600,000 to monitor the population: Ibid.

26 $1,500,000 for research on Pelagic: Ibid.

27 $650,000 for beaver research: Barbara Barrett, " 'Beaver' Earmark in Budget Draws Attention," McClatchyDC.Com, March 6, 2009, www.mcclatchydc.com/politics/story/63464 .html.

28 $1,700,000 for a honey bee: "Weslaco Bee Lab Funded," *Brownsville Herald*, http://home. ezezine.com/1636/1636-2009.03.12.08.34.archive.html.

29 Combined, the stimulus package: Paul Sherman, "U.S. Federal Deficit to Top 10% of GDP at End of 2009," CapitalBeat.com, January 27, 2009, http://capitalbeat.com/?p=781.

30 Other, possibly more: "Wrap-Up 7, Obama Sees Soaring Deficits, Pushes Big Goals," Reuters.com, February 26, 2009, www.reuters.com/article/marketsNews/idUSN264485032 0090226?sp=true.

31 According to the Congressional: Matt Cover, "Only 23 Percent of Stimulus Will Be Spent This Fiscal Year, Congressional Budget Office Finds," CNSNews.com, February 18, 2009, www.cnsnews.com/PUBLIC/Content/Article.aspx?rsrcid=43708.

32 of the $28 billion: Ibid.

33 of the $16.8 billion: Ibid.

34 More than $100 billion: Christian Broda and Jonathan A. Parker, "The Impact of the 2008 Rebate," VoxEU.org, August 15, 2008, www.voxeu.org/index.php?q=node/1541.

35 only 10 to 20 percent: Martin Feldstein, "The Tax Rebate Was a Flop. Obama's Stimulus Plan Won't Work Either," *Wall Street Journal*, August 6, 2008, http://online.wsj.com/article/ SB121798022246515105.html.

36 In the last quarter of 2008: "Japan: Worst Crisis since War's End," CNNMoney.com, February 16, 2009, http://money.cnn.com/2009/02/16/news/international/japan_gdp/.

37 When Japan Tried Obama's Program: "Barack Obama-San," *Wall Street Journal*, December 16, 2008, http://online.wsj.com/article/SB122938932478509075.html.

38 "If a country falls": Mark Skoursen, *The Big Three in Economics* (London: M. E. Sharpe, 2007), p. 213.

39 "Keynesian 'pump-priming'": "Barack Obama-San," *Wall Street Journal*, December 16, 2008, http://online.wsj.com/article/SB122938932478509075.html.

40 "I tend to believe": "Deficit Spending Stimulus Skeptics," Heritage.org, January 21, 2009, http://blog.heritage.org/2009/01/21/deficit-spending-stimulus-skeptics/.

41 "We're creating a real": "Economist, Nebraska Reps. React to Stimulus Plan," KETV.com, January 25, 2009, www.ketv.com/money/18561438/detail.html.

42 "That [large government spending]": Larry Elder, "Do Economists Agree with Obama?," TheAtlasphere.com, February 10, 2009, www.theatlasphere.com/columns/090210-elder -economists-disagree.php.

43 "This is probably the worst": "Harvard Economist: 'Stimulus Is Probably the Worst Bill That Has Been Put Forward Since the 1930s,'" Examiner.com, February 9, 2009, www.examiner .com/x-2304-DC-Republican-Examiner~y2009m2d9-Harvard-Economist-Stimulus -is-probably-the-worst-bill-that-has-been-put-forward-since-the-1930s.

44 "[T]he risks of a": "Deficit Spending Stimulus Skeptics."

45 "The calculations that": Ibid.

46 "My advice to": Ibid.

47 "Unfortunately, bailouts and": Ibid.

48 "The theory that": Ibid.

49 Even though Bush cut: Gerald Prante, "Summary of Latest Federal Individual Income Tax Data," TaxFoundation.org, July 18, 2008, www.taxfoundation.org/research/show/250.html.

50 the richest 1 percent: Ibid.

51 "We are in the": Steve Holland, "Obama: U.S. in Worst Crisis since Depression," Reuters. com, October 7, 2008, www.reuters.com/article/governmentFilingsNews/idUSN0749084 220081008.

52 "But I think what": Associated Press, "Obama Meets Congress Leaders on Economic Res-cue," Cleveland.com, January 23, 2009, http://blog.cleveland.com/pdextra/2009/01/obama _meets_congress_leaders_o.html.

53 "I want to say": Scott Wilson, "Obama's New Track: Blaming Bush," *Washington Post*, March 15, 2009, http://mobile.washingtonpost.com/detail.jsp?key=362202&rc=to&p=1& all=1#___1__.

54 "We've inherited a terrible": Ibid.

55 "We've inherited an economic": Israelis Picking a New Leader; Race Against Time for Rescue Plan; Obama Administration's Golden Parachutes," The Situation Room, "CNN .com, February 10, 2009, http://transcripts.cnn.com/TRANSCRIPTS/0902/10/sitroom.02 .html.

56 "By any measure": Wilson, "Obama's New Track."

57 "There are a lot of individual": "Remarks by the President and Economic Recovery Advi-sory Board Chairman Paul Volcker after Meeting," March 13, 2009, www.whitehouse.gov/

the_press_office/Remarks-by-the-President-and-Economic-Recovery-Advisory-Board -Chairman-Paul-Volcker-After-Meeting/.

58 According to the Federal Reserve: "How Much Is a Trillion?," Econbrowser.com, March 3, 2009, www.econbrowser.com/archives/2009/03/how_much_is_a_t.html.

59 "The Fed prints": Anthony Karydakis, "The Fed's Interest Rate Experiments," CNN.com, February 12, 2009, http://money.cnn.com/2009/02/12/news/economy/karydakis_debt.for tune/.

60 So even though: "March 13, 2009," "US Financial Data," March 13, 2009, http://research. stlouisfed.org/publications/usfd/20090313/usfd.pdf.

61 And mortgage interest rates: "Weekly Primary Mortgage Market Survey," FreddieMac.com, March 19, 2009, www.freddiemac.com/dlink/html/PMMS/display/PMMSOutputYr.jsp.

62 "The Fed is acutely": Karydakis, "The Fed's Interest Rate Experiments."

63 It's that top 1 percent: Gerald Prante, "Summary of the Latest Federal Income Tax Data," TaxFoundation.org, July 18, 2008, www.taxfoundation.org/news/show/250.html.

64 43 million American households: Gregory V. Helvering, "Spreading the Wealth and Killing the Goose," AmericanThinker.org, October 31, 2008, www.americanthinker.com/2008/10/ spreading_the_wealth_and_killi.html.

65 More than 20 million: Jessica L. Dorrance, Daniel P. Gitterman, and Lucy S. Gorham, "Expanding the EITC for Single Workers and Couples without Children (AKA Relief for Low-Wage Workers,)" law.UNC.edu, January 2007, www.law.unc.edu/documents/poverty/ publications/gittermanpolicybrief.pdf.

66 Gore noted that: "Federal Individual Income Tax Rates History," TaxFoundation.org, www .taxfoundation.org/files/federalindividualratehistory-200901021.pdf.

67 Among other changes: "Economic Policy of the George W. Bush Administration," Wikipe-dia.org, http://en.wikipedia.org/wiki/Economic_policy_of_the_George_W._Bush_admin istration#cite_note-Tax_Policy_Center:_Urban_Institute_and_Brookings_Institution-44.

68 So President Bush: Brian M. Riedl, "The Myth of Spending Cuts for the Poor, Tax Cuts for the Rich," Heritage.org, February 14, 2006, www.heritage.org/Research/Budget/bg1912.cfm.

69 in 2005, the Child: Ibid.

70 Now Obama has: Robert Steere, "Implementing 'Making Work Pay' Tax Credit Is No April Fool's Joke," CompleteTax.com, www.completetax.com/taxguide/news/09-294taxcredit .asp.

71 After Bush got through: Helvering, "Spreading the Wealth and Killing the Goose."

72 Today, the poorest: Ibid.

73 The Heritage Foundation: Riedl, "The Myth of Spending Cuts for the Poor, Tax Cuts for the Rich."

74 The second quintile: Ibid.

75 In 1980, the richest: Prante, "Summary of Latest Federal Individual Income Tax Data."

76 By 2006, their share: Ibid.

77 The top quarter: Ibid.

78 Since 1980, the share: Ibid.

79 At the same time: Ibid.

80 During Obama's presidential campaign: Matt Cover, "Obama's Tax Cut Is Actually a Spending Increase, Says Non-Partisan Group," CBSNews.com, October 15, 2008, www.cbsnews.com/public/content/article.aspx?RsrcID=37519.

81 The top 20 percent: "Should I Be Worried About the "Over-Extended" U.S. Consumer?," PHN.com, https://www.phn.com/tabid/674/Default.aspx.

82 "nameless, unreasoning, unjustified": Franklin D. Roosevelt, "First Inaugural Address," March 4, 1933, www.bartleby.com/124/pres49.html.

83 "it cannot be emphasized": George Bittlingmayer and Thomas W. Hazlett, "FDR's Conservative 100 Days," *Wall Street Journal*, March 19, 2009, http://online.wsj.com/article/SB123742216772378825.html.

84 "both Hoover and Roosevelt": Amity Shlaes, *The Forgotten Man* (New York: Harper, 2007), p. 7.

85 "created regulatory, aid": Ibid.

86 "frightened away capital": Ibid., p. 10.

87 "Another problem": Ibid.

88 "Roosevelt systematized": Ibid., p. 11.

89 "I should like to": Franklin D. Roosevelt, "Our Documents: Franklin D. Roosevelt's Address Announcing the Second New Deal," FDRLibrary.marist.edu, October 31, 1936, www.fdrlibrary.marist.edu/od2ndst.html.

90 "more of them had": Riedl, "The Myth of Spending Cuts for the Poor, Tax Cuts for the Rich."

91 "In other words": Ibid.

92 "A rising tide": John F. Kennedy, "400—Remarks in Heber Springs, Arkansas, at the Dedication of Greers Ferry Dam," Presidency.UCSB.edu, October 3, 1963, www.presidency.ucsb.edu/ws/index.php?pid=9455.

93 "Americans . . . are": Jeremy Rifkin, *The European Dream* (New York: Penguin, 2005), p. 43.

94 "there is a belief": Ibid.

95 "reconcile France with": Rifkin, *The European Dream*.

96 "two-thirds of Americans": Ibid.

97 When asked that question: Ibid.

98 "in Europe, a majority": Ibid., p. 41.

99 "The European Dream": Ibid., p. 3.

100 "the French experiment": Ibid., p. 48.

101 "the European model": Charles Murray, "The European Syndrome and the Challenge to American Exceptionalism," *The American*, March 16, 2009, www.american.com/archive/2009/march-2009/the-europe-syndrome-and-the-challenge-to-american-exceptionalism.

102 "providing generous child": Ibid.

103 "most carefully protected": Ibid.

104 "great time with": Ibid.

105 Citing Europeans' "self-absorption": Ibid.

106 "irreversible damage": Ibid.
107 "the American project": Ibid.

2. THE BANK BAILOUT THAT BOMBED

108 Though they're now wallowing: Christopher S. Rugaber, "Largest Banks That Received Aid Cut Lending," HuffingtonPost.com, February 17, 2009, www.huffingtonpost.com/2009/02/17/largest-banks-that-receiv_n_167748.html.

109 " 'Make more loans?' ": Mike McIntire, "Bailout Is a Windfall to Banks, If Not to Borrowers," *New York Times*, January 17, 2009, www.nytimes.com/2009/01/18/business/18bank.html.

110 "To borrow a line": Christopher Boyd, "Banks Won't Open Loan Spigots until Economy Mends," *Orlando Business Journal*, February 13, 2009, http://orlando.bizjournals.com/orlando/stories/2009/02/16/focus1.html.

111 "it's unreasonable to expect": Ibid.

112 "a slow start": Jon Hilsenrath and Liz Rappaport, "Consumer-Loan Plan Is Off to Slow Start," *Wall Street Journal*, March 19, 2009, http://online.wsj.com/article/SB123741859019977963.html.

113 "stillborn would be": Ibid.

114 "a month ago": Ibid.

115 "one reason for the": Ibid.

116 "AIG alone had $500 billion: Author interview with Barry Elias, April 5, 2009.

117 "government cannot do this": Deborah Soloman, "Geithner Banks on Private Cash," *Wall Street Journal*, March 23, 2009, http://online.wsj.com/article/SB123776474431608981.html?mod=googlenews_wsj.

118 "at a time when": Ibid.

119 "win-win-lose": Joseph E. Stiglitz, "Obama's Ersatz Capitalism," *New York Times*, March 31, 2009, www.nytimes.com/2009/04/01/opinion/01stiglitz.html.

120 "the government would": Ibid.

121 "the Obama Administration": Binyamin Appelbaum and David Cho, "U.S. Seeks Expanded Power to Seize Firms," *Washington Post*, March 24, 2009, www.washingtonpost.com/wp-dyn/content/article/2009/03/23/AR2009032302830.html?hpid=topnews.

122 "giving the Treasury Secretary": Ibid.

123 "impose greater requirements": Stephen Labaton, "Administration Seeks Increase Oversight of Executive Pay," *New York Times*, March 21, 2009, www.nytimes.com/2009/03/22/us/politics/22regulate.html?_r=1.

124 "the new rules will": Ibid.

125 "the debate on bank": Nouriel Roubini, "The U.S. Financial System Is Effectively Insolvent," Forbes.com, March 5, 2009, www.forbes.com/2009/03/04/global-recession-insolvent-opinions-columnists-roubini-economy.html.

126 " 'Thus,' he adds": Ibid.

127 "It may be necessary": Mark Memmott, "Greenspan Says Obama Administration May Need to Nationalize Some Banks," *USA Today*, February 18, 2009, http://content.usatoday.com/topics/post/executive+pay/63005211.blog/1.

128 (But the current): Johan Carlstrom and Nikals Magnusson, "Sweden's 'Mr. Fix-It' Bank Bailout May Be Model for U.S., U.K.," Bloomberg.com, March 2, 2009, www.bloomberg.com/apps/news?pid=20601109&sid=atrQkJTX1P50&refer=home.

129 "you take the banks": Tunku Varadarajan, " 'Nationalize' the Banks," *Wall Street Journal*, February 21, 2009, http://online.wsj.com/article/SB123517380343437079.html.

130 "temporary receivership": Ibid.

131 "after years of": Carter Dougherty, "Stopping a Financial Crisis, the Swedish Way," *New York Times*, September 22, 2008, www.nytimes.com/2008/09/23/business/worldbusiness/23krona.html.

132 It spent $18.3 billion: Ibid.

133 "We started . . . each other standing": Varadarajan, " 'Nationalize' the Banks."

134 "three or four regional": Ibid.

135 "framework of internationally": "RAW DATA: G-20 Communique Statement," Fox News.com, April 2, 2009, www.foxnews.com/politics/first100days/2009/04/02/raw-data-g-communique-statement/.

136 In the name of: Ibid.

137 "provide early warning . . . all firms": Ibid.

3. OBAMA'S MORTGAGE PLAN THAT WON'T HELP YOU

138 "up to 5 million": Phil Mintz, "Obama Sets $75 Billion Mortgage Rescue Plan," Yahoo News.com, February 19, 2009, http://news.yahoo.com/s/bw/20090219/bs_bw/feb2009db20090218582414.

139 "assist up to": Ibid.

140 About 27 percent: Associated Press, "Obama Unveils $75B Mortgage Relief Plan," CBSNews.com, February 18, 2009, www.cbsnews.com/stories/2009/02/18/politics/100days/economy/main4808886.shtml.

141 Obama wouldn't be: Ibid.

142 His plan allows: Alan Zibel, "Housing Plan Aims to Help 9M, but Leaves Out Many," YahooNews.com, March 4, 2009, http://finance.yahoo.com/news/Obama-administration-launches-apf-14540623.html.

143 "owe so much more": Marilyn Lewis, "Help for on the Brink Homeowners," MSNMoney.com, March 5, 2009, http://articles.moneycentral.msn.com/Banking/HomeFinancing/help-for-on-the-brink-homeowners.aspx.

144 "You can modify": Associated Press, "Obama Unveils $75B Mortgage Relief Plan."

145 "provide their most recent": Zibel, "Housing Plan Aims to Help 9M, but Leaves Out Many."

146 "only homeowners in good": J. W. Elphinstone, "Meltdown 101: Will Obama's Housing Plan Help Me?," March 4, 2009, www.google.com/hostednews/ap/article/ALeqM5ip
Za-UuiRALM9rXphRa2IN0Fs_ywD96NGUT00.

147 "at risk of imminent": Ibid.

148 "Fannie and Freddie": Peter Barnes, "Obama's Foreclosure-Prevention Plan Faces
Hurdles," FOXBusiness.com, March 4, 2009, www.foxbusiness.com/story/markets/obamas
-foreclosure-prevention-plan-faces-hurdles/.

149 "as much as $1,000": Dawn Kopecki, "Obama Rescue Plan Said to Be Limited to Homeown-
ers Most in Need," Bloomberg.com, March 4, 2009, www.bloomberg.com/apps/news?pid=
20601070&sid=aN4NFR0MfE4w&refer=home.

150 Homeowners themselves: Ibid.

151 "mortgage lenders and investors": Barnes, "Obama's Foreclosure-Prevention Plan Faces
Hurdles."

152 "will not save": Mintz, "Obama Sets $75 Billion Mortgage Rescue Plan."

4. OBAMA'S HEALTH CARE CATASTROPHE

153 "President Obama pledged": David Martin, "Obama Calls for Health-Care Reform in 2009,"
CNN.com, March 20, 2009, http://edition.cnn.com/2009/HEALTH/03/20/obama.health
.care/.

154 "focus only on extending": "Three Big Problems with Obama's Health-Care Plan," *Wall
Street Journal*, December 21, 2008, http://online.wsj.com/article/SB122990539802425297
.html.

155 The nurse population: "Nursing Shortage Fact Sheet," American Association of College of
Nursing; www.aha.org/aha/trendwatch/chartbook/2008/08appendix2.pdf.

156 All told, 70 percent: Jackie Calmes and Robert Pear, "Administration Is Open to Taxing Health Benefits," *New York Times*, March 14, 2009. www.nytimes.com/2009/03/15/us/
politics/15health.html?hp.

157 http://www.nytimes.com/2009/04/27/health/policy/27care.html?_r=3&em

158 "A study by the Rand": Ibid.

159 "Barack Obama will accelerate": Ibid.

160 "Most medical records are": Barack Obama, "Barack Obama and Joe Biden's Plan to Lower
Health Care Costs and Ensure Affordable, Accessible Health Coverage for All," Barack
Obama.com, www.barackobama.com/pdf/issues/HealthCareFullPlan.pdf.

161 "Canadian patients . . . are": Brett J. Skinner, "The Trouble with Canadian Healthcare,"
The American, December 6, 2008, www.american.com/archive/2008/december-12-08/the
-trouble-with-canadian-healthcare.

162 "while Americans spend 55 percent": Ibid.

163 327 percent more: Ibid.

164 Doctors in the United States: Ibid.

165 And there are 14 percent: Ibid.

166 the average waiting . . . seventy-seven days: Ibid.

167 6.7 per 100,000: Colon Cancer Canada, www.coloncancercanada.ca/.

168 4.8 per 100,000: National Cancer Institute, www.cancer.gov/cancertopics/types/colon-and -rectal.

169 41 percent of cases in Canada: Colon Cancer Canada, www.coloncancercanada.ca/.

170 only 34 percent in the United States: National Cancer Institute, www.cancer.gov/cancer topics/types/colon-and-rectal.

171 "What is going on": "Colorectal Cancer: Treating It—A Moral and Legal Dilemma," Colorectal-Cancer.ca, May 15, 2009, www.colorectal-cancer.ca/en/news-and-resources/colo rectal-dilemma/,970.

172 In British Columbia: Ibid.

173 Sylvia de Vries: "The Horrors of Rationed Health Care in Canada," The Globe and Mail (Toronto), March 11, 2008, http://prairiepundit.blogspot.com/2008/03/horrors-of-rationed -health-care-in.html.

174 "Lindsay McCreith" Nadeem Esmail, " 'Too Old' for Hip Surgery," Wall Street Journal, February 9, 2009, http://online.wsj.com/article/SB123413701032661445.html.

175 "Shona Holmes": Ibid.

176 "In Alberta, Canada": Ibid.

177 Brian Sinclair: Chinta Puxley, "Inquest Called into Death of Homeless Man after 34-Hour Wait in Winnipeg ER," Canadian Press, February 4, 2009, www.winnipegfreepress.com/ canada/breakingnews/39056162.html.

178 To improve services: Esmial, " 'Too Old' for Hip Surgery."

179 cancer death rates: "Table 1: Leading Causes of Death, Canada, 2004, Males and Females Combined," Public Health Agency of Canada, www.phac-aspc.gc.ca/publicat/lcd-pcd97/ table1-eng.php.

180 And heart disease deaths: "Leading Causes of Death," Centers for Disease Control and Prevention, www.cdc.gov/nchs/FASTATS/lcod.htm.

181 "Canada's model of universal": Author's interview with Ken Lee, March 31, 2009.

5. OBAMA'S BLUEPRINT FOR POLITICAL DOMINATION

182 In largely Hispanic: Foon Rhee, "Obama Talks Immigration," Boston Globe, March 18, 2009, www.boston.com/news/politics/politicalintelligence/2009/03/obama_talks_imm.html.

183 he's "very committed": Gebe Martinez, "Has Obama Forgotten Immigration?," Politico. com, March 4, 2009, www.politico.com/news/stories/0309/19564.html.

184 "illegal residents who have": Charles Babbington, "Obama Says Immigration Overhaul Still Needed," March 18, 2009, www.google.com/hostednews/ap/article/ALeqM5hEx 3tiPJhZQLVqjNmHR_oP6FZMuwD970PMT80.

185 "We're going to start": Martinez, "Has Obama Forgotten Immigration?"

186 "before the ink was dry": Martha Zoller, "Controlling the Census: The Obama Administration's Power Grab," HumanEvents.com, February 12, 2009, www.humanevents.com/article .php?id=30672.

187 Gregg had opposed: Mark Whittington, "Obama to Seize Control of Census," AssociatedContent.com, February 9, 2009, www.associatedcontent.com/article/1459209/obama_to _seize_control_of_census.html?cat=9.

188 "The last thing": "GOP Sounds Alarm over Obama Decision to Move Census to White House," FOXNews.com, February 9, 2009, www.foxnews.com/politics/first100days/2009/02/09/ gop-sounds-alarm-obama-decision-census-white-house/.

189 "I've always remembered": Ibid.

190 Associated Press, "Official: Obama Taps Grove for Census Director," April 2, 2009, http:// www.tulsaworld.com/news/article.aspx?subjectid=338&articleid=20090402_338_0 _WASHIN679936.

191 "we're ready to pay": Sam Hananel, "Companies Seek Middle Ground on Union Card Check," March 22, 2009, www.google.com/hostednews/ap/article/ALeqM5i-uuyg_cknu QUXeX4h-43g4wqzfwD9739I7G5.

192 "got a first hand": FoxNews.com, March 25, 2009.

193 "I will make it the": Ibid.

194 "some employers abuse": John T. Palter, " 'Card Check Bill Is Union Power Grab," *Dallas Morning News*, March 18, 2009, www.dallasnews.com/sharedcontent/dws/dn/opinion/ viewpoints/stories/DN-palter_19edi.State.Edition1.217ea25.html.

195 "why unions are on": Ibid.

196 "the problems of": Kris Maher, "Key Senator Won't Support Union Bill," *Wall Street Journal*, March 25, 2009, http://online.wsj.com/article/SB123792023652828061.html.

197 "Senator Specter said he": Ibid.

198 "one change [Specter] supports": Ibid.

199 "there may be": Dick Morris and Eileen McGann, *Fleeced*, p. 81.

200 "take actions to encourage": Josiah Ryan, "Speaker Pelosi Backs Senate Amendment to Regulate Talk Radio," CNSNews.com, March 6, 2009, www.cnsnews.com/public/content/ article.aspx?RsrcID=44588.

201 "primarily to gender, race": Ibid.

202 "I centainly can't tell": Jim Inhofe, "Inhofe: Localism Is a Threat to Freedom of Speech," *American Chronicle*, March 8, 2009, www.americanchronicle.com/articles/view/93765.

203 "Localism": Brian C. Anderson, "The Unfairness of a Fairness Doctrine," *Los Angeles Times*, March 3, 2009, www.latimes.com/news/printedition/opinion/la-oe-anderson 3-2009mar03,0,3110313.story.

204 "localism . . . also could": Ibid.

205 "comprised of local": Jim Boulet Jr., "Obama Declares War on Conservative Talk Radio," AmericanThinker.com, November 17, 2008, www.americanthinker.com/2008/11/obama _declares_war_on_conserva.html.

206 Anderson calls localism: Anderson, "The Unfairness of a Fairness Doctrine."

207 Media reform groups: Matthew Lasar, "Obama's FCC Chariman Pick Hailed by Reform Groups," ArsTechnica.com, January 13, 2009, http://arstechnica.com/telecom/news/2009/01/obamas-fcc-chairman-pick-hailed-by-reform-groups.ars.

208 "Barack Obama believes that": Ibid.

209 "leadership, the FCC's": Ibid.

210 "take actions to encourage": Ryan, "Speaker Pelosi Backs Senate Amendment to Regulate Talk Radio."

211 "any effort to encourage": Boulet, "Obama Declares War on Conservative Talk Radio."

212 "Restore local . . . public broadcasting": Ibid.

213 "diversity in [station]": Matt Cover, "Durbin: 'Right-Wing' Radio Hosts Wave 'Bloody Shirt' over Broadcast Censorship," CNSNews.com, March 12, 2009, www.cnsnews.com/PUBLIC/Content/Article.aspx?rsrcid=44895.

214 " 'affirmative actions' to": Ibid.

215 "What is most concerning": Inhofe, "Inhofe: Localism Is a Threat to Freedom of Speech."

6. OBAMA SENDS MESSAGE: THE WAR ON TERROR IS OVER

216 "avoid[ed] the terms": Associated Press, "Napolitano Avoids Terror Terminology," CBSNews.com, February 24, 2009, www.cbsnews.com/stories/2009/02/24/national/main4826437.shtml.

217 "an unprecedented level": Barack Obama, "Memorandum for the Heads of Executive Departments and Agencies; Subject Transparency and Open Government," WhiteHouse.gov, www.whitehouse.gov/the_press_office/TransparencyandOpenGovernment/.

218 "presumption in favor": Barack Obama, "Memorandum for the Heads of Executive Departments and Agencies; Subject Freedom of Information Act," WhiteHouse.gov, www.whitehouse.gov/the_press_office/FreedomofInformationAct/.

219 "organizing and directing": Pauline Jelinek, "Pentagon Announces Charges in USS Cole Bombing," USA Today, July 1, 2008, www.usatoday.com/news/topstories/2008-06-30-2475186758_x.htm.

220 On February 5, 2009: Catherine Herridge and Associated Press, "Charges Dropped Against USS Cole Bombing Suspect," FoxNews.com, February 5, 2009, www.foxnews.com/politics/first100days/2009/02/05/sources-charges-dropped-uss-cole-bombing-suspect/.

221 The United States had sought: Catherine Herridge and Associated Press, "Military Judge Refuses to Halt Trial of USS Cole Bombing Suspect," FoxNews.com, January 29, 2009, www.foxnews.com/politics/2009/01/29/military-judge-refuses-halt-trial-uss-cole-bombing-suspect/.

222 According to U.S. intelligence: "Profile: Abd al-Rahim al-Nashiri," HistoryCommons.org, www.historycommons.org/entity.jsp?entity=abd_al-rahim_al-nashiri.

223 "critics are . . . saying': Myra MacDonald, "Pakistan Agrees to Shariah Law to End Swat Fighting," Reuters.com, February 16, 2009, http://blogs.reuters.com/pakistan/2009/02/16/pakistan-agrees-to-shariah-law-to-end-swat-fighting/.

224 "a surrender to the Taliban": Ibid.

225 "it means that there": Ibid.

226 "According to certain": Indrani Bagchi, "In Search of 'Good' Taliban," *Times of India,* March 5, 2009, http://timesofindia.indiatimes.com/India/In-search-of-good-Taliban/articleshow/4226199.cms.

227 "any kind of Talibanism": Ibid.

228 "They point out that": Ibid.

229 "received a hero's": Sherin Zada, "NATO Cautions Pakistan over Truce with Taliban," YahooNews.com, February 17, 2009, http://news.yahoo.com/s/ap/20090217/ap_on_re_as/as_pakistan.

230 "is certainly reason for concern": Ibid.

231 "the agreement still needed": Ibid.

232 "repeatedly pushed some of": Tom Hamburger and Josh Meyer, "Eric Holder Pushed for Controversial Clemency," *Los Angeles Times,* January 9, 2009, www.latimes.com/news/nationworld/washingtondc/la-na-holder9-2009jan09,0,6643509.story.

233 "angry lawmakers demanded": Ibid.

234 "instructed his staff": Ibid.

235 "I remember this": Ibid.

236 "strong opposition to": Ibid.

237 "Overall, the two groups": Ibid.

238 "These terrorists took away": Joseph F. Connor, "Hearing Statement of Joseph F. Connor," United States Senate Committee on the Judiciary, January 16, 2009, http://judiciary.senate.gov/hearings/testimony.cfm?id=3629&wit_id=7569.

239 Why did Holder ignore . . . for the pardon?": Ibid.

240 "as something President Bush": Andrew McCarthy, "Lawyer's Lawyer, Radical's Radical," *National Review,* March 9, 2009, www.judicialnetwork.com/cgi-data/in_the_news/files/227.shtml.

241 "extreme and implausible": Ibid.

242 "in fact, the practice was": Ibid.

243 "it had arrested": Ahmd Al-Haj, "Official: Yemen Releases 170 al-Qaida Suspects," Yahoo News.com, February 8, 2009, http://news.yahoo.com/s/ap/20090208/ap_on_re_mi_ea/ml_yemen_al_qaida_suspects.

244 "after signing pledges": Ibid.

245 "local tribal leaders": Ibid.

246 "increase [Bush's] reluctance": Ibid.

7. THE UNITED STATES SENDS AID TO HAMAS . . . YES, HAMAS!

247 The U.S. contribution makes up: Joel Mowbray, "Lawmakers Worry Whether U.S. Can Keep Gaza Aid Away from the Hamas," FoxNews.com, March 2, 2009, www.foxnews.com/politics/first100days/2009/03/02/lawmakers-worry-gaza-aid-away-hamas/.

248 "UNRWA openly collaborates": Caroline Glick, "Column One: Entrapping Netanyahu," *Jerusalem Post*, February 26, 2009, www.jpost.com/servlet/Satellite?pagename=JPost%2FJP Article%2FShowFull&cid=1235410729960.

249 "I am sure that": "UNRWA's Hamas Employees," HonestReporting.com, www.aish.com/ jewishissues/mediaobjectivity/UNRWAs_Hamas_Employees.asp.

250 May 2004 . . . rockets at Israel: Ibid.

251 According to Congressman: "Teaching Rocket Science," *New York Post*, May 6, 2008, www .nypost.com/seven/05062008/postopinion/editorials/teaching_rocket_science_109621 .html.

252 "discovered there small-arms": Arlene Kushner, "UN Dollars for Terror," FrontPageMag .com, August 18, 2004, www.frontpagemag.com/Articles/Read.aspx?GUID=F80544EB-508B -42F8-9AE4-4C06C508B2A2.

253 "So pervasive is this": Ibid.

254 The European Union contributes: Ibid.

255 "thirty confirmed fatalities": Herb Keinon and Tovah Lazaroff, "UNRWA Offers Political Cover to Hamas," *Jerusalem Post*, February 25, 2009, www.jpost.com/servlet/Satellite?cid= 1235410706632&pagename=JPost%2FJPArticle%2FShowFull.

256 "UN issued a revised report": Ibid.

257 "One of [the banks]": Claudia Rosett, "Can We Give to Gaza Without Giving to Hamas?" *Forbes*, March 5, 2009, www.forbes.com/2009/03/04/gaza-hamas-clinton-opinions -columnists_claudia_rosett.html.

258 "that may be indicative": Ibid.

259 In 2006, Under-Secretary: Ibid.

260 "we have worked": Ibid.

261 "a considerable portion": Jonathan D. Halevi, "Aid to Palestinian Authority Used for Terror-ists," Jerusalem Center for Public Affairs, March 4, 2009, http://jcpa.org.il/Templates/show page.asp?FID=575&DBID=1&LNGID=2&TMID=99&IID=22002.

262 "This aid serves as": Ibid.

263 "it is directly": Asaf Romirowsky, "How UNRWA Supports Hamas," *inFocus*, 2007, www .jewishpolicycenter.org/article/53.

264 The UNRWA employs: Ibid.

265 "UNRWA workers are permitted": Ibid.

266 "Instead of a condemnation": Ibid.

267 Said Sayyam . . . military structure of Hamas: Ibid.

268 "there have also been widespread reports": Ibid.

269 "allowed terrorist groups": Mark Silverberg, "Gaza's Quandary," www.familysecurity matters.org/publications/id.2310/pub_detail.asp.

270 "destroyed during bomb-making": Romirowsky, "How UNRWA Supports Hamas."

271 "UNRWA's job is to": Asaf Romirowsky, Barry Rubin, and Jonathan Spyer, "UNRWA: Refuge of Rejectionism," GLORIACenter.org, May 8, 2008, www.gloriacenter.org/index .asp?pname= submenus/articles/2008/rubin/5_8.asp.

272 "UNRWA schools become hotbeds": Ibid.

273 "the exact opposite": Ibid.

8. CHRISTOPHER DODD AND CHARLES RANGEL: FROM IDEALISTIC REFORMERS TO PRIVILEGED INSIDERS

274 "I came back": David Welna, "Dodd's First Race Was Call to Service, Legacy," NPR.org, October 8, 2007, www.npr.org/templates/story/story.php?storyId=14694831.

275 In 1967, Thomas Dodd: "The Undoing of Dodd," *Time*, May 5, 1967, www.time.com/time/magazine/article/0,9171,899472-1,00.html.

276 "He said to me": Elizabeth Bumiller, "Dodd's Other Campaign: Restoring Dad's Reputation," *New York Times*, September 24, 2007, www.nytimes.com/2007/09/24/us/politics/24dodd.html.

277 "contrary to good morals": "The Undoing of Dodd."

278 Accepting $8,000 . . . 2009 dollars: Ibid.

279 "backdoor law practice": Jack Anderson and Drew Pearson, "The Washington Merry-Go-Round," Bell McClure Syndicate, March 20, 1967, http://dspace.wrlc.org/doc/bitstream/2041/53122/b20f02-0320zdisplay.pdf.

280 For example, according to: Ibid.

281 Another witness: Ibid.

282 the annual salary: Ida Brudnick, "Salaries of Congress: A List of Payable Rates and Effective Dates, 1789–2008," Senate.gov, February 21, 2008, www.senate.gov/reference/resources/pdf/97-1011.pdf.

283 In 1965, it increased: Ibid.

284 "There is an interesting": Anderson and Pearson, "The Case of Sanford Bomstein," Bell McClure Syndicate, March 15, 1967, http://dspace.wrlc.org/doc/bitstream/2041/53114/b20f02-0315xdisplay.pdf.

285 Dodd's Juvenile Delinquency Subcommittee: Ibid.

286 "received help in the": Dave Altimari and Matthew Kauffman, "Chris Dodd: A Few Real Estate Deals among Friends," *Hartford Courant*, March 15, 2009, www.courant.com/news/politics/hc-doddproperty.artmar15,0,4867366.story.

287 "We were friends": Ibid.

288 "it would have been": Ibid.

289 "Mr. Downe Doled Out": N. R. Kleinfield, "Living Poolside, and Wanting More; Insider-Trading Charges and the Southampton Summer Set," *New York Times*, June 16, 1992, www.nytimes.com/1992/06/16/nyregion/living-poolside-wanting-more-insider-trading-charges-southampton-summer-set.html?sec=&spon=&pagewanted=3.

290 Dodd has been: Landon Thomas Jr., "At Hearing, Pointed Questions about What Led to a Bailout," *New York Times*, April 4, 2008, www.nytimes.com/2008/04/04/business/04scene.html?scp=2&sq=edward+downe+pardon&st=nyt.

291 "Having a relationship financially": Altimari and Kauffman, "Chris Dodd: A Few Real Estate Deals among Friends."

292 Dodd claims that: Ibid.

293 His salary in 1986: "Senate Salaries since 1789," Senate.gov, www.senate.gov/artandhistory/history/common/briefing/senate_salaries.htm.

294 "had exploited insider trading": Ronald Sullivan, "S.E.C. Reaches Settlement with Socialite," *New York Times*, September 15, 1994, www.nytimes.com/1994/09/15/business/sec-reaches-settlement-with-socialite.html.

295 "the example[s] of Ed's": David Lightman, "Dodd Helped Friend Secure Presidential Pardon," *Hartford Courant*, February 24, 2001, http://christopherfountain.wordpress.com/2009/02/22/dodd-and-his-pardon/.

296 personal access: Marc Lacey and Don Van Natta Jr., "Access Proved Vital in Last-Minute Race for Clinton Pardons," *New York Times*, February 25, 2001, www.nytimes.com/2001/02/25/us/access-proved-vital-in-last-minute-race-for-clinton-pardons.html?scp=5&sq=edward+downe+pardon&st=nyt.

297 "bypassed the Justice Department": Ibid.

298 "Politics rather than": Ibid.

299 "It would have been": Altimari and Kauffman, "Chris Dodd: A Few Real Estate Deals among Friends."

300 William Kessinger was: Kevin Rennie, "Dodd's 'Cottage': A Cozy Purchase," *Hartford Courant*, February 22, 2009, www.courant.com/news/opinion/editorials/hc-rennie0222.artfeb22,0,3796755.column.

301 When the property was sold: Ibid.

302 Dodd told the *Hartford Courant*: Ibid.

303 "Someone might also": Ibid.

304 "In 1993, Irish planning": Kevin Rennie, "Dodd's Explanations Misleading, Incomplete," *Hartford Courant*, March 22, 2009, www.courant.com/news/opinion/editorials/hc-rennie-dodd-aig-houses0322.artmar22,0,1723577.column.

305 "According to the Irish": Altimari and Kauffman, "Chris Dodd: A Few Real Estate Deals among Friends."

306 "Two years after": Keving Rennie, "Pardon for a Friend, a Good Deal for Dodd," *Hartford Courant*, March 8, 2009, www.courant.com/news/opinion/editorials/hc-rennie-dodd-house0308.artmar08,0,4360050.column.

307 He speculated that: Altimari and Kauffman, "Chris Dodd: A Few Real Estate Deals among Friends."

308 "These were pretty": Ibid.

309 New development plan for Sunflower site stirs officials By JOHN L. PETTERSON The Kansas City Star, June 12, 2002 http://www.kansascity.com/mld/kansascitystar/3448952.htm

310 "Candidly, our thinking": Ibid.

311 http://www.portfolio.com/news-markets/top-5/2008/06/12/Countrywide-Loan-Scandal

312 Dodd and Countrywide *The Senator should take the witness stand. Wall Street Journal* October 10, 2008, http://online.wsj.com/article/SB122360116724221681.html

313 march 23, 2009 *Dodd's Wife a Former Director of Bermuda-Based IPC Holdings, an AIG Controlled Company* By Kevin Rennie

314 "getting away with murder": Deal Journal, "Mean Street: What's More Shameful than AIG? The U.S. Congress," *Wall Street Journal*, March 20, 2009, http://blogs.wsj.com/deals/2009/03/20/mean-street-whats-more-shameful-than-aig-the-us-congress/.

315 "Are these guys": Ann Woolner, "AIG Bonus Tax Idea Feels Great, Stinks as Law," Bloomberg.com, March 25, 2009, www.bloomberg.com/apps/news?pid=20601039&refer=colum nist_woolner&sid=a4n5b.9iX6Bw.

316 "out of touch": "Rangel Says Feds behind A.I.G. Bonus Were out of Touch," NY1.com, March 28, 2009, www.ny1.com/content/top_stories/96420/rangel-says-feds-behind-aig-bonuses -were-out-of-touch/Default.aspx.

317 "Someone screwed up": Ibid.

318 In 2007, Rangel submitted: Alan Finder, "Study Finds Record Education Earmarks," *New York Times*, March 24, 2008, http://query.nytimes.com/gst/fullpage.html?res=9801E1DA13 3DF937A15750C0A96E9C8B63.

319 "You don't agree": Sheryl Arrkiss, "Is Rangel's 'Monument to Me' Worth It?," CBSNews.com, September 14, 2007, www.cbsnews.com/stories/2007/09/14/eveningnews/main3261346 .shtml.

320 "I would have": Ibid.

321 "a new 'Charles B. Rangel' ": Ibid.

322 "We call it the": Ibid.

323 And so did City University: David Kocieniewski, "Rangel Pushed for a Donation; Insurer Pushed for a Tax Cut," *New York Times*, January 2, 2009, www.nytimes.com/2009/01/03/ nyregion/03rangel.html?scp=21&sq=Charles+Rangel+Center+for+Public+Service&st= nyt.

324 "one was sent to": Ibid.

325 "Drug companies, hospitals": Matt Viser, "Hospitals, Firms in Healthcare Back Kennedy Institute," *Boston Globe*, January 20, 2009, www.boston.com/news/local/massachusetts/ articles/2009/01/20/hospitals_firms_in_healthcare_back_kennedy_institute/.

326 Although Rangel had been: David Kocieniewski, "Republican's Question Rangel's Tax Break Support," *New York Times*, November 25, 2008, www.nytimes.com/2008/11/26/ nyregion/26rangel.html?_r=1&scp=2&sq=nabors&st=nyt#secondParagraph%23second Paragraph.

327 as the *New York Times* disclosed: David Kocieniewski, "For Rangel, Four Rent-Stabilized Apartments," *New York Times*, July 11, 2008, http://www.nytimes.com/2008/07/11/nyregion/ 11rangel.html.

9. THERE IS NOTHING LIKE A NAME . . .
TED KENNEDY, JR., THE SENATOR'S SON

328 In the year 2000: Melody Peterson, "Bristol-Myers Delays F.D.A. Review of a Blood Pressure Drug," *New York Times*, April 20, 2000, www.nytimes.com/2000/04/20/business/bristol-myers-delays-fda-review-of-a-blood-pressure-drug.html.

329 25 million Glucophage prescriptions: Lindsey Tanner, "Study: Diabetics Face Drug Danger," MedTech1.com, May 15, 2002, http://medtech1.com/success/device_stories.cfm/25/1.

330 Every minute that generic: "Congress Watch Director Frank Clemente Opposing the Bristol-Myers Squibb Monopoly Patent Extension," Citizen.org, www.citizen.org/congress/reform/drug_patents/bmsg/articles.cfm?ID=6490.

331 In 2001, the company spent: "Lobbying Spending Database," Center for Responsive Politics, https://www.opensecrets.org/lobby/clientsum.php?lname=Bristol-Myers+Squibb&year=2001.

332 The manufacturer, which: Juliet Eilperin, "Bristol-Myers Presses for Patent," *Washington Post*, November 28, 2001, www.washingtonpost.com/ac2/wp-dyn?pagename=article&node=&contentId=A25330-2001Nov27.

333 Provide advice re: "BMS Report Images," Center for Responsive Politics, https://www.opensecrets.org/lobby/client_reports.php?lname=Bristol-Myers+Squibb&year=2001; See Marwood's 2000 lobbying disclosure form for BMSL.

334 "healthcare advisory and financial": "Marwood Group," www.marwoodgroup.com.

335 The Marwood Group LLC: "The Marwood Group LLC," BusinessWeek.com, April 7, 2009, http://investing.businessweek.com/research/stocks/private/snapshot.asp?privcapId=9638663.

336 If the currency of Washington: Jeffrey Young, "Ted Kennedy Jr.'s Firm Sues over Political Intel," TheHill.com, November 20, 2007, http://thehill.com/leading-the-news/ted-kennedy-jr.s-firm-sues-over-political-intel-2007-11-20.html.

337 Edward M. Kennedy, Jr.: Michael Maiello, "Ponying Up to Camelot," Forbes.com, April 10, 2004, www.forbes.com/forbes/2004/0419/054.html.

338 The $10 billion Chicago: Ibid.

339 When the dispute became: Ibid.

340 In Senator Kennedy's home state: Raphael Lewis, "Cahill Fund-Raisers Gain Pension Funds," *Boston Globe*, February 11, 2005, www.boston.com/news/local/articles/2005/02/11/cahill_fund_raisers_gain_pension_funds.

341 Rubin even disputes: Ibid.

10. STEALTH LOBBYISTS: THE FORMER CONGRESSIONAL LEADERS WHO SECRETLY INFLUENCE FEDERAL POLICIES AND SPENDING

342 There are now 15,150: "Lobbying Database," Center for Responsive Politics, www.opensecrets.org/lobby/index.php.

343 "beneath" him: David D. Kirkpatrick and Sheryl Gay Stolberg, "Daschle's Ambitions Collided, Friends Say," *New York Times*, February 4, 2009, www.nytimes.com/2009/02/05/us/politics/05daschle.html?hp.

344 "He's got a lot": Christopher Lee, "Daschle Moving to K Street," *Washington Post*, March 14, 2005, www.washingtonpost.com/wp-dyn/articles/A32604-2005Mar13.html.

345 "You can't be advising": Kirkpatrick and Stolberg, "Daschle's Ambitions Collided, Friends Say."

346 "Daschle is merely": Ibid.

347 Our health care: Alston + Bird LLP, "Health Care Legislative & Public Policy," www.alston.com/health_legislative/.

348 http://www.alston.com/services/serviceparent.aspx?service=326.

349 Ibid.

350 "efforts to rescue": Timothy J. Burger, "Mitchell's Firm Worked for Dubai Ruler in Jockey Case," Bloomberg.com, January 27, 2009, www.bloomberg.com/apps/news?pid=20601087&sid=aa7hdtvtfYxc&refer=worldwide.

351 Iraq Reconstruction: "Iraq Reconstruction," www.dlapiper.com/iraq_reconstruction/.

352 According to Bloomberg News: Burger, "Mitchell's Firm Worked for Dubai Ruler in Jockey Case."

353 In the past: U.S. Department of Justice, "Exhibit A," www.fara.gov/docs/3712-Exhibit-AB-20081215-12.pdf.

354 "to help my clients": "Obama Aide Joins Ogilvy as Adviser," *New York Times*, January 26, 2009, http://dealbook.blogs.nytimes.com/2009/01/26/obama-aide-joins-ogilvy-as-adviser/.

355 "meeting Ogilvy clients": Jeanne Cummings, "Daschle, Obama Aide Joins K Street," Politico.com, February 18, 2009, www.politico.com/news/stories/0209/18928.html.

11. THE SHEER CHUTZPAH OF COUNTRYWIDE FINANCIAL EXECUTIVES

356 "gall, brazen nerve": Leo Rosten, *The Joys of Yiddish* (New York: Pocket Books, 2000).

357 "delinquent home mortgages": Eric Lipton, "Ex-Leaders of Countrywide Profit from Bad Loans," *New York Times*, March 3, 2009, www.nytimes.com/2009/03/04/business/04penny.html.

358 For example, PennyMac recently: David Mildenberg and Linda Shen, "PennyMac, Led by Ex-Countrywide Head, Buys FDIC Loans," Bloomberg.com, January 7, 2009, www.bloomberg.com/apps/news?pid=20601087&sid=aVYn.SXOHh48&refer=home.

359 "It's like Jeffrey Dahmer": Gail Collins, "The Rant List," *New York Times*, March 4, 2009, www.nytimes.com/2009/03/05/opinion/05collins.html.

360 PennyMac is headed by: Ruthie Ackerman, "Countrywide Execs Get New Home at PennyMac," Forbes.com, March 24, 2008, www.forbes.com/2008/03/24/pennymac-countrywide-update-markets-equity-cx_ra_0324markets29.html.

361 "lawsuits against Countrywide": Liptor, "Ex-Countrywide Leaders Profit on Loans Gone Bad."

362 "Countrywide obscured the": "Brown Sues Countrywide for Mortgage Deception," Office of the Attorney General, June 25, 2008, http://ag.ca.gov/newsalerts/release.php?id=1582.

363 the company has telemarketers: Liptor, "Ex-Countrywide Leaders Profit on Loans Gone Bad."

364 "whole loan losses": Ackerman, "Countrywide Execs Get New Home at PennyMac."

365 "role model": Liptor, "Ex-Countrywide Leaders Profit on Loans Gone Bad."

12. PAY TO PLAY: NO-BID CONTRACTS EXCHANGED FOR CAMPAIGN CASH

366 "act of official": Brad Bumsted and Walter F. Roche Jr., "Ending 'Pay-to-Play' a Top Issue for GOP," *Pittsburgh Tribune-Review*, January 10, 2009, www.pittsburghlive.com/x/pittsburghtrib/s_606620.html.

367 Take a look: Tracie Mauriello, "Rendell Contributor under Investigation," *Pittsburgh Post-Gazette*, January 7, 2009, www.post-gazette.com/pg/09007/940033-85.stm.

368 It seems his company: Sheryl Gay Stolberg, "Richardson Won't Pursue Cabinet Post," *New York Times*, January 4, 2009, www.nytimes.com/2009/01/05/us/politics/05richardson.html.

369 He also granted: David A. Patten, "Burris Donated Thousands to Blagojevich; Won Contracts," Newsmax.com, December 30, 2008, www.newsmax.com/insidecover/roland_burris_donations/2008/12/30/166509.html.

370 He gave Blagojevich: Ibid.

371 "how the association": Eric Lipton, "Trade Group Confirms Deal with Tiny Firm for ID Cards," *New York Times*, April 28, 2006, http://query.nytimes.com/gst/fullpage.html?res=9905E5DF103FF93BA15757C0A9609C8B63.

372 trips that cost: Eric Lipton, "In Kentucky Hills, a Homeland Security Bonanza," *New York Times*, May 13, 2006, www.nytimes.com/2006/05/14/washington/14rogers.html.

373 Or maybe it was: Ibid.

374 The *Indianapolis Business Journal:* "City Cuts Property in Play," *Indianapolis Business Journal*, August 23, 2008, www.ibj.com/html/detail_page_Full.asp?content=19054&NoFrame=1.

375 Her husband, Daniel Mulhern: Chad Selweski, "Granholm Supporters Helped Her Husband Secure Wayne County Contracts," *Macomb Daily*, January 13, 2002, http://204.176.34.196/macombdaily/article.asp?ID=2971927.

376 three-quarters of the: John Chase, Ray Gibson, Sbr S David Kidwell, Ray Long, and Jeffrey Meitrodt, "The Governor's $25,000 Club," *Chicago Tribune*, April 27, 2008, http://archives.chicagotribune.com/2008/apr/27/business/chi-blago-big-donors-bd27apr27.

377 "a unique and innovative": Robert O'Harrow Jr., "Federal No-Bid Contracts On Rise," *Washington Post*, August 22, 2007, www.washingtonpost.com/ac2/related/topic/The+White+House?tid=informline.

378 In 1992, his office: Dana Heupel, "Burris' Contracts to Contributors," January 5, 2009, http://illinoisissuesblog.blogspot.com/2009/01/burris-contracts-to-contributors.html.

379 More than half: Ibid.

380 After leaving his seat: John Chase and Ray Gibson, "Burris Practiced in Political Arts," *Chi-

cago Tribune, January 8, 2009, www.chicagotribune.com/news/local/chi-burris-record-08
-jan08,0,4656666.story.

381 As a private citizen: "Roland Burris: Not a Virgin in a Chicago Whorehouse," FreeRepublic
.com, January 8, 2009, www.freerepublic.com/focus/f-news/2160983/posts.

382 $290,000 contract to scour: Chase and Gibson, "Burris Practiced in Political Arts."

383 A Philadelphia firm: Ibid.

384 Another company, ACS Healthcare: Ibid.

385 "approval from state hospital regulators": Ibid.

386 "was room for more": Ibid.

387 His old law firm: Ibid.

388 Once in office: Ibid.

389 "bought his job": Chase, Gibson, Kidwell, Long, and Meitrodt, "The Governor's $25,000
Club."

390 A Chicago engineering firm: Ibid.

391 A Chicago pharmacist: Ibid.

392 Six months after: Ibid.

393 A Chicago architectural firm: Ibid.

394 Ali Ata, Blagojevich's: Ibid.

395 ACS State & Local: Ibid.

396 The Ballard law firm: Chris Freind, "Ballard's $773,000 'No Contract' Work," *The Bulle-
tin*, January 9, 2009, www.thebulletin.us/articles/2009/01/09/top_storiesdoc4966eef74061a
740614583.txt.

397 "the turnpike is in": Ibid.

398 Ballard's chairman, Arthur Makadon: Ibid.

399 In all, the Ballard firm: Ibid.

400 DRPA has paid: Ibid.

401 Before Rendell was elected: Ibid.

402 The Ballard firm itself: Ibid.

403 Ballard Chariman Arthur Makadon: Ibid.

404 Partner Ken Jarin donated: Ibid.

405 David Cohen, a former: Ibid.

406 The Philadelphia Future Political: Ibid.

407 When Boscov's, a Pennsylvania-area: Chris Freind, "Rendell, His Political Friends—and
More State Contracts," *Philadelphia Bulletin*, December 5, 2008, www.freerepublic.com/
focus/f news/2143459/posts.

408 Citing Boscov's "reputation": Ibid.

409 Or was it the fact: Ibid.

410 Bailey donated $75,000: Ibid.

411 Earlier, at another firm: Ibid.

412 And don't forget the $599,000: Mauriello, "Rendell Contributor under Investigation."

413 But it appears that Governor Richardson: Martin Z. Braun and William Selway, "Grand Jury

Probes Richardson Donor's New Mexico Financing Fee," Bloomberg.com, December 15, 2008, www.bloomberg.com/apps/news?pid=20601103&sid=aL0GGUluJeT8&refer=us.

414 On March 19, 2004: David Alire Garcia, "Richardson Battles the Politics of Perception," *New Mexico Independent*, January 5, 2009, http://newmexicoindependent.com/13964/unlucky -bill-richardson.

415 Three months later: Ibid.

416 Later that same year: Ibid.

417 "over the same time period": Ibid.

418 Richardson hired Rubin: Braun and Selway, "Grand Jury Probes Richardson Donor's New Mexico Financing Fee."

419 In 2006, CDR and two: William Heisel, "CDR, at Root of Richardson Probe, Is No Stranger to Suits," *Los Angeles Times*, January 6, 2009, http://articles.latimes.com/2009/jan/06/busi ness/fi-cdr6.

420 From 1998 to 2003: Trip Jennings, "Malott's Firm Has Seen Boom in State Auditing Contracts under Gov," February 4, 2009, *New Mexico Independent*, http://newmexicoindependent.com/17322/malotts-firm-has-gone-from-bit-player-to-powerhouse-in-winning-state -business.

421 Another principal at Mallott's firm: Ibid.

422 For example, Meyners failed: Ibid.

423 "revealed widespread misuse": Ibid.

424 In 2007, it became the first: "Regional and State Employment and Unemployment Summary," U.S. Bureau of Labor Statistics, February, 2009, www.bls.gov/news.release/laus.nr0 .htm.

425 She and her husband: Selweski, "Granholm Supporters Helped Her Husband Secure Wayne County Contracts."

426 "did not work for the county": Ibid.

427 A month after Jennifer left: Ibid.

428 A few months after his wife's: Ibid.

429 The competing firms bid: Ibid.

430 A two-day, $15,000: Ibid.

431 An eight-month contract: Ibid.

432 A monthly leadership program: Ibid.

433 "the use of negotiated": Gajan Retnasaba, "Do Campaign Contributions and Lobbying Corrupt? Evidence from Public Finance," August 2006, http://papers.ssrn.com/sol3/papers .cfm?abstract_id=1003890.

434 Reviewing the impact: Ibid.

435 The study's "rough estimate": Ibid.

436 "an ever growing": James A. Kahl and Lawrence H. Norton, "State and Local Government Contractors Beware: Political Contributions—Even from Your Executives and Their Families—Can Cost You Business," April 25, 2007, www.wcsr.com/resources/pdfs/poli law042507.pdf.

13. SLOW SURRENDER: HOW OUR BANKS AND INVESTMENT FIRMS ARE OPENING THE DOOR TO MUSLIM EXTREMIST DOMINATION

437 "that Muslims living in": Paul Sperry, "Shariah Showdown on Wall Street," FrontPage Magazine.com, July 9, 2008, www.frontpagemag.com/Articles/Read.aspx?GUID=D0A52 215-262C-4438-A3CD-8073D0DE26CB.

438 "killing is to continue": M. Taqi Usmani, *Islam and Modernism* (New Delhi, India: Adam Publishers & Distributors), May 4, 2005.

439 "If the purpose": Ibid.

440 "At least in my": Ibid.

441 "The issuing company": Ibid.

442 "financial statements of": Ibid.

443 Unfortunately, several of these: Frank J. Gaffney Jr., "Shariah's Trojan Horse," *Washington Times*, December 6, 2007, www.frontpagemag.com/Articles/Read.aspx?GUID=0948CAB2 -4DD5-41CE-AC4C-90B9F05D191F.

444 "three of the largest": Gaffney and Yerushalmi, "Covering Up for Shariah-Compliant Finance."

445 The 2.5 percent tariff: Gaffney, "Shariah's Trojan Horse."

446 "deducted and given": Glazov, "Shariah Finance."

447 They have even coined: Gaffney, "Shariah's Trojan Horse."

448 "dozens of radical Islamists": Glazov, "Shariah Finance."

449 "radical Islamists trained": Paul Broun, "Congressman Paul Broun Hosts Shariah/Islamic Finance Briefing," Broun.house.gov, January 17, 2008, http://broun.house.gov/apps/list/ press/ga10_broun/ShariahBriefing.shtml.

450 "first retained in 1999": Gaffney, "Shariah's Trojan Horse."

451 Until recently he advised: Paul Sperry, "Showdown on Wall Street," July 9, 2008, Front-PageMagazine.com, www.frontpagemag.com/articles/Read.aspx?GUID=D0A52215-262C -4438-A3CD-8073D0DE26CB.

452 "has repeatedly endorsed": Paul Broun, "Congressman Paul Broun Hosts Shariah/Islamic Finance Briefing."

453 "runs a Shariah-compliant": Sperry, "Showdown on Wall Street."

454 "a Saudi-tied front": Ibid.

455 "if trends continue": Gaffney, "Shariah's Trojan Horse."

456 Shariah Law authorities: Gaffney, "Covering Up for Shariah-Compliant Finance."

457 "key drivers of this": Ibid.

458 The Center for Security Policy: Frank Gaffney Jr. and David Yerushalmi, "Covering Up for Shariah-Compliant Financing."

459 "to make it possible": Jamie Glazov, "Shariah Finance," FrontPageMag.com, April 15, 2008, www.frontpagemag.com/Articles/Read.aspx?GUID=A228AF1E-A0E5-429A-9AA8-BF 9CEEC8F366.

460 "The Shariah experts": Ibid.

461   The first company: Gaffney and Yerushalmi, "Covering Up for Shariah-Compliant Finance."

462   "Wall Street is jumping": "The Risky Business of Islamic Finance," *Investor's Business Daily*, February 27, 2008, www.ibdeditorials.com/IBDArticles.aspx?id=289008131344615.

463   "Citibank and Goldman Sachs": Ibid.

464   "The Dow Jones Islamic Index's": Gaffney and Yerushalmi, "Covering Up for Shariah-Compliant Finance."

465   "footbaths in public institutions Gaffney, "Shariah's Trojan Horse."

466   "beheadings, stonings, floggings": Ibid.

467   "to legitimize Shariah": Glazov, "Shariah Finance."

468   "create Islamic enclaves": Ibid.

469   "Those entering into": Cal Thomas, "Surrender!," HumanEvents.com, July 8, 2008, www.humanevents.com/article.php?id=27394.

470   "Islamic legal principles": Ibid.

471   "seems unavoidable and": "Archbishop: Adoption of Shariah Law in U.K. Is 'Unavoidable,'" FoxNews.com, February 7, 2008, www.foxnews.com/story/0,2933,329389,00.html.

472   Incredibly, Muslims in the: Ibid.

473   "Muslim women are prohibited . . . of their children": Thomas, "Surrender!"

474   "Shariah-compliant schools": Gaffney, "Shariah's Trojan Horse."

475   In December 2007 . . . "the killing of many people": Vincent Giola, "Shariah Banking: The Silent Jihad Against the West," ChronWatch.com, May 3, 2008, www.chronwatch-america.com/blogs/964/Shariah-Banking—The-Silent-Jihad-Against-the-West.html.

476   "there is, of course": Glazov, "Shariah Finance."

477   He cites the example: Ibid.

478   "Western involvement is key": Ibid.

479   "jumped into [Shariah-compliant financing]": Ibid.

480   "once [Shariah-compliant finance]": Glazov, "Shariah Finance."

481   The current flirtation: Baron Bodissey, "Exposing Shariah Finance," April 15, 2008, http://gatesofvienna.blogspot.com/2008/04/exposing-shariah-finance.html.

482   "it is very likely": The McCormick Foundation and the Center for Security Policy, "Shariah, Law and 'Financial Jihad': How Should America Respond?" www.scribd.com/doc/9930309/Jihad-Report.

483   Even after the market crashes: Charles Watson, "Cashed-Up Sovereign Wealth Funds Wait for Rock Bottom," InvestorDaily.com.au, www.investordaily.com.au/cps/rde/xchg/id/style/5867.htm?rdeCOQ=SID-3F579BCE-F3F1CFD2&rdeCOQ=SID-3F579BCE-09256BC7.

484   "there will be": E-mail from Frank Gaffney to authors, February 23, 2009.

485   "preferred stock": Jamie Glazov, "No Bailout for Jihad," FrontPageMagazine.com, December 23, 2008, www.frontpagemag.com/Articles/Read.aspx?GUID=B0152451-565E-4F35-A293-D6E7A39EB8BD.

486   "by anyone's definition": Ibid.

487   "whatever AIG is doing": Ibid.

488 "intentionally promotes Shariah": Ibid.

489 "To help achieve": Ibid.

490 "is to review": Ibid.

491 Under the program: Ibid.

14. HOW BILL CLINTON GOOFED . . . COSTING YOU $60 BILLION

492 It's estimated that their blunder: Edmund L. Andrews, "Oil Company Revives Suit on Avoidance of Royalties," *New York Times*, March 3, 2007, www.nytimes.com/2007/03/03/business/03royalties.html?n=Top/News/Business/Companies/Anadarko%20Petroleum%20Corp.

493 which usually run between: Ibid.

494 So, in 1996: Ibid.

495 Deepwater oil production: Marc Humphries, "Royalty Relief for U.S. Deepwater Oil and Gas Leases," September 18, 2008, http://fpc.state.gov/documents/organization/110359.pdf.

496 In the *next* two years: H. Josef Hebert, "House Votes to Recoup Lease Royalties," *USA Today*, July 27, 2007, www.usatoday.com/news/topstories/2007-07-27-1953281366_x.htm.

497 By 2000, the Interior Department: Ibid.

498 By 2006: Humphries, "Royalty Relief for U.S. Deepwater Oil and Gas Leases."

499 By the time all the oil: Ibid.

500 Patricia Minaldi: Andrews, "Oil Company Revives Suit on Avoidance of Royalties."

501 Sustaining Minaldi's ruling: Nick Snow, "Appeals Court Backs Earlier Kerr-McGee Deepwater Ruling," *Oil and Gas Journal,* January 14, 2008, www.ogj.com/display_article/350304/7/ONART/none/GenIn/1/Appeals-court-backs-earlier-Kerr-McGee-deepwater-ruling/.

502 The intent of Congress: Ibid.

503 "If the court's interpretation": Ibid.

504 the Government Accountability Office: Andrews, "Oil Company Revives Suit on Avoidance of Royalties."

505 At a time when: Tom Doggett, "Lawmaker Urges US Govt to Fight Oil Royalty Ruling," Reuters.com, November 1, 2007, www.reuters.com/article/companyNewsAndPR/idUSN0145493420071101.

506 "will result in the oil": Ibid.

507 In July 2007: Humphries, "Royalty Relief for U.S. Deepwater Oil and Gas Leases."

15. TARMAC HOSTAGES: HOW AIRLINES IMPRISON YOU ON THE RUNWAY

508 "food, water, electricity": Marilyn Adams, "Airlines Hope to Block Flier Bill of Rights," *USA Today*, December 10, 2007, www.usatoday.com/money/industries/travel/2007-12-10-stranding-law_N.htm.

509 In the first ten: Ibid.

510 During the same: "Passenger Rights," *Washington Post*, January 12, 2008, www.washington-post.com/wp-dyn/content/article/2008/01/11/AR2008011103506.html.

511 Passengers have a right: Kate Hanni, "Canada Got Their Airline Passengers Bill of Rights Why Can't We Have Ours!," FlyersRights.org, September 15, 2008, www.strandedpassengers .blogspot.com.

512 Guaranteed customer notification: "Bill of Rights," JetBlue.com, www.jetblue.com/p/about/ ourcompany/promise/Bill_Of_Rights.pdf.

513 "the air and toilets": Tom Zeller Jr., "Held Hostage on the Tarmac: Time for a Passenger Bill of Rights?," *New York Times*, February 16, 2007, http://thelede.blogs.nytimes.com/2007/02/16/ held-hostage-on-the-tarmac-time-for-a-passenger-bill-of-rights/.

514 After hours of sitting: Scott McCartney, "Runway-Bound: A Holiday Flight Becomes Ugly," *Wall Street Journal*, January 6, 2007, http://online.wsj.com/article/SB116804368966768690 .html.

515 "after eight hours": Ibid.

516 "according to airline officials": Ibid.

517 This "pivotal decision": Ibid.

518 "allowed about 20": Ibid.

519 "conditions in the": Ibid.

520 The chairman of the House Committee: Mike Collins, "Airlines Get 500 Million in Your Tax Dollars and Passengers Get Nothing," StrandedPassengers.blogspot.com, September 22, 2008, www.strandedpassengers.blogspot.com/.

521 While the task force: "DOT Tarmac Delay Task Force Declines to Set Time Limits," November 14, 2008, www.atwonline.com/news/story.html?storyID=14709.

522 The doctrine of: Steve Surjaputra, "Proposed Rule Would Allow Passengers to Sue over Tarmac Delays," Tripso.com, December 4, 2008, www.tripso.com/today/proposed-rule-would -allow-passengers-to-sue-over-tarmac-delays/.

523 The airlines have ratcheted: Center for Responsive Politics, www.opensecret.org/industries/ indus.php?ind=T110.

524 For example: Charlie Leocha, "American Airlines May Have Violated Ethics Rules," Tripso. com, January 30, 2009, www.tripso.com/today/american-airlines-may-have-violated -ethics-rules/.

525 It requires airlines to: "Proposed Bill of Rights for Airline Passengers," FlyersRights.org, www.flyersrights.org/billofrights.html.

16. THE SILENT CATASTROPHE: POST-TRAUMATIC STRESS DISORDER IN OUR MILITARY

526 In January 2009: Jason Leopold, "Obama Proposes Bigger VA Budget as Pentagon Grapples with Widespread Panic," TheVeteransProject.org, February 26, 2009, www.theveterans project.org/?p=336.

527 "terrifying. We don't know": Barbara Starr and Mike Mount, "Army Official: Suicides in January 'Terrifying,'" CNN.com, February 5, 2009, http://edition.cnn.com/2009/US/02/05/army.suicides/.

528 Twenty-four soldiers: Ibid.

529 Colonel Kathy Platoni: Ibid.

530 "the highest annual level": Ibid.

531 One hundred and twenty-eight: Ibid.

532 Marine suicides also rose: Ibid.

533 "there is still a huge": Ibid.

534 10 percent of the returning soldiers: Associated Press and Reuters, "1 in 10 U.S. Iraq Veterans Suffers Stress Disorder," MSNBC.com, March 1, 2006, www.msnbc.msn.com/id/11609834/.

535 Out of 222,620: Associated Press and Reuters, "1 in 10 U.S. Iraq Veterans Suffers Stress Disorder."

536 Of those diagnosed: Ibid.

537 In their study: Carl A. Castro, Dave I. Cotting, Charles W. Hoge, Robert L. Koffman, Dennis McGurk, and Shephen C. Messer, "Combat Duty in Iraq and Afghanistan, Mental Health Problems, and Barriers to Care," New England Journal of Medicine, 351, no. 1 (July 1, 2004): 13–22, http://content.nejm.org/cgi/content/full/351/1/13.

538 RAND says that: Office of Media Relations, "One in Five Iraq and Afghanistan Veterans Suffer from PTSD or Major Depression," Rand.org, April 17, 2008, www.rand.org/news/press/2008/04/17/.

539 The study also found: Ibid.

540 And 7 percent have: Ibid.

541 RAND estimates that: Ibid.

542 "There is a major": Ibid.

543 "produces a wide": William M. Welch, "Trauma of Iraq War Haunting Thousands Returning Home," USA Today, February 28, 2005, www.usatoday.com/news/world/iraq/2005-02-28-cover-iraq-injuries_x.htm.

544 "feel depression, detachment": Associated Press, "1 in 8 Returning Soldiers Suffers from PTSD."

545 "Jesus Bocanegra": Welch, "Trauma of Iraq War Haunting Thousands Returning Home."

546 "Lieutenant Julian Goodrum": Ibid.

547 "Sean Huze": Ibid.

548 "Allen Walsh": Ibid.

549 Sergeant Danny Facto: Sangay Gupta, "Combat Stress: The War Within," CNN.com, July 1, 2004, http://edition.cnn.com/2004/HEALTH/07/01/post.traumatic.stress/index.html.

550 "You can't just say": Ibid.

551 Ninety percent report: Ibid.

552 The New England Journal: Kelley Beaucar Vlahos, "Iraq War Takes Toll on GIs' Mental Health," FoxNews.com, September 25, 2004, www.foxnews.com/story/0,2933,133490,00.html.

553 "There are no clear": Ibid.

554 "Robinson said men": Ibid.

555 "I know from walking": Ibid.

556 "Some talk about fathers": Ibid.

557 "I wasn't functioning": Ibid.

558 "After struggling through": Ibid.

559 "The message was": Ibid.

560 "Of those whose responses": Castro, Cotting, Hoge et al., "Combat Duty in Iraq and Afghanistan, Mental Health Problems, and Barriers to Care."

561 "In the past five years": Shankar Vedantam, "A Political Debate on Stress Disorder," *Washington Post*, December 27, 2005, www.washingtonpost.com/wp-dyn/content/article/2005/12/26/AR2005122600792.html.

562 "because the increase": Ibid.

563 "we have young": Ibid.

564 Those who are: Ibid.

565 "once veterans are": Ibid.

566 "adversarial relationship": Ibid.

567 "they are unwilling": Ibid.

568 "what they [the VA]": Ibid.

569 The RAND Corporation: Office of Media Relations, "One in Five Iraq and Afghanistan Veterans Suffer from PTSD or Major Depression."

570 "If PTSD and depression": Ibid.

571 "many are worried": Ibid.

572 "the military create a system": Ibid.

573 "Only about one": Gregg Soroya, "Many War Vets' Stress Disorders Go Untreated," *USA Today*, May 10, 2006, www.usatoday.com/news/health/2006-05-10-veterans-disorders_x.htm.

574 "We are not . . . prepared for this": Vlahos, "Iraq War Takes Toll on GIs' Mental Health."

575 "The [Veterans Administration] . . . fixed now": Ibid.

576 "establish quality standards": "About the Defense Centers of Excellence," DCOE.health.mil, www.dcoe.health.mil/default.aspx.

577 "can deal with everything": Jeff Schogol, "Outreach Center Created to Aid Veterans and Families," *Stars and Stripes*, January 16, 2009, www.dcoe.health.mil/NewsItem.aspx?ID=27.

578 "service members can talk": Jeff Schogol, "Pentagon Hopes Stories Help Troops with PTSD," *Stars and Stripes*, February 9, 2009, www.stripes.com/article.asp?section=104&article=60587.

579 *Ajax* by Sophocles: Ibid.

580 President Obama's budget request: Paul Sullivan, "Veterans for Common Sense Statement Responding to President Obama's Fiscal Year 2010 VA Budget Request," Veteransfor CommonSense.org, February 26, 2009, www.veteransforcommonsense.org/articleid/12424.

581 The VA says: Ibid.

582 "provides greater benefits": Ibid.

583 The VA lauded the additional: Ibid.